"This is a courageous book about a topic for a long time neglected in restorative justice research and reflection. A well designed empirical study provides the reader with a wealth of victims' narratives and deep insights in the relational process towards forgiveness and how forgiveness contributes to justice experiences."

—*Ivo Aertsen, PhD, Professor of Criminology, University of Leuven*

"In *Violence, Restorative Justice and Forgiveness: Dyadic Forgiveness and Energy Shifts in Restorative Justice Dialogue*, Marilyn Armour and Mark Umbreit make a giant leap in the restorative justice discussion. Restorative justice practitioners have historically been reluctant to discuss forgiveness because it deflects the conversation from justice and it might place an emotional burden on victims or survivors of crime victims. Armour and Umbreit use the idea of a shift of emotional energy to reflect many of the emotional changes that can occur in victim-offender mediation dialogues. They develop a model of the flow of energy from preparation of participants to the dialogue to the aftermath. They create a new language for discussing the VOMD that will not fully please forgiveness researchers nor restorative justice practitioners, yet it makes a practical and conceptual leap that brings both communities into fuller contact with each other. The 20 cases are fascinating reading, and this is a truly new way of speaking about and thinking about the VOMD. This is well worth the read!"

—*Everett L. Worthington, Jr.*,
Author of Forgiveness and Spirituality in Psychotherapy:
A Relational Approach *(with Steven J. Sandage; APA Books)*

of related interest

The Forgiveness Project
Stories for a Vengeful Age
Marina Cantacuzino
Forewords by Archbishop Emeritus Desmond Tutu and Alexander McCall Smith
ISBN 978 1 84905 566 6 (Hardback)
ISBN 978 1 78592 000 4 (Paperback)
eISBN 978 1 78450 006 1

The Psychology of Emotion in Restorative Practice
How Affect Script Psychology Explains How and Why Restorative Practice Works
Edited by Vernon C. Kelly, Jr. and Margaret Thorsborne
ISBN 978 1 84905 974 9
eISBN 978 0 85700 866 4

Restorative Theory in Practice
Insights into What Works and Why
Edited by Belinda Hopkins
ISBN 978 1 84905 468 3
eISBN 978 0 85700 847 3

What Have I Done?
A Victim Empathy Programme for Young People
Pete Wallis with Clair Aldington and Marian Liebmann
Illustrated by Emily Wallis
ISBN 978 1 84310 979 2
ISBN 978 1 84985 734 5 (Large Print)
eISBN 978 0 85700 211 2

Restorative Justice
How It Works
Marian Liebmann
ISBN 978 1 84310 074 4
ISBN 978 1 84985 726 0 (Large Print)
eISBN 978 1 84642 631 5

The Pocket Guide to Restorative Justice
Pete Wallis and Barbara Tudor
ISBN 978 1 84310 629 6
eISBN 978 1 84642 748 0

VIOLENCE, RESTORATIVE JUSTICE AND FORGIVENESS

Dyadic Forgiveness and Energy Shifts in Restorative Justice Dialogue

MARILYN ARMOUR AND MARK S. UMBREIT

Jessica Kingsley *Publishers*
London and Philadelphia

First published in 2018
by Jessica Kingsley Publishers
73 Collier Street
London N1 9BE, UK
and
400 Market Street, Suite 400
Philadelphia, PA 19106, USA

www.jkp.com

Library of Congress Cataloging in Publication Data
A CIP catalog record for this book is available from the Library of Congress

British Library Cataloguing in Publication Data
A CIP catalogue record for this book is available from the British Library

ISBN 978 1 78592 795 9
eISBN 978 1 78450 795 4

ACKNOWLEDGEMENTS

The authors are appreciative of the contribution of Ted Lewis, MA, Restorative Communications Consultant, Center for Restorative Justice and Peacemaking for his assistance with the review of archival materials and with the conceptualization of the Dyadic Forgiveness model. We also thank him for the interviews he conducted with victim participants for this project. We are also appreciative of the contribution of Jennifer Blevins, Research Assistant, Center for Restorative Justice and Peacemaking for her preparation of materials for submission to the Institutional Review Board. Finally, the authors thank Sarah Ryan for her assistance in analyzing the 20 victim participant interviews, doing the sample demographics, creating the diagrams for the final report and editing it. The research that led to the preparation of this manuscript would not have occurred without the generous support of the Fetzer Institute and the authors are extremely appreciative of their involvement in this study.

CONTENTS

FIGURES

PREFACE

Restorative justice has emerged internationally as a viable response to the harm caused by crime. Its acceptance and promotion are underscored by the fact that the United Nations (2000) has adopted a set of principles that encourage use of restorative justice programming by member states. In addition, the Council of Europe (2001) supports its use in criminal matters while the American Bar Association (1994) promotes the use of victim offender mediation (VOM), which is the oldest, most widely used and empirically grounded form of restorative justice, in courts throughout the United States.

Restorative justice begins with the crime or wrongdoing and the far-reaching consequences for the victim, offender, and others. For the victim, there is a common response referred to as 'victim unforgiveness' (Worthington and Wade, 1999), which occurs as the victim ruminates about the transgression and its consequences. Specifically, resentment, bitterness, hostility, hatred, anger, etc. can coalesce over time into a cold complex of emotions called unforgiveness. Unforgiveness can be described as the emotional consequence of the perceived distance between desired justice and the victim's sense of injustice. Restorative justice endeavors to decrease that distance, and the lack of resolution associated with unforgiveness, by opportunities for face-to-face meetings between victim and offender. Indeed, forgiveness and involvement in a restorative justice intervention have been shown, under experimental conditions, to be statistically equivalent in reducing levels of unforgiving motivations, anger, and arousal, and in increasing levels of empathy, forgiveness, positive emotions, and control (Witvliet *et al.*, 2008).

Although forgiveness and reconciliation are important philosophical objectives for many within the restorative justice movement, little attention has been paid, until now, to defining or examining how these terms function in various contexts. The purpose of this project is to explicate dyadic forgiveness in victim offender dialogue (VOD), also called victim offender mediated dialogue (VOMD), by studying behaviorally implicit forgiveness and the process of victim and offender shifts in energy from the time of the crime through the restorative dialogue.

The project has four sections:

1. *A review of the literature on forgiveness in restorative justice with particular attention to the construct of dyadic forgiveness and the interpersonal dynamics of influence*: This section highlights the difficulties with forgiveness in restorative justice, the lack of information on implicit forgiveness, and the importance of energy shifts in behavioral change. A model of the change process in VOD for victim and offender dyads of seriously violent crime is proposed as a starting point for the project. This model is derived from a systematic review and retrospective analysis of restorative justice cases and archival materials on VOD.

2. *A qualitative study of 20 victims who experienced a positive emotional energy shift as a result of their participation in a VOD with their offender*: Data were collected largely from victim survivors (family members) of murder cases. These cases serve as exemplars of dyadic forgiveness. Each of the victim's narratives is summarized in their words and then analyzed using the model of the change process proposed in Section 1. Although every case is unique in the circumstances of the crime and context for the VOD, the analysis highlights the dynamics across all cases that allow for openness in dyadic engagement, transfer of the victim's pain to the offender, positive energy shifts in both victim and offender, and transformation of the victim's pain. Particular attention is given to the processes leading up to the dyadic dialogue as well as what occurs for victims in the aftermath of the meeting.

3. *A cross-case analysis and discussion of the findings about dyadic forgiveness from the 20 victim case narratives*: The model proposed in Section 1 is expanded and reworked based on the findings. Shifts from negatively to positively charged energy are noted both in terms of a series of graduated shifts that build on each other and core shifts that significantly transform the direction and quality of the energy. Dimensions of verbally explicit and behaviorally implicit forgiveness in dyadic forgiveness are identified. In addition to information on the study's methodology, this section is subdivided into findings on the a) crime and its impact, b) victim motivation and VOD preparation, c) the dyadic dialogue, d) resolution and post-dialogue outcomes, and e) dyadic forgiveness. The section concludes with a formulation about dyadic forgiveness and its processes and key attributes based on the results from the literature review, the VOMD study, and the study of 20 victims.

There is a significant literature on individual, unilateral, and intrapsychic forgiveness. This literature centers on the forgiver's motivations, tendencies or characteristic traits to forgive over time and across situations. The literature of dyadic forgiveness is exceedingly limited. Yet many victims of seriously violent crime report dramatic personal change in attitude toward the offender and in healing after meeting with an offender. Part of the dearth in information is because forgiveness in restorative justice is not a part of the agenda for victim change. Restorative justice facilitators do not ask victim participants to forgive or to report experiences of forgiveness. Indeed, the maxim in the restorative justice field is that forgiveness is less apt to occur the more it is prescribed. Because it is deliberately made "irrelevant," restorative justice has placed the examination of forgiveness outside its own field of inquiry.

Although this position is understandable, the concept of forgiveness in restorative justice cannot be ignored. It is a potent and promising outcome of the interpersonal nature of the dyadic dialogue. Our taboos around it, as well as ignoring or downplaying its existence, deprive us of much needed knowledge in a world beset with few avenues for repair and sustained healing. The restorative justice field offers an unusual opportunity for studying dyadic forgiveness because of its focus on wrongdoing, accountability, humanization, and amends making. This project seeks to open the door on the concept and importance of dyadic forgiveness. Instead of a focus on public acknowledgement of forgiveness or forgiveness as a goal, the project examines shifts in victims from negatively to positively charged energy as a result of dyadic engagement and as an indicator of dyadic forgiveness.

REFERENCES

American Bar Association (1994, Approved August 1994). 'Policy on legislative and national issues.' In American Bar Association (Ed.) *Policies and procedures handbook* (p.730). Chicago, ILL.

Council of Europe: Commission of the European Communities. (2001). *Report from the Commission on the basis of Article 18 of the Council Framework Decision of 15 March 2001 on the standing of victims in criminal proceedings*. COM (2004) 54 final/2, 16.02.04. Retrieved January 7, 2010 from http://europa.eu/bulletin/en/200012/p104015.htm

Umbreit, M. (2013) *Being with the energy of forgiveness: Lessons from former enemies in restorative dialogue* (film). Center for Restorative Justice and Peacemaking, St. Paul, MN. Available from https://www.youtube.com/watch?v=8OUnOpbmb7g

Umbreit, M.S. Lewis, T. and Blevins, J. (2015) *The energy of forgiveness: Lessons from those in restorative dialogue*. Eugene, OR: Cascade Publications.

United Nations: *Basic principles on the use of restorative justice programmes in criminal matters*. (ECOSOC Rex.2000/14). New York.

Wivliet, C.V.O., Worthington, E.L., Root, L.M., Sato, A.F, Ludwig, T.E. & Exline, J.J. (2008). 'Retributive justice, restorative justice, and forgiveness: An experimental psychophysiology analysis.' *Journal of Experimental Social Psychology 44*, 1, 10–25.

Worthington, E.L., Jr. and Wade, N.G. (1999) 'The social psychology of unforgiveness and forgiveness and implications for clinical practice.' *Journal of Social and Clinical Psychology 18*, 385–418.

1 ■

DYADIC FORGIVENESS IN RESTORATIVE JUSTICE

A Review of the Field and a Proposed Model

PURPOSE

The purpose of the study on the paradox of forgiveness is to examine the process of energy flow in implicit forgiveness by examining restorative justice dialogues. This section is a review of the literature on forgiveness that pertains to and contextualizes the study. It is also a review and retrospective analysis of restorative justice cases to ascertain key dimensions of implicit forgiveness, underlying conditions that foster that forgiveness, and the process of energy flow in restorative justice dialogues.

INTRODUCTION

Amidst a falling crime rate, including violent crime, the recidivism rate for prisoners who have served their time remains stalled (Durose, Cooper, and Snyder, 2014) suggesting that punishment, through incarceration, does little to effect behavioral change. Similarly, relatively few initiatives help heal crime victims who years after a violent offense continue to live restricted and fear-laden lives. For example, studies of family members of homicide victims have found that 66 percent could not find meaning after five years (Murphy, Johnson, and Lohan, 2002), endured post-homicide distress that did not dramatically lessen over time (Thompson, Norris, and Ruback, 1998), and were significantly more likely than other direct crime victims to have lifetime posttraumatic stress disorder (PTSD) (Freedy, *et al.*, 1994). Studies of sexual assault victims showed a slower recovery rate from sexual than nonsexual assault (Gilboa-Schechtman and Foa, 2001), increased vulnerability to panic disorder (Leskin and Sheikh, 2002) and chronic posttraumatic stress if psychological disorders were also present (Darves-Bornoz, *et al.*, 1998). In contrast to victims of minor crimes, victims of violent crime suffer significantly more distress, including loss of confidence (41% vs. 11%), loss of self-esteem (37% vs. 2%), sleeplessness (27% vs. 9%), and headaches and other physical symptoms (41% vs. 5%) (Strang, 2002).

An alternative and complementary approach to prison and punishment for violent crimes is restorative justice, which is rapidly gaining mainstream attention. It is a promising response because it acknowledges the interpersonal nature of crime. Using a variety of formats, it brings together victim and offender for a mediated dialogue. Using the negative energy from the crime that generated a forced, involuntary relationship, restorative justice offers the opportunity to channel that negative energy into healing through a process of accountability that allows victims to transfer the pain from the harm done to offenders, and offenders to use that pain to give back to victims through remorse-driven responses and behaviors. Restorative justice has a longstanding record of effectiveness. Victim offender mediation (VOM), which is the oldest restorative justice practice, has shown for over 40 years that it achieves a 25 percent to 32 percent reduction in recidivism (Umbreit and Armour, 2010, pp.132–133). Family Group Conferencing (FGC) has demonstrated the ability to reduce posttraumatic stress symptoms in victims by 33 percent at six weeks and by 40 percent at six months (Angel, 2005).

Because of the powerful potential in restorative justice to shift the negative energy from crime to positive energy for healing the harm done, and to generate change in and between victim and offender, many view restorative justice as a movement that explicitly furthers forgiveness and reconciliation. This pairing, however, is problematic and counterproductive to the restorative justice movement because it alters the objective of restorative dialogues for victims, which is to restore the victim's emotional and material losses. It also disturbs the safety that must accompany any meeting between the offender and victim by directly or indirectly prescribing/imposing the outcome for victims. Indeed for many victims, terms such as "forgiveness" and "reconciliation" are interpreted as devaluing their criminal victimization, or as judging their legitimate anger and rage as inappropriate (Murphy, 2002). Moreover, those who are unable or unwilling to forgive might experience a double victimization, first from the crime and second from the shame associated with their failure to forgive (Exline, *et al.*, 2003, p.13).

Restorative justice, therefore, works within a paradox. On the one hand, forgiveness and reconciliation represent a potent and promising outcome of the process of facilitator-assisted dialogue and mutual aid between crime victims and offenders. On the other hand, the more one talks about these concepts, the more likely they will be heard as behavioral prescriptions or even as a moral imperative and the less likely victims will participate in dialogues with offenders and have the opportunity to experience naturally occurring elements of forgiveness and reconciliation (Umbreit, 1995).

There is strong consensus in the restorative justice practitioner community, therefore, that forgiveness cannot be pushed. Proponents of restorative justice recognize that mislabeling restorative justice as forgiveness could serve as a disincentive for victims to meet with offenders because of the expectation of benevolence. However, there is also recognition that the concept of forgiveness in restorative justice cannot be ignored. To that end, Armour and Umbreit (2006) have proposed a model that defines the dimensions of forgiveness in restorative justice. Because restorative justice is systemic in focus, it is built on the tripartite representation of victim, offender, and community and suggests that the place, definition, and significance of forgiveness will vary depending on the needs of people in each of the three groups and the relationships of the stakeholders to one another.

Forgiveness in restorative justice includes the following dimensions: (1) From the victim's perspective, forgiveness refers to the unburdening of negative emotions associated with the trauma and/or the releasing of bitterness and vengeance while not condoning or excusing the offender (Umbreit and Armour, 2010, p.126); (2) From the offender's perspective, the experience of being forgiven is associated with feeling accepted as human by representatives of the community (e.g. victim, facilitator, other dialogue participants) and is the outgrowth of engagement in a process of the offender's accountability, remorse, and reparation. The acceptance is symbolic of being reinstated in the community as a moral citizen (ibid., pp.126–127); (3) Forgiveness involves a bilateral process that creates change in both victim and offender as a result of their impact on each other (ibid., pp.128–129); (4) Victim forgiveness is implicit and its communication is not dependent on the use of explicit language or the occurrence of specific behaviors. It is a by-product of the interaction between victim and offender that is communicated through a shift in attitude (e.g. letting go of anger) or behavior (e.g. no longer fighting against an offender's parole) (ibid., p.128).

As reflective of the model's emphasis on the processes of forgiveness and the implicitness of its expression, Umbreit has recently proposed that restorative justice embodies the "energy" of forgiveness regardless of formal outcome or expression and shown the nature of this energy by having participants of restorative justice dialogues share their experiences via media (*Being with the Energy of Forgiveness: Lessons from Former Enemies in Restorative Dialogue,* Umbreit 2013) and through narrative in *The Energy of Forgiveness: Lessons from those in restorative dialogue* (Umbreit, Lewis and Blevins).

This study extends the bilateral component of Armour and Umbreit's model and Umbreit's recent work on energy by examining in greater detail, through victims' accounts, the flow of energy in restorative justice dialogues that is involuntarily birthed by crime or wrongdoing and positively harnessed in the service of healing when it is unimpeded by preset agendas for forgiveness. Besides its unique contribution to the restorative justice community, this investigation adds to the forgiveness literature that, heretofore, has minimally examined the significance of bilateral (hereafter referred to as dyadic) forgiveness or forgiveness that is the result of transactional or dyadic interaction between the person responsible for the transgression and the person who was harmed.

TYPES OF FORGIVENESS

Historically, the focus on forgiveness has been unilateral and has centered on the substance of the drive or motivation to forgive. Proponents have identified that forgiveness may be either decisional or emotional. Decisional forgiveness is a behavioral intention to act less negatively and more positively toward an offender (Worthington *et al.,* 2012, p.2). Emotional forgiveness is a process in which positive other-oriented emotions replace negative emotions (p.2). It often involves an affective transformation (ibid., p.5) whereas decisional forgiveness can leave the forgiver with unresolved or negative emotions. Whether a decision or a change of emotion, both types of forgiveness, which can co-occur, see the outcome as an internal or intrapsychic phenomenon. Influences on this phenomenon include the forgiver's inclination or disposition to forgive, which is the tendency or characteristic trait of an individual to forgive over time and across situations (Worthington *et al.,* 2012, p.16).

Clinical interventions to foster forgiveness have reflected this division between decisional and emotional forgiveness and have focused on the individual, sources of motivation and his/her psychological changes. Psychoeducational forgiveness interventions, for example, have focused principally on groups of individuals who attend time-limited groups that promote forgiving others. Change is motivated either by encouraging forgiveness through affective and cognitive empathy, humility, and gratitude

(Sandage and Worthington, 2010, p.42) or through stressing the benefits to participants' social, emotional, relational, and physical wellbeing (ibid., p.43). Attention to the dynamic of empathy reflects, in part, studies that have empirically and consistently demonstrated that empathy is either a causal mechanism of forgiveness (McCullough *et al.*, 1998) or a core factor (Wade and Worthington, 2005). In contrast to restorative justice, these clinical interventions have focused solely on the individual who was harmed. Engagement with the transgressor, in these circumstances, has been internal to the participant rather than actual or dyadic.

Individual versus dyadic forgiveness

The dyadic construct as embodied in restorative justice practices introduces the possibility that the drive or motivation for forgiveness may grow out of the interaction between victim and offender. This construct does not preclude the co-existence of decisional or emotional forgiveness or that forward movement, even in dyadic forgiveness, may be initiated by a decision or involve emotional forgiveness, but the process by which change occurs and the movement toward positive relational energy is dependent on the actual interaction or dialogue between victim and offender.

Clinical interventions that foster dyadic forgiveness have targeted conflicts in close relationships including, among others, intimate partners, workplace relationships, and friendships (Fincham, Beach, and Davila, 2004, 2007). Results from these studies do not transfer readily to restorative justice interventions, which are usually based on a one-time transgression between persons who do not intend to reconcile and who have limited, if any, prior history.

Although generally confined to close relationships, there is growing interest in transgressor dynamics related to forgiveness and an expansion of forgiveness concepts to include self-forgiveness and forgiveness-seeking (e.g. Sandage, *et al.*, 2000), guilt (e.g. Baumeister, Stillwell, and Heatherton, 1995), and offender apology (e.g. Exline, DeShea, and Holeman, 2007). Similar to studies of victim forgiveness, the focus has been on motivation, with increasing evidence that guilt is the pivotal dynamic in the offender's incentive to seek forgiveness. Likewise, the emphasis is on unilateral activity, the individual, and intrapersonal change. The victim exists only as the object of harm in the offender's mind (e.g. Riek, Luna, and Schnabelrauch, 2013).

Leading researchers who focus either on those wronged or those responsible increasingly call for a fuller treatment of the experience of both parties with an emphasis on the dynamics of the relationship as well as the experience of both parties (e.g. Riek *et al.*, 2013, p.14); Worthington *et al.*

(2012, p.30). Lack of attention to interpersonal transactions leading to forgiveness can be attributed, in part, to the fact that clinical interventions tend to focus on only one party and controlled studies most often use student populations and hypothetical scenarios (e.g. Wenzel and Okimoto, 2010). Indeed, when students are asked to respond to survey questions on the basis of real experience, the range of transgressions is large, making it difficult to ascertain if the forgiveness response is mediated by the severity of the offense (e.g. Wenzel, Turner, and Okimoto, 2010).

Consequently, knowledge about dyadic forgiveness and the interpersonal dynamics of influence require applied research with populations of victims and offenders unimpeded by the explicit or implicit decree to forgive, which, in some religions, is considered critical to the victim's relationship with God and the afterlife. It is also important that the energy or bilateral movement toward forgiveness be undisturbed by warnings to the offender, for example, not to ask for forgiveness because that places responsibility on the victim to meet the offender's needs (New Hampshire Department of Corrections Victim Services Office, n.d.). Although the power of forgiveness is embedded in the fact that it is freely given, to place rules around transactions can also disturb the natural flow or spontaneous give and take between victim and offender that may otherwise lead to a positive place.

Explicit versus implicit forgiveness

There is no commonly accepted definition of victim forgiveness. Meanings assigned to the concept vary between forgiveness as a release of negative emotions toward the offender (Di Blasio, 1998; Hill, 2001), as a replacement of negative, unforgiving emotions with positive, other-oriented emotions (Worthington, 2003), or as an emotional transformation (Malcolm, Warwar, and Greenberg, 2005). In contrast, there appears to be general agreement that the need to forgive arises in response to reducing unforgiveness, which is the emotional consequence for the victim of the perceived distance between desired justice and the sense of injustice. It is described more specifically by Worthington, *et al.* (2007, p.292) as a state that occurs following an injustice in which the victim experiences ruminations about the offense that generate unrelenting bitterness, anger, vengefulness, fear, and depression. Many acts reduce unforgiveness or the injustice gap (Exline, *et al.*, 2003) including, among others, seeking vengeance, seeing justice done, letting go and moving on, turning the issue over to God, and forgiveness. Worthington claims that there is increasing consensus that forgiveness involves reducing unforgiveness, that it is a process rather than an event, and that the internal experience of forgiveness in victims can be distinguished from its interpersonal context (Worthington *et al.*, 2007, p.292).

A core but unexamined issue in definitions of victim forgiveness is the presumption that the outcome, which is forgiveness, is acknowledged or expressed overtly. This presumption likely reflects the fact that most research focuses on interventions designed to foster forgiveness or uses controlled studies with non-clinical populations where claims of having forgiven are in response to leading survey questions that specifically inquire about forgiveness. In restorative justice interventions, however, forgiveness is intentionally not part of the agenda. Victim participants are not asked to forgive, nor does the facilitator of the dialogue inquire about whether or not forgiveness has occurred. This prohibition is based on the belief that by keeping forgiveness in the background and the focus, instead, on creating a safe place for dialogue, many, if not most, victims will feel safe enough to travel the path of authentic forgiveness if that outcome is what happens and what they truly desire. Because it is deliberately made "irrelevant" (unless victims specifically request help with forgiving), victims may not identify or be explicit in the dialogue with the offender about having forgiven him or her despite having released negative emotions, replaced those emotions with positive feelings, or experienced an emotional transformation.

The challenge, therefore, is to understand the dimensions of implicit forgiveness by using methods, consistent with restorative justice principles, which do not require the explicit acknowledgment that it has or has not occurred. Indeed, requiring explicit acknowledgment might obscure a valid response because the need to "claim" its existence or communicate it to the offender could likely trigger a host of concerns for the victim, such as excusing, exoneration, forgetting, and reconciliation, that are popularly associated with the assertion of forgiveness (Enright and Fitzgibbons, 2000). The focus on explicit forgiveness also generates concern about the victim's ability to sustain forgiveness (due to confusion about forgiveness as a process), and questions, therefore, about its authenticity.

The purpose of this study, therefore, is to study the process of dyadic forgiveness in the context of restorative justice by examining shifts in emotional energy between victim and offender in preparation for and during the dialogue. The focus on flow and course of emotional energy leaves forgiveness per se underground, which is where it actually resides in restorative justice interventions.

RESTORATIVE JUSTICE AND MORAL RECTIFICATION

Studies of unilateral forgiveness have repeatedly found that empathy is the only psychological variable shown to facilitate victim forgiveness when induced experimentally (McCullough, 2001). Indeed, research has shown that empathy completely mediates the apology–forgiveness connection (e.g. McCullough *et al.*, 1998) and reduces the injustice gap by helping victims to see themselves as less innocent as human beings and their offenders as less evil (Exline, *et al.*, 2003; Worthington, 2003).

This well-established finding has recently been confounded by findings that suggest that dyadic forgiveness is mediated by changes in the victim's sense of justice that facilitate benevolent feelings toward the offender (Wenzel and Okimoto, 2010). Historically, the goal of seeking justice has been considered antithetical to forgiveness since justice is associated with payback or an eye-for-an eye approach whereas forgiveness is associated with the cancellation of a debt or mercy (Karremans and Van Lange, 2005, p.291). If justice is seen as larger than retribution and inclusive of fairness procedures and human values personified by the concern for the welfare of others, then forgiveness and justice reside in a similar domain as compatible. Indeed, if justice is more of a social construct about human values than a victim's need for justice, it could be positively associated with forgiveness (ibid., p.295) and the act of forgiving could help restore a sense of justice in the victim (Wenzel and Okimoto, 2010, p. 402). This conceptualization, however, requires that forgiveness be viewed as part of a mutual or dyadic process of accountability that includes the offender taking ownership, as in coming to terms with what he or she has done and its impact on the victim and expressing remorse (Andrews, 2000; Wenzel and Okimoto, 2010, p.402). It also requires a change in heart of both parties but in consultation with each other (Andrews, 2000, p.81).

Wenzel and Okimoto (2010) maintain that, for the victim, a transgression is more than a physical hurt or material harm but rather is a violation of values presumed to be shared. Responses to an aggression must restore those values through re-establishing the social consensus with the offender about the values violated and repair the perceived consensus for the victim about relevant values (Wenzel *et al.*, 2010). Forgiveness in this regard echoes Armour and Umbreit's tripartite representation of forgiveness in restorative justice; they claim that from the offender's perspective, the experience of being forgiven not only involves the victim and offender but is commensurate with being reinstated in the community as a moral citizen (Van Biema, 1999). The offender's reinstatement is an outgrowth of his or her engagement in a two-way process that furthers accountability, remorse and reparation (Armour and Umbreit, 2006, pp.126–127).

Wenzel and Okimoto (2010) have shown, through forgiveness-induced controlled studies, that the act of forgiveness is motivated by more than a decision or an emotional response but is also an attempt to restore a sense of justice based on trust in a consensus with the offender about shared values. They contend that the restoration of a sense of justice plays a critical role in the expression of forgiveness usurping feelings of empathy and reappraisals of the transgression and forgiveness. Rather, it is related to the offender's explicit and credible acknowledgment of responsibility but more importantly, to the victims' perception that offenders share relevant values with them (ibid., p.415). Hence, feelings of justice satisfaction may require both meeting the victim's needs as well as addressing the offender's values (Gromet and Darley, 2006, p.377). In support of this conclusion, victims who have met with offenders report being more satisfied with the justice process, feeling more fairly treated, and having fewer negative emotions after meeting with offenders, as compared with traditional criminal justice processes (e.g. Latimer, Dowden, and Muise (2005); Sherman *et al.*, 2005).

The findings provide a heretofore unrecognized dimension of dyadic forgiveness, that is, the victim's need for justice. This is another basis for the energy shifts that may occur between victim and offender in restorative justice interventions where the sense of injustice and issues of retributive, procedural, and human justice are prominent. Moreover, the findings about the victim's need for justice are compatible with Armour and Umbreit's (2006) assertion that the offender has a need to be morally reinstated in the victim's eyes. If this need motivates offenders to prove through their remorse and contrition that they are not monsters but rather deserving and credible as human beings, the reaffirmation through dialogue of what they share together might reassure the victim of their common commitment and adherence to a morally derived social compact and reinstate the offender as worthy.

THE ENERGY OF FORGIVENESS

The concept of energy derives, in the scientific world, from physics and the work of Robert Mayer who advanced the idea of different forces and how they are related to each other (Caneva, 1993). Mayer maintained that energy cannot be destroyed but can be transformed. In support of this idea, he postulated that forces are causes to which the equation that cause equals the effect is applicable since in the chain of causes and effects a number expressing the energy flow can never become zero because causes are indestructible. Moreover, since causes can assume various forms they are also qualitatively convertible. A force, for example, that causes the fall of objects is related to motion as cause and effect; they are convertible one into the other. Hence, since energy is constant and has the capacity to be converted into various forms, that is, negative energy (crime) may be transformed into positive energy (healing, implicit forgiveness).

The concept of energy, as it relates to forgiveness, also derives from Chinese culture. Energy refers to the life force that flows through the body's meridians and sustains all living things. It holds that everything in the universe is governed by five natural elements (wood, fire, earth, metal, and water) that are interrelated aspects of energy and function in harmony and balance with each other. Chi rests on the principle that disease reflects blocked energy.

The field of mind–body medicine, also derived from Eastern religions, is significant to the energy of forgiveness as well because of its focus on the use of mind through meditation and mindfulness to restore the flow of bodily energies in the service of healing for damage done physically, psychologically, and emotionally. Associated with mind–body and the connection with the brain is emerging interest in the neurobiology of interpersonal experience and the flow of energy and information among people. Siegel (2012), for example, maintains that relationships and neural linkages interact to shape the mind and that communication is based on the sharing of energy that has informational value between people based on prior learning. This "information" consists of swirls of energy that have symbolic meaning (p.6). The weaving together of modes of information processing is called integration, which is considered "the heart of health" (ibid., p.9). In contrast, lack of integration likely contributes to individuals who become stuck in their growth and development (ibid., p.10).

These derivations on the energy concept have direct relevance to forgiveness in restorative justice. As derived from physics, the facilitated meeting between victim and offender likely sets off forces, that if channeled, convert energy stored from the crime or negative energy associated with crime and the offender into positive energy. The dialogue itself works to release and redirect blocked energy or chi by correcting the imbalance of pain between victim and offender generated by the crime. The engagement of victim and offender is motivated by the desire for healing and the use of openness associated with the holistic mind–body paradigm to access the energy and regulate its flow. Finally, the focus on sharing between victim and offender of vital information is, in effect, a sharing of energy that shifts understanding such that there can be integration of the harm for both victim and offender. This is supported by the field of interpersonal neurobiology.

The concept of the energy of forgiveness draws from and is promoted by formulations from these diverse backgrounds.

ENERGY SHIFTS

Support for positive energy shifts as manifestations of forgiveness are most evident in the neurological and cardiological research on the health aspects of forgiveness. For example, forgiveness studies show changes in lower resting diastolic blood pressure and cortisol levels (Worthington *et al.*, 2007, p.297) and cardiovascular reactivity patterns. Forgiveness interventions have shown reductions in anger-induced myocardial perfusion defects in cardiac patients (ibid., p.299) and in affective and sensory pain for individuals suffering from chronic low back pain (Carson *et al.*, 2005). Moving beyond self-report, studies on brain physiology using electroencephalographic techniques or functional brain imaging tools and functional magnetic resonance imaging have made it possible to investigate the neural bases of the decisional and emotional components of forgiveness involved in the modulation of behavior, in moral evaluation and in adopting forgivingness strategies (Worthington *et al.*, 2007, p.293).

As an indicator of positive energy shifts, a recent study on the neural correlates of forgiveness examined re-appraisal-driven forgiveness (consistent with mental perspective taking and empathic concern) and subjective relief by using functional magnetic resonance imaging (MRI) to map regional brain activity when forgiveness was granted to an imagined offender (Ricciardi *et al.*, 2013). Researchers found activation in a brain cortical network responsible for perspective taking processes, appraisals and empathy, suggesting that these processes may play an important role in reducing negative affect. As a counterpart, a study of receiving forgiveness found that offenders not only prompted increases in positive emotions but receiving forgiveness and/or experiencing reconciliation stimulated less furrowing of the brow muscle associated with negative emotion and more electromyography activity of the zygomatic muscle indicative of smiling (ibid., p.297).

Although this study of implicit forgiveness is not focused on physiological indicators or neuroanatomy, research into neuro-correlates suggest that shifts in the energy associated with the transgression and shifts in the energy created by dialogue between victim and offender can likely be seen neurologically regardless of whether the forgiveness response is implicit or explicit. To that end, findings from brain mapping studies support the focus on energy shifts as a valid medium for examining implicit forgiveness in a dyadic context.

METHODOLOGY FOR ARCHIVAL REVIEW

Having situated the study of implicit forgiveness in the literature on forgiveness, the next step for the study is to develop beginning theory about the flow of energy in restorative justice dialogue. This theory can be used to guide interviews with 20 restorative justice victim participants who have experienced emotional transformation as a result of meeting with offenders and letting go of negative and life depleting energy (e.g. implicit forgiveness). The evolving theory will be augmented by results from (1) retrospective accounts with these participants about their experience of meeting with the offender and (2) data from a study of 60 victim–offender dyads who participated in victim offender mediation/dialogue.

The following section is a beginning formulation about the flow of energy in implicit forgiveness. It comes from a review of victim and offender participant transcripts, case notes, and videos from restorative justice dialogues. There were 30–40 videos from past dialogues that were originally reviewed and selected for closer analysis by Marilyn Armour and Mark Umbreit. Subsequently, Armour reviewed 20 transcripts from interviews with victim and offender participants about their experience of going through the dialogue process. Armour also reviewed 11 transcripts from interviews with David Doerfler, the founder and initial director of the VOM/D program in Texas. These interviews were conducted with Doerfler in 2002 prior to his leaving the VOM/D program and focused on a review of his cases, his conceptualizations of the dialogue process and his role as facilitator of these restorative justice dialogues. Ted Lewis, restorative justice practitioner and Communications Consultant for the Center for Restorative Justice and Peacemaking spent a week with Armour in a detailed analysis of selected materials from videos, notes, and transcripts. Together they created a beginning formulation of the flow of energy concept resulting in implicit forgiveness. Their discussions were audiotaped and transcribed as data to be used in conceptualizing the flow of energy in restorative justice dialogues as well as the identification of key dimensions and underlying conditions of implicit forgiveness.

GLOSSARY OF CONSTRUCTS

What follows is an alphabetized glossary of constructs specific to the findings from the review of archival materials and pertain to the energy flow of implicit forgiveness in restorative justice dialogues. Figure 1.1 shows the energy flow from the crime through the dialogue.

Completion

Completion refers to a time, usually at the end of the dialogue, when all relevant information and interaction has been brought into the shared conversation such that the victim's story and the offender's version of the crime and its impact are complete. The completion happens because victim and offender allow the process to guide them to the point where they are done with whatever they have needed to do with each other.

It consists of three dimensions: (1) reckoning, (2) balance, and (3) expression:

1. *Reckoning* refers to the accountability process and the settling of accounts between stakeholders that are otherwise unbalanced due to the transgression. Victim and offender must both reckon with themselves about what occurred and with each other. Reckoning commonly involves uncovering layers of accountability through conversation and the configuring and reconfiguring of the meaning assigned to the transgression so that it is shaped, changed, and re-altered until it leads to the end point of completion.

2. *Balance* refers to equity and equilibrium and the restoration between victim and offender of being in right relationship to each other. It also connotes that the energy that was otherwise churning with movement, intensity, and pressure is calm and at rest.

3. *Expression* refers to behaviors that occur, frequently toward the end of the dialogue, when victim and offender feel compelled, even driven, to convey thoughts or feelings in words or by gestures and conduct about the meaningfulness of their encounter. They may reach out to hug each other without having declared any intention to do so. There may be smiles, laughter, a squeeze of the hand, and statements of gratitude. The expression, in whatever form, has symbolic overtones in that it often reflects a joining and affirmation of each other at a core level.

Whether the expression is one-way or shared, it connotes an understanding that the past, as it was, no longer holds sway over the person.

This is the point where, in some dialogues, a victim may spontaneously offer forgiveness or the offender may ask for it. In the context of the dialogue, the victim's expression may connote an unburdening and transformation of the pain and/or acceptance or moral reinstatement of the offender. The offender's question may likewise be an expression of his desire for moral reinstatement as human, worthy and deserving, and an inquiry as to how the victim sees and experiences him subsequent to their conversation.

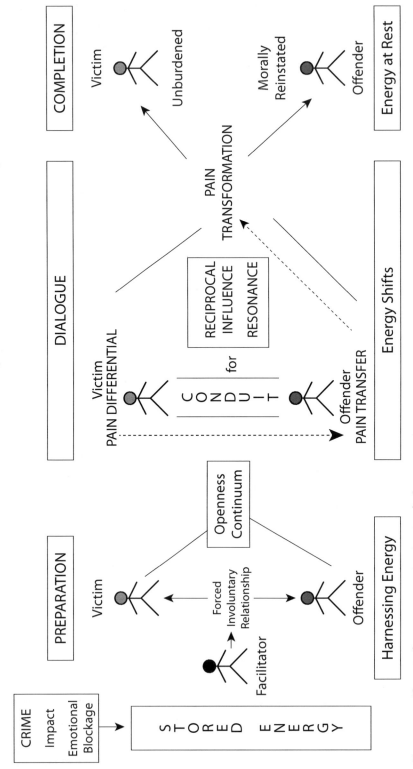

Figure 1.1: Energy flow in restorative justice dialogue

It is easy to confuse "forgiveness" as a code phrase for these more basic needs with popular meanings such as "pardon" or "mercy." Indeed, we have few other words, if any, to ask the question, "Can we be complete?" or to express the positive energy felt toward another who has taken the pain from the transgression as his own. It is possible, therefore, that there is no word to describe the sense of completion, the magnetism of victim and offender toward each other after a transformative encounter, or the positive energy that gets birthed off of the transformation of energy. Consequently, the word "forgiveness" may be all that we currently have in our limited lexicon to express the powerfulness of what happens relationally to participants who go through this process. The term "implicit forgiveness" is used in this study to best define the phenomenon that occurs.

Conduit

A conduit is a channel created by victim and offender for sharing thoughts, feelings, and reactions. It is the repository for what is happening in the space between the participants. It is co-constructed by victim and offender. The strength of the channel and the flow through it are conditioned by the degree of openness and authenticity each person brings to the dialogue and the quality of sharing between them. A positive flow, for example, will accelerate giving and receiving. If a person is more guarded, it will take longer to create a genuine dyadic flow. Although the conduit is established by the key stakeholders engaged with each other, the facilitator serves as the container for the energy from each of them until they meet. As such, the facilitator symbolically holds the energy in one place as it heats up prior to the dialogue.

Dissonance

Dissonance, specific to cognition, refers to discomfort experienced when victim and/or offender hold two or more contradictory beliefs, ideas, or values at the same time or are confronted with new information that conflicts with existing beliefs, ideas, or values (Festinger, 1957). In the universal human striving for internal consistency, the discomfort motivates or energizes participants to reduce the dissonance by (a) increasing the validity of the original belief to outweigh the conflicting belief, (b) reducing the importance of the conflicting belief, or (c) changing the conflicting belief so that it is consistent with other beliefs and behaviors (ibid.). In relationship to energy flow, dissonance creates a field of energy due to the tension of opposing forces. That energy provokes movement to reduce the opposition created by contradictory elements.

Dissonance is fundamental to restorative justice because meeting with the person responsible for the harm done to self and others and looking for assistance with healing is dissonant with cultural expectations. There may be both pre-dialogue dissonance related to the decision to pursue a meeting with the offender as well as dissonance that occurs during the dialogue because of information or experiences with the offender that contradict previously held understandings or attitudes.

Dissonance can occur for the offender as well. For example, from the offender's pre-dialogue perspective, it is likely that the victim could regard the offender as someone who could give him or her something worthwhile after having taken from the victim so deeply. Likewise, there is pre-dialogue dissonance around the fact that the dialogue is built on opposing truths: the pain associated with the transgression could be made worse by coming together but the only way, perhaps, to reduce or remove the pain is to come together. Beyond these contradictory realities, there are experiences throughout the dialogue that create dissonance. For example, victim or offender may have drawn conclusions about each other's character from scraps of information gleaned from behaviors in the courtroom, comments made by witnesses to the crime, or reports in the media. In seeing and experiencing the other in the face-to-face dialogue, new information or behaviors may contradict the old picture causing a quandary about which reality is genuine and forcing a choice, that is, movement, in order to reduce or resolve the discomfort or dissonance.

This process may occur repeatedly. Either party may recognize, as a result of the interaction during the dialogue, that they have information about the crime itself or about the devastating consequences that only they know. However, that information may be difficult to share. Their awareness of what they know and the need by the other for what only they know creates dissonance; if they withhold it, it becomes, in effect, a secret given what the other needs. If they share it, they lose control over what otherwise may be private. The confrontation created by co-existing but contradictory realities generates tension that forces choices (movement) in beliefs and responses to one another continually throughout the dialogue. In restorative justice, each choice allows for resolution of the tension and movement forward until the dialogue is complete.

Energy shift

Energy shift refers both to minor or graduated shifts and to a pivotal or core shift. Both graduated shifts and the core shift refer to a change emotionally and/or relationally in the quality of the interaction. The movement can be either negative or positive but it propels the energy in a different direction. The shift(s) can be caused by something novel or jarring that throws off what the participant had previously understood. They can be caused by oneself. For example, a participant may have an unexpected and illuminating insight. The shift may also happen because of what the other person said or did or occur as the result of a series of exchanges between victim and offender. Frequently, the resolution of dissonance creates an energy shift. Both before and during the course of a dialogue, there are usually numerous graduated or benchmark shifts that are relatively minor in the entirety of the conversation. These shifts can allow new information to reform old perspectives so participants can shift out of more guarded or protected spaces. The realignment of thoughts or beliefs can further openness and moving forward. They may not reach awareness in a person's remembrances of the dialogue but they help fertilize the pivotal or core shift(s). Not uncommonly, a core shift(s) occurs during the dialogue. This shift may have the quality of a climax or crux point that is decisive in fulfilling the needs of participants.

Openness continuum

The openness continuum refers to varying degrees of psychological openness versus guardedness (being closed) that participants bring to the dialogue. Greater openness helps participants to be more available psychologically and emotionally to each other and to be impacted by the dialogue process. The amount of openness in each participant is a product, in part, of their disposition or idiosyncratic characteristics (e.g. disposition for empathy, forgiveness), their preparation experience, and their trust in the facilitator. It includes histories that predate the crime, the discomfort that has developed since the crime, their inner values and resources for coping, and their growth since the preparation meetings. These conditions can inhibit or facilitate the flow from negative to positive energy. Moreover, the flow is affected by the ratio of openness to guardedness in a 2 x 2 quadrant when both participants are included. For example, a victim who is more open will be impacted differently based on the offender's position on the openness continuum. If the offender is more open as well, each person's openness will likely be augmented. If they start at different points, however, there may be less movement, at least initially, because of their mismatch, which may impact their responsiveness to each other and reduce the possibility for necessary energy shifts.

Pain differential

The pain differential refers to the disparity between victim and offender in the amount of pain each carries as a result of the harm done by the offender. Victims frequently feel the differential as a sense of injustice. Specifically, "Why should I be the one to carry the load of negative consequences of this crime?" The pain differential carries the energy from the impact of the transgression but that pain is stuck or lodged in the victim at the start-point of the dialogue because the offender, who caused the pain, has little or no visceral awareness of it either in terms of the damage he or she has done to the victim and/or the immensity of the ripple effect on other people's lives. As such, the pain cannot be resolved by the victim because it does not belong to that person. Rather, the pain belongs to the offender who is responsible for it. Consequently, whatever efforts the victim may have previously made to move the negative energy are likely futile.

Pain transfer

Pain transfer refers to the sharing of pain and suffering with the offender through the victim's story of the offense and its impact on his or her life. In telling the story fully, the victim transfers the negative energy to the offender. It also refers to the offender's embodying of the pain through their becoming deeply aware of the harm they have caused. Offenders may be self-aware without the direct sharing from the victim simply because they alone know the full story of what they did to cause harm. Through fully experiencing and reliving the victim's anguish, the offender takes on the burden of the pain and the responsibility for what they have done. Symbolically, the pain becomes theirs. This movement allows the pain to be shared. At a personal level, the pain transfer is about accountability, the taking of ownership for the harm caused and, consequently, relieving or rectifying the pain differential as a way for things to be made right again. Being accountable refers not only to ownership but to hearing the pain to the extent that the victim feels heard well by the offender. The pain transfer can only be fully understood in the complementary process of pain transformation whereby pain is both diffused and changed into something new.

Pain transformation

Pain transformation refers to the profound and radical change in the participants as a result of the successful transfer of pain from the victim to the offender. It is a point in the dyadic process where negatively charged emotional energy is diffused and replaced with positively charged emotional energy. This diffusion and positive shift may have begun during preparation or even before. However, it is during the pain transformation that it reaches a climax of actualization. Acting on the pain through the victim's unabashed relating of their narrative releases the stuck negative energy and the offender's acceptance of and response to the story begins to transform its valence. The victim, now unburdened of the pain from the offense that never was theirs, commonly feels visible, acknowledged and empowered. Moreover, in feeling heard, they may also feel safer. The offender, most often, feels and may express deep remorse about what they did to another human being. Their remorse may reflect a deepening awareness that helps strip away their denial so that they see themselves as well as the damage done more fully. Their remorse may also reflect having to answer to themselves and to the victim in ways that require a much higher standard of personal integrity and self-identity. This breakthrough is dyadic: the victim cannot feel truly seen without the offender letting them in fully. The offender cannot truly know what they have done without the victim's telling of their story. In this regard, victim and offender heal each other because the movement required could not happen without the other.

Paradox

A paradox is a statement that is self-contradictory because it often contains two statements that are both true, but in general, cannot both be true at the same time. In the context of restorative justice, paradox refers to the seeming contradictions that collectively comprise the operational truths within which restorative justice functions. Indeed, the concept of forgiveness in restorative justice contains multiple moral paradoxes. Paradox specific to the flow of energy works psychologically to reduce resistance to change (i.e. the movement of energy) because the change or change agent is unspecified. A facilitator's genuine neutrality about forgiveness, for example, communicates to the victim that it is okay to forgive and it is fine not to forgive. There is nothing to resist and no way to fail, therefore, relative to the issue of forgiving. This positioning leaves the facilitator's preference and the victim's correct behavior intentionally ambiguous, which paradoxically spurs or fosters movement in restorative justice because there is nothing to block it. In a different vein, the paradoxes that underscore forgiveness in restorative justice also generate movement because the co-existing but contradictory statements create dissonance or conflicting realities that do not resolve. Some of the multiple paradoxes include the following:

- When the concept of forgiveness is used as an explicit intervention, many victims will, at best, feel unsafe or even preached at. Some may feel quite offended. On the other hand, the more forgiveness remains in the background with the focus on creating a safe place for dialogue, the more likely victims will feel safe enough to travel the path of authentic forgiveness if that is what they truly desire.

- Forgiveness cannot be pushed in restorative justice but neither can it be ignored. As much as restorative justice maintains that forgiveness is not an intentional part of the process, the decision to bring victim and offender together for a healing dialogue requires that attention be given to forgiveness-generating elements such as empathy and remorse that are critical for forward movement. Moreover, to show no interest in forgiveness, particularly if it is desired by the victim or asked for by the offender, would negate the purpose and meaning of the dialogue.

- Forgiveness can be done solo but it is part of a dyadic process. This paradox reflects the idea that the victim's pain emanated out of and is tied to a forced, involuntary relationship. Moreover, the concept of forgiveness, itself, is embodied in a relationship. Does the attempt to address it outside of that relationship or without expression to the offender leave it incomplete? There is clear evidence that it is possible to experience the positive energy from forgiving when the victim elects to address the discomfort of their unforgiveness without involving the offender.

- Forgiveness can be willed but it is often discovered. This paradox suggests that forgiveness can be decisional or intentional in terms of the victim desiring the peace of forgiveness and assuming the responsibility to make it happen and/or to communicate having been able to forgive to the offender. It can also elude desire or be a transcendent gift that no one directs, but arrives serendipitously, without forethought from the victim or expressed desire from the offender.

- Forgiveness can occur but without forgiveness language. Society popularly associates forgiveness with mercy, pardon, and a history of favors that bypasses the process associated with dyadic forgiveness. Consequently, it is difficult for victims to verbally express explicit forgiveness without triggering associations, which confuse and compound what they are doing. Restorative justice maintains that expressions of forgiveness are not necessary for forgiveness to have occurred. This paradox is similar to the quandary that accompanies the tale of the tree that fell in the forest, but if no one heard it, did it fall? It raises a myriad of questions. If forgiveness remains covert, how can anyone know if forgiveness has occurred? Are there behaviors that each party perceives as equivalent to forgiving? If evidence shows that unforgiveness is reduced after a restorative justice dialogue, is that finding sufficient to determine that forgiveness, or some forgiveness, has occurred?

- Forgiveness requires that to be freed from past and present pain, participants have to re-enter past and present pain. In restorative justice, both victim and offender have to open to the pain of the transgression in order to move the energy of forgiveness from its blocked and negative state toward a positive state. However, there is no guarantee that entering that pain will result in the desired response, which is necessary for full or unblocked movement. There is no real security, therefore, in taking the risk but only the knowledge that not taking it reduces the quality and quantity of possible healing.

- Forgiveness embodies the reality that negative pain can be transformed into something positive. However, in the face of a violent and life-changing transgression, it is paradoxical that dealing with the negative energy from a crime so horrific could produce positive or life-giving energy, particularly from the offender who may have produced death.

Reciprocal influence

Reciprocal influence refers to the quality of communication between victim and offender during the dialogue and the fact that their giving and receiving goes both ways and is usually done in return for a similar act. In giving and receiving together, they encourage forward movement in the dialogue. Reciprocal influence often manifests as triggering a sequence of statements between the participants. One person makes a statement that triggers a statement from the other person that triggers a statement from the first person, etc., etc. The give and take is spontaneous. Unexpected statements are said and heard as each person thinks of something in reaction to the other's statement that has heretofore not seemed relevant to the history of the crime or its impact. However, the person receiving the statement in present time feels compelled to share the thought and therefore it becomes part of the mix.

This dyadic volleying produces various outcomes. There is a synergy of reciprocating influence where the momentum drives the movement forward in an upward spiral. It also deepens the responses, each to the other, which enlarges the story that they share. Moreover, the reciprocal triggering of interaction sustains the conversation taking it in new, unplanned, and seemingly unrelated directions. When the dialogue is finished, however, a review and reflection of the process reveals the linkages between trigger points that logically connect all the way to the point of completion. Moreover, after the transfer and transformation of pain has occurred, the statements between victim and offender appear triggered by a reciprocating empathy that further humanizes each to the other and energizes the forward movement toward completion.

Resonance

Resonance refers to the sympathetic vibration between victim and offender, which amplifies the shared quality of what is occurring between them including the strength or power of their words and feelings. It can be part of the dyadic volleying but usually emerges out of participants' openness to hearing each other fully. As such, the resonance is often referred to as "heart-to-heart" energy because of its intensity and intimacy. Moreover, resonance accompanies deep empathy, even bonding, which creates the energy flow between victim and offender that moves toward forgiveness.

Stored energy

Stored energy refers to the original energy produced by the transgression. It is existing energy that is fed by circumstances of the offense as well its impact on participants' lives and ongoing emotions, such as anger and the rumination it generates. Stored energy can be blocked/uncommunicated or released/communicated. The harm from the transgression builds a deep reservoir of blocked energy for both victim and offender. Though stored and likely blocked, the energy from the transgression is unstable, chaotic, and moves erratically in participants' lives prior to the dialogue. During preparation, the facilitator works to harness it so it can be used in the service of a healing connection by both directing the energy connected to the pain differential and channeling the energy so that it can flow between victim and offender. The facilitator also strives to develop greater openness in the participants so the energy can flow well in the dialogue. In this regard, the facilitator promotes the ability of participants to speak from the heart, thereby giving up the control that can allow the release of stored energy to fuel healing. The fostering of depth is also encouraged to ensure that the dialogue has enough energy to assist in the release of blocked or negative energy. Finally, the time limits on this one-time dialogue (i.e. roughly two to six hours in length) help create an energy surge in terms of the stored energy.

The constructs of completion, conduit, dissonance, energy shift, openness continuum, pain differential, pain transfer, pain transformation, paradox, reciprocal influence, resonance, and stored energy feed the energy flow of forgiveness between victim and offender in restorative justice dialogue. These constructs interact with each other in ways that produce feedback loops and a positive or upward spiral of movement.

ENERGY FLOW DYNAMICS IN RESTORATIVE JUSTICE DIALOGUE

The following description is a preliminary formulation of the dynamics of implicit forgiveness in restorative justice that shift the negative energy created by crime and transgression into the positive energy known as the energy of forgiveness. As illustrated in Figure 1.1, the process is underscored by external paradoxes that permeate forgiveness in restorative justice and by contradictions between what was known before versus new information and perceptions. These paradoxes and contradictions create dissonance, which, in an effort to resolve it, generate movement, pushing and transforming the negative energy into positive and healing forces.

Crime and its impact

A transgression births a forced and involuntary relationship between victim and offender that carries negative energy related to (1) the crime committed, (2) its impact on the lives of victim and offender and others who are connected to them, and (3) the emotional blockage of efforts to satisfactorily resolve the pain from the harm done (i.e. unforgiveness). The blockage exists, in part, because victim and offender attempt to handle the ensuing fallout outside the relationship. The relationship, though created by the crime, paradoxically is needed for resolution. Although the energy may accumulate over time due to the victim's rumination and a growing sense of injustice or the offender's increasing shame and powerlessness to make amends, it remains stored until, if ever, affective avenues become available.

Preparation

During preparation, the facilitator works separately with victim and offender so that they are ready for the dialogue. Because they both know that the facilitator is meeting with the other person as well as themselves, they symbolically are engaged in dialogue, to some extent, already. Moreover, their decision to enter into the formal dialogue is recognition that their original relationship was forced, but this time their engagement is voluntary. These realities, along with the review by the facilitator of the transgression and its impact on their lives, release the stored negative energy, making it available for movement. The surfacing of this energy is unnerving because it has little direction and limited release. It may have a churning or chaotic quality. The facilitator's work is to harness this energy and channel it in the direction of what each person needs from the other and what each person must be prepared for and ready to do in the dialogue.

In addition to the facilitator's actions, preparation is a time to assess the relative openness or guardedness of each person generally and in response to meeting with and truly hearing each other. If an offender and victim are highly guarded, the flow of energy in the dialogue will likely be restricted and the movement limited. If an offender is guarded but the victim is quite open, the mismatch will have implications for whether or not the pain, fully held by the victim, will be received, that is, transferred, or whether the offender will block it, thereby creating a vacuum around the pain that, in effect, allows no real movement other than a continuation of the pain held by the victim. A core purpose of preparation, therefore, is to move participants further along on the openness continuum through creating dissonance. If an offender, for example, believes that the victim hates him, a facilitator might disturb the certainty of the offender's belief by sharing that in his last meeting with the victim she was curious about his upbringing or concerned about his health in prison. The contradiction between the offender's belief and the facilitator's portrayal creates dissonance and discomfort, which can only be resolved by the offender making the decision to cling to his old beliefs (i.e. to be guarded) or to consider that the victim may actually be different than who he thought she was (i.e. to be open). Greater openness is also achieved through the building of trust with the facilitator who allows both victim and offender to lean on that trust so that they can, more easily, enter a risk-laden and unknown territory with the other person.

Dialogue

There are a variety of dynamics that occur between victim and offender that lead to energy shifts during the dialogue. Indeed, some of those shifts may have occurred prior to the dialogue itself and contribute to positive movement. Aside from the interaction related to the pain differential, pain transfer and pain transformation, there is no linear sequencing or cause-and-effect relationships. Victim and offender must construct a conduit between them for the flow of energy to travel from each to the other. The conduit, however, gets built through moments of resonance where what one person says vibrates and resounds in the other through hearing deeply and on many levels. Systemically, the conduit is also the mechanism that allows the message to resound because it guides it straight to the heart of the other. . Similarly, the conduit is the product of each person being triggered over and over again in a reciprocal or back and forth manner by what the other person has said. Concurrently, the conduit helps channel what is said so it is more likely to activate a continuous and spontaneous exchange due to the participants' dyadic or reciprocal influence on each other. This intimate experience often has its own layered process where, unimpeded, participants allow the triggering set off by the other person's comments and reactions to continue until it reaches a natural end. This parallel free-associating teaches participants a lot about each other. It also opens them up further to themselves and one another.

There may be numerous energy shifts throughout the dialogue as a result of questions asked and/or the giving or receiving of new information about the crime, its antecedents, the victim's or offender's life, having new insights that bring clarity to otherwise murky territory, and reacting or seeing the other person react in unexpected ways, etc. These shifts are often generated by dissonance-fueling contradictions between what was known before and what is evident in the here and now. These contradictions resolve as participants reconfigure, that is, shift, their perceptions in response to circumstances that assist in their sense-making and internal resolution. In this regard, the dialogue itself is a meaning-making process where the meaning made for both is the product of a shared process.

The pivotal or core shift in the dialogue, however, has to do with the pain differential associated with the crime. Until the dialogue, the pain from the transgression, like stored energy, has been held solely by the victim. In this regard, the energy associated with the crime has been unbalanced. Moreover, it cannot be resolved by the victim because the pain does not belong to him or her. Rather, the pain belongs to the offender who is responsible for the transgression. In telling the story of the crime and its impact, the victim, in effect, gives the misplaced pain to the offender. Because the offender was not the recipient of the crime, he or she has no way of knowing the damage done without the victim's story. Anything imagined by the offender is likely far from knowing, let alone feeling, the victim's truth. As the offender experiences the victim's pain – pain he or she caused – the pain gets acted upon and transferred from the victim to the offender. The pain inside the offender produces a self-confrontation. Instead of it being abstract or imagined, the offender now really knows his or her impact and has to be accountable for it. If the offender is open, the new knowledge cuts through whatever denial is still operating. The pain felt by the offender is likely sharper than any suffering heretofore experienced.

The natural response to the pain is remorse. As it is expressed and flushed out, it may be accompanied by other insights about oneself and how he or she has lived life. For the victim, this transference, if authentic, can be profound. Relieved of the pain differential, which has been accepted by the person responsible for that pain, the victim is available emotionally to experience the offender's humanity toward him or her. In the ensuing conversations, that humanity may be deepened as the offender, who has also released negative energy, is increasingly forthcoming and genuine. It is at this point that the pain becomes transformed as a result of its being acted on through the victim sharing and the transfer of it to the offender.

Completion

The dialogue is complete when the injustice, that is, inequity, between victim and offender that was caused by the transgression and embodied in the pain differential is rebalanced. The equity in the relationship, that is, being in the right relationship, is re-established by the fact that the victim is unburdened or freed of the misplaced pain and the offender, in accepting it, is symbolically reinstated as a moral and worthy person. The energy has shifted and is no longer negative between them. Because the work that they needed to do with each other is finished, the energy, for the time being, is at rest. The implicit forgiveness that attends this completion is often expressed verbally as gratitude and nonverbally in smiles, tears, warmth, inquiries, or reminders about future actions and mutual caring. Usually, there is no desire or need to meet again.

CONCLUSION

This preliminary formulation of the process of implicit forgiveness in restorative justice is not inclusive or reflective of many dialogues. However, it offers an initial model that can be tested and reworked in the upcoming analysis of interviews done with victims who participated in restorative justice dialogues and who have experienced forgiveness toward the offender outside of a preset agenda.

This review has two purposes. The first purpose is to situate the upcoming study in the relevant research on forgiveness with emphasis on the significance of implicit forgiveness in restorative justice cases. Although there are over 900 studies on forgiveness, little attention has been paid to bilateral or dyadic forgiveness outside of close relationships infused with history and the desire for reconciliation. Moreover, most research has focused on clinical interventions with the person transgressed against such that the actual dyad is not a part of the energy shift that results in forgiveness. Recent findings related to the forgiveness and the re-establishment of shared values in the eyes of the victim, however, support the current study and the transformation of pain that reinstates the offender as a human being with moral worth.

The second purpose is to postulate a beginning model of the energy flow of dyadic forgiveness in restorative justice dialogue through a review and analysis of archival materials. The model includes a glossary of constructs that evolved from the review and a hypothesized depiction and description of the energy flow that converts stored negative energy from the crime into healing through energy shifts created by dissonance-fueled paradoxes and contradictions that foster resolution in a positive direction.

REFERENCES

Andrews, M. (2000) 'Forgiveness in context.' *Journal of Moral Education 29*, 75–86.

Angel, C. (2005) 'Crime victims meet their offenders: Testing the impact of restorative justice conferences on victims' post-traumatic stress symptoms.' Doctoral dissertation. University of Pennsylvania, PA.

Armour, M.P. and Umbreit, M.S. (2006) 'Victim forgiveness in restorative justice dialogue.' *Victims & Offenders 1*, 2, 123–140.

Baumeister, R.F., Stillwell, A.M., and Heatherton, T.F. (1995) 'Personal narratives about guilt: Role in action control and interpersonal relationships.' *Basic and Applied Social Psychology 17*, 173–198.

Caneva, K.L. (1993) *Robert Mayer and the Conservation of Energy*. Princeton, NJ: Princeton University Press.

Carson, J.W., Keefe, K.J., Lynch, T.R., Carson, K.M., *et al*. (2005) 'Loving-kindness meditation for chronic low back pain.' *Journal of Holistic Nursing 23*, 3, 287–304.

Darves-Bornoz, J.M., Choquet, M., Ledoux, S., Gasquet, I., and Manfredi, R. (1998) 'Gender differences in symptoms of adolescents reporting sexual assault.' *Social Psychiatry and Psychiatric Epidemiology 33*, 111–117.

Di Blasio, F.A. (1998) 'The use of decision-based forgiveness interventions within intergenerational family therapy.' *Journal of Family Therapy 20*, 77–94.

Durose, M.R., Cooper, A.D., and Snyder, H.N. (2014) *Recidivism of Prisoners Released in 30 States in 2005: Patterns from 2005 to 2010*. Special Report. US Department of Justice, Bureau of Justice Statistics.

Enright, R.D. and Fitzgibbons, R.P. (2000) *Helping Clients Forgive: An Empirical Guide for Resolving Anger and Restoring Hope*. Washington, DC: American Psychological Association.

Exline, J.J., DeShea, L., and Holeman, V.T. (2007) 'Is apology worth the risk? Predictors, outcomes, and ways to avoid regret.' *Journal of Social and Clinical Psychology 26*, 479–504.

Exline, J.J., Worthington, E.L., Jr., Hill, P., and McCullough, M.E. (2003) 'Forgiveness and justice: A research agenda for social and personality psychology.' *Personality and Social Psychology Review 7*, 337–348.

Festinger, L. (1957) *A Theory of Cognitive Dissonance.* Stanford, CA: Stanford University Press.

Fincham, F.D., Beach, S.R.H., and Davila, J. (2004) 'Forgiveness and conflict resolution in marriage.' *Journal of Family Psychology 18*, 1, 72–81.

Fincham, F.D., Beach, S.R., and Davila, J. (2007) 'Longitudinal relations between forgiveness and conflict resolution in marriage.' *Journal of Family Psychology 21*, 3, 542–545.

Freedy, J.R., Resnick, H.S., Kilpatrick, D.G., Dansky, B.S., and Tidwell, R.P. (1994) 'The psychological adjustment of recent crime victims in the criminal justice system.' *Journal of Interpersonal Violence 9*, 450–468.

Gilboa-Schechtman, E. and Foa, E.B. (2001) 'Patterns of recovery after trauma: The use of inter-individual analysis.' *Journal of Abnormal Psychology 110*, 392–400.

Gromet, D.M. and Darley, J. (2006) 'Restoration and retribution: How including retributive components affects the acceptability of restorative justice processes.' *Social Justice Research 19*, 395–432.

Hill, W.E. (2001) Understanding forgiveness as discovery: Implications for marital and family therapy.' *Contemporary Family Therapy 23*, 369–384.

Karremans, J.C. and Van Lange, P.A.M. (2005) 'Does activating justice help or hurt in promoting forgiveness?' *Journal of Experimental Social Psychology 41*, 290–297.

Latimer, J., Dowden, C., and Muise, D. (2005) 'The effectiveness of restorative justice practices: A meta-analysis.' *The Prison Journal 85*, 2, 127–144.

Leskin, G.A. and Sheikh, J.I. (2002) 'Lifetime trauma history and panic disorder: Findings from the National Comorbidity Survey.' *Journal of Anxiety Disorders 16*, 599–603.

Malcolm, W., Warwar, S., and Greenberg, L. (2005) 'Facilitating Forgiveness in Individual Therapy as an Approach to Resolving Interpersonal Injuries.' In J.E.L. Worthington (ed.) *Handbook of Forgiveness.* New York: Routledge.

McCullough, M.E. (2001) 'Forgiveness: Who does it and how do they do it?' *Current Directions in Psychological Science 10*, 194–197.

McCullough, M.E., Rachal, K.C., Sandage, S.J., Worthington, E.L., Jr., Brown, S.W., and Hight, T.L. (1998) 'Interpersonal forgiving in close relationships II: Theoretical elaboration and measurement.' *Journal of Personality and Social Psychology 75*, 1586–1603.

Murphy, J.G. (2002) 'Forgiveness, reconciliation and responding to evil. A philosophical overview.' *Fordham Urban Law Journal 27*, 1353–1367.

Murphy, S., Johnson, L.C., and Lohan, J. (2002) 'The aftermath of the violent death of a child: An integration of the assessments of parents' mental distress and PTSD during the first 5 years of bereavement.' *Journal of Loss and Trauma 7*, 203–222.

New Hampshire Department of Corrections Victim Services Office (n.d.) *For Your Information… Apologies, Amends and Accountability.* Accessed on December 19, 2014 at www.nh.gov/nhdoc/divisions/victim/documents/apology-amend.pdf

Ricciardi, E., Rota, G., Sani, L., Gentili, C., *et al.* (2013) 'How the brain heals emotional wounds: The functional neuroanatomy of forgiveness.' *Frontiers of Human Neuroscience 7*, 839.

Riek, B.M., Luna, L.M.R., and Schnabelrauch, C.A. (2013) 'Transgressors' guilt and shame: A longitudinal examination of forgiveness seeking.' *Journal of Social and Personal Relationships, 31*, 6, 751–772.

Sandage, S.J. and Worthington, E.L.J. (2010) 'Comparison of two group interventions to promote forgiveness: Empathy as a mediator of change.' *Journal of Mental Health Counseling 32*, 1, 35–57.

Sandage, S.J., Worthington, E.L., Hight, T.L., and Berry, J.W. (2000) 'Seeking forgiveness: Theoretical context and an initial empirical study.' *Journal of Psychology and Theology 28*, 21–35.

Sherman, L.W., Strang, H., Angel, C., Woods, D., *et al.* (2005) 'Effects of face-to-face restorative justice on victims of crime in four randomized, controlled trials.' *Journal of Experimental Criminology 1*, 367–395.

Siegel, D.J. (2012) *The Developing Mind: How Relationships and the Brain Interact to Shape Who We Are.* New York: Guilford.

Strang, H. (2002) *Repair or Revenge: Victims and Restorative Justice.* Oxford: Clarendon Press.

Thompson, M.P., Norris, F.H., and Ruback, R.B. (1998) 'Comparative distress levels of inner-city family members of homicide victims.' *Journal of Traumatic Stress 11*, 223–242.

Umbreit, M.S. (1995) *Mediating Interpersonal Conflicts: A Pathway to Peace.* West Concord, MN: CPI Publishing.

Umbreit, M.S. and Armour, M.P. (2010) *Restorative Justice Dialogue: An Essential Guide for Research and Practice.* New York: Springer.

Van Biema, D. (1999) 'Should all be forgiven?' *Time 153*, 55–58.

Wade, N.G. and Worthington, E.L., Jr. (2005) 'In search of a common core: Content analysis of interventions to promote forgiveness.' *Psychotherapy: Theory, Research, Practice, Training 42*, 160–177.

Wenzel, M. and Okimoto, T.G. (2010) 'How acts of forgiveness restore a sense of justice: Addressing status/power and value concerns raised by transgressions.' *European Journal of Social Psychology 40*, 401–417.

Wenzel, M., Turner, J.K., and Okimoto, T.G. (2010) 'Is forgiveness an outcome or initiator of sociocognitive processes? Rumination, empathy, and cognitive appraisals following a transgression.' *Social Psychological and Personality Science 1*, 4, 369–377.

Worthington, E.L., Jr. (2003) *Forgiving and Reconciling: Bridges to Wholeness and Hope.* Downers Grove, IL: InterVarsity Press.

Worthington, E.L., Jr., Hook, J.N., Utsey, S.O., Williams, J., *et al.* (2012) 'Decisional and emotional forgiveness: Conceptualization and development of self-report measures.' Unpublished manuscript. Accessed on August 14, 2017 at http://static.squarespace.com/static/518a85e9e4b04323d507813b/t/51ddacc8e4b0c8c25ec46f3d/1373482184627/Decisional+and+Emotional+Forgiveness+.pdf

Worthington, E.L., Jr , Van Oyen Witvliet, C., Pietrini, P., and Miller, A.J. (2007) 'A review of evidence for emotional versus decisional forgiveness, dispositional forgivingness, and reduced unforgiveness.' *Journal of Behavioral Medicine 30*, 291–302.

2

VICTIM CASE NARRATIVES AND ANALYSIS

INTRODUCTION

The following section consists of 20 victim stories and their analysis based on the model developed in Section 1. Each case has been summarized from the interview transcript and presented chronologically, covering the time from the crime to after the dialogue up to the present day. The summary is used as the foundation for the case analysis. Each case is analyzed in three parts: Crime and Its Aftermath, Preparation and Dialogue. Victim participants lost loved ones to vehicular homicide and murder in nineteen cases. One person was the direct victim of a shooting. Collectively, the cases demonstrate the wide range of circumstances that attend severely violent crime and the deeply personal motivation to pursue a restorative justice, victim offender dialogue (VOD) with the person responsible for the crime. In all instances, victim participants were pleased with their decisions to meet with the offender. They found that the positive dialogue outcome was maintained even when, in some cases, offenders subsequently reoffended or did not keep the commitments they made to the victim.

MARIA'S STORY AND ANALYSIS

Maria's son, Marcus, was shot and killed by a 16-year-old boy at a party. Maria describes her path to forgiveness as so gradual she was almost unaware it was happening, until she was face to face with Donny. Maria had multiple serendipitous experiences, which pushed her to meet with Donny, an experience she sums up as "beyond belief." Maria was able to share with Donny true forgiveness, transferring her pain to Donny as he held her crying. They have continued to meet and share with others the unique relationship that Maria, Marcus, and Donny share together.

My son was murdered, shot three times in the chest and once in the head by a 16-year-old boy at an after-hours party. I hated the man who killed him. I wanted him to go to prison for the rest of his life, never to step on the same piece of earth that I stepped on. He was an animal and he deserved to be caged. The fact that he was 16 meant nothing to me. I hated everybody at that time.

When I first got the news, I couldn't sleep. I'd lay awake and listen for a key to turn, a knock at the door. I'd drive down the street, looking to see if I could see my son. I did that for a long time—months, maybe years.

My family didn't talk about it and haven't for 21 years. Everyone thought that I was the strong one, I didn't need nobody. "She'll pull through this." People thought, "Well, if I bring up your son's name, it's gonna hurt so I'm not gonna do that. I don't want you to cry." The truth is that those tears would likely have been tears of joy instead of sadness because someone else is thinking of your child. So no one talked about it and I wasn't going to bring it up with them. I was angry, angry with everyone for a very long time.

It took two years to get to the trial but after the murderer was sentenced, I fell upon a page in a book entitled "Two Mothers." It was about two angels in heaven and because of the similarity in the color of their crowns, they recognized they had both been mothers here on earth and started talking about their sons. One mother said, "I would have taken my son's place if I could have." The other mother fell on one knee and said, "You are she, the mother of Christ." The mother of Christ wiped a tear from her cheek and asked, "Tell me of your son so I may grieve with you." The other mother said, "My son is Judas Iscariot." After I read it again, I heard from within myself the declaration, "I want mothers whose children were murdered and mothers whose children have taken life to come together and heal." At first, I thought, "No. That can't happen. I don't want it to happen. It's not going to happen." I threw the idea away. But over the years, that declaration was all I kept hearing. "This is what you're to do." In order to make the vision happen, however, I made up my mind that I had to go and meet Donny, to make sure I had forgiven him.

After I found out about the VOD program, I went to the director and told him I wanted to meet Donny. At first Donny said no but after some months he said yes. I didn't have any hopes or expectations, I didn't know if I was gonna try to punch him out or not. We each participated in four preparation meetings that lasted two hours each. The facilitators for the dialogue wanted to make sure I knew why I wanted to meet with Donny and why Donny wanted to meet with me, what we would talk about, what we wouldn't talk about, what we wanted as an outcome. After they met with me they would meet with Donny and tell him what I said. Then they'd meet with me again and tell me what he said. Everything had to be in order before the meeting could take place. The first thing the facilitators said was, "Maria, he's such a nice guy." I said, "What? I don't wanna hear that!" I wanted to hear that he was an ogre.

I didn't feel any changes in me during the preparation meetings. I know we were both being honest but I didn't feel any differently. Those meetings just made me comfortable enough to be able to go and meet him. I did attend a program with victims and offenders for ten weeks and by the time it was over, I was thinking differently about offenders and murderers because I had heard their whole story. Also I spent time talking with another mother whose child had been killed and she helped me to see that he wasn't a monster.

That mother, who was also a friend, went with me to the prison for the dialogue. The night before she asked me to watch a DVD. It was about a guy who had taken someone's life but said he didn't do it. Now he was writing children's books and he was being let out of prison to go and share about his books. Watching that DVD changed something in me. I had wondered what it was like in prison. So through this DVD I got to see the guy in prison, his changes and some of the things he went through. I thought "Wow! Now this man is writing books and they're letting him out."

The next morning, we went to the prison. As I was walking up the ramp into the building I said to my friend, "I can't do it. I'm not ready." But my friend just pushed me up the ramp. I had to go to the bathroom because I was really crying. We went through the metal detector and a huge metal door. We couldn't see anyone working it and it shut by itself. I thought, "Whoa. We're really in here now." I told one of the guards, "Look, I'm the type of person who cannot tolerate dryness. Nothing is gonna happen here if you don't bring me some lotion." I thought that would end everything. Then we asked for cups for bottled water that the facilitators brought and the guard brought enough cups for everyone but Donny. I said, "Wait a minute. Where's his cup?" She answered, "Oh, he can't get a cup." I countered her by saying, "Well, what does that look like, us sitting here drinking water when he can't? That's not right." She finally brought in the cup. I didn't realize it at that time, but something had changed.

So she brought the cup and the lotion. My friend looked at the lotion bottle and told me to look at it again. The name of the lotion was

Beyond Belief. That's exactly what happened. It was unbelievable. I'm waiting for them to bring this man in who's taken my son's life exclaiming about the name of the lotion and then there was a knock at the door and I knew it was him. He entered and we shook hands. The first thing I said to him was, "Look, I don't know you. You don't know me. You did not know my son. My son didn't know you. So we need to lay a foundation. We need to get to know one another." That opened the conversation up and we talked for two hours. I know that something had already changed for me to say that. The forgiveness had started even if I was not aware of it.

I had told him in court that I forgave him. But as the years went on, I knew that I hadn't because he was on my mind too much. Even though I had repented all the things I had said or felt about him and said out loud that I had chosen to forgive him, I don't think I really recognized a heart change.

Donny and I met three or four times. In the first meeting, I saw Donny and my son had a lot in common. I didn't get all the answers I wanted, but I felt a little more comfortable with him. Comfortable enough that when he asked me if he could hug me, I said yes. We both walked around the table to get to each other and I became hysterical. I remember that I was falling and that he had to hold me up. He was just holding me and not allowing me to fall on that floor. That experience became a bond. He whispered to me saying, "I believe you're gonna be the person to help me to cry." During the dialogue I had talked to him about shedding tears and how men think they're not supposed to cry. I said to him, "Your tear ducts are just like my tear ducts. There's some things that you can just get rid of in your life. They may be small or they may be big. You just need to shed some tears and let some things out." So when he said, "I think you're going to be the person to help me to cry," I said, "Yeah. I'm gonna be that person." When he left the room, I bent over and said, "I just hugged the man that murdered my son. I just hugged the man that murdered my son." My friend came over to me to lift me up. But when I stood up, I began to feel a stirring that was moving in my feet and moving up, and moving up, and then it left me. I felt it leave me. Instantly, all that anger, the hatred, the bitterness, animosity was gone. I knew that it was over with and I have been free ever since. I had been dealing with all that stuff for 12 years. That first meeting was "beyond belief."

We got to know each other a little more each time we met. I still had the forgiveness in me. We were asked to speak to the other prison inmates about what had taken place in our meeting and we did that together. In the first meeting we'd had, he talked about his life as a child which brought up a lot of memories about my son. Marcus was reading at a 12th grade level in sixth grade and so was Donny. Marcus had to dress differently because he went to a private school and Donny's mother sent him to school in suits. He told me that he would never do anything to hurt me again, that he'd always be open and Donny said to me, "Me and your son have done a lot of the same things. We've been through a lot of the same things. We probably could've been friends." He told me he would be honest with me. Anything I wanted to know, that he would be willing to tell me. I told him, "In court, I'd forgiven you but today, I truly forgive you." He asked, "How can you do that ma'am?" I said, "Because of who is within me."

This is what I had to go through to get to what my calling is. I had to forgive myself also because how could I forgive someone else if I can't forgive me? I just saw the guard from the dialogue a couple Saturdays ago. We were at this function and she came and said, "What if I say the word lotion to you?" I said, "Lotion??" She said, "What if I would say 'Beyond Belief'?" I just started screaming out loud. I knew who she was! She was the guard that gave me the lotion! She told me she had known my son. "Me and Marcus used to play together with his cousin that lived down the street!" Amazing.

Analysis: Crime and its aftermath

Maria's journey to forgive was deeply connected to her dynamic relationship with God. For years, she prepared for the session with Donny knowing that her destiny lay in moving closer to the person who had murdered her son Marcus. At the same time, she harbored hatred and anger toward Donny and, in some ways, wrote off the world at large. Her family avoided ever mentioning Marcus both believing that Maria was strong and needed no one while concerned that the mere mention of his name would cause profound hurt. In reaction, Maria also decided not to speak about him to her family, sealing in her aloneness. Her days were spent searching for her son, unable to believe that her only child was really gone. The futility of her efforts created a powder keg with little relief but ready to explode.

The first shift in energy occurred when Maria came upon the poem "Two Mothers." As a devout Christian, the message of forgiveness and healing between the mother of Christ and mother of Judas was unmistakably relevant to her quest for relief. Rather than enveloping it, however, she struggled to accept what was otherwise an unacceptable idea. "That can't happen. I don't want it to happen. It's not going to happen." But the dissonance grew, requiring some sort of resolution because Maria kept hearing what she perceived as a divinely guided message that "This is what you're to do." In response to its incessant call, Maria decided she had to meet Donny. This movement gave direction to the energy amassed as a result of the murder and sealed off, in part, due to her isolation, anger, and obsessiveness.

Maria's decision to meet Donny was strongly compelled by her finding of the poem "Two Mothers." Maria had told Donny she forgave him at the trial. She had worked on forgiving him through repenting for her anger and reminding herself that she had made the choice to forgive. Her heart, however, knew better. She recognized that something was awry because she was unable to stop thinking repeatedly about him. This incongruity was like a stone in her shoe. She had resolved that she had to truly forgive Donny before feeling worthy to lead a group that brought together mothers of both victims and offenders. She determined, therefore, that she had to meet Donny in person to know for sure that her forgiveness was real and complete.

For Maria, there were energy sources that both blocked and compelled movement toward a forgiveness that felt whole. Besides the negative energy generated by the crime, she felt personal anger toward Donny and a generalized anger toward the world. A possible outlet with her family was blocked by the mutual silence about Marcus, causing additional and unresolved resentment, becoming another source of negative energy. Although her discovery of the poem "Two Mothers" opened the door to possible resolution, energy was further generated by the tension between her reluctance and her desire to move forward with the message generated by the poem, which was to bring together mothers of victims and offenders. Finally, there was a build-up of energy from struggling to fully comply with her religious prescription to forgive coupled with her guilt because her statement of having forgiven Donny was less than completely authentic.

Preparation

The purpose of dialogue preparation, in part, is procedural, allowing for the building of an agenda for the meeting, an assessment and refinement of each person's expectations, and an awareness of concerns that might hinder the sense of safety necessary for full sharing. This preparation process helps harness the stored energy to be used in the service of a carefully constructed meeting with the other party. The unspoken mission of preparation, however, is to help both victim and offender remove those barriers that could block fully hearing and experiencing each other, thus limiting the potential healing influence of the dialogue.

The formal preparation process increased Maria's comfort and sense of safety with the process but did little to expand her receptiveness to Donny.

Indeed, in some ways, it positively exacerbated her conflicted feelings toward him because the facilitators' remarks that "he's such a nice guy" inhibited her from concluding that he was an ogre. This pull toward seeing Donny anew was strengthened by hearing first hand the personal stories of offenders over ten weeks. Like a drip of water that keeps wearing down the sharp edges of a rock, Maria realized that she was feeling differently about offenders in general after hearing stories and spending time repeatedly with inmates and murderers like Donny. The pull toward greater openness was also furthered by the constancy of her friend who kept pushing her forward. Maria unquestionably trusted her friend's guidance because her child too had been killed. This friend tracked her every step of the way encouraging her to see Donny as more than a monster. Indeed, on the eve of the dialogue, her friend showed her a film about a murderer and the possibilities for his future, which again changed something in Maria. The film juxtaposed the murderer's criminal act and life in prison against the good he was doing in writing children's books. Being released from prison symbolically served to reward the murderer's transformation. For Maria, the synchronicity of this person's story placed in front of her by a trusted friend coupled with its message of hope generated yet another energy shift that expanded her openness to the experience of meeting with Donny.

Maria's vacillation, however, reappeared full force as she inched closer to the actual encounter with Donny. Her friend literally had to push her up the ramp into the prison as she exclaimed, "I can't do it. I'm not ready." Her crying jag in the privacy of the bathroom before going through security spoke to the tremendous import and consternation of what she was about to do. The realness of her decision to elect to meet the person face to face who had killed her son and whom she had only known in her mind hit her yet again as the metal door invisibly shut itself, sealing off the back door. Finally, she tried to buy time threatening to stall or even quit the dialogue until she got hand lotion and cups for the bottled water she had brought for drinking. This effort, however, was thwarted by events that continued to move her forward. She was diverted by her friend to see the message contained in the name of the hand lotion a guard brought her called "Beyond Belief." When the cups arrived for the water, she surprised herself by remarking on the injustice done to Donny because there was no cup for him. She recognized the inhumanity of the prison noting that he was expected not to need water like the rest of them. In her protest, she elevated Donny, moving him out of the position of "other" and moving herself into a position of caring for and about him.

Dialogue

Maria moved toward Donny from the time he entered the room. Besides shaking hands with him, she set the terms between them, noting that in spite of how profoundly they were already engaged in each other's lives, they did not know each other. Maria observed that her dictate that they needed to use their time together to lay a foundation was proof positive that she was amenable to a positive relationship and that again there had been an energy shift, which unbeknownst to her was the start of emotionally forgiving him. Using this conduit, they moved away from the forced involuntary relationship established by Marcus' murder and instead began to build a relationship marked by mutuality. As Donny talked about his life as a child and Maria talked about raising Marcus, Maria noted the similarities between the two and their upbringing. As children, they were both bright, reading at levels way beyond their years. The children's mothers had both dressed them for school in formal suits and uniforms. As they talked, Donny also saw how alike they were. "Me and your son have done a lot of the same things. We've been through a lot of the same things. We probably could've been friends."

Beside their commonalities, they shared intimately what was festering inside both of them. Maria told Donny that she questioned whether her forgiving in court was heartfelt. She reassured him that today she could truly forgive because she carried God inside her. Donny too assured Maria that he would tell her the truth and was willing to answer any question she had. But he too confessed that he'd struggled against himself, unable to cry and shed the sorrow he carried inside. This admittance, in effect, acknowledged the pain differential, the fact that Maria had unfairly carried the pain of the crime alone, and the need to rightfully transfer the major pain to Donny as the person responsible for it. Maria ministered to his need and desire to cry, pulling him toward her. She reminded him that his tear ducts were like hers. As the mother of the person he had killed, she uniquely could enter his psyche, gently guiding him past his blockage by giving him permission to rid himself of his own pain. As if invisibly bonded, Donny allowed Maria's gift to grow inside so that now he felt the pull toward her in response. He asked her for a hug and she responded, the two of them moving in concert toward each other and around the table that had stood between them. Their physical touching was electric. Without provocation, Maria became hysterical, transferring the enormity of her pain to Donny who, in turn, accepted it, literally holding her up so she did not fall. That experience became a bond as Donny declared, "I think you're going to be the person to help me to cry." As if sealing their future, Maria responded, "Yeah. I'm gonna be that person."

Struck by the contradiction of having just hugged the man that murdered her son, Maria bent over as if to catch her breath. As her friend lifted her up, Maria felt the negative energy she had carried for so long literally move up and out of her body. She described the unburdening and transformation of her pain. "Instantly, all that anger, the hatred, the bitterness, animosity was gone. I knew that it was over with and I have been free ever since." There was no explicit verbalization of forgiveness at that point. Rather, Maria symbolically forgave Donny by receiving his hug and literally coming apart in his arms. This act physically expressed her letting go of her mistrust but also conveyed to Donny her moral reinstatement of him in the world as acceptable. Indeed, Maria tested the genuineness and staying power of her forgiveness each time she met with Marcus.

Maria has marked the dialogue with Marcus with the phrase "Beyond Belief." Although the phrase expressed the profoundness of their first encounter, it also contained a subtext, which is that the journey to each other, in Maria's eyes, had been divinely guided. From the discovery of the poem "Two Mothers," Maria felt she was led to the message that she had to meet Donny. She was then led, through a series of events and symbols, to open herself to Donny. Though ambivalent about proceeding, Maria's surrender was analogous to a conversion in which she both released and transformed the toxic energy that had remained inside her from the murder of her son. The sudden appearance, long after the dialogue, of the prison guard who had given her the hand lotion called "Beyond Belief" was, from her perspective, an additional divinely guided symbolic act reminding Maria that she had been accompanied all the way.

For Maria, the transformation of her pain was accompanied by moving Donny from his prior banishment into becoming an active part of her ongoing life. Today they hold Marcus between them and publicly present their story and union in partnership. Maria continues to follow the mandate embodied in the poem "Two Mothers" but her internal world is now congruent with her external mission, creating a personal wholeness that wasn't there before.

BRIANA'S STORY AND ANALYSIS

At a local festival, an argument broke out between two groups of friends. When Big Jon singled out a smaller member of the opposing group, Felix stepped up as an opponent of equal size. Felix suffered a massive injury to his brain stem due to a punch from Big Jon that resulted in his hitting his head on a rock. After several days on life support, Briana made the decision to withdraw care. Briana saw the difference between the support for Felix and the total lack of support for Big Jon.

Briana felt sadness for Big Jon, despite his actions, and decided to meet with him, as a mother meets with a son. Briana spontaneously shared her hopes and dreams for Big Jon, that he become the type of man he never had in his life growing up, the type of man Felix may have become. While Briana never felt compelled to forgive Big Jon, she was able to let go of the pain she felt and the hurt towards her own son for putting himself in the situation that ended his life.

My son hung out with a group of guys that met up with a different group at a local festival. A fight ensued as a result of words exchanged between the members of both groups but it wasn't a fair fight due to the difference in size between the two main fighters. After my son, Felix, criticized the leader of the opposing group for picking on someone smaller, the leader, Big Jon, suggested Felix stand in for the smaller guy. Felix agreed so the choice was his but several times he said, "This is stupid. Let's not do this. If you want to fight me, I'll fight you but this is just so stupid." Felix thought he had talked Big Jon down but Big Jon decided to go forward. He gave Felix such a hard undercut that it lifted Felix's large 260 pound body up a bit so that he fell at an angle hitting his head on a rock and crushing his brain stem.

After several days on machines, I signed the papers to discontinue life support, never to speak to my son again. The night before he died, however, I had a visitation dream. Felix approached me in a hospital gown loaded down with tubes. He said, "Mom, what happened? I don't know what happened. Mom, don't be mad at me." I believe my son never realized he'd been punched out and did not suffer. His worry about my reaction just shows how close we were.

I was numb and shut down for a long time. My family and friends gathered around both to cry with me and help me move forward. One friend insisted I attend a support group for homicide survivors, driving me back and forth weekly for three months to be sure I went. I attended this group for two-and-a-half years, eventually becoming its facilitator, a position I held for nine years.

But there were big changes in how I related to the world. My anger triggered quicker, much quicker. My judgment about what constituted real versus insignificant problems shifted. If folks were concerned about issues at work I'd ask, "Are you kidding? This is nothing." I mean, "People, come on. You just fix it." I didn't drink but I overate to quell the pain. I couldn't stand the quiet in our home that had been so full of laughter. My son had been a master chef. The guys would buy all kinds of groceries for Felix who cooked almost non-stop. After he died, my friends dwindled down. Being with me stirred up guilt because their children were still alive. I particularly missed hearing about the fun activities or behaviors of their children. Silently I'd plead with them thinking, "Don't take that away from me. I want to know."

I saw Felix's friends suffer too. One of his buddies committed suicide and two others became big alcoholics. Because I worried that Felix's murder might spark more hatred and retaliation, I decided to speak at a gathering, telling his pals, "Not one of you has lost more than I lost that night. So none of you trump me. None of you. I say, 'No retaliation.' And if you do something and I find out about it, you will have hell to pay from me." Briana gradually learned more about the fight that took her son's life. Big Jon was disturbed at the festival. He had just broken up with his girlfriend and was being taunted by another guy. Big Jon was so upset with this guy that when he punched my son, he exercised no restraint. I never said anything to the guy who teased him because I love him and worried that the information would hurt him.

Big Jon had three hearings and I attended all of them with my boyfriend, my sister and 7 to 12 of Felix's friends. I saw that Big Jon was always alone. At first I was curious about the lack of support but then I began to wonder about his family. After the third hearing, I insisted the victim advocate get me information on his family. I wanted to know, "What does a mother look like whose son would hit somebody they don't know so hard?" Big Jon had no family at the trial either. The emptiness around him was palpable as my family and I read beautiful impact statements about our relationships with Felix. Although Big Jon and Felix were both biracial, the judge noted the marked differences between them. "You couldn't have two young men who were brought up so dissimilarly." I learned at that time about Big Jon's background. He'd been in permanent foster care since he was 11 after being taken away from his mother many times because she was a drug addict. He never knew who his father was. Although I pushed for a maximum sentence, I felt very sorry for Big Jon because he lacked the loving and kind environment Felix had, as well as a meaningful relationship with his mother. I knew then that I wanted to talk to Big Jon and learn more of his story so I could understand where his rage came from and how he could hit Felix so hard that it would cause his death. Even before knowing about the VOD program, I wanted to encourage him to participate in prison programs so that he would not hurt someone again. I also wanted him to know Felix, the person he had killed.

After I expressed my desire to meet Big Jon at the support group meeting, the director told me about the VOD program. I had no intention of meeting with him to benefit myself. Rather I believed that since he had no mother, I was uniquely situated to talk to him as a parent about making different choices going forward. So I decided to pursue the dialogue with three provisions: I could talk with Big Jon about the punch he gave my son, how important it is for children to be loved physically and emotionally in order not to be angry, and the importance of a support group. I then went through the preparation process so I was ready to meet him.

At the time of the dialogue, I felt sick to my stomach in anticipation of meeting Big Jon. My brother and sister came with me for support. I had expected a young man who looked wild and crazy but instead he walked in like a regular kid. My heart just broke because he looked like any other kid that Felix would have brought home to stay at our house. In fact he looked smaller than the 6 feet 4 inch, 190 pound buff man I had met in court. I decided prison had taken its toll on him. Not wanting to forget anything, I had carefully planned what I would put in front of him and the topics to be covered. For example, I brought pictures of Felix as well as the birthday and Mother's Day cards he had given me. I wanted Big Jon to know the person he took from me. But I saw that my making him open each card and read it was tortuous for him, like rubbing his nose in it. I felt bad because he seemed to be saying, "I never felt like this for anybody. I could never write these words to anybody." Indeed after he finished looking at the cards, he put his head down on the table and cried.

I realized Big Jon had been sorry for what he did from the moment he was sentenced. Indeed, when he was taken from the courtroom he had turned to me and whispered, "I'm sorry." I whispered back, "Okay." Big Jon's pain in response to understanding the love Felix had for me brought me to tears as well. Without warning, I found myself saying, "I don't hate you. I am sorry you did not get what my son got. You should have. You deserve that and every kid deserves that. I want you to find someone who will love you, someone you will marry and have a baby with. I want you to remember me sitting here talking to you about this and I want you to be a good dad. Hold your babies. Be there for them. It's what you didn't get. It's why my son isn't here." I hadn't planned to say these things but the words kept flowing. "Not until the day that you hold that baby in your arms will you know what you took from me. It isn't what you took from my son. It's what you took from me. I don't get him anymore. I love him a lot and I'm sorry somebody didn't love you." I told him that I speak to inmates at different prisons. I ask how many of them have kids. I scold them, telling them they are not a father because they did not parent their child. I say, "Who's hugging your baby tonight? Who's giving them a kiss goodnight and making sure they're worthy of someone's love?"

I told Big Jon that Felix had that love. In fact, at the time of the fight, Felix's only motive was to help someone who would otherwise have gotten hurt. I admonished Big Jon saying that had he not been so angry and ready to fight, the blow that killed my son never would have happened. Instead their encounter escalated to a point where there was no choice. There had to be a fight. I knew, however, that Felix never would have thrown the first punch because he had promised me, years ago, that he would restrain himself. So I turned the spotlight on Big Jon and said, "My son is not here anymore to keep this promise to me but you can keep it. I want you to look me in the eye and promise me that you will never throw the first punch again." Big Jon agreed saying, "I won't, I promise you." I check on him periodically. He's out of prison now and evidently has not been back in the correctional system.

I don't forgive Big Jon for what he did because forgiveness, from my perspective, would wash it away. Indeed, I didn't even see forgiving Big Jon as relevant since Felix participated in what happened and, in some ways, his death was a fluke. If anything, I felt I had to forgive my son because he did not walk away from his decision to fight. I told Big Jon that I wanted him to have a wonderful life and to live it in honor of Felix who was no longer able to live his life. Although I expected the meeting would help Big Jon, I was surprised it was so positive for me and relieved some of the burden I'd been carrying. It calmed me down and gave me the chance to express everything I wanted to say to Big Jon. I left knowing that he had accepted it all and that he was sorry and promised to live a better life. He struggled with his obstinacy not understanding why, in his mind, he had to kill Felix to learn important stuff and exclaiming he was sorry that it took me losing my son for him to learn it. "That was unfair to you."

I have no regrets about meeting with Big Jon, what I shared or additional things I wanted to say. I felt my deep love for Felix, my gratitude for the tightness between us, and my grief about the abrupt ending before I was done being a mom. I told Big Jon about all I'd lost, including the fact that I would never hold my grandbaby but then I stopped. I could see his physical writhing in response to what I was saying, as if I were putting a knife into him and turning it. So instead I reminded myself to appreciate that I had had Felix for 22 years and our relationship was closer and more rewarding than people who have their children their entire life.

Analysis: Crime and its aftermath

At some point in her life, Briana made a personal commitment to live within the parameters of an intentionally built moral and principled existence. Her philosophy grounded how she mothered her son Felix and what she expected from him, her reasons for meeting Big Jon and gave direction and purpose to the conversation between them. Her motivation was steeped in sensitivity to social injustices and efforts to correct circumstances that gave one person an unfair advantage over another.

In recalling the fight that led to Felix's death, Briana felt the inherent essential wrong was pitting opponents of unequal physical size against each other. She had sensitized her son to see the same injustice such that Felix volunteered to replace the homeboy because he was close in size to the fighter from the other side. Felix again reflected Briana's value base by trying for agreement with the other man not to fight. "This is stupid. Let's not do it." Circumstances, however, resulted in the disastrous resolution. There was no way to protect the smaller man except to be the substitute fighter. Moreover, without agreement from Big Jon to step down, the fight, in effect, was inevitable. The final injustice, in Briana's eyes, was an unexpected blow from Big Jon after Felix thought he had dissuaded him. Because Briana had years ago extracted the promise from her son that he would never give the first punch, she knew that Felix had not provoked Big Jon. Rather, Big Jon had taken advantage of Felix's belief that the proclivity to fight had been dissipated and struck him when he was unaware and ill prepared for the attack.

Although Briana lost her son, her strong sense of responsibility and stance against revenge and more violence emerged over and over again. She had to make the decision to remove the life supports that completed his physical death. She confronted Felix's buddies trying to stop them from potentially retaliating against the men in Big Jon's group. "Not one of you has lost more than I lost on that night. So none of you trump me. None of you. I say, 'No retaliation.' And if you do something and I find out about it, you will have hell to pay from me." Briana also learned the back story about how Felix's pal had needled Big Jon prior to the fight but determined to keep the information to herself rather than inflicting more pain. "He's a really good kid. I love him. We just never speak of it."

Briana's pain and excruciating sadness were more central than her anger. In many ways she turned off her feelings. She missed her only child profoundly. Although he'd been her son, they had navigated the world as a unit, together and as companions. The way he had lived his life was life-giving to her. Felix's friends would stay over at the house on weekends and there was always laughter. His cooking, though messy, created the base for wonderfully fun gatherings. Now nothing had Felix's touch. Everything was too quiet, just an empty echo of the past. Briana hated it. She overate to subdue the pain.

But the loss of Felix was compounded by the loss of her girlfriends who pulled back because there was too much pain. No one would talk about their children so the sharing that previously had been life-giving also disappeared. Briana pulled deeper into herself, noting changes in how she related to the world. She was emotional, quick to anger and had little patience for what now seemed trivial. She had some protectors, however, who continued to stay close by. Her fiancé accompanied her through the criminal justice process and sat beside her in her meeting with Big Jon. A friend from the Department of Corrections insisted on taking her back and forth to a support group for three months and also served as a support during her dialogue. But Briana also fought for herself and her sanity. She stayed in the support group, eventually becoming a group facilitator and giving back as a way to help others. She also tried out different therapists, selecting one who could understand her pain because she too was a mother.

Briana's activism and care for others inhibited the emotional blockage of anger-related energy associated with crime. She stayed watchful over the impact of Felix's death on his friends. She sought out like-minded people such as her friends, the therapist and support group members to help unpack her reactions, see her through the legal process, and navigate being indefinitely suspended in life without Felix. Her strong sense of purpose allowed her to write for herself the next chapters of her future and to exercise choice in ways that mitigated, even blocked, her descent into being victim-minded or identifying as a victim.

Preparation

During the time she was in the support group, Briana went through the criminal justice process. She had repeatedly questioned how one blow could have killed her son and concluded that Big Jon must have been exceedingly rageful to hit Felix that hard. The illogic of the circumstances that attended his death emerged anew during the pre-trial hearings. Briana attended, encircled by family and Felix's friends. In contrast, Big Jon stood alone with no support. Briana's concern for Big Jon and his lack of family grew exponentially at each of three hearings. Her energy started to shift from herself to Big Jon as she noted the stark and unjust contrast between her world and his. She demanded that the victim advocate who was her support find out where his family was. Again, at the sentencing, she noted the absence of his mother and father, questioning still further the gross unfairness and incomprehensible reality. "How does your son get sentenced, go to prison and you're not in the courtroom? How does that happen?"

The dissonance between Big Jon and Felix's upbringing ate at Briana. Their similarity began and ended with the fact that they were both biracial men in a dominantly White world. Otherwise, their backgrounds diverged radically. Big Jon was orphaned, in effect, by both his parents and raised from infancy in poor, abusive and loveless homes. In comparison, Felix had a kind and loving environment with strict discipline, guidance and a solid awareness of how special he was to his mother. As Briana saw these opposites, she began to understand the deprivation he had suffered and the possible source of Big Jon's rage. It was this inquiry and sense of wrong that opened Briana up to Big Jon as a human being and wanting to know why he had hit Felix so hard. The dissonance and sense of unjust life circumstances that humanized Big Jon laid the groundwork for Briana's commitment to his getting what he needed in prison to never hurt someone again.

Briana's decision to move forward with the dialogue happened as she moved from being a member to being a facilitator of the survivor group, a role that involved giving back. Similarly she had a lingering desire to give Big Jon the guidance he'd never received from his mother. Throughout this time, Briana had worked to make sense out of what had happened and was sure that the explanation lay in Big Jon's childhood and the extreme psychological deprivation he suffered. In her decision to meet with him, she had no wish to gain anything for herself. She just wanted to help him make different choices going forward. Her agenda was set—she'd talk with him about his angry punch, why children need to be loved, and encourage him to attend a support group.

Dialogue

When Briana saw Big Jon, she felt an immediate shift in her heart toward him. Instead of the wild muscular man she expected to meet, she was moved by his youthfulness and vulnerability. She continued to get caught between her expectation and the reality of what she saw in front of her. For example, Briana had wanted Big Jon to understand and appreciate the fine character of the person he had taken from her. But as she strategically laid out the pictures of Felix for him to see and requested that he read the special cards Felix had given her, her heart melted. Watching him take in Felix's love for her opened another door for Briana as she took in his utter loneliness and the fact that Big Jon had never experienced anything comparable from anyone in his life. The dissonance between the expected and the real again interrupted her pre-planned agenda when she told Big Jon she would never hold her grandbaby. She found it hard to watch as his body struggled against the pain he was feeling.

In these instances, Briana was thrust into responding to Big Jon as a mother would respond to a hurt child soothing his pain, teaching him about life, and taking care not to make it worse. Briana drew on her awareness that crime does not start in a vacuum but exists in a larger social context that, in Big Jon's situation, included missing essential emotional support as a child.

She also was propelled by the dissonance that accompanied the juxtaposing of Big Jon's upbringing against Felix's experiences. She spoke, therefore, to Big Jon's loneliness telling him he was deserving and should have been loved and that he must find that love and give it as well to his children. "It's what you didn't get." She spoke a broader truth, reminding him that Felix was gone, in part, because he was loved and therefore not angry, angry enough to hit someone so hard that they died. Moving far away from her pre-programmed dialogue plan, she continued to respond to Big Jon, intuitively speaking as a wise woman about the legacy he must play out with his child—to now give that child what he did not have and to know from his love for his own offspring what he took from Briana. And finally she extracted from Big Jon the same promise she had obtained from her son, to never again throw the first punch. Besides telling him that she hurt for what he did not have and truly wanted his life to be good, she placed on him a loving mantle—to live the life her son could no longer live and to live it well in honor of the man he had killed.

The unexpected shifts identified by Briana in her responsiveness to Big Jon, however, were actually shifts in the movement of pain in the context of their dyadic exchange. Briana shared pictures of Felix and the cards he had sent her that expressed the love between them. These mementoes conveyed the pain differential from the crime that she alone had carried. Her sharing of that pain through cards and pictures reflecting the profound loss of the relationship between her and Felix produced a transfer of the pain into Big Jon. In response, he put his head on the table and cried. At that point, the past became present as Briana recalled that Big Jon had whispered to her that he was sorry as he was taken from the courtroom after the trial. As the transfer of pain occurred, Briana too had tears. Unexpectedly she found herself ministering to him. She told Big Jon that she cared for him and wanted better for his life. In response, Big Jon validated the meaning Briana had made of his behavior—specifically, that the rage from numerous life long injustices had caused his punch. He spoke about his fighting throughout his life because he was so angry. Realizing what was missing, he said, "I didn't have a mom like you. I wish I'd had a mom like you." Resonating with the truth of his statement, Briana replied, "I wish you had too, cause then Felix would still be here." The volley between them continued with Big Jon knitting the pieces together in an apology and show of responsibility: "I don't understand why I didn't learn this stuff before. Why did I have to kill Felix for me to learn this stuff? I'm sorry it took you losing your son for me to learn it. That wasn't fair to you." Each time Briana or Big Jon spoke, it triggered reciprocally more introspection, honesty, and sharing, increasing their openness to each other still further.

Relieved of carrying the pain from the crime alone, Briana was freed up to pass on insights, encouragements and requests that Big Jon had never experienced, thereby reducing some of the dissonance or gap she had felt between Felix and Big Jon but also transforming the pain. That transformation through the giving and receiving of her mothering also allowed Briana to complete her mission and experience her own completion in giving Big Jon what she knew had been missing from his past. Briana never felt she had to literally forgive Big Jon. After all, it was Felix who agreed to fight. Yet the dyadic encounter and flow of energy between them allowed movement in the pain differential and repurposing of the negativity from the crime toward positive ends. Briana, who had planned the meeting as an intervention on Big Jon, left feeling surprisingly calmed and complete. These indicators confirmed the internal shifts in energy between them. Besides leaving her unburdened, the lovingness in her messages to Big Jon about his deservedness also provided him with the moral reinstatement that accompanies dyadic forgiveness.

CASSANDRA'S STORY AND ANALYSIS

David was a local drug dealer, murdered by a customer, Bret, who couldn't pay his debt. Cassandra, David's girlfriend, knew Bret but after moving away from their small community saw no sense in holding onto the anger she initially felt. With Bret's release date getting closer, Cassandra feared they would run into each other in the town and the VOD was a way to meet in a controlled environment. While their meeting was relatively short, Cassandra saw that Bret had damaged his own life, and during their conversation the rest of the world disappeared as they shared how David's death had impacted them both. Cassandra shared that she had forgiven Bret long ago, and continues to wish him well in the world, knowing his life is forever impacted by the choices he made.

My boyfriend David sold drugs and was shot 18 years ago by Bret, one of his customers who decided to kill him rather than pay off his debt. David had actually offered to reduce the debt if Bret mowed his grandmother's yard or washed his car. We were all young and from the same small community. In fact, Bret and I knew each other from a distance. Bret was tried as an adult and went to prison when he was 16 or 17 years. I was so enraged that I insisted no one use Bret's name around me. I wanted him dead and was ready to do it myself. I held onto that anger for ten years, gradually realizing that it had spread and that I could easily jump to anger at any time because I had so much of it inside already.

Gradually, the anger subsided and I began to think about Bret. What was going on in his life now? What had been occurring for him the day he killed David? I had moved away for ten years but when I came back to my hometown I was in a different place. I realized, however, that others had not changed and were still living exactly the same way, which included the drug world. I'd tell them, "You're not gonna have a whole lot of happiness running around doing hateful things, saying hateful things, being hateful." As for me, I began to turn the other cheek. I actively worked to cultivate a personal philosophy of letting go of the wrongs done to me. I'd think, "There are so many more important things to do." If someone took something from me, I'd say, "Whoever took it must have needed it more than I did." And I pushed back against people who would try to rile me. Some of them, for example, were upset that Bret's mother was the lunch lady and served lunch to my daughter at her school. But I recognized that Bret's mother had to live with the stigma and burden that her son had killed David. The added realization that Bret's life had been on hold for the past ten years just reinforced my belief that it made no sense to continue holding onto such anger. So I told others not to be angry with Bret and that I had forgiven him a long time ago.

However, I pondered over the fact that when he got out, he would come back here and we might run into each other. What would happen if I saw him? Would I grab a can of peas and hit him over the head? I had been following his pictures annually on the Department of Correction's website. I wrote him a letter, put the letter "B" on it but never sent it. In the letter I had asked if he would meet me in the visitor's room at the prison, which I considered a safe controlled environment. I kind of forgot about it until I realized that he was getting close to his release date. In his pictures, his hair was suddenly cut short and he had shaved off his beard. I called the prison about seeing Bret. I knew I had to see him before running into him in the aisle of Costco. The prison referred me to Bret's case manager who then transferred me to the VOD program. The VOD facilitator who talked with me surprisingly had been the troop leader for my Girl Scout club when I was younger. I had slept over at her house many times and trusted her implicitly.

I learned a lot preparing for the VOD. I'm impulsive. I don't think before I act or speak. I had planned to go see Bret without ever thinking about what I wanted to say to him or wanted to hear from him. I would just see him and then quickly leave. The VOD facilitator stressed over and over again that this meeting was a process, not an event. That meant that I had to take the time to sit down and think about what I needed. Of course, I'd get frustrated and try to hurry things up but in the end, I had the chance to thoughtfully consider what I wanted and to get all the details nailed down—where to sit in the room, who would come in first, etc. I also had to decide who to bring as a support person. I weighed the possibility of asking someone who had known David but then decided it would be better if the person had no prior knowledge or personal connection to David and me. So I brought a girlfriend whom I met in recovery, which kept the focus only on Bret and me. Bret too had a support person and selected the priest who had officiated at David's funeral. Unbeknownst to Bret, this priest had been my priest growing up. He had met David when he occasionally accompanied me to church. So I felt very supported because I had the VOD facilitator, my girlfriend, and this priest.

The day of our meeting, I sat in the center of a round table with my support person and waited. The door to the room was in front of me. I wanted Bret across from me. I hadn't seen him since this sentencing 17 years earlier. However, I'd watched him age through his photos. As he came into the room, my whole body got hot and I could feel my chest expand. Then I felt an overwhelming sadness because I saw a man who took a life and in the process damaged his own. I felt sadness as well for all the people who had loved David and lost him. Both of us struggled to compose ourselves because we were overwhelmed with emotion and could not speak. But once we got the dialogue going, it flowed. Everyone who surrounded us at the table faded away. It was like having tunnel vision.

We met for two hours. I just couldn't understand why Bret had killed David. David wasn't mean to him. In fact, David would have told him to mow his grandmother's lawn or wash his car to work off what he owed. Bret assured me that what he'd done had nothing to do with David. He wasn't singled out. He had not been a jerk or a bad guy. In fact, in Bret's eyes, anyone could have been the target that day. To hear Bret admit that David had nothing to do with what happened was pivotal. It made my heart rest, rest a little more.

Bret did apologize but it was somewhat inconsequential. I told him out loud during the meeting that I knew I had forgiven him long ago. Unlike my family, I was not upset, therefore, that Bret was getting out of prison. I reasoned that Bret had hurt himself enough by having killed David. He'd lost his adolescence and young adulthood to the system. His father had died when he was in prison and he missed the funeral. His mother then lost her home. So Bret missed out a lot on his own life and had suffered enough in the ordeal. I felt he didn't need to suffer anymore. So forgiveness for me was letting go of the anger because it is toxic.

We took a cigarette break during the meeting. I hugged him and would have exchanged phone numbers. I told him then that I had followed him on the Department of Corrections website and noticed his hair. Bret told me that he had grown a beard earlier to avoid the predators in prison. As a 16-year-old, he was 5'2" and weighed 115 pounds. Because he was young and tiny, he was prone to becoming a victim. He learned to avoid gangs and negative influences and instead participated in writing classes. He's written short stories that I'd like to read. Overall, I felt he had become an interesting adult. I wouldn't mind seeing him again and catching up on what he's been doing. I saw him more as an individual in his own right than the person who killed David.

At the end of the meeting, I had a chance to talk briefly with the priest. He shared that he'd always had a soft spot in his heart for me. He remembers that in school I'd sit in the back of the room and ask questions no one, even the teacher, understood. Because I'd moved around a lot when I was growing up, I knew there was more than just Catholic stuff. And I always went against the grain. The priest felt in fact that I'd been severely misunderstood as a child. I know for me that we all want to be understood, loved, and cared for. We all crave being valued and respected. And if that care wasn't given, we are going to take it however we have to.

I left feeling I'd done what I needed to do. I felt lighter, less burdened. I wanted to embrace Bret. Others in my family and David's family, however, were upset that I met with him. None of them have said a word to me about it but I know they talk behind closed doors because my daughter tells me what they say. I've thought a lot about forgiveness. There's a Biblical quote that forgiven is the forgiver through the forgiving. That means I'm forgiven by forgiving. And that day I let it go. I've not run into Bret but I've wanted to know how things are going. It's got to be difficult finding work, applying for jobs, getting housing. I'm sure he has a lot of struggles but I hope he sticks with it.

I try to apply what I've learned to raising my daughter. I hear gun shots all the time in my neighborhood but I tell her and the neighborhood kids, "You can't fight on my porch. You can't yell at or be mean to each other." I also tell her to let me know if I've hurt her so I can apologize and change my behavior. I don't know I've hurt someone unless they tell me. And if I hear you and change, then you know I value you and the relationship. If I or others don't change then you know that the relationship doesn't matter.

Analysis: Crime and its aftermath

Cassandra, David, and Bret were all adolescents when David was killed. Although young, Cassandra's independence, contentious upbringing and lack of community roots thrust her into adulthood early. As she noted,

"Sometimes I feel like I'm four and sometimes I feel like I'm 1000 years old." Cassandra, consequently, grew accustomed to thinking things through for herself, often drawing conclusions that separated and isolated her from the adults around her.

After David's murder, Cassandra and her young daughter moved away from home and did not return for ten years. During that time, the size of her fury was so great that she tried to emotionally block and stuff it away by demanding no one talk about Bret in her presence. She did not care that Bret was 16, tried as an adult and sent to serve most of his young adult years in prison. However, these were also formative years for Cassandra. After living away from her family and reminders of the murder for over ten years, she formulated a personal creed and philosophy that allowed her to move beyond her rage. This happened long before doing the VOD with Bret. Indeed, it was the return to her small hometown and the stark contrast between her family and her own reformed outlook that propelled and solidified her humanitarian attitude toward others.

Cassandra's family and community were stuck in a morass of hatred fueled by past resentments and vengefulness, and associated with a drug culture. When Cassandra tried to counsel others to move beyond this way of life, family members would exclude and undermine her by making negative comments about her behavior behind her back and to her daughter. Cassandra dug in deeper, affirming again and again her decision to forgive, to cultivate compassion, and not contribute to the suffering of Bret or his family. When family members would warn her about his eventual release, she would tell them to let it go, that he had suffered enough.

These admonitions to "let it go" were steeped in a philosophy of forgiveness and Cassandra's decision to intentionally build a life that countered the community's norms. The ensuing, persistent and underground conflict, however, kept generating dissonance because it kept the past alive even in the presence of Cassandra's deepening certainty. In response, Cassandra found that holding ever more tightly to her beliefs helped reduce some of this discrepancy. Moreover, her commitment to live in accordance with peacekeeping values such as compassion generated a sense of mission that undergirded her life.

Preparation

Cassandra had already shifted the impact from the crime and reduced the emotional blockage caused by David's murder long before learning about VOD. Indeed, she had moved from refusing to acknowledge Bret's existence to curiosity about his life in prison to compassionately perceiving changes in his prison photos over time. This openness, however, was from a distance. The reality of his eventual release and return to the home community they both shared created fear about how she might respond even though she had grown so much. To prevent the "accidental encounter," she decided to visit Bret before he was released. Although such a meeting with a glass wall between them seemingly might reduce fear, the prospect of activating a connection generated still more fear and concern for her safety. Her ambivalence, therefore, was strong and she avoided this visit until time threatened to run out.

The VOD preparation process ironically furnished Cassandra with the safety she needed for meeting Bret. She had originally planned to see him just as a visitor, to go it alone as a fast in and out. Instead, the serendipitous presence of her former Girl Scout leader and priest surrounded her with support that she rarely experienced in her own community. Moreover, she was instructed to think through a myriad of details, which harnessed the energy associated with the crime. It also gave her more control including each question she wanted to ask, what she wanted to know and how she wanted to orchestrate seating for the meeting. The slow and deliberate care required to sort through such details not only deepened her investment but also underscored the intentionality that she had already chosen as the basis for her daily living.

Dialogue

For the meeting, Cassandra elected to sit at the center of a round table with her support person so she could see Bret before he saw her and positioned Bret so he would be directly across from her. Then she waited. When she saw him, her whole body felt inflamed and her chest expanded just as she had imagined would happen if she had met him accidentally at a store. But instead of the anger she expected to have, she felt an overwhelming sadness for all the people who had loved David and lost him but also for the waste of Bret's life in prison—"I saw a man who took a life and in the process damaged his own."

They began to build the conduit between them. Cassandra noticed that Bret was overwhelmed too and struggled for words. She also noticed, as they spoke, that everyone else in the room faded away giving her a kind of tunnel vision into him. Although Cassandra had previously moved from rage to curiosity, she was plagued by not knowing his motive for killing David. How, she asked, could Bret kill someone who had actually offered him a number of ways he could pay off his debt? How could Bret turn on someone who was working to help him? This contradiction carried all the unresolved pain she had felt for years. It also embodied the unspoken question: What did David do to deserve what happened to him? Cassandra asked Bret if he remembered the options David gave him to pay off the debt. He did, a fact that both validated Cassandra's perceptions and increased the reliability of Bret's responses to her questions. She followed up by asking Bret to explain what was happening in his life at the time and the circumstances that could have led him to kill David. Bret's response was believable, in part, because it mirrored and resonated with what Cassandra had already concluded. Specifically, Bret told her that he had had his own sadness, fears, and struggles and that "it could have been anybody that day." Bret's answer was like a warm, healing balm for Cassandra. David had not been targeted nor was Bret against him. Bret's response not only resolved the dissonance between David's debt-reducing offers and Bret's horrific response, but Cassandra experienced Bret's willingness to take full responsibility for his decision and for the pain he had caused. In response, she said, "To hear him say that it could have been anyone that day…it just made my heart rest, my heart rest a little more."

Although Cassandra had forgiven Bret long before their meeting in the sense of letting go of her anger, she experienced forgiveness on a different level because of their dialogue. Indeed, during a cigarette break, she hugged Bret and told him out loud that she had forgiven him. She also commented repeatedly that the dialogue "lightened me." The energy continued to flow between them unimpeded. They talked about their religious views and beliefs. Cassandra discovered that Bret had grown a beard in prison to protect himself from being victimized sexually. Because of his size, he had to constantly guard against predators. He also told Cassandra that he had worked to avoid the prison gangs and any negative influences by keeping to himself and enrolling in writing classes and writing stories. Bret's effort to dispel negativity matched Cassandra's own efforts to steer clear of the anger and hatred fostered in her community. Both of them resonated to their mutual need for protection, their decisions to semi-isolate, and intentionally build through their activities an affirming environment.

The pain transformation is evident in how Cassandra felt post-dialogue but also in how she saw Bret. Besides reporting that she felt lighter and less burdened, there is also evidence that Cassandra morally reinstated Bret through her wishes for more contact. Indeed, she found him to be "an interesting adult" and wanted to read his short stories. She wished they'd exchanged phone numbers. She saw him more an individual in his own right rather than the man who had killed David. If she ran into him today, she could smile, say hi, and give him a hug.

Although Cassandra had already moved ahead in terms of a shift in energy prior to the dialogue, her sense of resolution was not complete.

The VOD that included Bret moved her prior forgiving to a dyadic level which resulted in a transfer and transformation of the pain and a subsequent unburdening. The significance of dyadic forgiveness is demonstrated in Cassandra's instructions to her young daughter about their relationship and responding when Cassandra has inadvertently hurt her. "Unless you tell me I might never ever know that I hurt you… Then I can apologize and change the behavior. Otherwise, I might continue on. If I change the behavior it means I value you as a person and our relationship. If it doesn't stop than you know that individual doesn't value the relationship and you can leave it alone."

Before deciding to meet with Bret, Cassandra had embarked on a mission to combat the attitudes in her family and community that attended the aftermath of David's murder and kept its negativity alive. The decision to meet with Bret, even before the prospect of VOD, was a part of that journey. The dialogue with Bret helped change the meaning of David's death and humanize Bret. Indeed, by neutralizing Bret's hold on her life, she could continue to move forward. The dialogue also helped Cassandra achieve a congruence between herself, her beliefs and actions that empowered her further while distancing her from the unconstructiveness of others.

PAULA'S STORY AND ANALYSIS

Paula's father was violently murdered by one of her acquaintances shortly after spending Christmas with her and her family. Paula was plagued by nightmares and overwhelming anger towards Jessie. Paula felt ambivalent about meeting with Jessie and even more unconvinced he would be truthful, but she began preparation to address the fear she felt for herself about his release. For two years Paula dealt with her hesitation and ambivalence, finally settling on 40 questions she needed answered. Paula hoped Jessie's willingness to meet might indicate his willingness to fully engage in truth-telling. Jessie was able to share the impact the murder had had on his own life, which allowed Paula to begin to humanize him. Against protocols, Jessie asked for forgiveness and although Paula doesn't call what she experienced forgiveness, she described a type of compassion she felt towards Jessie and peace by fully honoring her dad's memory.

When I was young, I met a guy, Jessie, while dancing at a nightclub who wormed his way into my family's life. Although I only saw him a few times, I invited him to spend Christmas Eve at my mother's home and Christmas Day at my father's house because he had no place to go. It didn't take long to realize that he was a quite a liar. Jessie had told me he was an insurance agent but actually he had no job, no car, and no place to live. I quickly broke up with him. A few weeks later I got a call that my father had been violently murdered in his own home, a place he'd been working to repair since his recent separation from my mother. His brains were splattered all over the refrigerator.

I struggled to get information. The police called us in for questioning but refused to give us the specifics about what had happened. Because they were compiling a list of possible suspects, I told them about Jessie and his lying but they showed no interest. But a week later my mother got a phone call from the credit union that someone was trying to cash checks on my mother and father's account. My mother told the credit union to call the police who apprehended Jessie later that day. I next tried to get information from the coroner's office and the mortician at the funeral home. The mortician said there were only five wounds on his body. However, at the trial months later, we finally learned that my father had been stabbed 85 times and hit over the head with a hammer. There was nothing left of the back of his head.

I remained in shock for a long, long time, just crying and crying and amazed that the world didn't stop. It just went on as if no one cared. My biggest reaction was anger because we could not find any answers and no one was willing to give us information. I felt horribly stuck and as if my father's murder was my fault because I knew Jessie. Indeed the media reported the news as "Boyfriend of Daughter Kills Her Father." I was not able to control the rage I was feeling. I worried I'd lose my job because the slightest problem would send me reeling and wanting to scream, "Doesn't anyone know what I'm going through?" Horrible dreams bombarded me where I'd see my father just down the road, wake up terrified and then be flooded with the truth of the awful reality around me. I'd be scared to go to bed at night for fear I'd have those terror nightmares and was plagued by an awful sleep disturbance that could be easily set off by the news or a scary movie. If I see a body, it's my dad's body. I went to groups for over five years plus individual therapy to learn to control my anger but it's still unpredictable and will come out if the right situation presents itself. Frankly, I just didn't want to live anymore.

I knew about the VOD program but had huge reservations. My therapy group leader had even recommended it but I'd always say that I wasn't ready and would wait. I worried Jessie was still a liar, that I might feel even worse after meeting with him or that he would hurt someone else and I couldn't stop him. It began to dawn on me, however, that Jessie would be getting out of prison soon and I'd never get a chance again to meet with him. So even though I was terribly ambivalent, I agreed to do it because I wanted to get answers to all the questions rattling around in my head. I wanted to know what had happened at my father's home, why Jessie had killed him, if he was sorry, and last and maybe most important, was he going to come after me. One of the big issues was that Jessie claimed that my father had attacked him sexually. There was nothing to support that defense but it went public and fed the current frenzy that homosexuals were running around attacking people. I knew this was not the truth but it hurt my mother horribly because it was printed everywhere. I wanted to confront Jessie with his lie and also, in the name of my father, make sure he never attacked or murdered anyone again.

Getting ready for the meeting took two years. During that time, I fought with my hesitation, pulling on myself to be as receptive as possible. For example, my VOD facilitator interviewed Jessie on tape and then showed it to me so that I would assess his motivation and sincerity. I saw that his appearance had changed and how he talked which really prepared me for meeting him in person. When the facilitator asked him if he really wanted to do the meeting, he said, "Yes, this is something I really want to do." He wanted to make it right somehow, make something better come out of what he had destroyed. I also had the chance to review Jessie's daily life with a woman from the Department of Corrections—what he ate, information about his cellmate, how much trouble he'd been in, the transfers he had gotten to different facilities. These events started to answer some of my questions so I began to see that doing a meeting with him might be good for me. I also realized the gift I was being given to meet with someone who had murdered my loved one, did not have to meet with me, and yet was open to giving me what I needed. I used that to challenge myself: if I am nasty, I'll never get the answers I want. Since he might be willing to give me those answers, I need to be open to this process to get anything from it. His willingness to meet with me was a credit to his character and I found myself ever so gradually opening to him and to the meeting.

As I went through the process of getting close and then pulling back, my facilitator suggested I write down the questions I'd want to ask him, all the questions I'd obsessed about over the years and lay awake at night trying to answer. This assignment gave me a lot of time to think through thoroughly all I wanted to know. I ended up with 40 questions. I felt really, really good about my list and asked every one of them. Although preparation was a lengthy, back and forth process, going through it all really prepared me for the dialogue. I decided to have my husband attend as my support person. Because he did not know my father, my life prior to him was surreal but his love and respect for me was strong and he was willing to accompany me on this journey. My son had also grown up never knowing my father but aware of what had happened to him.

The day of our meeting, my husband and I arrived at the prison 40 minutes early. We spent some time just observing the prison yard, people walking, all the fences and little houses—things that made real the world I was about to enter and what I was about to do. When Jessie entered the room, I wasn't shocked. I knew what he looked like and what to expect from the video. What was shocking was the terror I suddenly felt and the thousand conversations rushing through at one time in my brain. "Oh, my God, here he is. This is the same guy that murdered your father. He's in the room with you. He's seated right there. How many times have you imagined what you'd do if he was in front of you? I'd kill him. But, no, you don't want to kill him. Well, maybe you do."

So we did our dialogue. We both told our stories because I felt it was important to remind him about what happened. I went first and he listened and responded even though he knew much of the information already. But when he told his story, I began to feel for him. He had really suffered both through the prison system and with his family. They had no contact with him anymore. His parents had no interest in him and his son wanted nothing to do with him. I realized that it's really easy to hate someone from afar but if they are saying they are sorry and explaining themselves, it makes a difference. There was humanity to what Jessie was sharing. It was sincere, not a lie, and he didn't do it to get something. He was doing this dialogue because he wanted to somehow make it right.

After telling our stories to each other, I asked my 40 questions and he answered all of them. He admitted that my father never attacked him. No one tried to touch his privates or came up from behind to do something to him. My father had said something rude to him and so he had murdered him. That was huge for me. It put my mind to rest. Besides learning the real story of the attack, I felt a change in my terror about my personal safety because, after being with him, I was able to feel safe again.

We talked for three to four hours. He openly apologized and that felt like a gift. He didn't have to be sorry or own any of it. He owned all of it. The compassion I felt was only because he was very sorry for what he did. He told me he would never again do anything like he had done to my father and I actually believed him.

He surprised me by asking for my forgiveness. In the preparation the facilitator had told him not to request forgiveness but he did anyway. At first I was pissed that he asked. But he talked about my sister and I remembered that at his trial, my sister had yelled at him that he would rot in hell and the courtroom went crazy with cheering. Her words really bothered him because he was quite certain he would actually burn in hell. I told him my sister is nowhere near forgiving him and that I wasn't ready to forgive him yet. But I understood that he asked because this was his one chance, just like it was my one chance to ask him all my questions.

I don't know if forgiveness happened or not. It means so many different things and there's so much pressure to forgive. If you don't it's like you're defective and will be miserable your whole life. But for me, a grace happened, a compassion happened, some type of forgiveness happened where I could see things through his eyes in a way I've never allowed before. The same thing happened for him. Is that forgiveness? You could argue yes. You could argue no. Does forgiveness mean you forgive everything Jessie did and let it go? For me that's a lie because some days it comes back, it's there in your face and I'm angry at him all over again. I think that's normal. Does that mean I don't forgive him? I'm a lot more at peace, the peace that comes from having answers to questions about something you cared so deeply for and that plagued you for 20 years, the peace that comes from not living in fear, the peace that comes from knowing what happened that night, the peace that comes from knowing I did right by my dad.

I didn't want to hang onto all those questions and all that fear. I no longer felt afraid of being in the room with him. Meeting with Jessie also changed my relationship with my husband. He had been angry but now he too felt at peace because he had the chance, in the meeting, to speak to Jessie. He told him never to hurt our family but reminded him that he wanted the best for Jessie. "I want you to succeed, to go out and get a job and not be unhappy and I don't want you to come looking for me." They kind of had a man thing but it gave my husband great relief because his job is to protect the family.

Analysis: Crime and its aftermath

The murder of Paula's father was exceptionally brutal both because of how he died but also because the murderer had fraudulently wormed his way into the sanctuary and intimacy of her family at a special and sacred time of year. Paula had befriended Jessie, bringing him into her home to share Christmas because he had no place to go. Her family's generosity toward him had been met with lies, deceit and ultimately the taking of her father's life. Paula felt tremendous guilt. After all, she figured, she had introduced Jessie to her father, thereby setting the stage for his murder. In her mind, the family trusted her and she had let them down.

Although she felt tremendously betrayed by Jessie and enraged, her deepest anger sprang from feeling thwarted as she frantically searched for answers in her effort to regain some modicum of control. Round and round she went, practically begging officials to tell her something. "How did this happen? What can I do to fix this?" Besides having been taken in by Jessie and his lies, she could get no information from the police or the coroner's office. Even the mortician hid critical details, such as the fact that her father was stabbed 85 instead of 5 times, and was repeatedly hit over the head with a hammer. Her unabated fury rose still higher when the media misrepresented her relationship with Jessie, claiming that the murderer was her boyfriend. Worse yet, the newspapers denigrated her father by reporting his murder was provoked by his homosexual advance toward Jessie. In Paula's world, she was surrounded by lies or refusals by those in charge to tell her the truth. Paula felt completely out of control. She'd fly into a rage at the slightest provocation, pushing others away with her anger because they couldn't understand what was happening to her. As hard as she tried, she could not regulate or channel it. If the right situation occurred, it zoomed out with no warning.

But it wasn't just anger. Paula had vivid and horrifying nightmares where she saw her father as if he were still alive and then would wake all over again to the shock and terror of what had happened. She felt plagued by flashbacks from the trial when she finally learned the results of the autopsy. She was scared to go to sleep for fear she'd see her father's wounds, the violence done to his body, the amount of blood and brains splattered around the kitchen. She believed as well that the murder of her father was directed at her and that Jessie would kill her when he got out of prison. Paula's fear and rage operated in tandem. When she felt fear she'd lash out but her anger only reinforced her sense of impotence, generating still more fear. Moreover, there was nothing to soften the trauma because she trusted no one.

Not wanting to live, she found some solace and release in the support groups she attended and later led as well as through individual counseling. Although these comfort zones served as valves for the release of some of her pent-up feelings, they did not stop the brewing of emotions triggered by the mental replays of her father's death and the countless unanswered questions generated in her head. Moreover, the synergistic relationship between her fear and anger blocked any emotional resolution, keeping her stuck in an endless feedback loop leading nowhere.

Preparation

Paula seemed ripe for doing VOD. The negative energy was not only stored but had been regularly fed without outlet for over 20 years. She was quite familiar with the process. An advocate she revered had frequently brought the idea to her attention. Members of her support group had successfully met with their offenders as well. But Paula was fearful and reticent about moving forward. She worried about Jessie's lying and that meeting with him could inflict more harm than good. Although seemingly ambivalent, she actually was nudging herself bit by bit toward Jessie and the opportunity he afforded. She had to work with her anger and cynicism, reminding herself that meeting him was an opportunity. She had to open herself so that what she learned about Jessie could make a difference. Learning about him from Corrections' staff, his daily life as a prisoner, and the trouble he'd experienced while incarcerated challenged many of her preconceived ideas. She labored to stay open to the process by acknowledging Jessie's openness and his decency in choosing freely to meet with her. "Not everybody gets someone who murdered their loved one who's standing there ready to take it."

The trustworthiness of Jessie's character was heightened by the authenticity of his responses to the VOD facilitator on tape. Paula's assessment from afar revealed a different person than she remembered at the trial. He actually wanted to make it right. Moreover, her chance to preview how he looked and talked further reduced her apprehension, opening the door within her for what might happen between them. Although we can only see Jessie's behavior through Paula's eyes, it appears that he too was coming to the meeting open minded and motivated to give. Because of the video, the VOD dialogue, in some ways, was already in process. Jessie knew that going ahead with the dialogue was dependent on Paula. She would be watching him and trying to decide whether to move forward based on his truthfulness. So he was in effect talking to her through the facilitator. In response, Paula could already feel the shifts inside her as she evaluated who he was, internalized his genuineness and felt his desire to provide what she needed. The video, therefore, influenced the upcoming dialogue by pulling them toward each other and increasing the openness of each to the other.

Indeed, Paula's propensity to pull back had changed over time to believing that the meeting with Jessie would be really good even if it went bad. A cruel residual from her father's murder was the number of questions that remained unanswered. This gap was the source of her anger. It left her unsettled and unable to construct what actually had occurred. In her mind, those who had the answers held the power and that included Jessie. Without answers, there was nothing she could fix. The facilitator's assignment to write down all her questions was a stroke of genius because the suggestion put Paula in charge of what she needed in order to feel whole again. Moreover, this elevation, along with the sheer number of questions, empowered her to counter the sense of impotency that had drained away part of her spirit.

Paula's movement through the preparation was driven by a number of dissonance-generating realities. As much as she did not want to encounter Jessie ever again, he held the answers she sought and therefore her relief in his hands. The facts that had made her fear for her life were discrepant with what she learned about Jessie and saw for herself. She therefore had to contend with the fact that she met someone who both had brutally killed her father and passed her stringent tests for believability and motive. Although her psychological protection lay, to some extent, in remaining on guard and angry, she could not heal without opening herself to being influenced by a murderer. Paula resolved the dissonance in each of these contradictions by shifting her weight toward a different and new reality.

Dialogue

In some ways, the dialogue between Paula and Jessie had previously begun. Paula already had felt a resonance with Jessie's desire to make things right. What surprised her was her panic at actually meeting with the man who had killed her father. She had to bring her remaining reticence up to date quickly and recommit to the openness she had established during preparation. Each set the stage by telling the other how the murder had impacted their lives and the suffering they and others had endured because of Jessie's actions. Each person's story resonated deeply, finding a home in the other's reactions. Because Paula felt truly heard, she took in Jessie's story, feeling his suffering and the high price he had paid over many years—"He didn't feel he had a friend in the world."

For Paula, however, the real sharing happened through her 40 questions. As she ceremoniously asked each one, she conveyed the torment of having no answer, no resolution of her pain, of being left to wander in the dark. In response, Jessie answered all of them, admitting to the specifics of what he'd done, and in so doing he transferred the pain from Paula to himself. His replies were illuminating and helped transform the pain for Paula. By the end, for example, Paula found herself no longer scared for her personal safety. Part of re-establishing that safety was learning for certain that her father never attacked Jessie sexually or came at him from behind. Rather, it was Jessie who got mad at Paula's father for a remark he had made. It was Jessie who murdered him from behind his back.

The back and forth between them not only generated a vital flow of information but also conveyed a powerful reciprocity. Paula experienced Jessie's open apology for what he did and his full ownership as a gift. "He didn't have to be sorry." In response she felt compassion and deep appreciation. "I felt sorry for him because he was very sorry for what he had done…" Jessie's sincerity was powerful. It not only helped both transfer and transform Paula's pain, but also enabled Paula to see Jessie's humanity. She then began to experience him differently. She could see, for example, that even in his request for forgiveness, he did it not to break a rule but because he was plagued by the terror that he would burn in hell. Even though not all of his answers were truthful, Paula could now excuse some of his responses stating, "He was pretty honest a good 75–80 percent of the time." In seeing his humanity and humanizing rather than monsterizing his behavior, Paula, in effect, morally reinstated Jessie.

Although Paula was clear that she did not forgive Jessie, she felt that something profound had happened in the dialogue. "Some type of forgiveness happened where I was allowed to see things from his eyes in a way that I've never allowed myself to before, and he, the same thing happened for him. It was huge." She cried hard after she finished the dialogue. "It was like tears of release or joy for finally having some peace about many of those questions that I've had for 25 years."

Paula had a strong sense of completion. She no longer felt fear or the sense of oppression that accompanied it. She was more at peace within herself, primarily because of "having the answers to questions that you never ever had for 20 years about something you cared so deeply about." She felt proud that she had taken every opportunity possible to make the best she could out of what happened in her life. She and her husband grew closer because he too felt more at peace. She also felt she'd set a wonderful example for her young son about tackling problems even if it's going to be painful.

CLYNITA'S STORY AND ANALYSIS

JoEllen and boyfriend Tyrone had a tumultuous relationship. Although it was never physically abusive, Clynita was afraid for her daughter, documenting every concerning encounter as JoEllen attempted to end their relationship. When Clynita learned that JoEllen had been viciously stabbed to death she immediately knew Tyrone was responsible. Clynita withered away, her husband emotionally unavailable; she felt desperate for answers only Tyrone had. They'd met before and Clynita was able to use their relationship as the conduit for their dialogue. Tyrone shared every detail, without emotion or eye contact. The dialogue was unusually short and when Clynita felt she had heard everything and was preparing to end the VOD and their connection, Tyrone's anger flashed hot. His reaction showed Clynita exactly what her daughter had experienced, an angry man desperate to control things. The experience filled in the missing pieces, freeing Clynita from Tyrone and in effect allowing her the ability to escape from Tyrone, something her daughter was never able to do.

My daughter JoEllen was stabbed 48 times by her ex-boyfriend Tyrone and left to die on the side of the road. They were very different. She was raised on a farm in a small rural town and trusted everyone. He came from a hard core, underprivileged family in the inner city and carried knives in case he needed to protect himself. They had met during her first year in college. Although Tyrone was an A student with no history of drugs or criminal behavior, red flags went up soon after they met. For example, we learned that he had slashed the tires of her car and bleached all her clothes, and done things that were harmful to her personal property. Eventually she broke off the relationship but Tyrone continued to destroy her things. We had to file police reports and get a restraining order to keep him away from her. Finally, he seemed to accept her decision and agreed with her that they would just be friends.

Their agreement didn't last long. Within days, he was waiting for her at her apartment after a male friend dropped her off. They texted back and forth and he finally persuaded her to leave her apartment and get in his car. She warned him in one of her texts saying, "You better not have a knife with you." Much of the rest of this story I learned when I met with Tyrone in prison. All we knew was that she didn't show up for work. When we called her cell phone, we got a message that her phone was no longer in service. Only after we went to her apartment to try to find her did we learn from police officials that they had found a dead girl whose identifiers such as tattoos, body weight and scars on her knee from surgery matched the description of JoEllen.

At first they thought it was a hit and run because a cement truck driver had found her on the median of a highway and called the police and paramedics. She was still breathing. A kind policewoman stayed with her, praying as she went to heaven. When I learned she had been killed, my first thought was Tyrone. I'd kept a log of his behaviors every time JoEllen told me anything, regardless of its significance. We'd been to the hospital together after he slashed her lip. Her father and I had gone to the police with her after he slashed her tires. So when I learned she'd been stabbed, I gave the police my information and said, "Go find him." The police apprehended him at his father's home, which was two hours away.

There were immediate consequences for me and my family. I've never felt any anger. Rather, I found myself absolutely numb like at the dentist. It was like I'd left my body and was looking down at me and my husband. My son who had been a perfect third grade student started to have problems. My husband completely shut down and was unavailable. I got severely ill to the point where I dropped 30 lbs. I just could not eat and was withering away to not much. I ended up in the hospital. Everyone thought I was having a stroke because the left side of my body was numb, I was thin and pale, and couldn't talk right. In reality I was having such bad migraines and was so tense that I had pinched a nerve which caused the numbness.

I couldn't sleep. I'd have visions in my head trying to figure out what had happened. I felt like I was truly starting to deteriorate. One night I asked JoEllen for help to get through all this, to help me sleep and to find some peace. I felt her hand slip into mine. It was warm and I drifted off, dreaming that we'd gone to the beach. She was wearing the bright tank top she'd had on when she was killed. She lifted it up and told me she was okay and not hurting anymore. There were no stab wounds. This and other similar dreams helped me to let her go.

But still I had no idea what had happened. I continued to feel like I was coming apart. I had the front of the book and the back of the book but knew nothing about what was inside the book. Why? How did it get to this point? Did anyone see what happened? I knew no details. I spent hours combing through police files, autopsy pictures and asked a ton of questions but it was never enough. It just made no sense to me. The court process happened and went pretty quickly. Tyrone was convicted of first-degree murder within six months. Immediately after he was sentenced I spoke with the official from the Bureau of Criminal Apprehension. I insisted that I have the chance to talk to Tyrone and get the answers I needed. He then introduced me to the facilitator associated with the VOD program.

It took two years before I could see Tyrone. During that time, I met with his father and learned the truth about his past. He had grown up in Indiana. His mother was a prostitute and he was the oldest of nine brothers and sisters. Each of them had a different father. Tyrone had to take care of them all. In his younger years, he had pushed his cousin off a deck. Although he would snap whenever he got frustrated or lose control, he seemingly had never hurt anyone before. His uncle was diagnosed as bipolar and had killed a cat, writing on the wall with the cat's blood. Recognizing his son's propensities, Tyrone's father declared to me that "Tyrone never had a chance."

In preparing for the dialogue, I was clear that my agenda was to find out what had actually happened between Tyrone and JoEllen to cause her death. I had to talk to Tyrone to get answers. I warned folks that I would stay the whole time if Tyrone was honest with me. But if he wasn't, I'd leave and never come back. Tyrone and I knew each other some because I'd insisted JoEllen bring him to the house so I could meet him when they first got together. Tyrone evidently was worried. In response to my warning, he would say to the facilitator, "I'm afraid to hurt her." But I was desperate. I had to have some kind of closure. Not knowing was eating at me and I couldn't imagine living the next 50 years ignorant about what happened to JoEllen. I knew myself well enough that I couldn't go on and be good to anybody else without fulfilling this selfish need of my own.

So I made clear to everyone that I needed honest facts. I didn't want this to be a waste of my time and I felt Tyrone owed me the truth. I asked the police commander to come with me to the VOD. He had become a good friend and I felt he would give me confidence and help ensure that Tyrone would be truthful.

At first I was excited to finally meet with Tyrone at the prison but when I walked in everything changed. I became small. Everything about JoEllen's murder came flashing back and I felt very vulnerable. I was surrounded by huge men of color who were not nice and I had to walk through the hall with them as the only female. I went through two sets of double doors and remember the clinking and thinking, "I'm trapped in this prison." The police commander must have sensed what was happening. He said, "This is a little intimidating isn't it? Just keep your head down." When I walked into the room where we were meeting, two security guards joined us. When we sat down at the table, I had the police commander to my right and a security guard beside him and on my left.

Tyrone walked in and I was shocked because he wasn't shackled. He sat across from me with his head down. I began to cry. Everything that had happened just came back on me. I couldn't stop crying and I couldn't breathe. I wasn't able to talk and worried I couldn't go on with the meeting. It took five minutes before I could compose myself. I finally looked up and said to Tyrone, "I need you to put yourself back at my house the night I made dinner, when we were sitting across the table from each other, and pretend that it's just you and I sitting at this table here, in the prison. I need you to tell me exactly what happened and how we got sitting at this table." And he did, including all the details he was afraid to tell me plus some that no one yet knew.

After JoEllen had gotten in his car, he drove out to the edge of town where the cornfields are very high. He tried to persuade JoEllen to come back to him but she was firm that their relationship was over. He reached into the back of the car and grabbed a knife and stabbed her in the abdomen. She got out of the car and started to run through the cornfield. But because of her recent knee surgery she wasn't fast. Tyrone chased her, stabbing her from behind. Tyrone said that right before he started stabbing her he had an out-of-body experience where he was watching it all happen but unable to stop himself. He'd never had such anger before. Eventually they got to the main road where there was a lot of construction. She ran to the grassy median. Tyrone got on top of her and stabbed her 48 times. Then he ran back to his car, got in it, and drove past her. She was still moving and he hoped someone would have found her and saved her. There evidently was a witness that drove by during the stabbing that never came forward. Tyrone was able to describe the car and who was in it but he'd never shared those details in court.

I felt Tyrone was telling me the truth. But the whole time he couldn't look me in the eye. He sat with his head down and his hands in his lap. I remember thinking, "Why hasn't he said he's sorry? Why doesn't he have any compassion for this meeting? Why isn't he crying? Why isn't he asking for my forgiveness." He looked so hardened. There was no emotion. As he finished telling me what happened, the security guard told us we had only 15 minutes left for the dialogue. The facilitator asked if I had anything I wanted to say to Tyrone. I said, "Thank you for telling me what happened. That is why I came and exactly what I needed. I don't ever want to hear from you again. I don't ever want to come back. I don't ever want to hear from you. Don't contact me. I will never contact you again."

There was a complete shift in him. He raised his arms up to the table and had that angry look at his face. I thought, "There it is. That's the shift of anger his dad was talking about." I said, "This is done," and they walked me out. The police commander asked, "Did you see that?" I replied, "That's exactly what I saw and that's a huge piece of closure for me." It confirmed that's what happens to him when the control is taken from him. I think he expected that this meeting would become a relationship, and that I would come to see him and forgive him. I had made up some stories too which were completely wrong. I thought Tyrone was going to cry and apologize, show me he's a 19-year-old boy who made a really bad mistake. Maybe I would give a hug on the way out. But that's not what happened or was supposed to have happened.

I left the prison feeling a huge lift, better than I'd felt in two years. I got exactly what I'd been waiting for, to hear what happened and to fill in the blanks. It was the hardest two hours I'd ever sat through but it was a relief. There was brightness in my life again. It was moving forward so I could keep living for myself, my kids and everything else. I felt completely free. He was the only one that had the key to open that book and tell what was in it. He gave me that key. I took my freedom and everything back from him when he told me. Everything made sense. I don't make up stories anymore in my head about what happened. "Did she do this? Did she do that? Was she screaming for us? Was she yelling for help?" I know now that she was doing all that. So my meeting with Tyrone was the number one shift in my journey. It probably saved my life. I'm thankful to him, very thankful that he gave that opportunity to me, cause he didn't have to. I never experienced anger, only sadness. For me it wouldn't feel natural to forgive him since I'm not angry and never was. I gained back the 30 lbs and I'm out doing things in the wilderness and with running that make me get out the bad and breathe in the good.

Analysis: Crime and its aftermath

The murder of JoEllen caused an immediate and severe stress reaction for Clynita. She found herself slipping away. Instead of anger, which is a source of energy, albeit negative, Clynita found that her energy was evaporating. She felt numb and dissociated from her body, almost as if she had lost herself. Indeed, with her loss of weight and inability to eat she felt that she was fading away. Her call to JoEllen for help is illustrative. Once she felt JoEllen's hand in hers, she felt more tethered in the world and could sleep.

Clynita knew almost immediately what she needed. Because of his history with JoEllen, she recognized that Tyrone was the likely killer. She therefore had details about their relationship, his propensity to anger, physical abuse and destruction of property and what had ultimately caused her daughter's death, but she knew nothing about what had happened between them to escalate matters to such a violent end for JoEllen. Clynita described this dilemma in terms that likely matched what she felt inside. She did not say that she was unable to finish the book without vital information. Rather, she pictured that she had the front and back covers of the book but there was nothing inside—"Everything in the middle was unknown." It was as if JoEllen's murder took her breath away and she was left empty and without form or substance, like a ghost. Clynita, therefore, was driven to get back what was missing both in information and about herself. Without the puzzle pieces she did not feel complete as a human being.

As soon as Tyrone was convicted, Clynita therefore began requesting to meet with him. "By the end of January when he was convicted, I was ready to walk out of court and go talk to him." Indeed, her initiative began much earlier than is usual for victim survivors. But Clynita had already been hospitalized and felt this was a wake-up call to figure out what had happened. She had some awareness that she needed Tyrone and what he knew so she could put herself back together. In some ways, her desire to meet soon was, in effect, the fight for her life. "I was looking for some kind of closure because I was physically and mentally not doing okay with not knowing… It was eating at me." Clynita had spent hours at the police station reading the files and talking to the police commander and official from the Bureau of Criminal Apprehension but that wasn't enough. She began pushing to see him and talk to him to get answers.

Preparation

Clynita had to wait two years before she could meet with Tyrone. There is no information about the delay or why preparation took so long. Perhaps Tyrone was resistant or wasn't ready for the dialogue. Perhaps the facilitator assessed that Clynita needed more time so that she was emotionally prepared to meet with Tyrone. Regardless, the delay was exceedingly frustrating for Clynita. During preparation, Clynita had conveyed to Tyrone the urgency of their meeting, relaying that she wanted to know everything that had happened on the day of her daughter's death and he had to be completely honest with her. She made clear that he owed this truth to her. She assured him that she would stay and listen to every horrific detail. However, if he lied or withheld information, she would leave and never come back. Tyrone, therefore, knew that Clynita could walk out at any time. By the time they met, Clynita felt confident that Tyrone would be truthful with her.

There is little information about the preparation process itself or its impact on Clynita. It appears that it had little effect in terms of her attitude or feelings toward Tyrone—"[My attitude] did not change because I didn't know anything of what he was about to say. I didn't know what he thought." For many victim survivors, preparation is a time for the harnessing of their negative energy and cultivation of openness so that the upcoming dialogue can be healing. For Clynita, there was little negative energy. She was quite neutral toward Tyrone. She just needed his information, information that she felt belonged to her and information that could release her and give her back her life.

Dialogue

Clynita knew ahead of time that the dialogue would last only two hours. Again, it's not clear if she chose this time limit or if it was imposed by the prison system or some other outside force. It appears she did not have a tour of the prison, which is commonly done to help victim survivors feel more familiar with the prison environment prior to the dialogue. Rather, Clynita experienced the setting for the first time when she arrived to meet with Tyrone. She was traumatized by the prison environment and the prisoners themselves, feeling her vulnerability as the only woman around—"I still almost have nightmares of going through two sets of double doors and the clinking behind me, feeling like I'm trapped in this prison." She again felt her strength slipping.

Even though security officers surrounded her, the confidence that she had built over the past two years seemed tenuous. She was flooded by the past. When Tyrone appeared, she was surprised he was not shackled.

She became hyper-aware of his hands and how they had taken JoEllen's life. She couldn't breathe or talk. She dissolved into tears and could not stop crying. Clynita was worried that she could not compose herself enough to do the dialogue, but in hindsight her explanation was that she was no longer numb and that she had released more in the initial five minutes of the dialogue than she did throughout the court process. In some ways, Clynita, through her tears, began to reclaim part of herself, part of what she had lost. Her feelings only surfaced as she sat across from Tyrone, suggesting that they were meant for him. Moreover, those feelings, in effect, were expressing the pain differential or the immensity of the pain she had carried since learning of her daughter's murder.

In some ways, the dialogue seems limited and even aborted. Clynita said almost nothing until the end when she thanked him and told him she'd never see him again. Tyrone responded with anger, the same anger that he likely felt when JoEllen refused an ongoing relationship with him. Because security had indicated to both Clynita and Tyrone that the session was almost over, it is possible that the process was scrunched. There was no time left to deal with his response. If there had been, Clynita might have challenged Tyrone's behavior and directly made the association to his response to JoEllen. Instead it is likely that Tyrone felt used. He gave Clynita what she asked for but his expectation of getting something back did not happen.

Clynita, however, felt transformed and free. Because he held the information she needed to feel whole again, he was her captor. His sharing it with her released her from his bondage and she began to come to life again. She could breathe now and her life moved forward. As such, her pain was transformed and she felt a deep sense of completion. Energy shifts did occur. Tyrone's response to Clynita's declaration was negative while Clynita felt a significant positive shift because of what Tyrone gave her. As such, there was a dyadic process and it had movement. Clynita's positive shift happened because of Tyrone but it did not happen "with" Tyrone. When Tyrone responded to Clynita as he had to JoEllen, she got to do what her daughter never did. She was able to leave and escape Tyrone. She completed her daughter's act.

Clynita did not vilify Tyrone in the information he gave about his own behavior. She humanized him. She saw that they both had had out-of-body experiences in relationship to JoEllen's murder. She recognized his history. She heard that he did not want to hurt her in what he shared. She acknowledged that he had a choice to meet with her and give her the pieces she longed for. Being open to Tyrone was never a goal or necessary in her eyes. She just needed the information. Clynita was never angry with Tyrone.

She saw him as a product of his circumstances—"He never had a chance." Rather than pity, she felt he was pitiful, beyond hope and doomed from the start.

For Clynita, forgiveness was irrelevant. After all, you can't forgive a dog that bites you and doesn't know any better. Moral reinstatement of Tyrone was also not useful. Clynita saw him as ongoingly dangerous. Prison was the right place for him. Tyrone and Clynita shared no common value base nor did any appear in the time and space they had for their dialogue. Clynita was cognitively open to other possibilities in terms of her comments about what was supposed to have happened between them but nothing materialized.

The VOD was done to retrieve information, information that was critical to Clynita's physical and psychological existence. Tyrone was only useful as the source of that information. Clynita had nothing to resolve between them. The only dissonance she experienced was her dependency on the person who murdered her daughter, a person she never wanted to see again and yet someone she needed. She resolved the dissonance by pushing for the meeting but remaining emotionally detached from him. The irony is that Clynita got what she needed because of and through the dyadic encounter. No conduit, however, was built between them for the transference of Clynita's pain to Tyrone. This was never part of Clynita's agenda. Rather she used the dialogue to take back from him what he owed her in order to fill herself in and to become whole again.

LILA'S STORY AND ANALYSIS

Lila's daughter was murdered on prom night by a young man, Jake, whom she met at an after-prom party. Lila describes the intense anxiety she repressed for the sake of looking strong and supporting her husband. Meeting with Jake was Lila's only way to answer the question, "Why?" and to make sure Jake knew the person he killed. Preparation was not an easy road; Jake initially declined, and later backed out the day before. An additional year went by before they met face to face and Lila describes seeing Jake as a person for the first time. Gradually Jake took ownership of the crime and of all the burdens Lila had been storing. By acknowledging his escalating violent behavior, Lila was able to shift the guilt she carried onto the person responsible and free herself.

My daughter Loretta was killed on her senior prom night by a 19-year old acquaintance she ran into at an after-prom party. This was one night I didn't give her a curfew. I figured she'd be safe because she was going to double date with her good friend. She hadn't dated much and actually had to be persuaded to go. I remember her dress, her long red gloves, and her telling me not to worry because she soon would be 18 years old. I went to sleep without waiting up for her. When she wasn't home by 4:00 in the morning, I figured she had spent the night at her friend's house because it was so late. It was only later that day that I got worried. After calling her friend I learned that they had gone to a number of after-prom parties including some with college students. Eventually Loretta's friend had gone home, leaving her with Jake, the acquaintance she had met at one of the parties.

By midday, my husband and I called the police to report that my daughter was missing. She always called home if she was late but we had heard nothing. We finally learned Jake's last name from an old girlfriend who was frightened that he might harm her if he found out she had given his identity. Evidently both Jake and his brother were known to be violent. Eventually we located Jake's uncle who took us to where Jake lived in a drug-infested neighborhood. No one was home but other tenants helped us gain entry. There was a pungent odor. After noting that the bed was stripped of sheets or coverings, we found a pile of blankets and saw Loretta's leg sticking out. My husband forced me out of the apartment. The police would not allow me back in no matter how much I begged. The funeral home director refused to let me see her body because he worried I'd fall apart. So we had a closed casket and I never got to see my daughter again.

Jake had blown out of town. He was on probation because of a burglary offense. He was found several states away with Loretta's belongings in his trunk. I never got to be at the trial. My husband and I were sequestered to sit outside the courtroom. Supposedly Jake was crying in the courtroom but I believed those tears were for himself, because he'd been caught, not for my daughter.

I was initially in shock that someone so young could do something so heinous. Jake had wrapped a necktie around Loretta's throat and used his hands to poke a hole right through her esophagus until she was gone. Then he bragged about the kinky sex he had had. I remember that the night after the funeral I sat alone and the sound coming out of me was like an animal, the grief was so deep. I felt like the waking dead and walking around in a deep fog. I was angry with everyone. I planned to hunt him down if he wasn't caught or given first-degree murder. In my mind I kept going over what Loretta had gone through and the house where it happened. I would wake up every night at 4 a.m., the same time Loretta had been killed. I had visited Jake's apartment repeatedly. I had to go to the closet where she was found and touch the floor to be sure she wasn't there. I became hyper-vigilant. Anytime I'd see young people getting into a squabble or fight, my heart would just start racing. I had chest pains and tremendous anxiety.

I ended up with acid reflux. I tended to stuff my feelings and be strong for others like my husband who was very teary. I felt I had to put on this mask and pretend I was handling it. Everyone kept telling me that I was strong even though I didn't want to be. I eventually found someone who helped me start a support group. There I didn't have to be strong. I could fall apart.

I wanted from the beginning to meet with Jake. I wanted to know why. Why did he kill her? Was it because Loretta was mixed or Black? I wanted to know what was going on for someone so young to do something like he did. I remember being his age and doing crazy things but to take someone's life? Someone sent me a transcript of the trial but the legal world is so different from your own personal questions. I just figured the prison system should let me see Jake and say what I want. I felt he owed me. I didn't even know about VOD until I heard a mother at a conference talk about meeting with the man who had killed her daughter. I asked her how she did it and she referred me to the facilitator. When I met the facilitator she told me I should write down all my questions. Then we would talk about the process. It was all foreign to me. I didn't know what she meant by "the process."

She told me she would need to talk to Jake to see if he would agree to the meeting. I was offended. I thought, "Why in the heck should he have the right to refuse me?" but the facilitator explained that if the process was not voluntary, I might not get what I wanted. She asked me about my hopes. I knew that my biggest need was to see if he had any remorse. At the trial he wouldn't look at me but I heard he was remorseful. Jake's initial reaction to meeting with me was "no way." But he really didn't understand what it was about. He thought I wanted to beat up on him. "Tell Mrs. Leander that I can't see her. I don't need her to come in and shame me and blame me any more than has already been done. I can't put my family through this. Tell her that I'm sorry. I would trade places with her if I could. I was on drugs and alcohol and I didn't know what I was doing."

I felt discouraged. The meeting had ended before it started. But the facilitator wanted to go talk to him and explain what doing a VOD was all about. She also told me I needed to prepare for the meeting and I should get some more counseling. I should also find a support person. I asked the man who helped me start the support group. Jake was also given the option to have a support person in attendance but he decided he didn't want anyone. Jake agreed to meet after he spoke with the facilitator and understood the purpose and meaning of doing a VOD. I found out later that even though he didn't have many friends in prison there was an older man he trusted who told him that he had an opportunity that "many of us will never be able to do." This man was his support and gave him the courage to finally meet with me.

I prepared for the VOD for a long time. The facilitator would visit with him and give me an idea of some of the things he'd said and then share with him some of my questions that he should think about. We kind of got to know each other through her. That helped a lot. I wanted to take some photos of Loretta with me in case he forgot what he left me with. I was afraid he might forget what he'd done. I wanted him to know who she was, who her family was. I also went to the police department to see the crime photos I never cared to see. I felt like I finally identified my daughter. They let me take a few of them with me to the meeting but they assigned a police escort to go with us. Actually I think the police woman was protecting those photos. It was important to me that he remember and understand what he took. The day before the scheduled meeting he backed out. Supposedly he was ill but maybe he made himself sick with the prospect of meeting with me. So I waited another whole year. I was afraid he'd back out again. I was fortunate to have a lot of support from friends who were watching and listening. My support group wondered why I would meet with him. They couldn't understand it. I said, "Because he's the only one that can answer my questions. Hopefully he will."

I remember the trip to the prison well. I traveled back ten years to when it all first happened. I felt I was in a soap opera. You are not actually in it but you are. I felt like I was above my body, looking down and watching myself. Driving to the prison I also felt all this tension from what I'd been carrying for so long. It was like a balloon that you blow up and it gets bigger and bigger, like you're about ready to pop. There had been a recent lockdown at the prison and he, therefore, would have to be brought in, in handcuffs and shackles. They could not use the usual room for meetings because it was full of contraband so we met in one of the classrooms. The warden who was waiting for us was pretty nervous. It was eerily quiet because of the lockdown. There wasn't a lot of movement.

I went into the room first. I had the photo album with me. The guards went to get Jake. I heard the clinking of the shackles. But something strange happened when he walked in. I called him by his name. I had never used his name but only referred to him as "offender." I had this image of a monster in my head. I didn't give him a face. But when he came in, the mask of monster that I had put on him came off. I was surprised. It was easier to see him as something else but now he's human, a real human being I'm dealing with. So that was a big shift. He sat down and I thanked him for coming. Thank goodness he kept his hands under the table. Those were the hands that killed my daughter. It was really quiet. You could have heard a pin drop. I felt my daughter's presence.

The facilitator asked me to go back to the day Loretta died. I went right back and shared what it was like for me and my husband, how we searched for Loretta and how much I loved her. She was my first born. Even though I knew he'd had struggles like a bad childhood, I wanted him to know that life hadn't been easy for her and we'd had struggles as well. I went through the album. I know this was hard for him because he was squirming in his seat but I felt that was right. He should. I wanted to see if what had happened meant anything to him or not. After I was finished he talked. He looked like he was looking at somebody from way back when he was 19. He said, "I was so messed up. I was so messed up." I was kind of surprised to see him go straight back to that time as if it were etched in his mind. In his story it was like he was in another zone. There were no words to really explain it and I don't know if he really knew. We never had a real answer as to why he did it. I told him that I knew he'd gone back after he killed her and took her out of the closet. I wanted to know if he remembered what he left me with, the condition of Loretta's body. He said, "She looked really, really bad." I could hear it in his voice, on his face that he didn't forget. I didn't need to show him the crime photos because he was visualizing it. It really meant something to me that he didn't forget.

As we talked the balloon got smaller and smaller. It was releasing somehow. I wanted to know if he thought about Loretta. He said he thought about her every day. The biggest thing I was unprepared for was that he took ownership. Jake told me he liked Loretta. He knew something was going on with him and he had had his hands around other girls' throats. He knew he was going to end up killing somebody. He said it didn't make any difference who she was, even if it were a sister of his. He said he was sorry and wished he could change places with Loretta. He was clear that what happened wasn't her fault. But he went further. He said, "It wasn't your fault." I had felt it was. After all, parents are supposed to protect their children. I should have protected her. I should have given her a curfew. And other people would blame me too—"If you were a Christian, this wouldn't have happened." So you live with all that. It haunts you. When he said, "There's nothing you could have done. It wasn't your fault," he took full ownership. He did not blame it on the drugs and alcohol. We asked about that and he knew exactly what he was doing. It was a gradual thing with this shifting and him taking ownership. Everything I was hanging onto, he took. It was like I was just literally letting him have it. Then he says, "It wasn't her fault. It was my fault. And it wasn't your fault." I wanted him to know what he left me with but he was actually owning it. He was taking it. And he listened. That was tremendous. I felt like I was literally handing over all of these burdens to Jake and he was willingly taking all that from me so I didn't have to live with it.

I was bothered all the way through the meeting because he kept his head down. At one point I said, "Jake, I need you to look at me." He said, "I don't feel I have the right to." And that was another big shift. He was feeling the remorse and the guilt. It made him more human to me. He talked about the shame he'd brought on his family and his not wanting to look at me. He finally did. I'd always thought that the eyes are the mirror to your soul. I could see in his eyes and I asked, "Jake, do you have any faith?" He didn't. I asked, "Have you ever asked Loretta for forgiveness?" He replied, "Oh, I couldn't do that. I couldn't do that." I just looked at him and said, "Yes, you can." That surprised me. It's like, "Did I just say that?" But I did.

I didn't plan to do that. Forgiveness was a foreign word to me. I felt that it wasn't up to me to forgive. That was up to the Lord. The facilitator had asked if I wanted an apology from him and warned me that he might not give that to me. For me it was just important that he hear me and look at me. I wanted him to have to see me. By the end my voice was softer, almost like I was talking to another child. I realized he was older now but he was a child at 19.

My meeting with Jake took all my fear away. A lot of unexpected things happened like telling him to ask Loretta for forgiveness. Our dialogue just took on a life of its own. I hope he got something from it. I know he did call his grandparents to let them know he'd done something good, something for which they can be proud. I think he held his head up a little higher. At one time I wouldn't have cared if he had changed or not. I wanted to kill him. But I did care. He knew he couldn't give me my daughter back but he gave me something, some kind of peace. I've been able to move forward. I don't feel as stuck. When I shared what happened with my husband, he teared up and said, "We always said there were two lives that were destroyed that night."

Analysis: Crime and its aftermath

Lila lost her daughter under the most normal of circumstances—her daughter's senior prom. Although Jake clearly took advantage of a young, naïve girl, Lila lived in a shadow land of guilt and responsibility for many years. She berated herself for not giving Loretta a curfew, for falling asleep before Loretta got home, and for not questioning her daughter's delay in returning home. She lived with the worry that others held her responsible. She tormented herself trying to decide what was normal behavior for a parent of a young girl going to her prom and what wasn't. Lila also bore a huge regret that she never again saw her daughter because others determined that she could not handle how badly Loretta looked—"The funeral director thought no mother should see their dead child. I didn't know I had a choice."

Lila stuffed many of her feelings. She felt she had to be strong for her family, particularly her husband who was suffering greatly and her three small children at home. At times she wanted to tell him, "Shut up. It's my turn." But she felt she had no choice. Eventually she founded her own support group. Only when her co-leader gave her permission to let go was she able to fall apart periodically. Lila describes storing up her feelings with no outlet as a huge balloon. It got bigger and bigger until it threatened to burst. She had lots of anger and was ready to hunt him down herself. She obsessed, imagining many things. For example, if she envisioned his having a family and children, she'd rage internally—"How dare he have children, if he would take mine." With no outlet for her feelings, she'd also ponder suicide—"I didn't want to live. I just wanted to die. I'd pray for a disease. If anybody was ill, I'd trade places with them, so I could go be with my daughter." Lila kept ruminating about how her daughter died and what kind of pain and torture she had endured. She would hear her voice, have feelings and again stuff them. She'd visit the apartment where her daughter died, looking for her daughter's spirit.

She put all the negative energy surrounding Loretta's murder into constructive action. Besides the support group she started for homicide survivors, she began working as an advocate for the Department of Corrections. She surrounded herself with caring people who knew firsthand what homicide survivors experience. She searched for answers everywhere, including the criminal justice system. But everything remained incomplete. She couldn't figure out how someone who was still a child at 19 could do something so brutal. This dissonance gnawed at her. The pieces didn't fit. In her efforts to determine why her daughter was killed, she kept returning to questions about Loretta's race and if it was a factor in her death. Lila was convinced that the answers along with any relief lay in Jake's hands. Lila seemed to sense that she and Jake were irreparably bonded by Loretta's murder. Try as hard as she could, there was no peace. She could not get to the other side without him.

Preparation

Lila had considered intermittently meeting with Jake. Once she met the facilitator, however, she realized there were many steps, some of which included her acceptance of the process as voluntary for both her and Jake. This requirement forced her to start thinking of Jake as his own person rather than a prisoner that she could beckon at will. Lila prepared for a long time not withstanding Jake's initial refusal based on his worries about what would take place between them as well as his subsequent backing out because he got sick. Ironically, Jake's behavior gave Lila a window into his fears and vulnerability. She had heard that he suffered during the trial but, at that time, was cynical about his motives. Now, with the help of the facilitator, she could begin to humanize some of his responses, understand the courage that it took to meet with her, and see his reactions as indicators of the weight he too carried. Lila's openness to the process likely grew as well from the facilitator's attitude and the carrying of information about each to the other as part of the facilitator's moving back and forth in her visits with Lila and Jake. As Lila said, "We kind of got to know each other through her." Importantly, Lila was impacted by the facilitator's response to Jake's resistance. Rather than backing off, the facilitator interpreted Jake's reticence as based on erroneous information and took the initiative to meet with him in order to increase his openness to the VOD process and what Lila needed. Jake's shifts and the facilitator's patience and success likely increased Lila's openness to Jake as well. Indeed, he had struggled with himself to move past his initial resistance and concern for himself to deciding to meet with Lila because it could help her. He experienced a kind of dissonance between not wanting to meet with Lila while receiving guidance from an older support person that this meeting would be an opportunity of a lifetime. Because of the amount of activity between them prior to meeting, the information shared and Jake's shifts, the tracks for the emotional conduit between them were already laid.

Lila's core motive in doing the VOD was to see if Jake had any remorse. Lila also wanted to use the meeting as an accountability process to ensure that he remember and never forget what he had done. Part of harnessing the energy that she had stored connected to the crime was planning out how she would make the memories stick. She decided to bring photo albums of Loretta and her family. That way she could guide his vision, introducing him on her terms to her daughter and her daughter's life before her death. She also got the crime photos so he could clearly see what he had done. Lila knew at some level that giving Jake the pain she carried and the pain that actually belonged to him rested on his accepting responsibility. Her hope was to increase the probability of that happening by painting a vivid picture of what he had taken from her when he killed her daughter. She therefore harnessed the energy she had stored for years and approached the dialogue with purpose and a steadfast attitude about what she wanted to accomplish.

Dialogue

As determined as she was, Lila was not prepared for her own shifts. For example, she found herself responding to him as a human being rather than the monster she had surmised him to be—"Now he's human. It's a real human being I'm dealing with." As she shared her story, she went back in time. She shared searching for and finding her daughter in the closet, her love for Loretta as a struggling single mother, and the impact of her death. Lila watched Jake's reactions closely. She wanted to see if anything mattered to him. When she went through the photo album of Loretta's life, she noted his squirming and felt some initial success in getting through to him.

After Lila spoke, Jake talked. Lila again was surprised because Jake without hesitancy went back to the same point in time as Lila, which helped establish the conduit of honesty between them. Lila's questions about his feelings and reactions to Loretta and to what he had done resonated internally and his responses were direct, personally revealing and heartfelt. Indeed, his responses served a twofold purpose, to both provide her with a mirror into how deeply he too had been impacted by what he'd done and to hold himself accountable in her presence for his choices, the violence he wrought and the pain he suffered internally for who he was and who he destroyed.

This sharing between them went beyond information. It was as if each pulled from the other personal truths that provoked still deeper self-revelations. Lila, for example, had carried immense guilt about what she might have done to prevent her daughter's death. Because of the years that had passed, her guilt had quietly settled down but played in the background. Unbeknownst to her, it likely played a role in her needing Jake to share some of the pain, through his feeling remorseful for what he had done to Loretta. Lila's awareness of the guilt she had carried came to life as Jake explicitly directed her to give him the burden. "There's nothing you could have done. It wasn't your fault." The conduit Lila and Jake built through these powerful and resonant exchanges allowed the energy to flow back and forth between them. They did a whole segment together about seeing. For example, Lila could ask Jake about his going back to the apartment and looking at Loretta while watching him visualize the condition of her body. She could comment on how he looked down rather than at her. They did another segment on worthiness. He could share how unworthy he felt and she could minister to him about asking Loretta for forgiveness. They also created shared meaning about forgetting. Lila could ask him to remember what she can never forget and he could reassure her that he had never forgotten what he did. They also served as healers to each other. He could convey his remorse through his words and his eyes and she could convey her humanity by speaking to him as a mother. The openness between them allowed these exchanges whereby each of them felt the pain of the other and responded in ways that were healing. Indeed, many of Lila's spontaneous and heartfelt responses to Jake were unexpected.

Ultimately, the back and forth flow and reciprocal influence they had on each other helped to move the pain from Lila to Jake and transform it. Lila had no more fear. She felt unstuck likely because Jake has taken such ownership for what she had otherwise carried alone. Lila was clear that there is still plenty of pain, particularly when she realizes that she has missed Loretta's growing up and getting married. However, she felt an obligation to share her journey with others. She eagerly talked about her VOD experience with her immediate family and support group and felt that it offered them hope for their own situations. She even accepted an invitation to talk about the dialogue with the parole board. Lila's reinstatement of Jake occurred in part through the trust of him that grew during the dialogue. She allowed him to attend to her and the guilt she had carried. She believed fully that he had taken ownership and the burden off her shoulders. She no longer doubted that he remembered exactly everything that had happened and suffered for it. Jake demonstrated the change in his status by calling his grandparents to publicly mark what he had done to make things right. His notifying them about his actions likely helped heal some of the shame he had brought on his family.

The significance of the dyadic dynamic between Lila and Jake was evident throughout the dialogue. Lila's need to see if Jake was remorseful expressed a cry that he shoulder some of the pain she otherwise carried alone. In some ways, her need was a statement that they were in an involuntary but unrecognized relationship because of Loretta. But Jake went further than Lila had hoped for. Specifically, out of his remorse came full ownership, which had no energy or life until it could be realized with Lila, the person to whom it was owed. For Lila, Jake's ownership was transforming. It not only lifted her guilt but changed the meaning of the story she otherwise carried. Although there is a strong, residual and abiding ache, what she now shares with others is redemptive because of the ownership that grew out of Jake's remorse. The dissonance between seeing Jake as a monster and his humanity toward her coupled with his expression of accountability clearly pulled Lila to seeing him anew. This experience led to still more openness to go further and deeper in the process. It is possible, for example, that his ownership and movement could have provoked still another positive challenge for Lila to move further ahead because Jake had removed so many of the encumbrances. All of these shifts within each of them and between them reflect the power of positive energy generated by the dyadic encounter and exchange.

RANDELL'S STORY AND ANALYSIS

Baird and Cameron had met earlier that day at a neighborhood picnic when Cameron discovered his sister had been assaulted by her partner. Baird and some others from the picnic accompanied Cameron to confront his sister's partner and as they were leaving her home, Baird flipped the vehicle, ejecting Cameron who died on impact. Randell was devastated by the loss of his son and the multitude of lies Baird told to escape responsibility. Randell could feel himself becoming addicted to the hate and he could see where that path had led his grandfather, after the death of his own son. For Randell, VOD was a way to finally hear the truth and hold Baird accountable. Prior to the dialogue Randell saw Baird as evil, but as they spoke and Randell felt sincerity and remorse those feelings began to dissolve. Their meeting led Randell to meet with the parole board twice and make a public statement of forgiveness. Randell and Baird continued to meet and when he was released began a voluntary relationship, sharing their story at Victim Impact Panels.

My oldest son, Cameron, was invited to a neighbor's picnic where he met Baird. While he was there, Baird learned his sister had been beaten by her partner who was a meth addict. Baird took off in his truck to confront him and invited Cameron and others at the picnic to come with him. Baird threatened the guy with a broken beer bottle but Cameron grabbed his hand just in time to stop him from hitting and possibly killing the man. Because neighbors had called the police, Baird and the others took off, driving recklessly to get away before the police came. The truck reached 100 MPH on a highway ramp, flipping the vehicle end over end. Cameron was ejected and killed on impact. Baird, who was drunk and high on drugs, wanted to escape the scene and leave Cameron's body. He called a friend with a tow truck but the highway patrol showed up and eventually handcuffed him to a gurney after he tried to flee the scene three times.

Baird tried to blame Cameron for his own death, saying that he was ejected because he wasn't wearing his seatbelt. Another passenger, however, was also ejected but unhurt so the story of the seatbelts didn't match. Baird then claimed he saw Cameron get up but another car ran over him and killed him. It took a long time to find out the truth about what had happened to our son.

But there was more shady stuff. A judge ordered a blood test for Baird but they gave him the wrong one. The file created on Cameron was supposed to contain the judge's order, the police notes, and the blood test results but when the officials pulled it out, there was not one shred of paper. Everything was gone. There was no evidence to back up Baird's use of alcohol and drugs that night. When questioned, the judge could not remember what she had written down at home and supposedly taken it to her office and turned it in. Because the evidence that might have resulted in a 30-year sentence for Baird was gone, Baird took a plea and received only ten years. At the hearing, we were threatened with being kicked out if we showed any emotion, including outcries and screams. But I was furious with the man.

I hated Baird horribly. At one point I had gone searching for him. I went to every bar he ever frequented and made sure everyone in town knew I was after him. I lashed out at him before the sentencing and said, "I hope you have a child someday. I hope every day that your child lives you're thinking that some drunk will kill your own child the way you did mine." To think that he planned to leave my son on the side of the road like he was a piece of trash stabbed me to the core. I couldn't imagine him being left there and then Baird lying about it to cover up what he did. He owned up to nothing. I felt someone, him or me, had to die. This was a constant thought. The hate became so intense I couldn't sleep. I began to get sick. I remember sitting in the doctor's office and hearing the cancer word. I knew it was brought on because of my intense rage. Hate becomes a drug. You become addicted to it. You learn to hate something so bad that it's constantly in your mind, 24/7, every time you're awake and even, subconsciously, in your sleep. Then I started having trouble with my heart, which was confirmed by the heart specialist. Hate can destroy. It consumed me.

But something else was also feeding it. Years ago, my grandfather's oldest son, Vince, had gotten into an argument with four other guys while they were in a boat on a small lake. One of the guys took an oar and hit Vince, throwing him overboard. My grandfather watched as they dredged the lake for his son and finally fished him out. No one confessed and no one was ever charged. This bothered my grandfather so badly that he turned from a mellow man into a mean, violent alcoholic. He died a young man. Now the same thing was happening to me. I was watching myself turn into that same person, a vile angry man. But I wasn't drinking.

My wife and I sought out counselors at a crisis and outreach center. Several of them talked to us about doing a dialogue with Baird. I wanted to understand what VOD was all about so I started volunteering for the group that was facilitating the dialogues. I worked on close to 25 cases. I would walk participants through the process and then meet with them before their VOD meetings. I wanted them to understand what they were going to do and to have a positive feeling that this would be healing. I saw that the process had a strong positive effect.

I wanted to do a VOD with Baird to get the truth. I saw him as the devil incarnate and felt he was evil to have walked away, leaving my son on the Interstate dead. His inmate number began with the letters 666, which in the Bible stands for the devil. My wife and I met twice with the facilitator. I knew her from the volunteer work I was doing and we got to be close friends. In preparing for the dialogue, the facilitator asked us if we wanted Baird to be in the meeting in just his jumpsuit, not handcuffed or handcuffed and shackled. My frame of mind was that I wanted to see him suffer. We thought we'd see real evil, so we requested that he come in handcuffs and shackles.

When he came into the room, he was shuffling with chains running down to his ankles. At that moment my heart stopped. I froze inside with fear because now I'm face to face with the monster. He sat across from me and my wife. I realized that meeting the guy who took my son's life was the hardest thing I'd ever done. I remembered that Baird had said that Cameron was a piece of shit. Specifically, at the time Cameron was killed, the officer at the scene had said to Baird, "Boy, you're doing better than your buddy over there." Baird had replied, "I don't give a fuck about him. He's no fucking friend of mine." So Baird comes in and this is the first chance I have to look at him. I anticipated seeing the devil but what I saw was a man who was afraid and scared of me, someone who was broken, ashamed, and hurting.

Baird started by apologizing. My sense of him as a monster began to dissolve a little, like a piece of crayon that you chip away at. He began to tell us the story of his life. His father was a drunk and absent, as was his grandfather. His father felt that drinking was his right. He could do it whenever he wished. Baird had no male figure in his life, no one to look up to. Everyone in the family was abused. His story began to break me down. I was overwhelmed at what I was hearing and seeing and asked for a break. I had to get out of that room. So we took a break and during that time I asked the guard to please remove the handcuffs and shackles. The guard told me that was not possible because of my order for him to be shackled during the dialogue. We resumed the meeting and everyone was in tears—Baird, me, and my wife. I could see the remorse in his eyes. I was getting some of the answers I needed about Cameron. I wasn't expecting to feel empathy for Baird but I did. I grabbed hold of my wife's arm and said, "I have to try to help this guy now. I have to do something." I told the counselors as well but had no idea what to do. By the end, he reached out to my hand and shook it. It was a mixed bag. I did accept his apology and shake his hand. I had a lot to think about.

Following the first VOD, I was still kind of angry. My cancer and heart problems persisted. I felt now that I had to make an important decision. I had to work on forgiveness. Ever since Cameron's death my wife and I had been speakers on victim impact panels. Every time we spoke and described the VOD, we'd get questions back or letters asking if I could ever forgive Baird for what he had done. At first I got angry and would toss the letters aside. I ranted out loud, "How could they ask me to forgive? Don't they know what happened? Don't they understand? Didn't I explain it well enough?" But then the issue of forgiveness began to eat on me just like the anger had done. For me, forgiveness is a complete, total letting go. I can't forgive and still hate. Forgiveness means you not only forgive but you've released it, all of it.

It came time for his first parole hearing. I took literally thousands of letters I had received from inmates. I laid them on the table in front of the parole board. The parole board knew me from the volunteer work I'd done with VOC and asked, "Wow Randell, what are you after?" I said, "I've reached a point where I want to forgive Baird. I can't carry this hate anymore. It's killing me. I want to tell him I forgive him and I would like you to grant him hours for him to speak with us at victim impact panels." No one had ever asked that before and they were shocked. They had to think about it. Unfortunately, when Baird joined us, he did not respond to their questions properly. He showed little remorse and was kind of arrogant. The parole board shut the hearing down before I could speak. They said to him, "That's it, we're done. We're not going to grant you parole at this time. Go back and take classes because this is not working out." I was devastated because I'd worked with myself to get to the point of wanting to forgive and I'm shut down. I'd have to carry it all with me for a while longer.

After four months there was a second parole hearing. I again walked in and told the board what I wanted to do. They said to Baird, "Mr. Spitz would like to make a request of you." They told him that I wanted him to speak with me and my wife on victim impact panels. I then had a chance to say to him, "I forgive you. There may be some days I don't like you or want to talk to you but I want you to know that forgiveness means that it's over. I can't take it back because then it wouldn't really be forgiveness, would it? Forgiveness has to come from the heart and it has to mean that you're done. You've reached your end point." Baird broke down in tears, his head on the table and sobbed. Then he looked up and said, "I'll do anything Randell wants me to do."

We did a second VOD after that parole hearing. I told him that he had nothing more to fear. He could not be charged with anything more. Now was the time for complete honesty. I told him that if he wanted my help the best thing he could do was be honest and truthful. I also shared that I needed his help very badly. He spoke and it felt like we were hearing the truth for the first time. The pain began to melt away. It's like you take an aspirin for a headache and it starts to go away. It felt like some of that was being lifted, the weight we had carried from all the stories we'd heard about our son that were not true. He told me he did call his friend who had the tow truck and his intent was to leave Cameron on the side of the road. He told us how Cameron got ejected, how the vehicle flipped in the air and how the roof of the truck had caved down so far it landed on the steering wheel and dash. He admitted to being drunk. I thanked him for letting me know the truth. I really needed it.

I believe he carried the weight of the lies as well. It ate on him too. I talked with him about this and he confirmed that it was a nightmare that he lives also. I think it was helpful for him to tell the truth and get it out in the open. Baird spoke with us on victim impact panels ten times after the second VOD. His stepfather brought him to the first meeting because he couldn't drive yet. He got out of the car, walked over to us and gave me the biggest bear hug I've ever received. "Thank you," he said, "from the bottom of my heart for forgiving me. I want you to know that I had in my cell a picture of Cameron all the time I was in prison. There was not one day that I didn't look at that picture and think how badly I messed things up."

Today, Baird sees me as a father figure, somebody who will be a straight shooter with him. He's turned his life around. After he got out of prison he went to college and graduated with a degree in mechanical engineering. During those years he'd call and ask to meet me. It was like when I used to meet with Cameron, just talk about what is happening in our lives and things that really matter. The relationship between us has just blossomed. We got an invitation to his wedding. I think what he's trying to do is let us live a little bit through his life because we'll never get to see Cameron get married. At the wedding an old man in a wheelchair came up to us and asked if I was Randell Spitz. He told me he was Baird's grandfather. He reached out his hand and said, "I want you to know that if you hadn't forgiven my grandson the way you did and the way you talked to him and spent time with him, this wedding wouldn't be taking place today."

Since I have forgiven I'm cancer free and my heart is good. I had no treatments and no chemotherapy. It's just gone. I couldn't have reached this forgiveness on my own. It came from a Higher Power. I do believe when this life is over and I see my son, he will say to me, "Dad, you did the right thing."

Analysis: Crime and its aftermath

Although the death of his oldest son weighed heavily on Randell, Baird's attitude toward Cameron and his wanton disregard for anyone's life but his own were the critical factors that sent Randell reeling. Cameron had answered Baird's call for help in confronting his sister's abuser. He had physically stopped Baird from killing this man, warning him, "Whatever you do, do not kill him." Cameron, who was not drinking or doing drugs like the others, likely tried to stop the out-of-control behavior. When he was thrown from the truck, however, Baird's only concern was for himself.

Randell could hardly stomach the amount of untruth that attended every facet of the accident. Baird tried to leave the scene. He lied to the first responders initially, telling them that Cameron wasn't wearing a seatbelt, and then asserting that he was on drugs, got up after being thrown, claimed he was hurting, and then was hit by another car. More maddening were the missing documents. The court had lost all the evidence including the blood draw so no charges could be made involving alcohol. Everyone who was supposed to be responsible had dropped the ball. Randell and his own sons went back and forth to court three times waiting for a conviction. They were left with a sentence of only ten years.

All of these circumstances made Randell's blood boil to the point of explosion. He hated Baird with every fiber of his being. Without an outlet, his hatred built to the point that it began to destroy his body. In addition, Randell carried a family legacy from his grandfather who too had lost his son as a result of a violent encounter with friends. What happened to Cameron sparked the generational trauma for Randell that had never been resolved. Indeed, there were many parallels that underscored the litany of lies, dishonesty, and cover-ups that Randell felt powerless to undo. Worst of all, he saw himself becoming his grandfather who, because of his grief and rage, turned into a vile angry man. These negative energies created a vicious circle. Randell felt stuck in a cesspool of hatred that had nowhere to go and fed on itself, growing larger and larger over time. The intensification of these energies created additional stress, which coupled with his obsessing began to destroy his body. Randell felt certain that the diagnosis of cancer and then a heart condition were brought on by his hatred of Baird, which, ironically, was now threatening to take his life as well.

Randell began searching for an outlet, something to relieve the pressure always building inside himself. His grandfather became an abject lesson for Randell about what not to do. He told his wife, "I can't go down this road. I can't go the same way my grandfather did, without knowing the truth." He talked with his mother about how his grandfather had dealt with his grief over Vince. His mother who knew well the lasting strain she had felt as a child simply said, "You know, there was no help."

Preparation
Randell and his wife reached out to crisis counselors who suggested the VOD program. Rather than move forward, however, he first approached the possibility of meeting by volunteering to help other VOD participants.

In some ways, he became a surrogate participant learning about the program and what to expect through the experiences of others. In some ways, his volunteering was like practicing. He wanted to get comfortable with the process. He tried to convince himself, by what he gave to other VOD participants, that the meeting would be helpful and that it would be possible to have a positive experience without pain or suffering alongside all his hatred. He may even have hoped that taking the journey alongside others would be enough. So strangely, his volunteering served as his preparation. VOD preparation, however, is usually a lengthy process of personal exploration and setting of appropriate expectations. Although Randell had worked on close to 25 cases, he only did two preparation sessions with the facilitator who was also a close friend. He approached the dialogue, therefore, with openness to what it might accomplish but with little change in his feelings toward Baird. In many ways he did not want to humanize him. He saw Baird as the devil and with growing evidence of real evil. He used the meaning of Baird's inmate number to back up his belief. The hold of these intensely negative feelings was, for Randell, dissonant with seeing others who he had helped have positive interactions with their offenders and achieve some measure of healing. He took these unresolved and discordant pulls into the meeting with Baird.

Dialogue

Although it wasn't evident in his comments prior to meeting Baird, Randell actually had been working toward greater openness within himself. Instead of the monster he'd been waiting for, he immediately saw and responded to a frightened, broken man who began the dialogue by apologizing. This act opened the door and together with Randell's response began to create the emotional conduit for mutual sharing. Specifically, the contradiction between Randell's choice of handcuffs and shackles for an evil-laden Baird and the person in front of him created such dissonance that he could not stay in the meeting without trying to correct what he had picked to do to Baird. His response to the story of Baird's upbringing overwhelmed him as well. The tears shared between Randell, his wife, and Baird coupled with Baird's remorse laid the groundwork for more and more truth-telling. As Baird was increasingly transparent about what happened with Cameron and his own life, Randell felt something crack in him. This reciprocity or dyadic influence pushed him to go further, such that he committed to helping Baird in the future. Baird reached out to shake his hand in gratitude for the opportunity to meet and for the meaningful connection they had made. In many ways, Randell was more surprised by his own internal shifts than by anything Baird did. He never expected to feel empathy, caring, or kindness, much less a desire to help Baird.

Although Randell felt his hatred soften, he knew he had further to go. He was not at peace. His medical problems continued. He began to experience the dissonance associated with a new contradiction that emerged as a result of his interaction with Baird. Baird had readily given him a heartfelt apology with no expectation of anything back. Randell, however, was still holding on to some of his hurt and anger. As such, Baird had set the bar higher and, in effect, had moved beyond him. Randell knew innately that "I had to make some type of decision in my mind now. I had to work on forgiveness." For Randell, forgiveness came from the heart and was absolute, a complete and total let-go. Even though he was challenging himself to move forward, Randell was not prepared to give that much. He laid out his dilemma to other prisoners when he spoke to them as a victim impact panelist. They responded back through their letters because they felt the incompleteness of what had happened between Baird and Randell. They questioned whether Randell could ever forgive Baird for what he had done. Randell raged at them internally for implying that he should forgive. But he gradually resolved his internal conflict by deciding that he wanted to forgive fully and elected to make a public declaration to the parole board and promise to Baird that would seal off the possibility of his taking it back. In so doing, he both released himself and gave to Baird. Randell could have questioned the credibility and sustainability of what he had gained in the first VOD given Baird's behavior at the first parole hearing but he didn't. He came back four months later ready to make the same request.

The second VOD occurred after the second parole board hearing and after Randell had publicly forgiven Baird. His gesture lifted the shame from Baird as he broke down sobbing. Now that Randell had held nothing back in his full utterance of forgiveness, he challenged Baird to do the same in their second VOD meeting by reassuring him that he was safely out of harm's way. As Randell re-activated the emotional conduit that had been established between them during the first VOD meeting, Baird gave the full truth about himself, Cameron and the accident. In so doing, he released both Randell and himself from the negative power of the lies that had caused them both to suffer greatly.

The flow and sequence of events between Randell and Baird was unique. Baird broke through Randell's resistance at the first VOD meeting by starting rather than finishing with an apology. Similarly, Randell gave Baird his full forgiveness during the parole hearing, which was subsequently followed by another VOD meeting and greater truth-telling from Baird. In both instances, the apology and forgiveness served as catalysts for greater shifts in energy. The VOD process was deeply healing for both men. By the end of the second meeting, Randell felt complete. Not only was the weight lifted so that he no longer carried around the negative energy that manifested as hatred, but his cancer and heart problems literally disappeared. Baird felt fully reinstated as a moral citizen both through Randell's forgiveness but also by his support with the parole board and his request to have Baird join him as a panelist, which Baird did repeatedly. The power of his reinstatement was manifest in his turn around which included graduating from college and getting married. Finally, the VOD process gave Randell something his grandfather never got. Because Randell decided to walk a different path, he also helped heal what otherwise would have been passed down another generation.

The positive energy generated by the VOD process continues and is reinforced by the satisfaction each man gains from the other. Randell is a father figure to Baird who responds to his guidance by living a productive and successful life, which in turn is richly rewarding to Randell and reinforcing of what he has done to help others.

MAYA'S STORY AND ANALYSIS[1]

(Part 1 with mom, Maya) On her way home from dinner, Kaitlyn was kidnapped, raped, and shot to death. Her father, Duncan, his wife Maya, and the entire town were heavily involved in the subsequent search. Eventually, the two men responsible, Jerry and Gregory, went to the police and confessed to their involvement. Maya was trapped by her grief, letting only bits escape at a time. When her husband Duncan proposed a meeting, Maya had no personal interest but she did feel it was important to be present and bear witness. Almost as a passive observer, Maya finally heard the real story of her daughter's last moments and insight into Gregory's life. Maya saw the meeting as part of her healing, but experienced no transformation. Maya's forgiveness came later, a decisional choice not to allow her life to end with her daughter's. After several additional meetings Maya felt she had reached a point where Gregory had nothing left to give her and she was free to re-engage in her life.

My daughter, Kaitlyn, was kidnapped by two boys while walking home after midnight. She had just completed her freshman year in college and had returned home to spend the summer with me, her father Duncan, and her

---

1   The VOD with Gregory was conducted with both Maya and Duncan (see next case), parents of Kaitlyn.

sister Eleanor. The boys took her 30 miles out of town, raped and killed her. There was a massive community effort to find her. People gathered at our home because word of her missing had spread rapidly. It was all over the news. At least 500 people searched for Kaitlyn. You couldn't go anywhere without hearing about it throughout the state.

Eventually both boys came forward and told officials where she was. One of the boys had talked to his sister and sister's boyfriend who was a lawyer. This man cautioned him that he couldn't remain silent about the whereabouts of Kaitlyn's body. The boy's father insisted he go to the sheriff and refused to let him stay at the house. When the other boy found out that his partner was going to the sheriff he raced to the sheriff's office as well. Each boy took the police separately to where they had left Kaitlyn's body. I didn't learn that the officials had found Kaitlyn's body until we walked into the courtroom for the boys' arraignment. There was only unbelievable hatred toward them from the community members who were there. I remember feeling pity toward them and compassion.

When I first learned what the boys had done, I had an uncontrolled, almost animal response. Had they been standing in the doorway I would have ripped the flesh off their bones. I've never felt that kind of anger in my life except at that time. It lasted 30 seconds and then I went numb. I felt like I was picked up out of my life. I could see what was happening but I wasn't in it. My thoughts were incoherent. I had no idea what I wanted because I was basically numb. Everything was surreal.

Folks at my workplace were very understanding. They told me to take whatever time I needed so I was off for six weeks. When I went back I just stayed in my little corner, collected the mail and answered phone messages. I didn't do much because I couldn't. For example, someone came to my work to speak to a representative and I was the only one available. I went into a panic. I felt that I couldn't talk to anybody who didn't already know what had happened. Even though I was surrounded by fabulous co-workers who were amazingly supportive, I'd put on my armor when I went to the office and sent out the message, "Don't talk to me because then I'll cry and can't work." I felt that precarious for almost a year and just refused to talk about anything personal. At lunch I'd go home, throw myself on the bed and sob and sob and sob. Then I'd get back up, wash my face, have a bite to eat, and go back to work. That was the only way I could cope.

I lost weight because I had no interest in eating. When people were searching for Kaitlyn, our home was the central location for getting supplies so folks brought in a lot of food for the search crews. We froze stuff and just ate off of the stash for six months because we knew we needed to eat. But no one was really interested.

Sometime during the trial, we received our first letter of condolence and pain from the parents of each of the boys. It was jarring and confusing because the division between us seemed to merge. I didn't know which side of the table to sit on, as parent of my daughter or with the parents of the boys who did it. My husband, Duncan, was the first person who brought up the idea of meeting with one of the boys, Gregory. The other boy, Jerry, was in a mental health facility and not available. This happened long before the VOD process was established in the country so it was unfamiliar territory and there were no clear procedures in place. I myself had no inner sense that I needed to meet but Duncan was clearly interested and had contacted a facilitator about his idea. Even though I had no particular need, I wanted to be at the table to see what was said. I realized that if Duncan went alone and then reported back to me, he'd never give me all the specifics. I remember thinking, "I'm going to want to know *everything*, all the fine points, facial expressions, body language." Since Duncan doesn't have a nose for details, I'd felt I had to go.

The preparation process went on for 15 months. We couldn't meet until Gregory was finished with the appellate process. During that time, the facilitator was meeting with all of us. He would review procedures for the upcoming meeting and share things he had learned from talking with Gregory. This information and his impressions gave us a bigger picture of who Gregory was and maybe why he had gotten involved with Jerry. However, I can honestly say that all through the preparation, I still wasn't committed to the idea of meeting with him. I was just going along to learn about Gregory's present life. However, I started to shift from going solely because of Duncan as I began to learn more from the facilitator about what would actually happen when we met. His repeatedly spelling out the procedures helped me relax so I could be more open to the process. It just kind of evolved and somewhere I decided it would be okay to go.

The day of the meeting I was very nervous. I wasn't afraid Gregory would hurt us verbally. The facilitator had already told us what Gregory would say and how he speaks. I was just really nervous to be face to face with the last person who probably saw Kaitlyn. It was kind of surreal and I was apprehensive. I don't remember having a huge reaction to Gregory either. One of the things that made me most nervous was wondering if I should shake hands or not and if I was alright with touching him. "Well, do I want to do that or not? What do I do?" I didn't have strong feelings of revulsion or caring. I was just really conflicted, ambivalent, and not knowing.

Gregory did most of the talking. We knew from the facilitator that Gregory, in response to a question, would answer it by starting way back in time to tell you the whole story. You had to be very patient because he was unable just to answer what you asked. He'd get there eventually but you'd have to listen to all this build-up. There had been so many different stories when we first found Kaitlyn, most of which came from Jerry. But Gregory's account had remained consistent. I believe that what he told us at the meeting was probably closer to what happened than anything we had heard. Up to that point, we knew very little. We had no idea how she had ended up 30 miles out of town. Gregory told us how he and Jerry met and what they had done that evening before they kidnapped Kaitlyn. His giving us that information answered a lot of questions and it gave me context, insight into his life, and a better idea of how it all happened.

There were some funny, silly things about the meeting. The way he drank his coffee bothered me. He'd slurp. I wanted to tell him to stop it. If I had been dating someone like him I would have said, "Okay, I'm done. I can't live with your slurping." At one point he got choked up. I had some Kleenex. I don't know if he asked for it or I gave it to him but I shared the packet of Kleenex across the table. As he started talking, I got more comfortable because what he said began to confirm my picture of who he was. I didn't believe he was the ringleader. If Jerry had not initiated what they did to Kaitlyn, Gregory would never have done it. Gregory had a girlfriend and a child. He didn't need to go rape a woman. I think Jerry was the person who had deep psychological issues that he was acting out.

I had all kinds of thoughts going through my head. For example, it seemed ironic that Gregory outweighed Jerry by 50 lbs but he saw himself as a victim of Jerry. I had wondered why Gregory didn't just crush him or get him out of the way. I began to see Gregory as someone who, maybe all his life, had been sort of manipulated. He had tears in his eyes when he started to talk about his own son. I made a small shift at that point. That was when I shared my Kleenex with him. By the end of the meeting I had a little more sympathy and understanding. I could understand intellectually why he ended up where he was but I didn't really bond with him.

Afterwards, I wasn't as nervous but I was exhausted. Duncan, Eleanor, and I went to get something to eat and talked about never really knowing the whole story. I realized that we are just going to have to live with not knowing, which was a sort of resignation but not negatively so. It's more like, "I guess that's the way things are." Our meeting definitely contributed to my journey but it wasn't a big "Ah-hah." People in the community assumed we had forgiven Gregory because they knew we were meeting with him. I would tell them, "No, no. That's a big jump." Duncan and I had not talked about forgiveness at all. We hadn't even mentioned it. I remember taking a walk, which was my habit each morning. I recalled that Kaitlyn was walking home when she was kidnapped. Walking is often my prayer time. That day,

I had an internal conversation with Gregory and Jerry. "You have killed my daughter and taken her life but you're not going to take mine. I'm not going to spend my life a sad, mean, bitter old person who just can't get over it." I think that's part of forgiveness, the decision that I'm not going to carry all that negativity around. I recognize in hindsight that it's an odd form of forgiveness but it's a gift you give yourself. Later on Duncan and I did talk about forgiveness but the first meeting with Gregory laid the groundwork for it.

We met two more times with Gregory over the next couple of years. The follow-up dialogues made a difference. It got easier to meet with him and more information came out. At one point, we were able to do a soft confrontation with Gregory about his raping Kaitlyn. Duncan was able to say, "You know, you raped my daughter." That was powerful. In subsequent meetings Gregory talked about Kaitlyn and how she was crying when he and Jerry took her out into the country. In fact, she was begging. Gregory really thought they were going to let her go but that didn't happen. This information gave us more pieces to the puzzle. But at some point, I felt it was all complete. Duncan wanted to go again but I felt I'd had enough. I was beginning to get involved in my life again and I didn't see any more need.

Duncan goes to see Gregory at least once a year. He sends us a Christmas card every year and sometimes a letter. He's brought his reading level from 3rd grade up to 8th grade. At one place he was interested in gardening. More recently, he's involved in training therapy dogs. He's very proud of his work. I'm pleased. I celebrate with him as a fellow human being. I'm glad he has something in his life that is positive. But it also makes me sad because I know he was taken out of public school and put into an alternative school where he met Jerry. If he'd been in school with someone who had good intentions in their life, his life would have been different. He's definitely a follower, an *excellent* follower. He's never in trouble. He's a model prisoner who could be influenced for the positive as easily as the negative.

My meetings with Gregory tuned me into the penal system and families who have family members in the system. I'm involved with advocating for gun violence victims like the people involved in the Sandy Hook incident. There's always this awkward moment. We are concerned about the teachers and students but what about the shooter and his mother, who he also killed? I talked with an acquaintance recently who shared with us that she had a brother who had killed someone when he was high on drugs. I knew this woman but no one knew her history because she is so ashamed. Had I not met with Gregory or met with his parents and Jerry's parents, which we did as well, I would not have been as aware of what prisoners' families are going through too.

So where am I today? My pain is still there. I visualize a closet that's full of crap you don't want to deal with. When the door cracks open, I slam it shut unless I'm really ready to deal with it. Although for many years stuff was falling out all over the place, I gradually was able to close that door. To what end would I pull it all out and look at it? My talking about what happened now is just an energy zapper.

Analysis: Crime and its aftermath

Kaitlyn's murder had a profound impact on Maya and her family but it also ripped into the presumed safety for the residents of the small, rural community where Maya lived. Consequently, the community was an active part of the effort to find Kaitlyn, involved in the criminal justice procedures for Gregory and Jerry, and became the historic repository for shared stories about the family's subsequent activities in response to the murder. Maya was fully in the public eye because the community considered the murder a violation of the town as well as a tragedy for the family. She was hyper-aware, therefore, of where she stood relative to the expectations of others, including her husband, co-workers, and community members. Efforts to self-define and honor her feelings, reactions, and what she needed were constant and frequently different from the others around her.

Maya had anger toward the boys who kidnapped, raped, and murdered her daughter, but it was intense and very short-lived. It was quickly covered over by a profound numbness so that she felt little other than surreal and dissociated from her life. This sense of distancing continued and served to protect her all the way through from more personal disruption. She also worked hard to compartmentalize and therefore exercise some control over her reactions to events. For example, she coped by limiting what she did at work to jobs that did not require much contact with the public. But at lunchtime, she'd let down briefly to sob in the privacy of her home before returning to work again. Her grief, though intense, was only allowed, therefore, at particular times. She'd keep people from triggering it by keeping them at bay so that they would not talk to her directly.

She found herself, from the beginning, with contradictory reactions to the boys who had killed her daughter. In contrast to the community's hatred, which was palpable at the arraignment hearing, Maya felt pity and compassion toward them. When she received letters from the boys' parents, she felt confused because she felt the similarity between what they were going through and herself as the mother of the victim. Because of her numbness, ability to stay with her sadness, lack of anger, and capacity to maintain the bigger picture relative to the boys and their families, Maya did not have a build-up of resentment or stored energy. Rather she felt derailed because of Kaitlyn's murder and Gregory and Jerry's ongoing presence in her life. It was as if she'd jumped the track she had set for her life and her primary goal was to get back on target.

Preparation

Maya, therefore, had no obvious need to meet with Gregory. The idea belonged to her husband who kept discussing it with a possible facilitator and nudging her about the possibility. "I finally said, 'What is this about? This sounds like you're going to do it, so what is it?' And he kind of told me about it." The only impetus for Maya to be part of this plan was her knowledge of their differences in how each of them took in and reported information. She realized that if Duncan learned new information about the murder or details about Gregory and Jerry, he would not share it fully by her standards. Rather than living with that possibility, she decided to be part of the preparation process but remained ambivalent until the end about participating in the VOD meeting itself.

Consequently, she was initially motivated to attend a meeting with Gregory only because of the dissonance created internally between not wanting to go but knowing that she had to go to get all the important information given her husband's proclivities. Maya had two experiences during preparation that likely increased her receptivity to a meeting. First, she got answers to questions about why and how Gregory had ended up with a partner like Jerry. Second, the facilitator continually reviewed exactly what would happen in the meeting with Gregory, which increased her confidence that being together would not harm her. The information she received about him and the lengthiness of the preparation likely gave her time to consider everything and helped humanize Gregory, which relaxed her apprehensiveness and also opened her up to the possibility that the meeting could be useful, not damaging or a complete waste of time.

She participated, however, as a curious onlooker. She had no major needs. She remained non-committal, neutral, watchful, and observant throughout the preparation and the dialogue—"I could get into Gregory's space but I didn't have a lot of sympathy. I could intellectually understand why he ended up where he was." Her ability to compartmentalize when and what she would respond to gave her more control. In terms of the preparation, she had decided her role—"I was just going along to learn what Gregory was getting into."

Dialogue

Maya and Duncan did the meeting together with Gregory. Maya was nervous to be face to face with Gregory and ruminated about the possibility of having to shake hands with him. She positioned herself as an observer, noting his behaviors such as how he drank coffee, answered questions with lengthy stories, or asked to share her Kleenex packet. Most of the information Gregory shared, she already knew. However, his account of what happened confirmed Maya's picture of Gregory's role in the murder of Kaitlyn. She saw him as a follower who was easily manipulated by Jerry. Besides believing his version over the countless iterations offered by his partner, Maya also learned the backdrop of Gregory's association with Jerry. As such, Maya was able to humanize Gregory and to see him not as an aggressor like Jerry but more as a victim of negative circumstances and influences. The information she received helped her make sense out of what happened and, as such, contributed to her meaning-making about her daughter's murder. However, she said little in the meeting, in part because Gregory communicated through monologues rather than through interaction. She gained the information by bearing witness to his accounts. When Gregory talked about his son, she said, "I don't think that was a big shift for me. I expected him to talk about his child. I probably had a little more sympathy for him than I had before."

Maya had several powerful experiences following the initial dialogue. The meeting laid the groundwork for a confrontation with herself about forgiveness. She realized that carrying around feelings of resentment, anger, or vengeance would rob her of her own life and determined that Gregory was not going to have that power over her wellbeing. This intentional decision to keep negativity at bay was, for Maya, her form of forgiveness.

Maya also determined that what she has learned from Gregory was likely incomplete but she needed to receive what she had been given and accept it as enough. This decision resolved the potential dissonance between what more there was to learn and her decision not to go after it. Her conclusion allowed her to feel less tormented by what was missing and, therefore, more complete. Maya met this challenge, in part, because she did not harbor residual anger toward Gregory. She believed his story of what happened and saw him, in part, as an innocent lamb and ill-equipped follower. His sadness about his own son had also touched her heart somewhat. Her version of radical acceptance, therefore, helped stop her stuckness because she realized that in humanizing him, which was a giving, she was releasing herself, which was also a giving. She generalized from that humanity by focusing her concerns on the penal system and its dehumanizing impact on other prisoners and their families.

Maya met with Gregory two more times. She learned a little more about her daughter's rape but quickly decided that she had had enough and had no more need to meet with Gregory. This decision was very different from Duncan's plan, which was to continue meeting on a periodic but regular basis with Gregory. Although independently made, it is possible that part of her decision was in reaction to her husband's decision to keep Gregory central in his world. There was potential dissonance for Maya, therefore, in continuing to attend meetings when she didn't need them. She couldn't close the door, which was her goal, if she was still meeting with Gregory. Indeed, to do so would have been contraindicated because it would have ripped the bandage off the wound over and over again.

The dyadic encounter during the VOD meetings was important to Maya's meaning-making and sense of completion. However, her experience with forgiveness was not derived from that encounter. Moreover, there was no strong focus in the meeting on conveying of the pain differential or on the transfer of her pain to Gregory. The transformation of the pain, therefore, was dependent on the dyadic interaction but it was done by herself and singularly. Maya definitely felt some compassion for Gregory but otherwise had little emotional involvement. Her need was to comprehend what happened. She did not expect anything for herself and wasn't looking for anything emotional between them.

From the beginning, her energy was stored from the murder but it was not burdensome. Maya consciously decided that the residue and what was unresolved from the murder should stay in the closet so that they didn't bring her down or control her world endlessly. Her plan was to move away from greater involvement, except through her husband's reports, and take charge of where she would put her energies. She did not need Gregory for that goal but she allowed herself to accept what he could give her. She had as much completion as she needed.

DUNCAN'S STORY AND ANALYSIS

(Part 2 with dad, Duncan) On her way home from dinner, Kaitlyn was kidnapped, raped, and shot to death. Her father, Duncan, his wife Maya, and the entire town were heavily involved in the subsequent search. Eventually, the two men responsible, Jerry and Gregory, went to the police and confessed to their involvement. Duncan, already heavily involved in the criminal justice community, pursued a VOD with the intention of helping his family, the men, and the entire community. As it was a relatively new program, Duncan approached VOD from more of a research perspective, potentially more focused on process than emotions. Ultimately, a dialogue was only appropriate with Gregory and he and Duncan

continued to meet several times a year for the next 20 years. Duncan felt forgiveness was never the purpose of meeting and feels a strong sense of respect and compassion towards Gregory for their mutual suffering. Their continued relationship is now with the intent of preparing Gregory to reintegrate into the community. Duncan and Maya were both present during the initial VOD. The following describes the encounter and subsequent visits from Duncan's perspective only.

My daughter Kaitlyn was kidnapped, taken 30 miles from our home, raped, shot, and killed. I had just finished having dinner with her during her time off from school. She met some friends later and walked home in the early morning hours. Two men, Jerry and Gregory, came forward with information and were subsequently arrested, tried, and sentenced to life imprisonment. Evidently, one of the men's fathers insisted he go to the sheriff because he had knowledge about the death and the whereabouts of Kaitlyn. The other man's father then said to his son, "Since Jerry is going, you'd better get there too." The men said they had only heard a story about the murder and had second- or third-hand information. Eventually it became clear that they were the murderers.

In the meantime, large search and rescue crews went out looking for Kaitlyn. The headquarters of the search initially was at our kitchen table but then the fire department took over. I knew most of them and also had good working relationships already with the police department. My wife, Maya, myself and my daughter Eleanor, of course, were the spokespersons to the volunteers searching for Kaitlyn. I doubt that is done in many locations. It was empowering because we were part of the search rather than isolated and left alone in an emotional abyss. By engaging this way, it took us out of the shock mode.

My daughter Eleanor decided to go to the arraignment. I had not even considered whether to go but I did not want her to go alone so I went with her, my brother-in-law and father-in-law. There was such visceral hate in the room toward the men. It emanated in some ways as support for our family. I'm glad we could be there with Eleanor, to have her in my arms and support and protect one another. I felt compassion for the two men when they came into the room bedraggled and with shackled hands and feet. The one anger I felt was at a judge who announced, before telling us, that there was a break in our case and that they had found Kaitlyn's body. That was a violation to tell others before us. From then on, however, we were informed of every move before it happened. We'd meet with law enforcement about the plan for the day and then again at the end of the day for an update. Everybody was amazingly supportive.

I had an acute stress reaction during the first three months but I was spared a long-term posttraumatic stress disorder (PTSD) reaction. I'd have the reaction every time I saw a gun or a woman in distress on television. Mainly, I felt gratitude for all the support we received. We were even included in the meeting with the prosecutors so we could hear what the plans would be for the trial.

Because of the crime, the publicity we received, and my expertise as a research professor, we were hired to look at violence in rural communities. I received lots of material for that project, including a packet of information from a restorative justice leader about restorative justice. That was the spark that informed me of the possibility of victims meeting with offenders and illuminated my vision of what could be done in my own case. This restorative justice leader later referred me to Marcus, who was an expert in victim offender mediation, and we began to meet at his home and discuss the possibilities.

Initially I just wanted Marcus to meet Jerry and Gregory. From my readings, I learned that the goal of restorative justice was for the victim to express and acknowledge the impact of the crime and its consequences, and to understand the offender's position and motivation. Who were these guys? What was their motivation? What prompted this, put it in motion? I saw restorative justice as a benefit to me, to Jerry and Gregory, and the larger community because the community was impacted too. Marcus and I had discussions about all of this. What I was envisioning had never been done in this state and very limitedly in this country. There were no protocols or authority to do it in any other country either.

We determined not to go forward with Jerry. Marcus and I both felt that it would not be productive given his psychological limitations and resistance from the prison system in the state where he was incarcerated. Maya, myself, and Marcus met many times and had numerous phone calls and conversations as part of preparing to meet with Gregory. I don't remember any big shifts. Because Jerry and Gregory were from my small community, I had good friends who were teachers in the alternative school they attended. They gave me information on their backgrounds and family histories. Consequently, we had a profile of these guys well ahead of time and there was little new that we learned during the preparation time.

Preparation for me focused on understanding the structure and procedures that were going to be followed for our VOD and ensuring that they were appropriate and in line with established restorative justice practices. I was aware that Marcus was adapting what he knew from nonviolent cases and therefore was inventing what was appropriate in severely violent situations along with me. The big shock for me was meeting with the Department of Corrections (DOC). I thought there would be resistance to the idea of my meeting with Gregory. Instead, the Commissioner lectured us on the benefits of restorative justice and did a number of things to make sure the meeting would happen. The Commissioner who took his place supported it too, even in the face of push back from Parents of Murdered Children. I was very aware of the systems that were involved here and how new such a meeting was for everyone. My appreciation of the role of systems came from working as a psychologist for a community leadership program that examined the role of systems within communities to determine what makes a healthy community. A close colleague from that work gave the homily at Kaitlyn's funeral and talked both about the personal impact of her death as well as the impact on the community.

Part of the VOD procedure is to do the meeting only after the criminal justice process is complete. This mandate provides some of the safety for the process so it is not interrupted or used, in any way, to advantage the offender. We had to wait 15 months, therefore, before we could go forward with the VOD because the appellate process wasn't finished for Gregory.

When it was completed, we set the date for the meeting. Prior to sitting down together, we had a tour of the prison where Gregory was incarcerated. The intent of the tour was to desensitize us to the prison experience. I walked into the actual meeting with confidence and comfort. My expectation was to share and receive information. There were no surprises. The most intense feeling I had was anger about the rape because it was clear from the evidence that Gregory participated in it. Our meeting was a first and we had determined, therefore, to allow it to be captured on tape. A film crew from the Canadian Film Board took the lead and eventually created a documentary about Kaitlyn's murder and our first VOD.

I'm still meeting with Gregory and have for over 20 years. I never saw him as a monster that came in chains to ensure that he would never be loose in the community. I've seen him three times this year because the DOC is trying to lower the prison population so he's being considered for release to a lower facility. Because he's being assessed for sex offender treatment, the issue of accountability is beginning to come up in his meetings with the DOC. Last year was the first time anyone other than me had a conversation with him about his crimes. I'm the only visitor he has. His parents died and his sister died of cancer. His contacts are with his roommates and their parents.

A big motivation for my visiting him is to say something to the parole board based on my experience with him. I can't say yet that I'll advocate for his release. However, in the future, I'm interested in how Gregory and I could contribute together. We've been talking about speaking jointly to a lifer's group he's part of. But there is no vehicle in the DOC for that so I'm pushing the door. I think the main limitation with VOD as it is currently practiced is that it only happens once or twice. My goal is to get to the point when I can say, "Hello, neighbor" to Gregory. That's happened in the confines of the DOC but not in the free world. I see how he's evolved but will only advocate for him when he's ready to be in a community. My next conversation with Gregory is to ask him for access to his records. He tells me he's not had one write-up. I want to help with his relocation and re-entry.

I've seen him three times this year because he's moving closer to the next stage. The DOC is trying to lower the population so he's being considered for release to a lower facility. A big motivation for my visiting him is to say something to the parole board based on my experience with him. I can't say I'll advocate for his release. Last year was the first time other than with me that he had a conversation with the DOC staff about his crimes. Because he's about to go into sex offender treatment, the issue of accountability is starting to come up with the DOC.

I have a lot of respect for Gregory, particularly because of the way he speaks about his work, his respect for the staff, his roommate, and the mentor he's become. He's blossomed in doing the dog rescue program where he puts dogs through extensive training to prepare them for adoption. I trust him because he's done no more harm. I'm gaining deeper respect and trust as he talks about his other offenses, including stolen property and taking responsibility for what happened. My empathy for him started when he was talking about his son. I realized that both of our children were at the town's lake at the same time and we were likely both watching them in the lake at the same time. Compassion came over the years as he talked about giving up rights to his son.

Because we met with Gregory, people in the community thought we had forgiven him. However, Marcus, during preparation, planted the adage that the less attention to forgiveness the more it's available. Forgiveness was not very relevant to me. I didn't carry a burden of vengeance. Moreover, because I grew up Lutheran, the belief is that forgiveness is not of one another but with God. I was exposed for a time to the work of Bob Enright, a professor with nationally recognized expertise on the topic of forgiveness, and was on a panel with other survivors. However, I'm not sure what forgiveness is. Many people forgive as a way to get the pain to go away. However, I'm more concerned with compassion. I believe you cannot eliminate the pain you feel but you can eliminate the suffering by dealing with the cognitions and patterns of thought that perpetuate it, including the mistaken idea that you must make the pain go away. If you realize that the pain can contribute to compassion and it's not just debilitating then it offsets the burden of the pain.

What have I gained by being with Gregory? The initial dialogue helped this longer journey where I continued to meet with him but the personal shifts have been small. Gregory, however, has given me his honesty and forthrightness. He's accepted my acceptance of him and he sees me as more friend than opposition. He's given me insight into prison life. I'm moving beyond forgiveness to the area of compassion and we've been able to establish some mutual compassion for the suffering both of us have because of the crime.

Analysis: Crime and its aftermath

Duncan was a well-known resident and civic leader in a small, rural community. When his daughter went missing, the town turned out in mass to search for her and show their support for the family. Volunteers, police, and fire departments as well as the sheriff's office turned their attention and resources to finding Kaitlyn. The boys who were responsible for her murder lived in the same community. Their families insisted that they report what they knew to the sheriff, thereby contributing as well to the communal effort. Everyone behaved as if the kidnapping and murder were a personal blow and violation to the safety, sanctity, and norms of the community itself.

Duncan had little reaction toward Jerry and Gregory other than relief when Kaitlyn's body was found and a brief acute stress reaction. What mattered to him was his anguish over the finality of his daughter's life. Indeed, he felt some compassion at the arraignment of the boys and tremendous gratitude toward the volunteers and public servants who searched for his daughter. He and his family members drew close and felt partnered and watched over by the community. Rather than being disempowered by his daughter's murder, the response of the community and his inclusion in all aspects of the investigation and trial actually buoyed and empowered him. He enjoyed the camaraderie with law enforcement and personal relationships with staff in the criminal justice system and quickly became an expert on violence in rural communities and the role of systems in their health.

As a psychologist and professor, Duncan kept a broad perspective on everything he witnessed. He observed early on, for example, that his reactions to the boys were different from others in the community. Because of his professional stature and position, he also had access to cutting-edge ideas. He was already deeply involved in the case and its legalities so he resonated internally to restorative justice when he was sent literature by a national spokesperson—"That's the spark that informed me of the possibilities and illuminated that whole vision and image of what could be done."

Preparation

Kaitlyn's murder happened before there were formal VOD programs. Indeed, victim offender mediation (VOM) for minor crimes was the only restorative practice that brought victim and offender together for a dialogue. Duncan immediately saw the implications of applying that practice to more serious crimes like his own and contacted the originator of the VOM initiative in the county as a possible facilitator. They began conversations about the possibility of using it in Duncan's case and thinking through the steps that would be necessary for a productive encounter. In effect, Duncan, in concert with the facilitator, was inventing VOD for severely violent crimes. Although the facilitator remained focused and professional in his role, Duncan also experienced the two of them as true partners in the formulation and design of this innovative application.

In his study of VOM, Duncan recognized that the overall goal of the practice was to share the impact of the crime on his life, get questions answered, and learn more about the offender. He also realized that his doing a meeting with Gregory could educate others and help heal the community that had also been affected. Although meeting with Gregory was important, Duncan was equally focused on the nuts and bolts of this new restorative justice application. He wanted to be sure that what he did followed protocol and felt exceedingly well prepared for the meeting. He was acutely aware of the fact that he was charting new ground. He, therefore, was keenly observant of the reactions from others including homicide survivors like Parents of Murdered Children and the DOC. "I was very aware of the systems that were involved here and how new such a meeting was for everyone." Instead of his own resistance, which was not present, he was mindful of the resistance from others who did not understand or support his desire to meet with Gregory. It is likely that the only dissonance he felt was between the adversarial model that decried any relationship between victims and offenders and the path that Duncan had chosen.

As a neophyte and advocate for the process, Duncan was quite open. He had few, if any, reservations about meeting Gregory and did not expect any surprises. The facilitator had met with Duncan and Maya as well as with Gregory on many occasions and had communicated information about each to the other. Duncan had also learned independently about Gregory's background from his schoolteachers, who still lived in the community. All of this preparation had served to harness Duncan's energy but it was not negative energy from the crime as much as it was generated by the excitement about his discovery and testing it out. Indeed, his openness to meeting with Gregory did not emerge out of vengeance or suppressed feelings in reaction to the murder. Rather, he was open to restorative justice and to the facilitator's guidance, which increasingly reinforced what he wanted to do. His openness was also guided by his understanding of what a restorative justice process could provide and the necessary prerequisites to its success. He understood, for example, the purpose of the prison visit, which was both to educate him about Gregory's life as a prisoner but also to desensitize him to the prison environment, thereby preventing the trauma that might occur if his initial exposure occurred at the same time as the meeting. Such trauma could reduce his ability to remain fully open in the dialogue. Duncan also saw himself as a pioneer who was using his own story to educate others about the VOD process. Consequently, Duncan and the facilitator arranged to have the meeting videotaped so it could be turned into a documentary at a later time.

Dialogue

Duncan approached the meeting with little apprehension. There were no surprises. Moreover, because he carried no emotional burden or reservoir of feelings about the crime, there was no strong need to convey or transfer the pain. Rather, Duncan's goal was just to share and be open to receiving information from Gregory. The only topic that sparked anger was his daughter's rape, which he covered in a single sentence saying, "You know, you raped my daughter." Duncan used this initial meeting to establish a relationship with Gregory and to start to build a conduit between them for its own sake. Indeed, he returned numerous times to meet with Gregory over the next 20 years and to establish a comfort between them that resembled a trusting neighborliness.

Although Duncan did not comment on the likely impact of his continued presence, it is possible that his returning year after year had the effect of establishing an accountability process whereby Gregory had to show Duncan that he was indeed trustworthy and had learned from his crime. Duncan commented that "Gregory's told me he's had not one write-up or very minor, if any… I trust him because he's done no more harm." He noted that he started to talk about his offenses to the Corrections' staff, took some responsibility, and was productive in his work to prepare abandoned dogs for adoption. To that end, Duncan is now involved in the process of Gregory's transfer to a lower-level facility, his assessment for sex offender treatment, and his possible release one day. He assumes he will be involved with Gregory the rest of his life and views what he is doing as helping the community as well as himself.

Duncan was clear that his goal over time was not a sense of personal completion. Rather, it was to have a repeated dyadic encounter with the goal of a relationship in the service of Gregory's eventual reintegration back into the community. Moreover, the intent of meeting was not to feel unburdened and at peace, since there never was a sense of burden. Indeed, the ongoing meetings with Gregory produced the energy that drives Duncan forward in his research and study. Part of Duncan's ongoing motivation today is to test out the possibilities of the VOD process. He says, "The limitation of the victim/offender dialogue is that it only happens once or twice…What can be accomplished once or twice? The dialogue set the stage for us to be comfortable continuing. [But] if restorative justice is going to work, or… if we're going to sustain restorative justice, what's the whole involvement? Where am I involved in [Gregory's] re-entry? At what time?"

For Duncan, the dyadic experience with Gregory was founded on a relational model of mutuality. He considers it a gift that "he has accepted my acceptance of him." Duncan sees his pain and how he handles it as his own issue and not a part of the relationship. Consequently, he does not look to Gregory to lessen it. In fact, he does not see his pain as problematic, only the suffering. Gregory's sharing of his world *through* their dyadic encounters has helped build compassion in Duncan toward Gregory that, from his perspective, can be used to offset the suffering they both share as a result of Kaitlyn's murder. Transformation, therefore, has been more about transforming their relationship than personal transformation. They have built a strong conduit over the years with spurts of empathy but with no transfer or transformation of pain except privately. The energy is positive and at rest most of the way. There are few energy shifts except in response to Gregory's feelings about his son and the mutuality of their feelings toward their children. Duncan's goal is to be in Gregory's life forever. The realization of this dream would constitute completion for Duncan.

As important is Duncan's other agenda, which has been the furthering of VOD as a restorative justice practice. He has made himself a test case for VOD and is continuing to use himself to push the boundaries of standard VOD protocols by accompanying Gregory through his incarceration and possible return to the community. His commitment to this mission was sparked by Kaitlyn's death but is guided, as well, by his need to give back. Indeed, it is likely that part of his completing himself was not through the dialogue with Gregory but through contributing from his experience to the larger community.

MICAELA'S STORY AND ANALYSIS ————————

Micaela's husband, Joel, was hit and killed by a drunk driver. Ronald had a long history of alcohol-related offenses but Micaela was caught between intense anger towards him and Joel's strong connection to the AA community, as a recovering alcoholic himself. Micaela wanted to give Ronald an opportunity to make amends, a major AA component, while also ensuring he knew about the life he took, not seeing any true benefit for herself. During the VOD, Micaela felt gratitude towards Ronald and felt a release of pain. She was cautious about trusting the experience. Micaela felt drawn towards forgiveness but hesitated, instead placing conditions on it, encouraging Ronald to finally make positive changes in his life and solidifying it by shaking the hand of the man who had killed her husband. Fourteen years later, after learning Ronald was back in jail, Micaela wrote him a letter, severing the connection forged through her conditional forgiveness.

My husband, Joel, was late one evening coming home from his job for supper. We had spoken in the afternoon about plans for Friday evening. I later went to pick up our two-year-old son, Scott, from daycare and heard on the radio that there was a crash involving two pickup trucks. It crossed my mind that Joel had a pickup truck but I thought, "That's not related to me." I picked up my son and went home. When he didn't appear I again wondered about the accident reported on the radio and started calling around. Finally, I decided to call the police station. They told me Joel was in the accident and they'd taken him to the hospital. They also told me to stay where I was and they'd send an officer to the house. Half my brain knew what they meant and the other half went into overdrive, thinking of other reasons they would come to the house. I called my family to have someone come to stay with Scott. When a policewoman came, I simply said, "He's dead, isn't he?" And she said, "Yes." People talk about out-of-body experiences and that's what it felt like to me. I suddenly felt like everything was kind of a dream. It wasn't really real.

At the time this happened, Joel and I were living together but we weren't legally married. We'd been together two-and-a-half years and had married each other in a little private ceremony but were considered common-law married. My brother-in-law and sister were the first to arrive at the house. He and Joel were like brothers and he was the first person to whom I said the words, "Joel is dead." I didn't cry or get hysterical. I was just suspended in an alternate reality. We went to the hospital to identify Joel's body and I remember walking down the hallway and my legs were like noodles, very wobbly. When I got to the door of the room where Joel was, I stopped. I couldn't move and just froze. Eventually, as I realized I had to go in, I got next to Joel's body and felt very peaceful. He had a little bit of a smile on his face. It was obvious he was dead but I felt like his energy was still close and I didn't want to leave. I knew I'd never feel this energy again with him.

When I got home, the house was full of people from Alcoholics Anonymous. That's when I learned that the other driver, Ronald, had been taken to the hospital as well and that he was drunk with a blood alcohol level of 2 point something. He was treated and released. As I looked around the house, I realized it was full of recovering people and that every single one of them had probably driven under the influence. Certainly Joel had. I remember saying, "I hope this is his bottom, whoever it is."

Ronald took an Alford plea, which allows someone to plead guilty without an admission of guilt. The judge refused to let him bond out of jail because of his past history and the fact that he'd taken a life. He'd had 20 prior alcohol-related offenses and had injured someone else as well. My first interaction with him was at sentencing. He had long hair, a ponytail and a scar on his face from the crash. He stood up at the end and said he was sorry, it was an accident and then he was taken to prison to serve a ten-year sentence.

In the time after the trial, I was very confused and sort of haunted by the thought that Ronald was someone Joel would have sponsored in AA. Then I'd have horrible negative thoughts like "despicable, scum" about him as a person. Mainly I was overwhelmed with grief and panicked about survival because of my young son. The first time I thought about meeting with Ronald was Christmas when I was pretty sappy. I began to wonder, "How is he doing with this? Is he feeling as horrible as I am? I need to go see him." I called the Department of Corrections but was told I couldn't visit because I was the registered victim. I dropped the idea.

Joel's death completely changed my life. The feeling of shock hung on for months. Sleep was horrible but waking up was worse. I didn't want to be here. I wanted to go wherever he was. My son kept me alive but I did everything in a fog. I got involved three months after Joel's death with a very close friend of ours. People likely saw it as a betrayal or that I didn't love Joel but the reality was that this man was my comfort. A lot of my crying and mourning was done with him. Grieving is just very lonely and people really push you to get on with your life. I tried not to have any shame about it, I did not feel that Joel, if he exists somewhere, would have cared. In fact, he would have wanted me to have that comfort. But the opinions of others were difficult. They believed I'd moved on and wasn't grieving anymore because I was in a relationship with someone else.

I remember my sister remarking that, after four years, she didn't understand why I was so angry. I didn't see it but I had moments when I wanted Ronald dead. I would remember being with Joel's body, laying my head on his chest, he's not breathing and his body was hard. I'd get pissed off when I'd think about Ronald being in prison breathing. He didn't have the right to breathe. If someone asked me what should be done with Ronald, I'd have to say, "He needs to die." Another day I'd say, "I don't care" because I didn't have the energy for it. On another day I'd be worried about him and think, "How is he doing? Who is he? What's he doing with all this?"

Joel's death also had a lot of spiritual impact on me. I was raised Catholic but left the church. However, I stayed open to different beliefs over the years. But after Joel was killed, everything I believed went out the window. I questioned if there was an afterlife. I started focusing more on spirituality than religion. I went to someone who channels with the dead and then to a shaman. I had this strong desire to find out if there is something after death and if Joel and I might still have some kind of relationship.

As time went on, people started reminding me that Ronald could get out at any time. I realized I might run into him and not know who he was. But I also knew enough about AA and recovery to know that he needed to make amends to me and a missed opportunity to do so could become the catalyst to continue his lifestyle of drinking and drugs. I also felt that he'd been protected from the reality of accident from my end. He didn't know Joel. He only knew his name. He didn't know me and he didn't know Scott. In a way, he didn't really know what he'd done. I thought to myself, "You can't kill someone and not know who you killed." It seemed unjust.

So I again called the Department of Corrections to convince them that they had to let me see Ronald. This time they told me about the VOD program and referred me to a facilitator. We started preparing for the dialogue. Most of the work was done on the phone because I lived too far away but we met a couple of times too. The facilitator also visited Ronald to see if he would be willing to talk with me. He told her that such a meeting was very important to him. He had wanted to write to me but prison rules forbade it. She asked me to start a list of questions. All through the preparation process I maintained that I was doing the VOD for Ronald. I wanted him to make amends, to give him that opportunity so that maybe he could get sober and do well in his life. But the facilitator kept pushing me, "What about for you? What do you need for you?" My needs weren't clear until we met. Everything otherwise was about changing or influencing Ronald. I was assured that I'd have the opportunity to tell Ronald about Joel and his life. The facilitator suggested I might bring photographs. Scott, who was six at the time, made an audiotape of questions and things he too wanted to say to Ronald.

I was very nervous to meet Ronald. Ironically, I had bought a new outfit because I wanted to look good for the meeting in a prison that looked like the fortress in the film *The Shawshank Redemption*. I felt intimidated because I was the first person allowed to do a VOD in that facility and I didn't want to do anything wrong. As soon as I got into the prison, I started crying. I figured the correctional officers would think I was a hysterical victim so I kept saying, "I'm okay. I cry easily. I'm alright." The facilitator took me to meet the warden. He looked like Herb from the sitcom *WQRK in Cincinnati* with his hairpiece and plaid pants. I thought, "Oh, my God, it's Herb." And then I found out his name was Herb. He said to me, "I don't know why you want to come in here and meet with this piece of crap." I just said, "I don't think I have enough time to explain," and left it at that.

I was still crying by the time we got to the room for the meeting. When Ronald came in, I caught my breath, like the air got sucked out of the room. I couldn't look at him. When I glanced up I saw that he wasn't looking at me either. He just sat with his head down. I appreciated that because I was overwhelmed being in the room with him. The facilitator just waited, allowing time for us just to be there. Ronald eventually made eye contact with me. It felt like a shock all the way through my body.

I did most of the talking initially. I told Ronald about Joel, who he was and our life together, crying through the whole thing. When it was his time, he surprised me because he didn't ask obnoxious questions about my relationship with Joel like he did during preparation. I interpreted this change as his deeper understanding of the purpose of our meeting and the inappropriateness of his previous questions. My first shift was seeing him in the meeting. In court he looked like a skuzzy guy but when I actually looked at him, I realized I was wrong. As we spoke together in the dialogue, there was another shift. He shared his perspective about the crash and I could see that he was eager to answer anything I asked him. It touched me that he wanted to do something for me. He also shared a lot of really bizarre things that had to do with synchronicity or "by coincidence." For example, he had gotten a flat tire the day before the accident at the same intersection where the crash happened. He then went to a bar while the tire was being fixed. When he and a designated driver left the bar there was an AA medallion in the parking lot. His friend, the designated driver, picked it up and tossed it to him saying, "When you're here next, you can turn this in for a free drink." He said that because this bar had a big jar where people would toss in their AA medallions and get free drinks. How strange was that given Joel's history?

He talked a lot about himself, which helped fill in gaps that I didn't know. He shared things I wouldn't have thought to even ask him. Of course

I wanted to know how the crash happened and if Joel suffered. He told me he was the first person to get to Joel in the truck and he was already dead. That gave me some comfort.

It also surprised me that I brought up the topic of forgiveness. I wasn't thinking along those lines but I felt I needed to give him something. He seemed now like a very pitiable person who'd had a lot of loss. My heart went out to him. The word "forgiveness" came to me but I sat there thinking, "I don't know about that." But I said to him, "Ronald, I want you to know that if you go on and get the help you need, and if you stay clean and sober, then I want you to know that I have forgiven you. If you don't do those things, then I don't." That was as good as I could do at the time. I had a sense of forgiveness but I was also resisting it. I was worried that if I forgave him it might mean that everything was all okay, which wasn't true. I couldn't just say, "Okay, now we're done."

At the end of our meeting, I had huge gratitude for Ronald but again I struggled. I resisted expressing it because it might be a betrayal of Joel, it might minimize who Joel was to me or diminish the reality of my loss. I just thought, "I can't feel that way toward this man who took the love of my life away from me." It just wasn't right. I decided to say nothing and Ronald left. But then I realized that I would not have the opportunity again to say anything. I might never see Ronald again. I remember saying to myself, "It's now or never." I walked over to where he was now sitting behind bars. The correctional officers were anxious because they didn't know what I was doing. I called Ronald over. He looked anxiously to the officers for permission to walk toward me, but they let him. Although we had bars between us, I looked up at him and said, "Ronald, I want to thank you for meeting with me today." I appreciated what it took for him to be there. He didn't have to have met with me but he did. I felt like I had been able to give him all this grief and I didn't feel judged for my relationship with Joel or have to defend why, after four years, I still love him and miss him terribly. So I grabbed Ronald's hand to shake it and he shook back. I can still see the vision in my head of our hands, of shaking his hand. I also had this thought in my head that I was touching the man who killed Joel. It was surreal but it felt right to do.

The meeting was an incredible event in my life. I had such a different vision of Ronald and saw him more as his own person with his own history. I felt very connected to him. It was a strange bond between us that grew out of the fact that Joel's death impacted both our lives. After the meeting, I so wished that he would do well. I no longer hoped he would suffer or die. I no longer wanted to beat him or beat into him how much pain I was in. That meeting became my touchstone. Whenever I'm now faced with having to do something that scares me, I think, "Oh my God, I don't have to be afraid anymore." I had been afraid to meet him. I'd been in a fog of grief for those four years and had so much pain so having that experience was a relief because it released some of that grief and pain. I felt a lot freer. I let go of the burden of wanting a man dead, obsessing about him, thinking about him, wondering about him and the fact that he didn't know what he did. It's funny. On the one hand this meeting was an extraordinary thing. On the other hand, it felt like this is how it ought to be.

For a while I floated. I felt like what happened between us was spiritual. I could feel that energy in the room and that we were both experiencing spirituality that was bigger than the two of us. Time just stood still and I had no idea how long we were there for. Although there was loads of grieving in the room, toward the close of our time it became more of a conversation than a dialogue. Indeed, by the end, it felt very natural to be done when we were done. I felt exhausted afterwards.

Although the meeting was a success, the anger and hurt lingered but I didn't recognize it until 14 years after our dialogue. I got a phone call that Ronald was back in prison with an OWI (driving under the influence of alcohol). I had asked that he send me a postcard every March 12th so I'd know he was doing alright but I never got any. Through the years, I'd wonder where he was. Occasionally I'd do a Google search but found nothing. So I'd give up. I was learning a lot about letting go. I had heard a man talk about his son who was killed in the Oklahoma City bombing and how he didn't like the word "forgiveness." He was trying to find a way to reconcile what had happened to his son and his feelings toward Timothy McVeigh. When he spoke about the meaning of forgiveness, he said that it meant that McVeigh owed him nothing, no apology, no restitution, anything. He believed that when he felt that letting go, then he'd be reconciled. This definition became my definition. I wanted to get to a place where I felt that Ronald owed me nothing. I thought I was there but I realized I wasn't after I heard this man's thoughts. My conditional forgiveness was based on the message that if he does well, somehow I'm going to feel better about all this. If I had really let go after the meeting, I wouldn't have cared one way or another that he was back in prison. Because I had such a strong reaction I realized I hadn't let go of him. I immediately determined that I had to find Ronald and tell him that my forgiveness was unconditional. I needed to take away the condition that I had put on it that day in the dialogue. I couldn't find him so I tried to do things on my own like visualizations and efforts to release the negative energy but it still remained.

When I got the phone call that Ronald was back in prison, I initially felt back in the pit, back to year one, a kick in the gut. I knew I needed to see him and find out what happened. A friend of mine met with him and reported, "He is the most criminal thinking person I've met. The only reason he'd like to meet with you is because he'd like to have a visit." My friend also told me that Ronald had distorted things I had shared in the meeting. Now he believed that I was a crack addict and that Joel had rescued me from my addiction. He also thought that Scott was a crack baby and that Joel had had a disease and shouldn't have been driving. All of this was bizarre and gave me a horrible feeling. I told myself that I didn't want what happened to Ronald to take away or lessen my experience with him 14 years earlier. I just concluded, "That's who he was then and that's what happened then." In lieu of meeting with him, I wrote him a letter. I said, "I wish you well. I hope you have a good life. You have nothing to do with me anymore so live the life that you choose." My son Scott, who was then 19, had wanted to meet with him when he came of age so he also wrote him a letter. My friend took Ronald the letters in prison and read them to him. That was my real release. I finally let him go.

The judge gave him a year in prison. A year later he was on probation for drug paraphernalia and something else. When we did the dialogue we were on a path together. I always pictured our relationship to Joel and what we did in the meeting as a ribbon of connection between us. With the writing of the letter, I was taking the scissors and cutting the ribbon. So now he's just like anybody else. He does exist in my life but there is not that emotional attachment to him anymore. What happened after the dialogue doesn't cancel out our meeting. I think he continued to drink and do drugs and started losing more and more of himself. For him to live with having killed someone, he has to make it less his fault. So he invented rationalizations and stories in his head so he didn't have to feel responsible. I understand that.

It was a very different kind of grieving sharing it with the man who killed Joel. That's where and with whom it needed to be addressed. There aren't normal opportunities to really communicate fully what happened. Being with Ronald was a way to do that. It was also an honoring of Joel, his life and who he was. I felt all the way through that my grieving needed to be with him. It allowed the grief to dissipate. It was like being a hot air balloon where you're weighted down on the ground. When I left the meeting, I felt like those weights were taken off the air balloon and I was floating. After the meeting I wrote the Director of Corrections, the Warden and other influential people and said, "You need to make sure that this program is available for any victim who wants it."

Analysis: Crime and its aftermath

The death of Micaela's husband, Joel, was surrounded by meaningful coincidences that colored Micaela's responses at the time he was killed and throughout the VOD process. Joel was an alcoholic with seven years' sobriety and an active member of Alcoholics Anonymous. His killer, Ronald, had 20 prior alcohol-related offenses, including a crash and injury to another person. As Micaela observed, "He could easily have been somebody who'd been in my house, because of his history with alcohol. Joel could have been his sponsor." Micaela and Joel's friends were AA members and Micaela was steeped in the philosophy and practices of AA. In response to his death, her house was full of recovering people and she realized that all of them had likely driven while drunk, including Joel. The AA model of readiness shaped even her initial reactions to Ronald as she noted, "I hope this is his bottom, whoever it is." Although Micaela did not know Ronald prior to the crash, the involuntary relationship that was formed by the accident took shape early because of their shared history with alcoholism, the role it played in Micaela's relationship to Joel, the role it played between Joel and Ronald, the role it played in Ronald's destiny, and, therefore, the role it played between Micaela and Ronald. Without realizing it, Micaela was already humanizing Ronald because of her understanding of alcoholism which Joel, the man Ronald killed, had paradoxically given to her.

Although Micaela and Joel had been together only two-and-a-half years, Micaela was deeply in love. The news of his death sent her into shock and an alternate and surreal reality where she went through the motions of living but was otherwise absent. Micaela missed Joel terribly and wanted desperately to be with him. She ached with loneliness and intense mourning, finding comfort in the arms of a close friend. That loneliness was exacerbated by having to raise her young son Scott alone and the reactions of others who either minimized the strength of her relationship with Joel because it was common-law or expected her to move forward quickly.

For the next four years, Micaela felt bombarded by contradictory feelings of rage, indifference, and concern for Ronald. She'd be livid one minute, furious that Ronald was alive instead of Joel and still breathing and then empathic, wondering how he, like she, was surviving in the aftermath of a crash that had permanently changed both their lives. She clearly was searching for an outlet for this complexity of emotions, something that would tie all the contradictions together. During a sentimental moment, she had considered meeting with Ronald, perhaps as a link to Joel. She intuitively had some awareness of the pain differential and the fact that what she was feeling should be shared with him. "I'm listening to music and crying and thinking that I need to go see him." Indeed her question,

"Is he feeling as horrible as I am?" conveys the pain she was in and her wish to transfer it so as not to be the one holding it alone. Her effort with the Department of Corrections, however, was not successful the first time.

She looked to spirituality as another channel for some relief. Micaela carried with her the memory of Joel's energy and how close she had felt to him at the hospital. "I didn't want to leave… I knew in my mind I was not going to have that feeling of him being here again." She consulted with a channeler, a spiritual medium, and a shaman searching for Joel and spiritual wisdom about life and the afterlife. These avenues again were not particularly productive. Micaela's drive for resolution continued, however, energized by her unremitting grief, anger, and lack of resolution. She increasingly sensed that she needed to do this work with Ronald.

Preparation

The impetus for meeting with him ostensibly came from Micaela's concern for herself and the worrisome prospect of accidentally running into Ronald after he was released. AA again fueled her determination. Specifically, Micaela was convinced that she had to give Ronald the opportunity to make amends as the avenue for his possible sobriety and recovery. Micaela's sense of obligation may have been tied to what Joel would have done or wanted her to do. Her strong desire to meet, therefore, may also have been a way for her to honor Joel, to complete this painful chapter in her life, and make something positive come out of the tragedy. She figured, however, that Ronald could not make amends if he didn't know anything about Joel and how he had impacted her life. She approached the VOD, open to how she might help Ronald, therefore, but with little awareness that the meeting could help her. Her resistance to the gentle confrontations by the facilitator about her own needs was, "Sorry, this is not for me, other than to see his face." Although the facilitator could not shift her motivation, she did help Micaela harness her energy by preparing her for the meeting. She had her write down possible questions, bring photographs to show Ronald and have Scott make an audiotape of his questions as well. The only negative event during preparation were some intrusive questions Ronald had posed to Micaela through the facilitator about her relationship with Joel.

Dialogue

Although she was nervous going into the prison, a humorous synchronicity happened as Micaela recognized the warden's physical similarity to a television character only to discover that he had the same first name. Although seemingly irrelevant, these occurrences became part of the juxtaposing of events which were perceived by Micaela as evidence that circumstances were being managed by forces beyond her control. Moreover, Micaela surmised that such synchronicity was also a communication to her about the correctness of the path she had chosen. Micaela's pain was prominent throughout. She started crying immediately and cried through the whole meeting conveying the pain that belonged to Ronald but that she had carried alone. Although she had seen Ronald in the courtroom, Micaela was overwhelmed by the power of his presence in the meeting room as if she were seeing him for the first time. She felt an additional jolt when their eyes met. In many ways their relationship, which she had mentally established in her mind, came to life. The nonverbals between them in the first few minutes of the meeting were an indication of the thick energy generated and magnified by the presence of both parties and the history that connected them. Both waited along with the facilitator for a sense of space for constructing a safe conduit for this energy to flow through.

Micaela began by recounting her love for Joel, his importance to her, the meaningfulness of their life together, and what Ronald had taken from her. Ronald then talked about the crash and the layers of loss that dominated his own life. They were both responsive to the magnitude of their mutual sharing as demonstrated by the flow of energy between them, their resonance to each other's stories and their reciprocal influence on each other. For example, in response to Micaela's pain, Joel expressed his eagerness to help and do something to lessen it. He shared information that Micaela had not even considered about the crash but it filled in the gaps for her. Micaela responded to his caring and prior history by noting a shift in her feelings such that she moved from seeing him as the skuzzy guy in court to someone who had suffered a lot yet could provide her with some comfort. The giving and receiving between them further opened the conduit of energy flow making a more empathic connection between them. This flow accelerated as they shared stories about alcohol and the role of AA and the amazing synchronicity of Ronald's flat tire the day before at the scene of the crash followed by the designated driver's finding of an AA medallion.

As Micaela shared her pain with the person it was meant for, she was relieved because she could own all her grief, her ongoing love for Joel and how much she missed him without feeling judged. She felt freer, unburdened, and had much less fear. For her, the experience was clearly spiritual. Time stood still. She sensed the shifts in energy between them. "A spiritual thing happened. I felt that energy in the room. It was bigger than the two of us. By the time we got to the end, it just felt like, yeah, we're done."

Without warning, however, this de-intensification process and movement of energy from negative to positive started another process, which was loaded with struggle and dissonance. Because of her gratitude and compassion, she found herself thinking spontaneously about forgiveness. She was shocked—"Oh, my God. I don't know about that. I don't know what to do with it." Confused by and worried about all the potential messages that might be conveyed by the word "forgiveness," she decided to reduce the dissonance by making it conditional. That way, Micaela could forgive Ronald, as she felt inclined to do, but she could also ensure that the word "forgiveness" wouldn't be misconstrued by Ronald as a pardon. Without realizing it, however, Micaela's conditional forgiveness created a hanging on for her that reduced the very freedom she had felt, and a threat for Ronald that undid the offer of her gift. This giving and taking back at the same time generated a new dissonance for Micaela but it took a while before it surfaced.

As Micaela left the meeting, she faced more difficult decisions because the success of the meeting eroded some of the traditional barriers between her and Ronald that otherwise mark the territory between victim and offender. For example, she wanted to express her gratitude directly, but again worried that doing so might betray Joel. She therefore found herself stuck in the middle of a new contradiction. The meeting had been successful in transforming her pain and she felt a reciprocal empathy toward Ronald. Indeed, Ronald had partnered with her to make pivotal shifts occur and she felt differently toward him because of his authenticity, sharing, accountability, and desire to give to her. However, he had also murdered the man she loved so much. She couldn't express her gratitude without feeling disloyal. This contradiction was further complicated by the fact that the VOD was over and there was no more time to try to resolve it. Indeed, if she did not express what she felt in her heart, she'd have to live with that unfinished business because she'd likely never get another chance. Micaela decided to push past her resistance, which included her repulsion to touching the man who had killed Joel. She shook Ronald's hand in front of everyone, which, in effect, helped to solidify who he had become to her during their meeting and his moral reinstatement in her eyes.

The problem with Micaela's conditional forgiveness surfaced, however, 14 years later when she learned that Ronald was back in prison because of alcohol and drugs. At that point, the strength of her reaction to the news awakened her to how she was hanging on and what she needed to do to fully release herself as well as Ronald. Moreover, after finding out how Ronald had distorted the reality of their VOD meeting, she was even more convinced that she needed to take away the condition she had put on her forgiveness. Her decision to undo her emotional attachment was not just about her freedom. It was also based on her desire to hold onto the power of her meeting with Ronald and her determination not to allow what happened subsequently to take away or lessen her experience. Her final act of writing him, wishing him well, and letting him go resolved the dissonance she had created earlier. This act of completion also allowed the agitated energy inside her to come to rest. Consequently, although Micaela had forgiven Ronald in the meeting and had reinstated him by holding him in high regard for the positive difference he made in her life, she revisited the concept of forgiveness and challenged herself to go further by unconditionalizing it. She wanted a way to make it final without being dependent on him. She still needed real completion because of the condition she had put on forgiveness and his relapsing.

In conclusion, Micaela needed the dyadic connection with Ronald in order to share the pain of Joel's death which Ronald caused and therefore must own. She needed the dyadic exchange in order to generate the flow of energy that allowed the give and take that could reshape their relationship and change the valence between them from negative to positive. The forgiveness Micaela felt grew of the dyadic bond and gratitude she felt toward Ronald for what he did to help transform her pain. As Micaela initially needed Ronald to complete what she could not do alone, she also needed him in order to revisit and redo the forgiveness that actually could unburden and release her fully. She achieved this through the letter writing, which allowed her to communicate within the dyad and to preserve what she and Ronald had earlier created together.

NORMAN'S STORY AND ANALYSIS

When Norman was six years old, his mother was murdered by Raul, both of whom were involved in a biker lifestyle. Norman tried to focus the anger he felt, first with drugs and alcohol but later through kickboxing. As he got older Norman was no longer able to channel the rage he held inside and saw it spilling out into his wife and young son. Norman hoped that in meeting Raul he would be able to empty himself of the hatred and stop it from affecting another generation. Although his intention was to vent his rage, upon seeing Raul, Norman felt his heart fill with love and the two men bonded immediately over their deep connection to God. Norman saw a potential future in Raul, one he had inadvertently escaped when his mother died and he was removed from the biker lifestyle. Norman's wife was able to fulfill his original intent to hold Raul accountable for the damage done, and Norman found a peace and forgiveness he didn't know he was capable of.

My mother raised me in a biker lifestyle. When I was six years old, Raul, who was her contemporary and a biker gang member, killed her. From then on, I was angry, angry at the world, at God, and everything else. I blamed everyone for what happened. I was very quick to fight, to resort to violence. I spent most of my childhood with my grandparents but there was little stability because we moved from house to house in numerous different states. I had problems with relationships because I was so angry. It's not that I would beat up anyone, and certainly not a woman given what had happened to my mom, but every little thing would irritate me, make me mad, and be a trigger to get drunk or high.

A good friend introduced me to kickboxing, which allowed me to vent my anger and kept me away from drugs and alcohol. I literally fought in a ring. I fought anybody and everybody. All of my practicing and hard work paid off professionally. But I still had that fire in my gut. I eventually learned that I was just fighting my feelings and myself. After a ten-year career of competing, I messed up my back so badly that I could no longer fight. The anger returned. I was right back to where I had been before I ever started kickboxing.

My anger affected my family horribly. I was irritated with every little thing my wife or the kids did. You couldn't step right, walk right, or talk right. I didn't hit or beat them. I just made them feel an inch tall. Ironically, I love my family in a borderline obsessive way. I would walk to hell and back if I thought it would better them. I began to worry that I might lose them unless I did something about my anger. I vowed I would not let what happened to my mother affect yet another generation in my family. So I decided to visit Raul, the man who had murdered her, in prison.

I'd always faced my problems head on except for this one. It felt it was time. I had to confront the demon that had controlled my life. I initially planned to rid myself of every bit of hate and anger that had built up for decades by spewing it onto Raul. I wanted to pour it on him like hot tar. I might even beat him within an inch of his life. After all, he was the rightful source of my rage. I just figured I'd get it off my chest and be done. I called the prison to see if I could get on a list to see him but the prison said no because a lifetime no-contact order was in place. I was directed to a facilitator with the VOD program.

The preparation lasted eight months. My goal was to let Raul know how badly he had affected me and how much I hated him. The facilitator warned me that I couldn't call him names, belittle him, or yell. I had to be respectful. She also told me that he was willing to accept my venting. My wife was my support and accompanied me to the meeting.

The moment we got into the room, my feelings changed completely. I was sitting at the table waiting for him, nervous and sweating, and getting ready to tell him what he'd done to me. That just totally did not happen.

The minute he walked in, I felt like crying. As soon as he sat down, God filled my heart with love, compassion, and forgiveness. All I could do was forgive him. I couldn't do anything else. As he started talking, I interrupted him and said, "You know, we don't need all the details. We all know what you did and why you're here. We know why I'm here. But you know what? I just want to stop the hate. We have to stop the cycle. If I continue to hate you and be angry at you, it's going to affect my wife and children. They will see it and then you've affected yet another generation in my family. I'm not going to let you affect my children. So I'm doing this for my children and me. I continued, "I forgive you for everything you've done and have no animosity. When I really step back and look, I know that everything happens for a reason. I was being raised in a biker lifestyle. If you had not killed my mom, I would either be dead or in prison because I would have known no different. God removed me from all that by taking my mom. He had plans for me. One of his plans is that I make sure my son becomes a successful person and doesn't grow up filled with hate and anger."

These thoughts poured out of me spontaneously in a blink of an eye. I had considered saying something about forgiveness after I was done venting but wasn't sure. I was not expecting to say what I did in the first ten minutes. My only explanation was that God was speaking through me. I had never discussed it with the facilitator. It did not come up during preparation. Imagine the look on Raul's face when I thanked him for what he'd done to me because it made me a better person. He was in absolute awe. He couldn't believe what he was hearing.

The pain and anger I had did not slowly go away. It didn't evaporate into the air. Rather it was like a cup of water that you just tip over and dump it out. It's gone. It's no longer in the glass. I'm sure that what I did was partly tied to Raul's openness and readiness to accept whatever I dished out. He too was filled with fear and anger toward himself. He had grown up consumed with hate. His dad beat him, his brother, and his mother. So he started giving back what he was given. He joined the biker gang and started killing people, including my mom. He had not been able to forgive himself. I saw that the anger and hate he had learned as a child was taught to me by him and what he did to my mother so I grew up with it but refused to pass that onto my child. His side of the story, therefore, was as important as mine. I also saw that his fear was like my hate. They were both poisons. Raul was fearful about what would come out of the meeting and he hated himself for what he'd done. One of the ways he felt he could forgive himself was to open himself up to me, to put his neck on the chopping block and say, "Do what you're going to do." So we each had a glass of poison. Rather than letting it just sit, ferment, and become more poisonous, we tipped the glasses up and dumped them out. It was just gone. Just that fast, the build-up from 20 years of hate and anger were gone in the blink of an eye.

Raul was already on a God-directed journey when we met but the meeting awoke my spiritual self. It opened my heart to God and the wonderful things that can happen when you're not filled with hate and anger. Raul gave to me through his actions, mannerisms, and the way he handled himself in this meeting. I felt his spirit and soul were starving, begging my soul for forgiveness and the affirmation that he was on the right path. What I got from him was priceless. He was willing to take whatever I was going to dish out, including beating up on him, because that's what God said he needed. It wasn't his words, therefore, but his demeanor of acceptance that was so powerful. Our souls talked. It was as if God brought us together to make both of us stronger.

The meeting lasted two hours. Before it was over, my wife stepped up to the plate. My grandmother had been against my meeting Raul so my wife felt she had to represent her. She told Raul that my grandmother, my mother's mother, would never forgive him and will hate him until the day she dies. She also shared how he had affected me and that it made her sick that he was still alive. My wife spoke the venting that I intended to speak. She did it in five minutes. I know God was speaking through her and saying what needed to be said but through someone else's voice, not mine. Raul received it pretty well even though he was not prepared to hear it from my wife. He said that he completely understood her feelings and that he was truly sorry for what happened. He took it in his stride and was very gracious about it.

At the end of the meeting, I reached across the table to shake Raul's hand and then said, "That ain't good enough." I walked around the table and gave him a hug and said, "Thank you for everything. God bless you and stay strong." Everyone just lost it and started crying and bawling. I was surprised that others were making such a big deal of something I just felt I needed to do. I would hope any other father or husband would do this much for his family.

Forgiving Raul emptied out all my hatred and anger. That empty space is now filled with love, joy, and excitement for my wife and kids. My son is a phenomenal athlete. He's only eight and he's the youngest Tai Kwando Black Belt in Michigan's history. He's a state and national champion wrestler. He just took second place in the largest kickboxing tournament in North America. Although he'd be a wonderful athlete regardless, my not being angry and filled with hate has let him be truly happy and enjoy what he's doing. He doesn't know how to hate, only to love.

The meeting changed everything. It absolutely changed me. My wife and I probably would have gotten a divorce, which would absolutely have affected my son. My family and I would not be where we are at today. For example, I was never a church kind of person or religious. But after the meeting, we started going to church and I became closer to God. As hard as it is to say and as bad as it hurts, I equally feel happy and blessed that my mom was killed because my son would not otherwise exist. I've become a better husband, which has influenced my wife to be a better wife and mother.

Moreover, I have a spiritual brother I didn't have before. If I have an issue, I can call Raul day or night and we will pray about it. I never had someone before that I could reach out to, who would not judge me or ask a gazillion questions. Raul has been out of prison now for two years. We talk together about once a month. We spoke together at my church. After that we exchanged phone numbers because we felt we might do more speaking together in the future, particularly about forgiveness and the power of Jesus through forgiveness. The world needs to hear our story. It might stop the conflicts that exist because somebody won't forgive someone else.

Analysis: Crime and its aftermath

Norman's mother was killed when he was just a young six-year-old child. He remembered it as "gruesome" and "grizzly" and as connected to a violent drug and biker lifestyle. He spent his entire childhood loaded with anger, which likely reflected the immense amount of inner pain he carried with no outlet—"I was angry at the world, angry at God, and angry at everything." Norman used fighting to siphon off some of the build-up but the anger was relentless and became a way of life. For a time, Norman channeled it productively by using it to fuel a ten-year career in kickboxing. That avenue wore thin, however, and he had to quit because of back problems. Within two years, the anger had again piled up and was spilling over into his marriage and relationships with his children.

Norman was caught in a vicious cycle. He rejected the destructive lifestyle of his mother and yet kept producing anger and destroying himself and those he loved with it as if it were a cancer he carried from her murder. The accumulation of stored energy from all the pain and anger reached a breaking point inside of Norman. He knew his anger was directly connected to his mother's murder but now it was seeping into his current family. He truly felt powerless to stop it, because, in part, it did not belong to him but rather Raul, the man who had murdered his mother. Moreover, the unrelenting and stuck anger likely reflected his emotional frozenness related to the trauma of losing his mother at such a young age. The dissonance for Norman was that he couldn't continue the lifestyle he was living and still have a family.

Preparation

Norman's primary reason for meeting with Raul was to give him the anger he'd carried since he was six years old. He had years of personal experience dealing with it and lots of self-knowledge. Although Norman's core objective was to stop the generational cycle of hatred, he knew only one way to achieve it, which was to spew it out onto Raul. Norman had avoided dealing directly with his anger so his decision to move forward was both desperate and courageous. In many ways, he'd been in an involuntary relationship with Raul for years and had a thousand mental dialogues with him. The eight months of preparation with the facilitator did not soften his resolve. His openness to Raul, therefore, was motivated by his intense need for relief but was also limited to using Raul only as a sounding board. He knew, however, that Raul was God-fearing and willing to be a sacrificial lamb, "to accept my venting in the way it was going to be presented." In some ways, Norman was more optimistic than open. Raul's openness to Norman and giving him what he needed, however, suggests Raul was sensitive to the pain differential and receptive to having the pain transferred to him. His openness may have also helped establish the conduit between them and had some impact on Norman and his response to Raul when they met.

Dialogue

Commensurate with his age at the time that the trauma occurred, Norman's drive to meet with Raul was more emotional than a mental quest to make sense of the murder and its impact on his life. Indeed, because the loss of his mother had a primal impact, the details of what happened were not central. Moreover, he was clear that his intention was to stop the intergenerational transmission of anger for his children. He had not planned to forgive or say anything about it. The topic of forgiveness had not been part of preparing for the dialogue. Yet, "in the blink of an eye," everything changed. Norman was not religious but felt that his forgiving Raul was God-directed and that God was speaking through him. His feelings of forgiveness emptied out the hatred he had carried and expected to spew on Raul. Some of the openness that did not happen during preparation expanded as a result of the dialogue and the introduction of God. Indeed, the power in Norman's shift was more the result of the dyadic encounter with Raul, the man responsible for the trauma and resulting anger he had borne since age six, than even the content of the dyadic dialogue.

Although Norman's forgivingness was meant to shift the burden he carried of intergenerational anger, he sensed that it went directly into Raul's soul. This sensing reflected the strong flow of positive intent moving back and forth that helped establish the conduit between them. The resonance between them was stark. Norman felt Raul's fear and self-hatred. Raul's hunger for forgiveness and affirmation matched his own craving to be freed of the negative energy expressed through his anger and hatred. In giving to himself, he gave to Raul. He felt the transmission of energies on a soul level with Raul. Besides his sharing of himself, his decades-long struggle to rid himself of the load he carried, and his determination not to hand it down to his family, he also felt Raul's absolute willingness to accept whatever God asked him to carry. Norman, therefore, felt the pain transfer but also had a sense that Raul's reactions to him were God-directed—"I went in there to confront my biggest fear and enemy and I came out with a spiritual brother." Indeed, Norman concluded that "God brought us together to make us both stronger." God, therefore, became the conduit between Norman and Raul.

Besides the God connection, Norman and Raul had similar histories of badness. Raul's badness came from his anger and killing. Norman's badness came from the murder of his mother and how it was currently expressing his hatred. They both were filled with hate and were lashing out at others. But Norman felt that the anger Raul carried was passed down to him through the killing of his mother. It was that anger that Norman worried he would pass on to his son. The negative link between them, however, was metamorphosed into positive life-giving energy. For example, although Norman and Raul were both committed to moving the history between them, it was the God connection between them that transformed the pain. As part of his sharing forgivingness and his transformation, Norman suddenly saw his life differently as well as the role God had played in the circumstances that befell him. Gratitude emerged in place of the resentment he'd always carried. He felt fortunate that, because of Raul, he was taken from the biker lifestyle through his mother's murder, that God removed him from being a fighter, and that he was blessed with a wonderful son who was freed of the hate and anger Norman had lived with. By giving himself these explanations, his internal dissonance was resolved, he had clarity, and his mother's murder now made sense. He saw the goodness that resulted from the tragedy. He expressed his thanks to Raul. The shift in Norman's thinking reciprocally impacted Raul. Specifically, the change he witnessed in Norman reinforced his own faith in God and humanity.

When Norman's wife expressed her own anger to Raul, Norman again experienced it as God-directed, that is, God speaking to Raul through her. He watched as Raul graciously received her feelings, understood them and apologized. Because of Norman's turnaround, Raul, who was considerably older, looked up to Norman as his mentor about Christ but Norman saw Raul as way ahead of him spiritually. "He was already on the right path." Indeed, Raul had a strong relationship with Jesus whereas Norman's historic anger toward God kept him distant from establishing any real connection prior to the meeting. For example, Raul, rather than cringing or suffering under the expected weight of Norman's anger, was open, understanding, and actually welcomed what Norman needed to do for himself. Raul's positioning likely unnerved Norman and helped shift the energy associated with Norman's anger.

By the end of the dialogue, Norman felt relieved of the anger and hatred that had been sealed off and stuck since age six. The poison in his system was gone. In its place he felt love, compassion, and forgiveness as well as joy and excitement for his wife and children. Raul was morally reinstated in several ways. Norman hugged him, thanking him for everything he gave that day. More importantly, Norman and Raul established an ongoing friendship that was maintained through emails, phone calls, and giving shared testimony in front of the congregation at Norman's church. The dialogue and transformation also rebuilt Norman's relationship with God— "It renewed my faith in humanity. It awoke my spiritual self. It opened my heart to God and the wonderful things that can happen when you're not filled with hate and anger."

The strongest sense of completion for Norman was the difference he saw in himself and his relationships with those he loves. He felt changed from the inside out and lives with the reassurance that the cycle of hate and anger will no longer be passed down to his son. The manner in which Norman achieved his goal was paradoxical. He had expected to rid himself of his anger and hatred by spewing it onto Raul. However, he had a long history where his spewing did nothing but reinforce and increase his negativity. Paradoxically, his forgiveness rather than his anger accomplished what he set out to do.

TERRI ANNE'S STORY AND ANALYSIS

Terri Anne's son, Peter, offered a ride to a stranger, whose ultimate goal was to steal Peter's car. When Peter refused, Chester, just 17 years old, shot and killed him. Terri Anne's entire identity was bound to Peter and now to Chester. Terri Anne acutely felt the injustice of her son trying to help another, who then turned on him. These feelings were tied up in her religious upbringing but were also racially driven. Six times Chester backed out, but the final time Terri Anne felt Peter was right beside her showing her this was the right decision. During their dialogue Terri Anne became a sort of mother to him, absorbing the trauma of his childhood while also holding Chester accountable. At the end of the dialogue Chester washed Terri Anne's hands in his tears, giving herself and her pain over to God and to Chester, where it belonged.

When my only child, Peter, was a senior in college, he gave a young man named Chester a ride. Chester insisted that Peter give him his car and when he wouldn't he shot him—"The dude wouldn't give me his car, so I just shot him." He didn't know Peter but said, "He was littler than me and I knew I could take him down." Chester's brothers turned him in because they thought they would get a reward. Chester was 17 when he murdered Peter. I couldn't believe a 17-year-old could walk around with a pistol, point it at someone and kill him. That's not how Peter was raised.

I got very involved in the criminal justice system. I read countless books, trying to understand how someone could do something so horrible to someone who was nice to them and gave them a ride. It took me nine years before I could say Peter's name without totally falling apart. That's how awful it was. I would wake up every morning thinking, "I hope he dies today." I never changed that feeling until the day I met him. Chester got 14 years flat time and mandatory release after 25 years. I got a notice 11 years into Chester's sentence that he was up for parole review. That letter took me to my knees. I was balling and squealing and, frankly, hysterical. I called Victim Services about it and was told that sending out these notice letters was automatic and done a year in advance. It became a reality, at that point, that he might get released.

I found out about the VOD program and decided to meet with a woman who was the first person in my state to have met with her offender in order to learn more about her experience and what was involved. After that, I started to meet with a facilitator who directed the program for the Department of Corrections. In court, it was clear that Chester was uninvolved and hardened. My goal, therefore, was to make him look me in the eyes and feel what he did.

The preparation for the meeting lasted one-and-a-half years. During that time, I examined a lot of emotions that I had buried. The intent of doing the work was to help you better manage your reactions to the offender during the meeting. I kept complaining to the facilitator about the injustice of having to do all this inner work when all Peter was doing was trying to be nice to Chester. However, the introspection helped me see how I felt about who I was. I'd been Peter's mother for 21 years. I had no identity other than Peter's mother. He was the focus of my life. My career came second because it supported my first priority. I was number three. So I had to totally rearrange those priorities after Peter's death. I knew I wanted the death penalty, however, and I never changed my opinion about it no matter what I learned about Chester.

During the preparation, the facilitator would have me fill out questionnaires and then journal about my feelings. He also shuttled back and forth between me and Chester. He would have us write letters to each other about our feelings about what had happened and the impact of the murder on our lives. He reviewed the letters prior to delivering them to each of us along with his notes. I knew from the established rules that I couldn't belittle Chester. But I also know that he'd been put down all his life and he didn't need that from me. So instead I told him how devastated and hurt I was. I poured out my heart. In response, Chester was cold. It was like Peter was a chair that he just moved across the room. I couldn't get over his lack of feelings. I would tell the facilitator, "He doesn't even call his name. He doesn't even acknowledge that he was a human." The facilitator would reply, "Well, you know, he's probably stuffed his feelings." I'd tell the facilitator that Chester needed to get them unstuffed. I had no mercy.

My own family was not supportive. I'm White and Chester is African American. My father was a Pentecostal minister and kept saying, "God made red birds and blue birds smart enough not to build a nest together. We don't associate with people of other colors." I grew up with that philosophy but that's not how I raised Peter. I never taught him color. My family, however, told me that if I had raised my son right, he wouldn't have given Chester a ride. When your family blames you for your son's murder, you move on. I stopped talking to them about my pain and grief and instead read lots of books about grief, victimization, and criminals. I probably have 3000 of them.

In doing the preparation, Chester backed out six times. I asked the facilitator to keep trying and finally he was persuasive enough that Chester consented to meet. The facilitator had told me to write down the questions I wanted to ask in the meeting. I just wrote why, why, why, why, why. That was my cry. "Why did you do that? He was trying to help you. How can you be that mean?" What no one knew, however, was that I had other plans for after our meeting together. I was going to leave the planet because I wasn't needed anymore. I couldn't live with the pain. I hated God, the world and the horse it came in on, and everything about life. I *hated* to wake up in the morning. I would pray to die in my sleep. That's how deep the pain was. I did not ever tell anyone my plan. There was no reason for me to be here. Paul was dead so why should I stay? I didn't tell the facilitator because it wasn't his business. I figured that when I had met with Chester I'd be free and could get out of here. I wouldn't wake up.

The night before our meeting, I walked the floor all night. I didn't close my eyes. I obsessed going over my questions and rehearsing what I would say, but nothing happened the way I expected it would. To begin with, a strange event happened as I checked out of the motel to go to the prison the next morning. I had ordered a red Corvette for Peter as a graduate present three months before he was killed. I had planned to give him the keys when he walked across the stage. After his death, I would freak every time I saw a Corvette. The sight of the car would trigger my anger and the injustice of having lost my son. But this time was different. When I went to leave the motel the day of the meeting, I found my car was sitting right next to a shiny new red Corvette. I took it as a sign from Peter that I was doing the right thing.

When we got to the meeting, the facilitator had everything in place. The table was six feet long and two to three feet wide. We were to sit across from each other. But I had problems with that arrangement. So I insisted we sit across at the long ends because I didn't want to be too close to him. I didn't want to breathe the same air. I worried that he might touch me with his long feet. I was just a monster. The facilitator convinced me not to change the arrangement because the meeting was being videotaped for later review by Chester and myself. The videotaping for post-VOD debriefing was standard practice in the early years of the program in my state. The facilitator was also worried that my making a change could impact Chester's willingness to participate. The facilitator said to me, "We worked very hard to get him to this place. You want to talk to him. He has finally consented to do it. We've got him here and he's standing waiting. It would be helpful if you would just work with us." Chester too had had last minute misgivings. He had written me a letter the night before. It was very terse and said, "Don't expect me to cry. I'm a grown man. I know what I did when I killed that kid." It was not sweet. The facilitator explained that Chester had a right to his feelings but that he was willing to talk to me. I figured that I wanted to talk to him badly enough that I would just deal with whatever he had said in his letter later, if at all.

Chester came in in handcuffs and shackles. I was pleased to see him bound because I didn't want him near me. He had killed my son. At the time of the meeting, Chester had accumulated 153 disciplinary cases while he'd been in prison. I had to get special permission to meet with him because he was so violent and would attack the guards. He was one of the worst prisoners in the facility. The warden told me, "He's worthless, not worth anything." Through my connections, I had also read Chester's juvenile records. He was first arrested at age 11 and then let go because of overcrowding in the juvenile facility and returned to his neighborhood. His mother had moved while he was imprisoned so from then on, he lived on the streets. When he was 12, he watched his brother stab a man to death in a drug deal. He was arrested again. He had nine felony convictions at the age of 17. He had five brothers in the same prison for murder. He'd had a terrible life but I didn't cut him any slack. He had killed Peter and would get no sympathy from me.

The facilitator had told me that I would start the dialogue and to write an opening statement. I started talking to him in a soft voice. Peter used to ask me to talk to him when he was sick because of my voice. He'd say, "You've just got the sweetest little voice." At any rate, I simply said, "Thank you for doing this. I won't be unkind to you in any way." Chester started crying. I just kept talking but to the right of me was a box of tissues. I handed him a tissue across the table and said, "Here." He just shook his head. He couldn't speak because of his tears. It was unbelievable that I had any bit of kindness in me but we went on for hours. I showed him Peter's picture and made him say his name. I asked that he keep Peter's picture in his cell for a year. I talked to him like a mother. I was aware that Peter had known love from me. He didn't know what it was like not to be loved, adored, and encouraged. It was never "if" you were going to college but where and when. But I knew what Chester didn't have before I met him because of reading his records. I just had no mercy for him until this day. So then my mothering of him just came out. I believe that I was the one to set the tone for the way the day would go.

We went through some of my questions but as we talked I felt I didn't need to ask all 77 of them. He had given me the information I needed. He had opened up to me and would have done anything in his power to bring Peter back. He said to me, "I wish I could give you something. I don't have nothing." That's when things switched for me. I said, "What you can do for me is turn your life around. I know how you've acted in prison. You've attacked the guards and choked them. You've been a terrible person. You don't have to do that. You can go to college in here. You can make something of yourself. That's what you can do for me." Chester was incredulous. It never crossed his mind that anyone would take an interest in him and care. He said to me, "I felt more love in that room the day I met you than I've felt my whole life." He never said he was sorry and I never said, "I forgive you." The way I describe it is to say that we came to a place of peace.

The meeting was extremely lengthy. I was just exhausted by the end. I had given him my soul. I'd relived the pain all over again and was drained. I had spent my soul, my heart, my brain, my head and I just couldn't do any more. I thanked him 17 times. But I also said, "You can do this. You can make something of yourself, better yourself." I just encouraged him in every way possible. I gave him a book called *Out of Madness: From the Projects to a Life of Hope*. Coincidentally, the author had lived in the same neighborhood as Chester. His mother was a crack addict and he was a writer. I gave him the book and said, "Look what you can do. I don't care if your mother used to smoke dope with you, you can make something out of yourself." When I said this to him, he was sitting across the table with his head down, just overcome with emotion. I heard God talking to me. "Terri Anne, put your hand across the table." I said, "No. I've sat here all day. I've tried to encourage him. I've given him a book. I've told him I'll write to him. I'm going to buy him a GED[2] book. I'm going to try to help him get an education. Now what do you expect of me?" I reminded myself that if I put my hand out, I'd be holding the hand that held the pistol that murdered my child. I felt I couldn't do it. So I said, "God, I can't do that by myself." I had my eyes closed but I stretched my hand across the table. I didn't say, "Give me your hand." God was just there. Chester took my hand in both of his, pulled it under his face and washed both our hands with his tears. At that moment I let out a guttural scream of anger, hate, and rage that I had contained for 13-and-a-half years. After my scream, no one in the room was breathing. You could have heard a flea roll across the carpet. It was the most powerful spiritual thing that has ever happened to me in my life. I thought giving birth was spiritual but it was just painful. At that moment the rage, hate, and anger just lifted. It was gone.

I still want Peter back every day. The pain of missing him and of the murder has never changed. If you saw me at the cemetery on his birthday you would think he had died just the day before. People think that just because you do therapy or forgive that you just forget about your loved one. Maybe the pain is a little bit less but I wish Peter were here holding my hand when I let go of life and I won't have that.

Chester and I continued to exchange letters but they still all went through the facilitator. He wrote me every day and I would write him one letter a month. I still have all those letters in a file drawer. After our meeting, I put money in Chester's trust fund that the inmates have for incidentals, sent him books and did everything to help him. As long as I communicated with him, he was not in trouble. He did not get another disciplinary case at all. None. However, Chester started calling me his godmother and telling me he loved me. Someone in the Department of Corrections decided he was forming an inappropriate attachment to me and forbade me to communicate with him anymore. I begged the person to reconsider, saying that the conclusions drawn by others about Chester's attachment were wrong. But it made no difference and I was forced to quit writing him. He was all right for about a year and then he lost hope again. Nobody cared. Nobody came. I had seen value in him and I believe he wanted to live up to that and not disappoint me. I warned the Department of Corrections that he'd slide back and he did. He started to get into trouble again. He attacked a guard. They finally let him out but he's been in trouble ever since. He's back in now.

---

2   General Education Diploma.

I'm a better person now than the day Peter was murdered. I was raised to be very racially prejudiced, very judgmental. God has worked wonders in my life since he softened my heart. God thought I was worth saving. God knew I was not going to survive so I guess God figured, "I gotta do something or she's going to kill herself, so let's let this work." I do lots of work in prisons now to try to help other guys turn their lives around. I often have one of the prisoners hold my hand in front of the others while I tell the story of what God did to help me reach over the table for Chester's hand. Their hands get sweaty. It's almost like they can feel what Chester and I were feeling.

Analysis: Crime and its aftermath

As a single mother, Terri Anne was completely devoted to her only child, Peter. Her role as mother was her sole identity and had been so for years. In many ways, he and she were companions and soulmates in their dedication to each other as mother and son. She had tended him well throughout his growing up, using her strong sense of the moral lessons in life as her guide. Peter's upcoming graduation from college was to have been a marker event in both their lives and Terri Anne expected he would be next to her as she aged. When he was murdered, there was nothing left in her life to hold her up. She had no meaning and wanted to be with him far more than continuing to live with no purpose. In her mind, she was simply Peter's mom. Her family cruelly exacerbated her aloneness and sense of injury by their righteousness about her mothering. Specifically, she felt disenfranchised because they criticized how she had raised her son, claiming that if she had done it right, he would never have offered a ride to someone of a different race, someone who was Black. Terri Anne, therefore, not only bore the pain from her son's murder but also the guilt given her by her family and the unnecessary aggravation from the insensitive way in which she learned that Chester might be released.

Terri Anne chafed under the idea that Chester had intentionally targeted her son as an easy mark and taken advantage of his kindness and offer of help. From her vantage point, Chester's behavior was incomprehensible. His coldness to the murder itself and reactions in court were seemingly detached, emotionless, and violated her deeply held principles about human beings and how they should treat each other. Terri Anne read voraciously in an effort to understand Chester's thinking—"I read books about criminals like *Inside the Criminal Mind* to try to understand how someone could do something so horrible when somebody was nice to them and gave them a ride." She also read loads of books on grief and victimization in an effort to figure out her own indescribable emotions. What she read offered little solace. She had ceased talking about her pain with her family, but, as always, felt determined to attend to Peter and what had happened to him just as she had when he was alive. For her, the circumstances of his death were far from complete.

Preparation

Terri Anne learned about the VOD program from her connections in the criminal justice system. As with everything else, Terri Anne researched it thoroughly before moving forward. Once she decided to meet with Chester, she prepared by learning everything possible about his past. As she absorbed the extreme deprivation of his childhood, the lack of any parenting, and the onslaught of constant trauma just to survive, she slowly realized, at a core level, that the true enemy responsible for her son's murder was likely the inequity between Chester and Peter's worlds. Specifically, Peter had been raised by a devoted mother and ensconced with strong moral principles and countless advantages whereas Chester literally grew up on the streets with no parenting and struggling only to survive from one day to the next. Although this realization did not change her daily wish that Chester die or resolve not to cut him any slack, it did begin to humanize him and give her direction for how to engage with him in the meeting so that she could reach him emotionally. Her determination grew stronger as Chester kept refusing to meet with her.

Although Terri Anne began to harness her energy in anticipating how to relate in the meeting, she also was intentional in deciding what to say to Chester in the pre-VOD letters she wrote. After having informed herself about his upbringing, she decided not to be destructive but rather shared the immensity of the pain she was living with. Even though Chester had little response, she never backed off but rather pursued him relentlessly.

As part of preparation, the facilitator had Terri Anne answer numerous questionnaires about herself and how the murder had affected her. It was through this process that she began to understand the significance of her mothering role and how lost she was without it. It also clarified for her the core question, which had to do with the inconceivability and immorality of hurting someone who was trying to help you. Indeed, it was Terri Anne's need to answer that question and resolve the dissonance embedded in it that mobilized her to meet with Chester. Her detailing of 77 questions to ask Chester and repetition of the word "why" embodied the core question but was also more a statement of her outrage than an actual question.

Terri Anne's privately held decision to commit suicide fueled her "go for broke" and "nothing left to lose" attitude in meeting with Chester. It was as if she had a mission to perform and then she'd be done, released, and ready to join Peter. Her mothering role had been taken from her. Indeed, for Terri Anne, the searing pain of no longer being needed matched the pain of losing her son and only child. Her hope was that "I won't wake up anymore, it will be over, and all this pain will be gone." Although Terri Anne had shared her pain through her letters, there had been no response from Chester to suggest, in any way, that he was open to receiving it. The pain differential, therefore, stayed stuck inside her as she endured his limited involvement, ambivalence about meeting with her, and a letter the night before the meeting warning her that he would remain walled off from her in the dialogue. As such, Chester and Terri Anne's openness to each other was seemingly narrow and tentative. Indeed, Terri Anne wanted badly to reach Chester but otherwise did not expect to be personally affected by what he gave her. Specifically, she was open to sharing the impact of what Chester did on her life and to being done with the pain but was not expecting or open to it being transformed.

Dialogue

Terri Anne's determination to take her own life and be with Peter after the meeting was interrupted by finding the red Corvette next to her car at the motel. Her interpretation of the synchronicity was that Peter approved of her decision to meet with Chester and she'd be fine. The conduit between them had already been established through the letters they'd exchanged and the facilitator's sharing about each with the other during preparation. Terri Anne likely felt that conduit as she visualized sitting across from Chester and struggled to get emotional distance by pushing the facilitator for more physical space between them. The facilitator's rebuke of her for her contrariness was actually a challenge to her to be more open. Chester may have also felt the conduit. Indeed, his letter the night before the meeting may have been his effort to establish emotional distance as well. At the beginning of the dialogue, therefore, both Terri Anne and Chester were in a stand-off but it reflected a similar worry about what would happen when they came together.

Chester's crying in response to Terri Anne's opening statement and her handing him the Kleenex is further evidence that they both had some earlier sense of what might happen when they met. In those first moments, Terri Anne discovered that she held kindness toward him and Chester discovered that he felt something akin to remorse. Moreover, in his sobbing, he showed Terri Anne his willingness to accept her pain and transfer it into himself. This exchange generated a profound shift for both of them, which resulted in Terri Anne talking to Chester for hours about what she had given Peter as a mother, who Peter was and the advantages he had, who she had been as Peter's mother, what Chester had taken from her but all in the context of what Chester had a right to as a child but never got. In making the comparison, she acknowledged what she knew about his background from the records she had read, and all the pain and relentless trauma he lived with along with the unfairness of what Peter got and Chester didn't. Chester just listened, absorbed Terri Anne's loving energy and cried as he let in her caring and the mothering he felt from her.

The resonance between them was deeply felt and the energy flowed back and forth so fast through their verbal and nonverbal exchanges that it was difficult to track. Although Terri Anne had come to the meeting determined to show no mercy, she really could not appreciate someone being raised so differently from Peter until Chester was in front of her and she could see he'd had nothing good in his life. She began to nurture him. Chester felt the enormity of what Terri Anne was giving him and asked what he could do for her. Terri Anne jumped on the opportunity and told him that he could turn his life around. With that comment, she reinstated him as someone who had potential and worth. She gave Chester hope for himself but also set up an expectation for him in paradoxical terms. Specifically, she told him that he could redeem himself and in so doing, he would help himself but also heal her. As such, she joined the two of them together but with the message, in effect, that he was obligated to her for what he took from her life. Although her intent was loving, she put a net around him with her expectation that he go in a different direction. She fed the possibility by talking to him about the positive lives that others from his neighborhood had built. She gave him a role model by telling him about the author of a book concerning his neighborhood, the similarity in background and talent between himself and the author, the fact that this person made it out of the inner city, and then presented the book to him as a special gift.

This feeding of hope, spoon by spoon, hour after hour became almost a birthing process in which Chester experienced feelings and profound caring like he'd never known before. Although Terri Anne was seemingly giving to Chester, another birthing was also happening. Specifically, Terri Anne was gaining back, through Chester, the mothering role she had lost. She literally watched Chester's transformation in front of her and how what she was doing was healing the wounds he had carried from his childhood. But something was incomplete. Terri Anne was spent and felt she had nothing left to give. She felt directed by God, however, to reach out to Chester across the table. At that point, the idea of giving of herself physically to the person who had killed her son created such revulsion and dissonance that she pulled back. She felt, at some level, that she couldn't reinstate him to that degree. Yet she saw that Chester was "sitting across the table with his head down, just shaking his head" as if he could hardly contain what he had been given and what he was feeling. She ultimately resolved her discomfort by asking for God's help to do his bidding and move past the barrier that was still between her and Chester.

Chester's tears and holding of their hands together while his tears washed over them touched Terri Anne's soul. He held her pain and all the anguish she had felt since Peter was murdered and she likely experienced his tears as healing. As she let him touch her with his love and gratitude, she felt her pain associated with the negative energy she had held transformed releasing all the rage that was stored inside her. Terri Anne experienced what she interpreted as their transcendent interaction as God directed and consequently indicated that she trusted what had happened implicitly. "It was just God that was there." She reflected that she now felt complete. Not only was she unburdened but she also believed, according to her perception, that God felt she was worth saving. Indeed, she felt that God had helped her convert her hatred to doing something worthwhile.

Subsequently, she carried her experience and connection with God into the prisons with the idea of using her story and what happened between her and Chester to reach other inmates. In many ways, her mothering, through her meeting with Chester, was restored but she now ministered to a much larger group. Terri Anne described her sense of completion and the energy between them as coming to rest by saying that she and Chester had come to a place of peace.

For a while Terri Anne continued to befriend and mother Chester. The judgment from the person in charge about her relationship with Chester was heartbreaking as well as witnessing his deterioration, as he again felt abandoned and alone. However, by that point, Terri Anne was limited by the prison system in what she could do to change the situation. Moreover, she had developed into her own person and was living a life filled with purpose and affirmation. In many ways, Chester and Terri Anne gave each other life and mutual healing through the dyadic encounter and dialogue. Neither would have, or could have, moved without the other.

PORTIA'S STORY AND ANALYSIS

Mabel and her roommate were brutally murdered by Jackson, a man with no connection to them, who broke into the house and stabbed both women and Mabel's boyfriend repeatedly. Portia, Mabel's mom, dedicated her life to the court case, the trial, and subsequent appeals. Portia was living her life numb, in a binding but involuntary relationship with Jackson. Portia felt compelled to forgive because of her faith. Jackson's upcoming execution date made preparation time limited. She anticipated a quick dialogue to share her decisional forgiveness but what she got was five-and-a-half hours of Jackson accepting responsibility for his actions. Portia was able to take back control over her life. Jackson requested and Portia agreed to attend the execution, sharing with her that he loved her and was thankful for her ability to show him love in return.

My daughter Mabel was murdered on her twenty-first birthday. Jackson also murdered her roommate and seriously injured Mabel's boyfriend Remy. Jackson was a rapist who had been released by mistake from prison three months before he killed Mabel. He had been stalking Mabel's roommate for a month. Mabel had alerted her boyfriend that she kept hearing something in the backyard but no one saw Jackson jumping back and forth over the fence into their yard. Jackson stabbed Mabel 28 times and she bled to death in a fetal position in the corner of her closet. She had screamed for Remy who tried to pull Jackson off of Mabel but Jackson then turned on Remy and stabbed him 19 times. Remy lost his left eye and almost died in the hospital. It was a horrific crime scene.

Jackson ran away from the house covered in blood. He told a friend that he had gotten into a fight with another drug dealer and was cut, needed to shower and change clothes. Jackson stuffed his clothes is a plastic bag and had a girlfriend drive him out of town so he could toss the bag with the knife and bloody clothes off a cliff but the police found it. Jackson was found guilty and given the death penalty for the multiple murders. I was in the courtroom with him for 13 months. I was so close to him at times that I could just reach over and touch him. I was fortunate because his attorneys who were court appointed came to me and apologized for having to defend him. In response, I'd say to them, "Don't apologize to me. You give him the best defense you can because I don't want him getting out of prison again through some loophole or mistake. You defend him like you've never defended anybody and that will be your thanks to me." At the trial Jackson kept looking around at Mabel's girlfriend's sister. Every time he would turn to look at her, I'd get in the way of his view so I could protect her because I didn't have my daughter any longer to protect. During that time and afterwards, I took jobs to support myself but never committed to them so that I would be available for anything that happened during the appeal process. I could not let him go. I could not let him get away.

With Mabel's death, I was thrown into a world that I knew absolutely nothing about and I had to become knowledgeable about all kinds of things.

Moreover, I had to find a place to put myself, to put my life in the middle of all the chaos. I literally lost myself and walked through the next 12 years deaf, dumb, and blind. Because of my numbness, my two other children suffered. They lost their sister and their mother in the same night. My son is still afraid to let me get close to him. He's very cautious and withdrawn. My daughter has come around some. Some people whose loved ones are killed never get past their anger or hatred or the question of "Why?" I never cared why. I had other relatives whose child was murdered and I watched them die full of hate and anger. I just thought, "God, please, please, please do *not* let me do that." The hatred and anger just destroys everything inside your body.

For a long time, Jackson was the focal point of my life. I felt a strong drive to sit down and talk. I tried to see him in jail but I wasn't allowed in. I tried again when he went to prison but I couldn't because I was the mother of his victim. I just wanted to see him even though I didn't know why. I think I just wanted to see what he was really like. In the courtroom all I saw was a monster. I'd look in his eyes and they were just vacant. The lights were on but nobody was home.

I thought about Jackson a lot. Because I'm Catholic, I also obsessed about forgiveness but I had a struggle with it. I didn't want to forgive him. One day, I was driving back home and listening to Christian radio. A speaker was talking about forgiveness, which sparked one of my many conversations with God. On that day, I was crying while I drove and exclaiming to God, "How could I ever forgive Jackson for what he did? How can I do that? There's no way I can do that." Surprisingly a voice answered from the back of the car and said, "You don't have to forgive what he did. You have to forgive him." I was shocked. I pulled off the side of the road and sat there. I just cried and thought, "How do I separate the two?" It took me five years before I could separate Jackson from Mabel in a way that I could forgive him. It wasn't an easy struggle because I fought it the whole way. I still didn't want to do it. I was instructed to do it.

At the time Mabel was murdered, the VOD program was not available to victims whose offenders were on death row. So even though I wanted to see Jackson, I wouldn't have been eligible. I had been vocal about wanting to meet with Jackson but had no idea how to accomplish it. Out of the blue, a facilitator called me who was with the Department of Corrections and asked if I would be willing to participate and that I'd be the first victim to have a dialogue with someone on death row and close to execution. I remember saying, "Oh my God, I can't believe you're calling me. I've been trying to do this for 12 years." There was little time for preparation because Jackson's execution date had already been scheduled. However, in the time we had, I found out a lot about myself that was sometimes not so pretty. I just had to look in the mirror and say, "Yeah, that's true too" and accept myself.

So I went into the meeting believing that I would be there just to tell him I'd forgiven him. I was planning to say, "I can never forgive you for what you did, but as a person I have to forgive you." I had expected the meeting to last 30 seconds but it went on for five-and-a-half hours.

When I went into the meeting I was apprehensive and tense. I didn't know what to expect but it was nothing like what I thought it would be. I sat down and then he sat down in front of me and started crying. In the courtroom he had no eyes but in the meeting I could actually see life in his eyes, which had not been there before. He was remorseful, I could tell. He had changed in a lot of ways too and I could see the changes. See, I grew up in the streets too so I knew what to look for and he couldn't fake everything, believe me. However, I know it was only with the grace of God that I was able to really see him as a person rather than the monster I had seen 12 years earlier. That was a big shift for me.

We had had some correspondence through the facilitator before the actual meeting that was traumatic. Jackson had apologized and said all kinds of things. I, of course, wasn't interested in apologies. I was set to go in and say, "You know what? God commanded me to forgive you and I forgive you, not for what you did because I could never do that. But as a person, I forgive you." At the meeting he said, "Well I don't deserve it." I replied, "No you don't. But you have it."

Jackson talked about the fact that he had become a Catholic. He had been going through catechism and classes to become Catholic. He learned that forgiveness was something that not everybody could give. I felt his becoming Catholic as another slap in my face. Now he's not only taken my daughter but now he's taking my God. I was totally offended. But then my whole demeanor changed. I felt this warmth and peace come over me. I started breathing and my brain came back. I was able to think clearly for the first time in 12 years. When I say it was a transformation I meant that literally. I came back to life. I had been walking around dead for 12 years. I came back to life right there on death row, absolutely back to life. I started to feel more at peace, which I hadn't felt in a long time. I felt more relaxed. I could breathe. I could think.

In the meeting, we just talked back and forth. He talked a little bit about his drug history and the changes he was trying to make while he was in prison. We also talked about some of the things he did during his sentence and how I fought him all the way. For example, he went to the state Supreme Court and tried to get a new trial because he was an abused child. He tried to be an organ donor from death row. He actually was working with Jack Kevorkian trying to get an organ bank from death row inmates all over the country. In my state it's a problem because of the effect of the lethal injection on an inmate's organs. So if they were to be executed they would have to have their organs removed while they are still alive. That means that a doctor would have to agree to be the executioner. Jackson explained that from his perspective, he wanted to donate his organs in honor of his victims. He wanted to take out some of the darkness that he put into the world and put a little brightness back into life. I told him, "I'm going to have to think about that. I don't think it's going to be allowed but if it is, I'd rather you be discreet because I still have two other children that I have to protect." I told him however that if it happened, I wouldn't fight him anymore. Thank goodness, it never went through.

Jackson also told me that he was an abused child but I told him, "I don't know anybody that's ever had a perfect childhood." I myself was raised in a totally dysfunctional home but none of my siblings ever killed anyone. So I said to Jackson, "I can't accept that as a reason you murdered my daughter. I'm sorry, but it's just not a good reason." I just couldn't allow him to use that as an excuse for taking the lives of people he didn't even know. Throughout the meeting, Jackson let me say whatever I wanted to say and I did the same. It was the first time in 12 years that he didn't have any control over my life. I had control of the meeting and I wasn't going to let him take it back. So the meeting for me was life giving. I took my power back. I got to tell Jackson what he had done to my family. I told him that my children had gone through hell. I told him that one man, one act, had affected five families on a single night. I said, "You have no idea what you've done and how it will never go away." He answered saying, "No, ma'am, I don't know." I told him, "It is astronomical the number of people whose lives you've affected." I could express to him the powerlessness, the hopelessness, and the helplessness about Mabel's murder and everything I had to deal with afterwards. For example, at the trial I was not allowed to have any part of anything. I was dependent on a whole room of strangers and they had my life in their hands and I couldn't say anything about it.

We also talked about the death penalty and his execution. Jackson agreed with me that his being executed was morally and ethically correct. He asked if I would be there and I said that I would. He was just very genuine. At one point we talked about his mother and he started to cry. I said, "Jackson, I'm really sorry that your mother hasn't come or called you. I can't imagine that my kids would do that or that I wouldn't be there whether I agreed with my child or not." Jackson started to cry and said to the facilitator, "Here she is, a person who should hate me and she's giving me more love than my mother ever showed me." That touched me.

When I walked out of there, it was like somebody had just lifted a thousand pounds off of my body. I walked out of there a new person. I found myself accepting him as a human being, which I never thought I would be able to do. That was a pretty big transformation right there in that death row chamber. It was horrible but it was life giving at the same time.

Two weeks later, me and my family attended the execution. Remy was with us. Jackson told everyone he was sorry. He told me that he loved me and thanked me for the last two weeks of his life. He had no family. His mother lived out of state and never came to see him even once. He talked with her a few days before he was executed but that was it.

After the execution I met with Jackson's foster mother. She had him from the time he was 14. She had asked to meet with me. I found out he had two daughters. His ex-wife would have nothing to do with him. He was extremely abusive and she was trying to keep the children from him. The foster mother was the only one who had tried to help him, hoping to change his life. She told me some of his history. She said that when Jackson first came to her home he would refuse to take a shower. He wouldn't take his clothes off. The other boys in the home would get him and scrub him down but he would fight the whole way. Then his foster mother found out that his mother had sexually abused him since he was eight years old. It must have been in the shower a lot. The foster mother would tell Jackson, "You go into the shower because you cannot be going without a shower for days. You go inside and lock the door and I will put a chair right here in front of the door and sit here until you are through. I will make sure nobody comes into the bathroom."

When his foster mother heard about the murders on the news, she was just devastated. She felt Jackson had a good heart but never had a chance. Learning his background was a different story for me. I was thankful the execution was over but my heart broke for her because she had seen something in him no one else ever had. It didn't change the fact that he had murdered my daughter and her roommate and almost murdered a third person. It was just sad and so tragic.

For me, forgiveness is between you and God, not you and the other person. I had to forgive Jackson because I wanted to live. I wanted to be able to love my children and grandchildren without any restrictions and ill feelings. It's a very private personal issue. Forgiveness goes against everything in human nature. It's a long hard process because you have to search your heart and soul to be able to give true forgiveness. I learned through this process to forgive other people but also to forgive myself. I felt God nearly beat me to death with forgiveness until I finally reached the point that I knew what he was talking about. What is most important is that my completion of the forgiveness happened on death row when I saw Jackson's eyes and his remorse and when I saw he was a human being and not a monster. The pain never goes away. It's just not as severe. It's an accepted part of my life but the dialogue gave me back my power. Forgiving Jackson took away the control he had over my life and gave it back to me. From there, I could take my life back because I was in control. I thank God every day for the meeting because my other children wouldn't even have a life today if I hadn't had that meeting.

Analysis: Crime and its aftermath

Jackson violently intruded into the home and encroached on the presumed safety of Mabel and her boyfriend who were celebrating a marker birthday into her adulthood. He similarly broke into Portia's world changing everything about her life forever. His extreme dangerousness and rage were indisputable and marked by the number of times he stabbed each of the girls and Remy. His deviousness was evident as indicated by his voyeuristic stalking, efforts to run away, lying to a friend so he could clean up after the crime, and disposing of the evidence out of town.

Portia directed all her energy to keeping a close and almost obsessive watch over Jackson to be sure he didn't slip through the cracks. Being a serial rapist, he should never have been released and certainly not as an early release parolee. Portia fought for a strong defense so that the outcome of the trial could not be undone by an appeal challenging the adequacy of Jackson's representation. She stalked him at the trial, making sure he had to see her whenever he turned around in the courtroom trying to engage the sister of Mabel's roommate. Portia kept herself available so that she could be present for any legal procedure. She was possessed and singularly responsible for tracking Jackson and tracking the system to be sure he did not get away.

Portia tried to quickly master a legal netherworld about which she knew nothing while feeling brain dead. Because of her numbness and fixation on Jackson, the rest of her life receded into the background. In that process, she emotionally abandoned her other two children and did little to take care of herself. Indeed, she felt like she became a different person because Mabel's murder changed the way she thought, did things, and treated others—"It changes the way you think about people. You're more cautious and suspicious. It's just there from now on." Portia's big concern was that she would not wind up with the anger and hatred that had consumed her relatives after their son was murdered by his wife on Christmas in his own home—"Some people never get past their anger, the hatred, or the question of why." Indeed, she had watched as their unrelenting anger destroyed their bodies and ultimately took their lives.

However, in the midst of her grief and numbness, Jackson remained a focal point. She tracked him, trying to see him first when he was in jail and later when he went to prison but to no avail—"I don't know what I was going to talk to him about but I just had that drive." Portia, however, was haunted by the blank look in his eyes and wanted to talk to him to see what he was like, whether as a monster or otherwise. It was as if part of her mission was to have an encounter with him. The seeming intent of such a meeting was also that he'd have to see her and in so doing be held accountable for what he did by the mother of the woman he murdered.

It was a long time, however, before Portia gained insight into her drive and her unfinished business with Jackson. The unfinished business had to do with forgiveness. Specially, being Catholic, she was supposed to forgive others in order to be forgiven by God. Portia was bothered, however, because she felt she had zero motivation or even ability to forgive Jackson until God directed her to forgive his being or soul, not what he did in killing her daughter. Although she perceived that her conversation with God clarified what God expected her to do, it left her in a quandary about how to separate the person from the act. After all, how she saw and felt about Jackson was directly related to what he had done. So she continued to fight because she still had no will to forgive.

In the aftermath of the crime, therefore, Portia fixated on Jackson as if with purpose but actually had no direction for the negative energy that kept spinning around without an outlet. She felt driven to see Jackson but didn't know why and couldn't gain entry. She was plagued by her God-given need to forgive but had no personal desire to do so. This state of affairs reinforced her sense of powerlessness and helplessness to be able to impact the circumstances that had permanently changed her world.

Preparation

The call from the facilitator inviting Portia to be the first person to do a VOD meeting with a death row offender was, for her, overdue. She had been waiting and preparing for 12 years. There were some letters exchanged plus an apology from Jackson prior to meeting him but it had little impact because of Portia's single-minded agenda. She simply wanted to encounter him so she could see who he was, express her forgiveness, clarify that she was not forgiving what he did and quickly leave. She had no need for answers or information.

In terms of preparation, the facilitator had worked with her on recognizing and accepting her own human failings as part of establishing common ground between Portia and Jackson in their upcoming meeting. Events prior to their meeting, such as Jackson's claiming her religion as his own or his attempt to donate his organs, were aggravating to Portia. They reinforced her view of Jackson as manipulative, hell bent on delaying his deserved execution as well as the necessity of her maintaining a close and vigilant watch over every move he made. Portia's openness to the meeting, therefore, was grounded in what she needed to do to complete her journey but she otherwise had little time for Jackson. Her struggle with the dissonance of viewing Jackson as a monster and inhuman and seeing him as human paralleled the tension between her not wanting to forgive and forgiving. Although none of the dissonance was resolved until the dialogue, her decision to move forward with the meeting was an important step in shifting her internal stalemate.

Dialogue

Portia and Jackson met on death row in a small confined space two weeks before his execution. They were separated by a glass partition and could only talk together using a phone. Indeed, the physical distance between them was slight. As such, Portia could readily see Jackson's face. Portia sat down feeling uneasy and nervous. She was not prepared for the genuineness and impact of Jackson's remorse and the change in his appearance since the trial. The eyes that had been so vacant before were now full of life and expressive. She felt a deep shift inside her as he moved in status from monster to human being. Even without her directly sharing the pain differential, his response and openness to her were evidence that he had taken the pain for what he had done into himself. This obvious transfer and spontaneous combustion of positive energies quickly established a stronger conduit between them than Portia had ever imagined and created an atmosphere of safety and openness for her as well.

Portia shared the forgiveness she had practiced and planned to give but the dialogue continued for over five hours. Each shared important parts of their journey and life story with the other but with conversation and commentary. Each of them let the other have the space to express and emote without trying to tightly control the dialogue. The dialogue, therefore, had a natural quality that took on the aura of getting to know one another. For example, they discussed Jackson becoming a Catholic, the changes he had made while in prison, the efforts Portia had made to block his attempts to delay his execution, his current motivation to become an organ donor and her concern for the upcoming publicity about his efforts and its impact on her other children. She told him a lot about how his killing Mabel had shattered her world, how disenfranchised she felt by the criminal justice system, and what he had done to her son and daughter.

The reciprocity between Portia and Jackson had powerful energy. Portia's concentration on Jackson over the years was as if he had absorbed part of Mabel and the last part of her and her existence resided inside the man who had killed her. Mabel's life, as such, was continued through Jackson, which created a distorted dependency for Portia in terms of what he held and what she needed for her freedom and completion. Consequently, although Portia needed to give him her pain, which rightfully belonged to him, he needed to give Portia the power, which he was still holding from the murder.

This transfer was accomplished in several ways. Specifically, as Portia shared and transferred her pain to Jackson, she did it in a way that simultaneously took back control by holding him accountable to her for what he had taken from her, and his many questionable decisions. Jackson responded with heartfelt sorrow as if Portia was the rightful judge of his actions and, as such, transferred his power over to her. For example, Jackson acknowledged Portia's indictment that he would never know what he really did saying, "No ma'am. I don't know." Portia's tone in holding Jackson accountable was instructional and declarative of a more honest reality. For example, she could both refuse to allow him to use his abusive childhood as an excuse, but could also tend the pain of his mother's cut-off. Within her show of accountability, Jackson felt Portia's love along with her refusal to cut him any slack. As such, the commentary they gave to each other on various issues served to reshape their current realities. Portia felt visible and acknowledged, which shifted her feelings of powerlessness. Jackson felt parented and accompanied, which likely shifted his sense of aloneness and the terror associated with his pending execution. This manifestation of their reciprocal influence on each other helped alter the nature of the energy between them, changing it step by step into a positive flow. Indeed, Jackson asked Portia to attend the execution and told her in the death chamber that the last two weeks of his life had been positive and that he loved her. For Portia, she rested within the paradox of being close and disclosing with the man who murdered her daughter while experiencing, for the first time, that he was not controlling her life.

Paula left the VOD meeting a new person. During their time together, Portia felt a significant shift in energy as she moved from apprehensive to relaxed and from numb to feeling her brain start to work again. She felt the newness of actually breathing fully and without impediment and had a deep awareness of having dropped the burden and sense of responsibility she'd carried since Mabel was murdered. "It was like somebody had just lifted a thousand pounds off my body." Indeed, her intense focus on Jackson over the years had been infused with negative energy, which bound her to him and reinforced her sense of powerlessness. As the negativity was transformed into something more positive, she experienced the release.

The irony of coming back to life while on death row was striking. She felt a similar paradox in the death chamber. Specifically, in her comments about the execution, Portia recognized how the pain she had carried was tied to Jackson's criminal status as a kind of negative energy identification. She said, "There was a pretty big transformation right there in that death row chamber. I felt that I had slept with him on death row for 12 years and I was ready to get out of there. It was horrible but it was life-giving at the same time." Perhaps the greatest paradox was that within the abnormality and horror of a state mandated death, the events, conversation, and growth within and between Portia and Jackson felt so natural.

Portia's reinstatement of Jackson was demonstrated by her acceptance of him as a human being rather than a monster. Indeed, it was through her acceptance that she manifested her forgiveness of him as a person. Her meeting with his foster mother post his death was a further expression of her acceptance. She was able to hear differently and with compassion now about his past, his victimization at the hands of his mother, and his response to the trauma. She could both feel for him and his foster mother and hold the emotional reality of his having murdered her daughter. Portia's journey, including her meeting with Jackson, stretched her way beyond what she had known prior to Mabel's death. Being able to contain and live within seeming opposites gave her a purview on life that allowed her to encompass more and more and to grow in her comprehensiveness as a human being. She could encourage Jackson's defense attorneys in addition to the prosecutor to excel. She could work toward forgiveness while fighting it. She could see Jackson as a manipulator and decide not to fight him over the organ donation. She could parent Jackson, cry with him about his mother, and accompany him at his execution while also believing that taking his life was a necessary penance for the life he took. Finally, she could hold all those worlds while moving into a space where she felt free and unencumbered in her living.

The dissonance between Portia's religion and its mandate to forgive and her resistance to that mandate had been partially resolved prior to the meeting through her conversation with God. Specifically, she had perceived what God had said as a directive to distinguish between Jackson's behavior and Jackson as a human being. Portia determined that she had to remove the association between Mabel and Jackson in order to accomplish God's bidding. Portia felt she had accomplished the separation and wanted to meet with Jackson, in part, to convey her forgiveness, thereby completing the task. Although Portia had come to terms with forgiving Jackson, her effort remained at a decisional level and arguably more centered in her relationship with God than with Jackson.

Jackson's remorse and acceptance of responsibility, however, revised and deepened her forgiveness by moving it into a relational and emotional realm. Moreover, God's instruction to forgive Jackson as a person emerged through the dialogue as Portia accepted Jackson for who he was and who he was becoming. This shift that was rooted in her ability to fully accept Jackson happened as a result of the quality of the dyadic flow between them. The movement from decisional to emotional removed the remaining dissonance and allowed Portia to achieve congruence both with her religion and within herself. Portia experienced this movement as God influenced. Indeed, it is through the dialogue that Portia also repaired her relationship with God specific to her struggle with forgiveness. As such, she finished the dialogue and execution with a sense of completion and wholeness.

LIZETTE'S STORY AND ANALYSIS

Karmen offered assistance to two young men one night at a gas station. Unbeknownst to her, Gamal and Antonio had stolen a car and were on the run. They intentionally misled her with the purpose of raping her, and afraid of being identified, shot and killed her. Lizette, Karmen's mother, gave Gamal and Antonio little emotional energy, focusing on her granddaughter and going back to school. Lizette felt she had done a lot of healing, especially after working in the prison system, but researching VOD as part of her dissertation showed her more healing was available. She was primed for it. Lizette and Karmen's now adult daughter met only with Gamal; Antonio was not appropriate for the program. Lizette sensed Gamal's need to tell her everything, including the forgiveness her daughter had given him moments before her death. Lizette's forgiveness came in parts, before they met with the release of negative energy, implicitly through physical touch during the dialogue, and then explicitly in letter form, cementing her hopes that Gamal would forgive himself one day.

My daughter Karmen stopped for gas on her way home from visiting a friend. She befriended two 15-year-old boys, Gamal and Antonio, who had filled their car with gas instead of diesel fuel and it wouldn't start. Karmen didn't know the car was stolen. In addition, one of the boys gave her a sob story that his father had kicked him out and he had nowhere to go. When she offered to give them a ride, they intentionally misdirected her down a lonely abandoned road and sexually assaulted her. At first, they figured they needed time to get away, so they shot her in the leg. When they realized she could identify them, they killed her.

She went missing for five days. At the time, Karmen was pregnant with her second child so we concluded that she had left town to think through her decisions. My husband and I were taking care of her daughter, Amanda. Although we justified her behavior, my husband and I both walked around the house with a sense of dread. We identified our jitters as anger for her irresponsibility and believed what was the least painful. I know now that we never really believed she left town to reflect on her life. On the first night I had said to my husband, "My head keeps thinking how mad I am with her, how angry I am." He replied, "My gut is scared to death." I then fessed up, stating, "I feel exactly the same way." My body was on alert for those five days. I couldn't eat and had trouble sleeping. I kept my granddaughter and myself as busy as I could. I process stress by talking so I stayed around people as much as I could as well.

We knew nothing until the police came to our home after they found Karmen and had caught the boys. I was out of the house with Amanda when they arrived. On my way home I remember seeing a sign that said, "Those who love the Lord never see each other for the last time." For some reason, I just knew I needed to hold that in my heart. As I drove in our driveway I saw all the cars. No one needed to tell me what they meant. I didn't want my husband to know I was home because he'd come outside to give me the dreadful news and I just didn't want to hear it in front of anybody else.

I remember just feeling hollow, having a dry mouth and eating through two to three sacks of Halls for weeks. In terms of the boys, they had long juvenile records. I figured they were thoroughly bad guys, really bad. Frankly I didn't give them a lot of my time. I had my granddaughter to raise now and was working to gain custody after her paternal grandparents refused to send her back from a Christmas visit. I felt in limbo for a long time—in limbo with the civil court system because of Amanda as well as the criminal justice system. Specifically, the boys hadn't been sentenced, they hadn't come to trial and we didn't know if we had custody. It was an awful way to feel. All I could do during the time was vegetate. I sat in front of a space heater in my den just so cold that I wished I could crawl into it.

I tried various things to cope. I attended a victims' group for about a year and tried to match my anger with theirs. Folks would say to me, "Boy, it's a shame those little bastards can't get the death penalty, that they are too young." When I found myself thinking the same thing, I realized I didn't fit in very well. The members were keeping me in a state of anger. Recognizing that I was a square peg in a round hole, I decided to quit.

I figured the one thing I could have some control over was school so I decided to go back and finish my college degree. That was something I could do for me. I decided that I wanted to be a grief counselor and an educator of deaf students. Because I had read voraciously about grief and loss, going back to school just seemed the right thing for me to do. I got my bachelors and my masters and began teaching in a community college. I wasn't thinking about Gamal and Antonio at all. One day someone asked me their names and I got them mixed up. I couldn't remember which one's last name was which. I thought, "Oh how horrible. I can't even remember their names." But that's how much emotional energy I gave them.

Following Karmen's murder, our family was rebuilding their lives. With school and teaching, I was happy, healthy, and fulfilled. The only difficulty in my life was that I had that hole there that was never going to be filled in. One day, I asked my students what they thought should happen to a mother who had recently killed her children. It was lethal, all the ugly awful things they were going to do to punish her for what she had done. That little conversation absolutely crystallized my thinking. I remembered the victim support group I had attended years earlier where the response of the members was to repay violence with more violence. It was like they wanted everyone to be on the same level but that level was low and amounted to "get mad and get even." I began looking for something that was non-violent.

A year later I discovered restorative justice by accident. I had gone to a Presbyterian meeting and found a pamphlet produced by the Presbyterian church titled *Restorative Justice: For Non-violence*. That title just grabbed me by the throat. I read it cover to cover and thought, "Oh, my goodness. This is what I've been looking for." At that time I was working on my doctorate, teaching and doing adjunct work at a university. I was also teaching in prison, which was more healing than anything I'd ever done. As I learned about restorative justice, I determined to focus on my dissertation research on the VOD program. I went through the VOD training to be a facilitator so I could see what was involved. I also interviewed victims and offenders who had done VOD meetings. That's what made me want to do my own. I actually felt that I had had enough of my own personal healing but when I realized that more could happen, it made me go from not needing to feeling that talking with either of the young men who killed Karmen would be the ultimate completion of my healing process.

I did preparation for about a year. Amanda, who was now 20 years old, decided to do the VOD meeting with me. The plan was to meet with Gamal because Antonio was not considered appropriate. We had a female facilitator assigned to us who checked in with us regularly. She had us do a lot of psychological inventories or questionnaires. The victim inventory was particularly helpful. It was ten pages long and we each had to answer very deep, soul-searching questions. We also had to answer the questions from the perspective of the offender, which was Gamal, as well. Doing these inventories was the first time I thought about Gamal as a human being. It was the first time I gave him that status in my mind and heart.

When I walked into the meeting, I actually wasn't that nervous. I had been in prisons many times to teach. I had been trained myself to be a VOD facilitator and I had interviewed VOD participants for my dissertation. So I felt really comfortable with the whole process. Our dialogue preparation and the meeting itself were being filmed for a documentary so I had a little nervousness about the taping but the crew had already been filming the preparation so they weren't strangers. If anything, we were excited to get started. Everyone in the room was keyed in on it and anxious in a good way, exhilarated, and incredibly supportive. It was like we had a cheering section with us and it felt wonderful.

At the meeting, Gamal was so remorseful and started crying from the very beginning. He never cried when he talked about his own upbringing and his abuse at the hands of others but he sure cried when he talked about what he had done. It was just more than he could bear. The new piece that came out of the dialogue for me was Gamal's sharing the information about Karmen's last words. She knew she was about to be killed and was pleading with the boys to spare her life. The last thing she said to them was, "I forgive you and God will too." The last moments of her life were the hardest for me to think about. It was a place I never went. Learning what happened at the end was amazing and incredibly helpful. Interestingly, I never actually asked Gamal about Karmen's last moments. I had asked him why he had committed a violent crime when he'd never been violent before except to himself. He misunderstood the question but once he started going down the road and talking about Karmen, I found it hard to stop him. I think part of me realized he needed to say it. Once we learned about Karmen's last words, it took some pressure off of me. Not only did I feel better but I think it relaxed him once he saw the shift in me.

I, of course, wanted to know about Gamal and his background. He talked about it in a matter-of-fact way. He also talked about the family of another inmate that had "adopted" him as one of them. We, of course, talked about our own family and ourselves and the impact the murder had had on all of us. It was painful for him to have to hear about all the damage and ripple effects of what he had done. We showed him pictures of the family and you could see the pain. It was hard for me to see his response because it felt a little like the football penalty where they all pile on top of a player.

Gamal was very careful. I think he had done a lot of reflection over the years about what he had done and how he felt about it. He tried very, very hard not to revictimize us with how he said things, how he framed them, how he couched them, and the language he used. A member of the film crew commented that Gamal and I were protective of one another. I knew exactly what he meant. Indeed, I've seen that protectiveness many times with offenders I've worked with in prison. That's one of the overarching reasons why I can see them as human beings and not monsters or judge them for just that one thing they did.

We never talked about forgiveness. I think it was clear to Gamal that I forgave him by the fact that I approached him for a hug. I reached out to him with my hands but I never used the language. When I got home, I wrote him a letter and said it to him in words. One definition of forgiveness is letting go of any negative emotional power that something holds over you. I had done that long, long, long ago. But when I did the preparation I personalized it for the first time. I mean, I obviously had let it go if I couldn't even remember the names of the killers. That astonished me. So in my letter I said, "It's probably obvious to you that I forgave you but I just want you to know, for sure, and I hope that some day you can forgive yourself." I always wondered about Gamal, however, and his pain and if there was support for him in the prison.

Gamal and I wrote four to five letters back and forth after the meeting. When he made parole, he sent me a long letter on a card. He had written lines on this card so that he could write straight. It was the tiniest little writing you ever saw in your life and I struggled to read it. He wrote *all* over the card. He also said, "I hope I don't offend you or hurt you by saying this but I would love if we could go and talk to offenders together, people on probation and especially juveniles." I would love to do that with him but it's cumbersome. I saw him again about a year ago after he was released. We talked quite a bit. I know that what he did still causes him pain. I don't know if he'll ever forgive himself. I think he tries to put it behind him but I don't know how much help and affirmation he gets. The facilitator kept in touch with him for a while but I think she too has lost touch with him.

Analysis: Crime story and its aftermath

The murder of Lizette's daughter, Karmen, catapulted Lizette into a flurry of activity. Caught initially between her anger at her daughter for her presumed irresponsibility and dread about the possible reasons for her disappearance, she burrowed into caring for her granddaughter, staying as busy as possible, and keeping as many people around her as she could. She also made the decision, early on, not to spend energy on the boys who had killed her. These early reactions defined how she would handle herself for many years. Specifically, she tried to fill the hole inside herself with distractions and distanced as much as she could by not giving the killers any of her emotional time. She felt successful because, over time, she couldn't remember their names or got them mixed up. Indeed, Lizette channeled her emotional energies into self-coping and caring activities for her family members.

Lizette's activism took center stage in her life. When she was threatened with the loss of custody of her granddaughter, she filed a civil law suit to gain it. She managed the slowness of the criminal justice system and existing in limbo by attending a homicide victims' support group. When she recognized the mismatch between herself and the group specific to cultivating anger toward the offenders, she left and decided that she could help herself through her grief and the aftermath of her daughter's murder by furthering her learning and returning to school. This turning outward was empowering because it gave her a stronger sense of control and a constructive way to deal with Karmen's murder.

Although Lizette, subsequent to the murder, was moving forward and feeling productive and fulfilled, there would be critical events that resonated internally as if she were also on a quieter journey. For example, in addition to her dissatisfaction with the support group, the conversation with her students about punishment for murder helped solidify her thinking on non-violence. Likewise, her discovery of restorative justice seemed to be an avenue to politically express her convictions. It was like having a trail that took her to new destinations, each of which further defined her next steps. The discussion with the students led to restorative justice, which led to her dissertation, which led to VOD training, which led to interviewing VOD participants, which ultimately led to her decision to do a meeting with Gamal. She made the decision early on not to let anger about the loss of her daughter build up inside her or determine her future. She saw the tie of anger to violence and refused to cultivate it in herself or to subscribe to the punitive agenda of the criminal justice system, which, from her perspective, repaid violence with more violence. She chose, therefore, a constructive rather than destructive outlet for her feelings and did not perpetuate the negativity of anger and resentment that many others have.

Preparation

Lizette's decision to do a VOD meeting with Gamal emerged from recognizing that her healing could go further. Because she had taken the VOD training and interviewed participants for her dissertation research, she now had knowledge about a possible avenue that was available to further complete her process. Moreover, she had already committed to working with victims and offenders of serious crime and to restorative justice as a non-violent response to violence. As such, openness to expanding her vision and comprehension was, by the time of preparation, an ongoing process. That openness conceptually included meeting with one's offender, but it was not personal and had not included Gamal whom she had intentionally detached from after Karmen's murder. Indeed, Lizette had positively engaged with offenders for years while keeping Gamal at a distance. The dissonance between her being open and closed became apparent in answering probing inventory questions from the perspective of Gamal. She realized she was feeling non-cognitive empathy for him for the first time—"I really thought about Gamal as a human being and gave him that status in my mind and heart."

For Lizette, her decision to meet with Gamal made good sense. Up to that point, she had used her energy to "do" things. She had attached it first to her processing her loss of Karmen and the amount of grief she felt and then directed it to her education and working in prisons, and ultimately to restorative justice. Once she had determined to do the VOD, she harnessed that energy and narrowed it to a focus on Gamal. However, she had little sense of needing much herself. Letters had been shared between herself, Gamal, and Amanda prior to their meeting and Lizette already knew that Gamal was remorseful. She felt, therefore, that the meeting would allow Gamal to express himself directly to her and Amanda, and that she could learn more about his personal history.

Dialogue

Given her familiarity with the VOD process, Lizette felt little anxiety about meeting with Gamal. She was already heavily involved with the filming which had begun much earlier and included scenes of preparing for the meeting. She, therefore, was comfortable, as well, with the filmmakers and actually saw them as key supporters who were accompanying her, Gamal, and Amanda through this unique experience. Instead of dread, she felt excited, in part by the magnitude of what they all were doing and the difference that the showing of film could make in the "free" world.

Gamal set the tone by crying from the moment he entered the meeting room and saw Lizette and Amanda. Because of the exchange of letters during the preparation process, the conduit between them had already been built. Moreover, both Lizette and Amanda had shared a lot about their pain in their letters. Consequently, Gamal's tears likely reflected, in person, the transferring of their pain into himself. Lizette immediately recognized and felt the enormity of his remorse but because she had already done a lot of healing over the years, her response to his heartfelt transfer of pain was not for her needs but rather concern for his wellbeing. Indeed, she responded to him in a motherly way, being careful not to give him more than he could handle. She noted that his tears were directed solely at what he had done to hurt her and her family, and felt how desperately he wanted to do something to help all of them. She felt his care, as well, in not wanting to cause any further harm and how sensitively he communicated with her and her granddaughter. "I know about me being protective of him, but I also realize that he was protective of me and us."

Lizette's core shift and transformation occurred as Gamal told the story of purposely misdirecting Karmen down a country road to rape and subsequently murder her. Just as Lizette had disengaged, over the years, from Gamal and Antonio, she had also sealed off thinking about Karmen's last minutes before she died. "That was just a place I never went." Indeed, the focus on this part of the murder story came from Gamal. Lizette let him continue because she felt he needed to talk about it. Karmen's words to the boys at the end of the story were pivotal for Lizette. Gamal's report took her right into the heart of the pain. Gamal's responsiveness and emotionality actually confronted Lizette with her own distancing that may have been natural given her time as a professional. In contrast, Gamal was experiencing and exploring for the first time. He could cry for Lizette's daughter and wasn't afraid to go into the pain, unabashedly transparent. Gamal's opening of this door, which was directly associated with forgiveness, helped open up something in Lizette that she had closed off and could now let herself have, given the new knowledge of Karmen's last words.

Lizette's personal encounter with that pain and with Gamal as the offender ironically served to reduce it. Gamal's account provided new truth and meaning-making, which helped relieve some of the pressure that Lizette didn't even know she had been carrying. Her relaxation had a resonance and reciprocal influence on Gamal who relaxed as well, moving both of them into a conversational territory where the back and forth energy flowed fluidly as they shared more fully about their lives. This critical event in the dialogue was an important dyadic moment that illustrates how what Gamal gave helped Lizette and her response, in turn, helped him. The truth-telling that occurred could only have happened through their dyadic interaction. Moreover, Lizette's use of the word "relaxation" in response to the impact of her response on Gamal is important evidence for the energy shift between them since it is an energy-dynamic term that means loose or loosen in Latin.

The palpable resonance of this story on both Gamal and Lizette increased the closeness between them. They exchanged information about their lives, the impact of Karmen's murder on Lizette and her loved ones, and things they had in common. What they learned about each other brought forth more pain in response to the empathy each felt for the other. Their responses to each other were caring and affirming of what they each had been through. At the end of the meeting, Lizette asked for a hug, which for her was both a reinstatement and a measure of forgiveness—"I think it was clear to him that I forgave him, by the fact that I approached him for a hug and that I reached out to him with my hands." Lizette was explicit about forgiveness in the letter she sent to Gamal after their meeting.

Clearly, Lizette's giving to Gamal helped her heal. Since Karmen's murder, giving, not getting, had been the source of wellbeing. She realized that no one could give Gamal what he needed but her. As such, her forgiveness mattered because she hoped that it would help him forgive himself. She was concerned about the amount and relentlessness of the suffering he endured. Lizette continued to follow Gamal when he was released. Even though he wanted them to talk about the crime together to juveniles, Lizette's primary interest remained focused on his emotional health and doing what she could to protect him from the severity of the rules from the criminal justice system that defined the conditions of his parole.

Lizette's meeting with Gamal was part of Lizette's larger vision about cultivating non-violence. Lizette's raising of Amanda was, in some ways, a replacement for her daughter. It kept her terribly busy for years. Lizette lived in the middle of the dissonance that included the violence around her from her crime, the criminal justice system's response and the crimes around her that stood in contrast to her deep commitment to non-violence. She had partly resolved the dissonance through restorative justice and her work in the prisons but she had not resolved it in her personal life. To do so, she had to go back into the pain of her daughter's murder, humanize Gamal, and allow the non-violent process to work on her through the blossoming of the dyadic connection between her and Gamal. The catalyst for her shift was her daughter's last words, which relieved her because, in her eyes, her daughter had accepted her fate and did not suffer. Her own forgiveness of Gamal had occurred years before their meeting. However, forgiveness took on new meaning, not only because of her daughter's final words but also because she realized that Gamal's suffering pre-empted her own and that of her daughter. She hoped that being explicit about her forgiveness might help Gamal to forgive himself, thereby reducing his pain.

THERESA'S STORY AND ANALYSIS

The morning Gerald was set to be sentenced to prison he raped and murdered Theresa's sister, Samantha. Theresa was determined to live her life, making healing a choice, which left her emotionally repressed. It wasn't until she was raising her own two daughters that she began to experience the injustice and rage associated with losing her sister. The content of Theresa's VOD with Gerald was extremely difficult, but Theresa was determined to feel everything. Her decision to forgive him was based more on a fear of regret than any mutual connection she felt. Gerald later sent Theresa a letter, reaffirming his remorse and waiving his trial, choosing to be committed to a sex offender treatment facility. The VOD was more a part of Theresa's journey towards healing than the culmination of it.

My sister Samantha was murdered by Gerald, a man who volunteered at a substance abuse treatment center where she worked. He had a history of sexual assault and killed her the morning before he was to have been sentenced and incarcerated yet again. It was his final act of revenge against the system. My sister and I were in college together. When she didn't show up for a night class, I went to her apartment and found her dead.

Gerald took a plea and I attended his sentencing hearing a month after her death. I'd never seen him before but he looked normal, chatting with his lawyer like he was at a business meeting. I looked at his hands, wondering how someone could kill someone else. I just couldn't comprehend it. But there were police all around and I realized that I could easily have a gun in my hand and shoot it at the back of his head and not feel any remorse. I'd never had that kind of feeling before. I remember thinking, "This is what vengeance feels like." Something about feeling that coldness was a significant moment for me. I vowed that I would not let my sister's murder make me a hard, cold, angry, bitter woman. I was only 20 years old and had my future in front of me but I realized that if I fed the anger, I could become that woman. I determined to fight my feelings of hatred. He was sentenced to 25 years but would be released in 16 years 8 months. I assumed that the memory of my sister's murder would have faded by then and I would have moved on.

Each of my family members, including my eight siblings, had their own process with the murder. For some of us, the outcome was for the better while for others it was worse. Each of us, however, became deeper people and are teachers or social workers, all in caring professions. My brother was the exception. He was close in age to my sister, became a chronic alcoholic, and unfortunately died of liver failure. Her death escalated his behavior and we couldn't really get him back.

After my sister died, I finished college. I figured that if I stayed in the game, didn't back off, isolate, and give up that I'd eventually heal. I wanted to get as far away from the crime as I possibly could, so completing school was part of my decision to move on and have hope. My sister had taken a course on death and dying the semester before she died. One of the assignments was to journal about what she would say to loved ones if she had a terminal illness. I memorized it because it was a message of hope—"I would like to tell everyone to live on and to learn to live fuller days, to have a positive attitude about my death and not to feel sorry for me. I'm at peace with God and I will continue to be happy and I want all of you to do the same." Had I not had her message to hang onto I would have felt sorry for myself and sorry for her and gone to a dark place that would have been hard to come out of. Her message gave me permission to live on.

I got married and we had two daughters. Having daughters who were sisters brought up a lot of the trauma, pain, and anger but I didn't understand what was happening or that I had stuffed my feelings because her murder was just too traumatic to feel. It seemed strange that I had only shed a few tears over it. I guess the anger and trauma seemed to have numbed me and was starting to have a hardening effect on me. But I felt a lot of anger that I had to raise daughters in a world where the sexual assault and murder of my sister could happen to girls. I began to realize that, regardless of my earlier commitment to reject anger, her death had made me bitter anyway.

At the ten-year anniversary of her murder, I determined that the health of my marriage and my daughters was at stake if I didn't look at some of this. I was feeling a generalized anger at men that was coming out on my husband who was otherwise kind and loving. One morning I got very, very angry at him. I went to our room, slammed the door, and threw a picture across the room. My little two-year-old daughter came walking in. It didn't hit her but she was really scared and started crying. My husband picked her up, looked at me and said, "I don't know what's going on here and why you are so angry but we need to get some help or I am going to need to take the girls and get some space from you." I was stunned. I had thought I could move on and not deal with it but here it was and it was hurting the people I love the most. At one point my husband said, "I know I'm not perfect but I don't think this has anything to do with me." I said back, "You've never had anyone brutally rape and murder someone you love and leave them there for you to find." That's when I finally realized the role her murder was playing in my life and that I needed help. That awareness was a really, really big relief because I knew all my feelings were just sitting in this big pressure cooker waiting to blow up and I had to deal with things before that happened.

I didn't know where to begin so I called the police and asked if I could look at my sister's folder. I'd never dug into the details of the crime before. The police connected me to a victim advocate named Loretta who herself was a homicide survivor. She gathered everything about my sister's case for my husband and me to see. We read statements, looked at crime scene pictures and all kinds of other stuff. The day was a good start for me. I remember saying, "I've turned a corner here and there's no going back to denial." As I faced the seriousness of what happened, I began to get curious about Gerald, the man who killed her, where he was right now, and if he had changed over the years. I realized he'd be coming out of prison soon and I wanted to know what he'd processed. When I mentioned my questions to Loretta, she said, "Well, that would be possible if you were interested in talking with him." I learned then that VOD was an option.

I was ready to do whatever was necessary to start healing. Over the years, I'd wake up in shock and start remembering things about the day I found her. But then those memories would disappear so I couldn't get them back. I'd convince myself that finding her wasn't so bad. She just looked like she was sleeping. Perhaps she hadn't suffered that much. Telling myself these things made my life livable but now it was time to face it all and not run away.

My daughters still talk about the season where I cried a lot. It was a time when everyone was getting me back. I framed a picture of Samantha and me and cried every time I looked at it. This happened for as long as it took because finally I was grieving her death, shedding tears over what happened to her, and the fact that she was gone. There were so many things I had to mourn—the fact that my sister was no longer a college student with me, that she wasn't able to graduate from college and be a teacher, that I wasn't going to experience nieces and nephews or a possible husband she might have had one day. Instead of just feeling anger about the injustice of her death, I could now feel deep sorrow. Although there was a ton of pain, it was a healing pain because I was releasing everything I had stuffed and buried. Moreover, each step I took made me want to take the next one because I started feeling more alive. With the pain came my desire to meet with him. Indeed, my reason for doing a VOD was that I wanted to feel something again.

I called Loretta and asked her to facilitate the meeting. She made contact with Paul who ran the local VOD program and together they met with Gerald to assess his eligibility for the meeting. They decided to proceed, which started the whole nine-month process. For me, it became the culmination of my forgiveness journey. Having processed through the anger and hate already, I now had to face actually talking to Gerald about the crime and asking what had happened. He had her last moments and I wanted to know what she had gone through. As part of my preparation, I continued to read about restorative justice and also about forgiveness. I kept thinking about the courtroom day and the Lord's prayer where it says, "forgive fellows who have sinned against you." Forgiveness felt wrong to me initially. Murder is too big to forgive and it hurt so many people besides me. But during this time, I also gained some clarity that simplified it. For example, I just had the desire to forgive Gerald for my own sake and because I've been forgiven for things I've done. I also felt that forgiveness would open up my whole world again to the people who matter and that I could care about others as well. So this meeting became a spiritual journey for me.

Coincidentally, the meeting was held on the same day I first met Loretta. She also had the same birthday as my sister and was motivated by her Christian faith as I was. We all drove to the prison and I felt very peaceful and thankful for the opportunity. Although my primary motive was my own emotional and spiritual healing, I knew he would be released soon and hoped this meeting would take him further down the road to some kind of peace. The meeting lasted from 9 until 3 in the afternoon. Although in court, I felt I could easily shoot him, I didn't feel anything overwhelming when he walked in and I had my first eye-to-eye contact with him. In the morning he told his story of killing my sister. I realized I would have more to grieve because now I'm hearing my sister's suffering. I again felt my commitment not to let this new information harden me. So while he talked, I just kept thinking that I was facing this information because I wanted to grieve it, forgive it, and heal. People who can suffer and cry have no idea what a gift that is. I'd lost that ability and now was getting it back.

Gerald was thorough and comfortable in telling me what happened to my sister. I learned later that his comfort was a reflection of his sexual offender treatment where the inmates have to tell what they did over and over again. It was hard, however, to hear about my sister's tears and her begging him to stop. Indeed, as he would tell me the details of what happened, I could talk to myself saying, "Okay, this is what happened" so as not to fall into my previous habits of filling in the gaps, denying things, inflating them, or minimizing them. By the time he was done, I felt all my questions had been answered. I'd been able to ask about his coming to my sister's apartment on campus. "Did she answer the door right away or did she ask who was there?" He said, "No, she asked who it was." So then I knew that she recognized who was at the door before she answered it but was obviously clueless about how dangerous Gerald was. She had fought him off, which contradicted the newspaper's account, but Gerald's version sounded more like my sister.

Because the morning was so hard and overwhelming, I was hesitant to go back and meet with him after lunch. But Loretta and Paul told me that the most healing part of a VOD for victims was telling the offender how they had been affected. So I stayed in and told my story, but I told it differently to him than I had anyone else because now I had the eyes and ears of the person responsible. Telling him how his actions impacted me was empowering. His listening, eye contact, and head nodding at the right times felt genuine. I began to see him less as an evil beast of a person and more of a human being who went in a horrible, bad direction. I also saw some humanity in him because he was willing to engage in this journey and have our lives intersect so I could come to some peace. Toward the end of our meeting, I shared Samantha's journal entry and one of her favorite Bible verses. I didn't know if the forgiveness words were going to come out of my mouth but there was a point that I just felt done. So I just stopped talking.

The facilitators asked if we had anything more to say. Gerald was nervous and fidgety. I could tell he had something on his mind. He looked at me and said, "I know this means really nothing in some ways but I want and need to say it. I am really, really sorry." His words just hung there. I was surprised and didn't know how to respond. I had read *What's So Amazing about Grace*, a book of short stories about people who had gone through tough forgiveness stuff and the mercy and grace of God. There was one story about a murder where a person had apologized and the other person regretted not saying, "I forgive you." When I read the story I thought, "If that comes my way, I would love to have it in my heart to be able to say, 'I forgive you.'" The ability to do that seemed really, really freeing, like it would be a key to get out of living with a lot of bitterness in my heart for a long, long time. I wanted to say it and I wanted it to be genuine but I didn't really know if it was going to come out of my mouth or not. I just looked at him and said, "I forgive you and I will need to continue to be on that journey probably the rest of my life." It was a good thing for me. I needed to say the words.

I had brought a medallion with me from a treatment center that had been named after my sister, as well as a little New Testament. I hoped it would bring Gerald peace as it had me. I also felt, as part of that peace that I wanted to touch and shake his hand, so I said, "Could I touch your hand and shake your hand?" He just right away said, "No." I replied, "That's okay." That is how our meeting ended. I did get a follow-up about why he wasn't able to let me touch his hand. He told the facilitator that he just felt really dirty.

I received a long letter from him a few years later. He had been rejected for mandatory release and was committed to Trunk Bridge for Sex Offenders. He explained that he gave up his right to a trial about being committed to this facility and instead admitted to everything. He is still there to this day. In the letter, he wrote, "I'm sorry" for 26 different things that came up during our meeting. He also said, "These are things I couldn't express in the meeting but I need to express now." He specifically apologized for every one of them.

Overall, our meeting was not between two people connecting. There were a couple of back and forth exchanges but I was scared and did not want him to feel any kind of bond with me. I knew he was a rapist and a murderer. My meeting was very victim centered and never about what he would get from it. The only back and forth dialogue happened in the last hour when I knew the meeting was coming to a close and we both had things that needed to be said.

The day was kind of surreal to me. In hindsight I would wonder if it really happened or was I making it up. It really did happen. I'm thankful for every bit of it and have no regrets. It had a big impact on both my husband and me. Some of it happened in the meeting and some of it happened before and after doing the VOD. I had more grieving to do after the meeting because of what it opened up. However, I'll never be able to go back and see Gerald as a ruthless animal. He'll always be human to me now. I know he grew up with years of abuse that my sister got caught in. The meeting also affected how I see my daughters. I wanted to go through the VOD so that they would grow up not to hate men and to have faith and hope. Both of them are lively and opinionated and at the same college together. That reality brings up a little jealousy and this longing to somehow get those years back with my sister that we could have lived together. Anger has never been a coping skill for me, however, since the meeting with Gerald. Instead, I have to acknowledge this sadness about my sister and me so it doesn't create its own little world. Indeed, those moments don't control me anymore as long as I'm just honest about them. I used to worry I'd never live a normal life again and that a normal life was important. Now I feel like I want to live engaged and I don't necessarily want just normal life.

Analysis: Crime and its aftermath

Theresa was a college freshman on the brink of her adulthood when her sister, Samantha, was killed. Her murder upended what had otherwise been a peaceful, fun, and productive time for her. Suddenly she came face to face with the horror of finding her sister's body, the evil intentions of a vengeful, serial predator, and the reality that she would have to chart her own path alone and without the security and close companionship of her older sister. Her experience in the courtroom with Gerald was a moment that defined her reaction to her sister's murder and her future identity. Specifically,

Theresa realized that she could easily shoot Gerald and feel no remorse but only hatred and coldness. Her self-identification with Gerald's vengefulness and what she could become frightened her. She determined never to allow the murder to turn her into a hardened, bitter, and angry woman.

Believing that she was honoring her sister's edict to move on, she intentionally put the murder and her feelings aside, finished college, and married five years later. Indeed, Theresa credited her sister with her decision to "live on and move on" and felt proud that she did not allow the murder to make her a victim who felt sorry for herself or take her to a dark place that would have been hard to break through. Instead, she accomplished her goal, which was to live a normal life as an antidote to becoming bitter. The irony is that she had to stuff her feelings and dissociate in order not to be consumed by hatred or controlled by anger. She had little awareness of the cauldron inside herself until the birth of her two daughters, whose existence as sisters was a stark reminder of her loss. In spite of her resolve, she began realizing that she felt little or nothing and was becoming hardened. She began having marital problems and felt a generalized anger toward men, which culminated in a rage attack. Her throwing of a picture scared her two-year-old daughter and propelled her husband into action. Her husband's limit-setting in response to her out-of-control behavior provoked her realization that her free-floating anger was about both the brutal rape and murder of her sister and visceral onslaught of having been the one to find her body.

With this initial release of stored energy and new awareness, Theresa faced a pivotal but dissonant moment. Her husband's threat to leave endangered the normalcy of the life she had built. Moreover, this goal of normalcy had tied her to her sister and gave her a sense of being worthwhile. Theresa realized that if she continued as she was, she would lose that normalcy. However, if she fully faced the impact of her sister's murder, she might also lose her normalcy. Either option was problematic. Her continuing to stuff and deny her feelings assured her bitterness while resurrecting the crime and the true loss of her sister had no known or guaranteed result.

The disparity between where she thought she had put the murder mentally and where it really was shifted her awareness. In spite of her reluctance and sense of foreboding, Theresa made the decision to open herself up to her grief. This was a healing shift point before the meeting that brought her to terms with her inner emotions. Specifically, this undertaking opened her to her emotional self, the reality of her sister's murder and loss, and her denial of the larger impact of the murder. In many ways, this opening was the life-changing event and core energy shift for Theresa.

Preparation

Theresa's decision to lift the emotional lid on her sister's murder brought forth the reality of Gerald who otherwise had been banished from her mind and even the idea of forgiveness—"The whole idea of forgiveness was on the scene pretty quickly with me… I knew this was going to have to be part of this journey but it was going to have to be an honest one." With Loretta as her guide, she began to feel again as she finally grieved the tragic loss of her sister. Theresa's decision to meet Gerald was a part of her healing plan. In referencing it, she said, "I wanted to feel something again… I remember thinking, 'Whatever I need to do to start healing from this, I want to do it.'" As she broke through her denial and minimization, she began learning and trusting that the pain that emerged actually was leading her to whatever next steps she needed to take on this journey and those steps led directly to Gerald. Upon hearing her questions for Gerald, Loretta introduced her to the possibility of a VOD meeting. Theresa started reading about restorative justice—"I was really excited to be exposed to all this literature…[It was like] when a student is ready, the teachers appear. I was hungry and eager to learn and heal and grow." Feeling spurred on by the process and the role that forgiveness could play in her life, she decided to go forward with meeting Gerald. For Theresa the VOD was part of an evolutionary process toward greater openness to life and something more than just a "normal" life.

There was some dissonance in her push to move forward. Although she had spent time reflecting on and contemplating forgiveness, it felt wrong to Theresa. Concomitantly, however, it was also becoming part of this life-giving process that began to take its own path and had its own energy. Similarly, as Theresa opened the door on her sister's murder, she realized that she knew nothing about Gerald so he was an unfinished part of the story. Her lack of knowledge was not about denial. Rather, she had to have dyadic engagement with him to complete her process. However, she did not feel open to seeing him personally.

Although the preparation took nine months, it fit hand in glove with her ongoing mourning for her sister and her sense of awakening through the pain to life. "Meeting with him was somewhat of a culmination of an emotional forgiveness journey rather than one that started it." Consequently, the preparation focused less on her feelings and more on her expectations and the kinds of questions she wanted to ask him. Samantha was clear that she had no interest in building a relationship with Gerald. Rather, this would be a one-time endeavor focused solely on her needs.

Dialogue

The meeting filled in a lot of details for Theresa. She learned about her sister's last moments. However, the giving of information did not grow out of the interaction between Theresa and Gerald. Rather he was dispassionate in reciting his story as she fought internally to absorb his brutality and her sister's struggle and suffering. In contrast, Theresa noted that she was sharing her story differently than usual because she was saying it directly to the person who was responsible for her pain. She watched his body language as he absorbed the pain differential and felt empowered by what she had done.

The conduit between them existed only for this telling of each person's story and conveying the pain. Indeed there was little responsiveness or energy flow between them except at moments along the way and toward the end when the flow accelerated because of limited time. Indeed, the VOD was not about connection and dyadic engagement but rather about managing the bond so that what happened between them did not raise expectations for additional or closer contact.

There is some evidence that Gerald transferred Theresa's pain to himself during the meeting. He listened, made eye contact, and nodded his head at critical points as he heard Theresa's story. She felt his responses were genuine and could feel her opinion of him change from evil beast to human being who went in a horribly bad direction. She also recognized his humanity by virtue of his willingness to meet and help her through embracing the VOD process. Moreover, as he recognized that this meeting would be his only time to directly apologize, he also said he was truly sorry, which contributed to a sense of completion for Theresa. The true transfer of pain, however, happened after the meeting and was reflected in his letter when he apologized specifically to Theresa for each thing he had done based on what she had enumerated in the meeting—"These were things I couldn't express in the meeting, but I needed to express now." Through this exercise and ritual, Gerald expressed some remorse and, in effect, held himself directly accountable to Theresa.

Theresa had been in a struggle with the concept of forgiveness since lifting the lid of her denial. She had convinced herself that she needed to give it in order to receive it from God. She also believed that giving it would further her path with her children as well as herself. The forgiveness she felt she could give, however, was decisional rather than emotional. She felt pressured in response to Gerald's apology and their limited time together to act on what she did not feel. She was caught in a double bind. If she said it, she might regret it and if she didn't say it, she might regret it. She pondered, as well, the consequences of forgiving or not forgiving him. Theresa's dilemma was also caused by the fact that true forgiveness is commonly seen as an intimate sharing which she did not feel. Indeed, she was resolute about keeping any emotional connection distant. Consequently, despite their physical presence to each other, she could not make the decision about forgiveness from within the relationship because she was not that close. Indeed, she had to lean on a homicide survivor's account in a book to motivate her still further. Because her choice, therefore, had to be decisional rather than dyadic, she could only use logic about possible outcomes, which generated more internal conflict.

Theresa resolved the multiple forms of dissonance by making forgiveness an ongoing process, which took away the expectation of finality. As such, she responded to the pull for forgiveness by giving it but claiming that it would be an ongoing journey for her.

Theresa did not expect a sense of completion from the meeting because she experienced it as just the next step on her course for healing. She had already transformed the pain prior to the meeting by putting her anger in a different place. However, she did find that the meeting changed the availability to her anger such that now she goes straight to the pain underneath rather than getting stuck in it. Moreover, because of putting pieces about the murder into place, her grieving the pain of her sister's loss and numerous other consequential losses became paramount over the pain from the crime.

Theresa was able to do everything she had planned for in the dialogue. She expressed forgiveness and gave Gerald the medallion and New Testament as symbolic mementoes from their meeting. She wanted to touch and shake his hand as well to convey a sense of peace between them. Gerald, however, refused because he did not feel acceptable in the aftermath of what he had done. Indeed, he refused to be morally reinstated. He not only turned down Theresa's request but also gave up his right to a trial thereby cementing his permanent incarceration in a facility for sex offenders. As such, Gerald declared, in effect, that he saw himself as unfit societally and undeserving of moral reinstatement. Although sensitive to his humanity, Theresa, too, saw him as having severe problems and likely being an ongoing danger to society.

Theresa did the major part of her healing and transformation prior to meeting with Gerald. Moreover, the dyadic relationship was minimal between them on both sides. Gerald was flat in his affect and not ready to receive a connection whereas Theresa was conflicted and not ready to give it. However, she needed the dyadic encounter to complete her journey. Indeed, she had pushed herself in her own healing as far as she could go alone but needed a connection with Gerald to complete the next step in her process.

Her getting the full story of the murder from the murderer himself and not removing herself emotionally from the horror solidified her strength and commitment to face life differently from that point on.

KEISHA'S STORY AND ANALYSIS

Her entire life Keisha was told lies about the identity of her biological father. Almost by accident, she learned of his whereabouts and his death after he and two others were killed by a drunk. For four years she researched his life, craving the knowledge she didn't know was missing. Keisha's emotions were full of contradictions: anger at the drunk driver, Adam, but also towards her father for not being a part of her life. Keisha was struck by the fact that no one had represented her father during the trial and she saw VOD as a way to honor his life. Keisha's mother who was diagnosed with terminal cancer accelerated preparation. Keisha was able to find empathy in similarities between herself and Adam and hold Adam accountable for his involvement in denying her a relationship with her father. Keisha felt that God had the ability and the capacity to forgive Adam and they've continued the relationship, sharing with others the deep connection and healing they experienced together.

As a private detective, my job is to solve crimes through locating missing data. I never expected it to be about my own life. Specifically, I discovered several years ago that I had a half sister who had recently died in a car accident. Coincidentally, I also found a picture of my biological father's headstone along with an appellate court's decision that a drunk driver named Adam had killed him and two other people while they were biking. This information turned my world upside down. A man I thought to be my actual father had raised me, but, at age 16, my mother told me that she had had an affair and that my biological father had died in Vietnam. Actually it turned out that my stepfather was my biological father's superior officer in the military. He told my mother a lie, which was that my biological father had been sent to Vietnam and was killed in the war. He and my mother agreed not to tell me anything about this man. My mother and stepfather divorced, however, when I was five and my mother, believing my stepfather's lie, told me about my real father and his alleged dying in Vietnam when I got older. My mother knew nothing about my biological father's background or family. She had no pictures of him and didn't even know his real name. My mother was truly shocked when I found him.

I spent the last four years researching his life. I found that I had family on the East Coast and Illinois, that I look like my real father, and that he had been a military police officer and a homicide investigator like me, except that I work for the defense. I also learned that our personalities are similar and that my father grew up with a stepdad under comparable circumstances to my own. I wanted to know who this man was, why he was a biker, and the mitigating circumstances that led him to be riding his motorcycle in Webster Falls and being killed by a drunk driver.

The most difficult part for me was discovering that my real father was alive the whole time I was growing up and that he actually had lived only two blocks away from me. My first reaction was anger that he was dead and that I had been denied the opportunity to confront him about his leaving my mother and me. I got into the library archives and read all the newspaper articles about the accident, trying to understand what had happened. I also ordered all the court records, which my mother read with me because she too needed to have answers and closure. I learned that Adam had had a .22 blood alcohol level; that no one was present at his trial to stand up for my father or to say that my father's life mattered or had made any difference. None of the bikers he'd known came to court because bikers don't do that. It hurt deeply, therefore, that he'd died and nobody said, "This person's life was important."

I further learned that Adam during the legal process had written letter after letter to the judge taking no responsibility and expressing no remorse. I started writing him a letter but I wrote and rewrote it over and over again because I could not express what I wanted to say. I was angry at him but I also had empathy and understanding because of my own circumstances. I, too, had been an alcoholic and quit drinking only after I discovered that Adam had killed my father. I identified with him because I too had drunk and drove but hadn't gotten caught. I also understood, as a private investigator, that we tell our clients to keep their mouths shut in court, fight like hell, and appeal anything you can to avoid 35 years in prison. So I felt conflicted in my feelings and reactions. Because I'd never been given a chance to speak at his trial, this letter was my way of writing a victim impact statement. At the same time, I didn't know if Adam's lack of remorse was actually his fighting for his own life and reducing the prison time he'd been sentenced to serve.

While struggling with the letter, I started poking around on the Department of Corrections' website. I inadvertently found the VOD program and contacted the staff for information because I wanted to face this man. I had no idea what I would say but I felt internally that I had to meet with him to have closure. I also realized that I needed to tell him who my father was, that his life mattered to me, probably more than anyone else.

I prepared for approximately six months working with two chaplains who were to facilitate the meeting. During this time, my mother was diagnosed, unfortunately, with terminal cancer. I, therefore, almost backed out but I knew I had to meet with Adam and that my mother too needed closure before she died. The chaplains serving as facilitators sped up the process. I went through every emotion with them. They were consistent and focused, and I trusted them implicitly. My big concern was whether Adam was truly remorseful. What I had read told me nothing. I needed to see his eyes, hear the tone of his voice, see his facial expressions, and engage in an intimate face-to-face conversation to truly know if he was remorseful or not, which would determine the direction of what I was going to say to him. Right before doing the meeting, my mother and I drove to the scene of the accident at Webster Falls and put three crosses on the side of the road. In effect, we buried my father.

The meeting lasted two hours and 15 minutes. It was an intense time walking into the prison and down a very long corridor to the meeting room. However, I felt like I was ten feet tall. My chin was up, my shoulders back, and I was *so* proud of myself. The setting was very private, such that other inmates were not watching either of us. When Adam came into the room, the very, very first thing I noticed were his eyes. He had the softest, most peaceful and loving eyes and I knew right then and there that he was a Christian. He looked nothing like his prison photo. Rather he was fit, strong, and very muscular. He was the same age my father would have been if he were still alive. I introduced myself and shook his hand but he would not look at me. He had enormous shame, guilt, and remorse, which I could see immediately.

I'd asked prior to the meeting that he begin the dialogue. He'd written a one-page letter that he had folded, creased, and re-creased over and over again. That showed me his nervousness and fear. All of his body language and tone of voice showed true remorse. I now could see the direction of the meeting. After he finished, I told him that I was a Christian and a recovering alcoholic. I could see the relief on his face. I shared further that I also drove drunk in the past and would not harm him. However, I wanted to share my father's story and how much he mattered to others and me. I told him about my father, the similarities between us, the things that hurt my father in his life, and his accomplishments. I also shared my history that included the abuse I endured because I wasn't my stepfather's real child, the lies I'd been told, and how I learned about and searched for my father. I made clear that Adam was responsible for my father not being in my life and for taking away the opportunity to have found him and confronted him or possibly to have had a restored relationship with him.

Adam told me that he was also a Christian and active in Alcoholics Anonymous. He wrote letters to different AA groups and had used his experience with my father to give testimony to help others about drinking and driving. He took full responsibility for not listening to the courts, his family, or friends. He also told me that his son who lived near Webster Falls had seen the three crosses on the side of the road and asked if I had placed them there. I shared that I had buried my father that day.

I told Adam all about my father because nobody did in court. I stood up for him. Then, I turned the topic to Adam and me and how his killing my father had affected me. I enumerated all the things he took from me, including the opportunity to ask my father all the questions of "why." You know, "Why did you do this?" "Did you ever look for me?" "Did you ever actually find me?" "Or were you ever scared to approach me because you abandoned me years earlier?" I named every question I had for my father and after each one I said, "You took that from me. You robbed me of that opportunity and that chance."

I also talked about forgiveness. I told him that I could not forgive him for killing three people because that harm was only between him and God. However, I could forgive him for never being able to get answers to questions I had of my father. I can't describe how I could say it with such certainty but I told him I forgave him and that I could live with not having those answers. I also asked for the letter he read at the start of the meeting. He bowed his head and started to cry as if he was unworthy of my forgiveness. I remember saying, "God's forgiven me for so many things that I have done and for the harms I've caused other people and I can forgive you." I was trying to tell him that he could let the burden go and that the slate was clean for me and for him. As I reached across the table for the letter, I laid my hands in an embrace on top of his hands and he started to pray. For the first time in my life, someone prayed for me. He prayed for my healing. He prayed for my heart. He prayed for my protection. He prayed for my safety. He prayed for my comfort. Never once did he pray for himself. That's how we ended the meeting.

It was magical. I have never been in a situation where I had to earnestly forgive someone and have it make such a powerful impact on my life. It wasn't something I was prepared to do. It just happened. His praying was so genuine, honest, and healing. I felt I had done what I set out to do. This long, long journey that started before I was 16 all came to an end right then and there. I asked if I could write him a letter because I felt our connection wasn't over. He responded that he would write me back. We write each other once or twice a month. For Celebrate Recovery, I gave my testimony about our meeting, the healing it brought me, and the closure it brought my mother. I sent my testimony to him, which he shared with the AA group he attends at the prison. Now he's working on his testimony so I can read it for him at my

Celebrate Recovery and other Celebrate Recoveries in my area. Of course his testimony is about his killing three people, one of which was my father.

Doing this meeting was something I felt I had to do regardless of the outcome. I relied on my instincts and true faith. I would never have had the closure I felt without eye-to-eye contact, hearing his voice, voice fluctuation and tone, and seeing his eyes and body gestures. It had to happen this way to have the magnitude of closure I've had. This whole part of my life had been such a driving force in terms of my dysfunction, poor choices, failed relationships, and the daddy issue but now it was done. I put an ending to all of it.

I was able to share this experience with my mother and bring closure to the end stages of her life. The real test for me was discovering if, after the meeting, I had let go of the questions about my past. On my mother's deathbed I considered asking her questions to determine if she had kept secrets from me or if I believed that she didn't actually know about the whereabouts of my real father. Specifically I planned to ask if, in fact, my real father might have found my mother and if she knew he lived down the street from me. I decided to believe her and did not ask. I believe now that I actually was the one being tested in terms of my trust and I passed it. I really *did* let it go.

I feel I found my father, how he lived his life, his frame of mind when he joined the motorcycle gang, and I stood up for him. I'm so proud of completing this journey, being my father's voice, and putting it all behind me. It gave me an enormous amount of closure. I had no idea how heavy that burden was when I walked into the prison but when I walked out, it was just, wow! It was a breath of fresh air and it was just over. It was very freeing. The pain was truly gone. That hardness in me, that darkness and what I carried around for so many decades has opened up. I'm filling my life now with healthy things and a lot of goodness. To take all the tragedies, trauma, abuse, and failed relationships and see them turned into something so beautiful and something that can be used to help others is amazing. All of those events now are just events.

Analysis: Crime and its aftermath

Keisha lost a biological father that she never knew in a drunk driving accident. Moreover, his death happened years before she unexpectedly found out about it. It was her discovery of his death, paradoxically, that gave her the knowledge that the man, in fact, was her biological father. She, therefore, started her journey with a dissonance-generating reality based on lies that she didn't have a father while he was alive but got a father because he had been killed. As such, her reaction to the crime and its impact was negligible. Rather, her personal loss centered on the finality of the opportunity to have had any relationship with her father.

Much of her reaction to the knowledge about the existence and concomitant loss of her biological father focused on making sense out of her past. Indeed, it had to be rewritten because the reality now of having had a father exposed all the lies she had been told by her mother and stepfather about who her father was and how he died. Additionally, she had to deal with her mother who had told her a false story about her father's death that her mother thought was true. She further discovered that her father, instead of being killed in Vietnam, actually lived close by throughout her childhood. She teetered, therefore, between feeling shocked, angry with her abusive stepfather for his deception, abandoned by her real father, and a compelling drive to get information about him.

As a private investigator, she started researching his life—"Why did he go from being a military police officer into a biker? I pounded a lot of biker stores." She learned that he had a son, that her biological father too had lied to her mother about his past, that he had joined a motorcycle gang, and about the numerous similarities between them. She corrected her childhood conclusion that her stepfather might have sent her real father to Vietnam to be killed. She also gained understanding about her stepfather's abusive reactions to her as a child and the emotional currents connected to the numerous unspoken but pivotal truths that had directed much of her prior life. Indeed, she released much of the stored energy inside her as she proceeded in her personal investigation. She also quit drinking after discovering how her father died and the link between her alcoholism and distorted past.

Having determined who her father was, she turned to dealing with the fact that no one spoke for him as the victim of a horrific crash that killed three people—"No one said his life mattered, his death matters, that any of it matters." It was as if her father's existence came and went without anyone noticing. Because Keisha was a private investigator for the defense, she knew the court system well, including the fact that, as her father's daughter, she would, at least, have given a victim impact statement. She also felt robbed due to the fact that "I was never given the chance to speak in trial."

Keisha's digging into the injustices dealt her and her father during the trial generated lots of anger. Whatever might have been possible for her with her father was taken from her with his death. Her reactions were compounded, however, by the fact that she had been an alcoholic and defense investigator, which gave her understanding and empathy for Adam's predicament. The dissonance between the various realities emerged as she tried to write him a letter. "I was angry, but yet, then I understood… I couldn't put it into words because I couldn't draw which emotion I was really feeling." Motivated by feeling robbed of the opportunity to speak at Adam's trial and blocked in her ability to express her feelings to him, she discovered the VOD program. She'd known she wanted to meet with Adam even before reading the court transcripts. "I felt internally just [that] this is something I have to do. I have to do this. I have to have this done."

Preparation

Keisha prepared for six months before meeting with Adam. The chaplains assigned to facilitate the dialogue knew that the meeting was critical to both Keisha and her ailing mother and sped up the process because of the gravity of time. Keisha reports that "I went through every emotion with them…their professionalism created a bond of trust…they were consistent…they were focused." These relationships helped open her to the process. Moreover, Keisha had already humanized Adam because of her background and knowledge of the court system. She recognized that she had driven drunk herself many times and that he had to posture himself according to his lawyer's dictates during the trial. Consequently, she started the preparation with some openness to Adam already.

However, she felt stymied about whether or not he was remorseful, which made it difficult for her to determine how open she would be in the meeting. The numerous discoveries she had made naturally opened her to learning more and to expressing her pain and anger to Adam who, in effect, could be a container for sharing what she had learned about her father, the lies she had otherwise carried, and the dashed hope of ever confronting or having a relationship with her father. She couldn't anticipate, however, what might be possible because she had no direct information with which to assess him. Although the court records had indicated that he had no remorse, it was equally plausible that he could admit nothing, at the time, without incriminating himself. She felt a mix of anger and compassionate thinking, therefore, which was dissonant and confusing. Moreover, in anticipating the dyadic power of the dialogue ahead, Keisha wrestled with a core dilemma. If she shared little or nothing, she'd close down a possible opportunity and walk away with little return. If she confronted Adam and he wasn't remorseful, he would be yet another father figure who abandoned her. She went through preparation, therefore, with additional dissonance created by needing to put everything she knew and felt in a safe place but feeling unable to assess Adam's availability to receive it. Her vulnerability was heightened because she was about to lose her other parent as well.

Dialogue

The initial dyadic encounter served to quiet Keisha's concerns and speculation. She read Adam's body language immediately and felt reassured from his eyes and demeanor that he was genuinely remorseful and available to do the work with her. She also noted that he was close to her father's age and resembled a fit biker, which was also reflective of her father. Although Keisha had not yet shared her pain, Adam began the dialogue by reading a letter that he'd painstakingly written to her that conveyed the importance he gave to the meeting and the depth of his repentance. As she listened and saw his conscientiousness, Keisha made her first emotional shift, releasing much of her previous apprehension. Moreover, Keisha reciprocally completed the conduit between them, noting the common bond they already had by virtue of shared religious values and their joint commitment to recovery. She instilled even more safety and the possibility of greater openness by reassuring Adam that she would not harm him. She felt the resonance of her words as he responded with relief.

It was critical for Keisha to give Adam the entirety of her story because everything about her past and present was so interlaced. If she had left something out, the story would have been distorted. The fullness of her account and having it heard allowed her to integrate the disparate parts of her life with the man responsible for her father's death. She gave him her pain in telling him about the various chapters of her life, including her recent discoveries. She focused first on her father's mattering and giving voice, as she was not able to do at the trial, to who he was, including how he became a biker and his struggles and accomplishments. Indeed, the actuality of her father's life was and would remain imaginary since she never knew him. However, she now also had a real emotional reality about him as if she had known him well and she communicated that reality to Adam. Indeed, Adam knew nothing about the man he had killed. Keisha also shared her own history, the abuse from her stepfather, and the sordidness about her real father who abandoned her and her mother and was never in her life. In describing her father to the man who had taken his life, she brought him to life for both of them. This telling allowed his life to matter as well as his death and gave her father's life meaning.

Keisha was clear that when Adam killed her father, he took away hope specific to any opportunity ever to challenge or get to know her father. She dealt with this second source of pain by using Adam as a surrogate father and doing with him what she might have done with her own father. She listed every question she might have asked him and ritualistically followed each question with the statement, "You took that from me. You robbed me of that opportunity and that chance." As Keisha held Adam accountable for the answers he took from her, she unburdened herself by giving him her pain and the responsibility for the missed opportunity she would never have. As such, she began an integration process in which she began to make more sense to herself.

Having deposited her pain with Adam, she spontaneously realized that she could live without the answers and moved to forgiving him for taking her opportunity away. As she unexpectedly shared her forgiveness, Adam reciprocated with his tears. His expression caused Keisha to reciprocate further. She ministered to his sense of being unworthy by lifting him up with her words and joining them in their shared humanity as two people who, like everyone else, make mistakes and cause harm. As such, she reinstated him as worthy. Adam's tears, however, also indicated that he was accepting Keisha's pain and allowing it to be transferred to him. As she, in response, laid her hands on his and he reciprocated through praying for her, he, in effect, said to her, "I will hold this pain for you." As such, he transformed the pain into deep caring. Keisha experienced this transfer and the transformation of her pain as healing and magical. Although Adam was not responsible for all of her pain, he was the only one left in her life who could receive it. The plunge they mutually made into greater depth was the result of the dyadic energy between them.

Keisha felt complete. She had come to the end of her journey. In many ways, her whole life had been a disenfranchised burden given to her by her mother and stepfather through lies, secrets, and distortions. She unburdened herself by giving her pain to Adam and was able to let her suspicions go. She tested her shift into a trusting place in the world with her mother and found that it held. The energy she had expended since childhood was at rest. The meeting with Adam had resolved her issues with her father. Indeed, Keisha reconstructed a father–daughter relationship that had new and rich meaning such that it helped move her out of a painful past. The VOD gave her a safe and powerful vehicle to reconstruct this positive narrative. It served as a catalyst to ground out the negative excess charge within her and open her to the positive gifts of the transformative experience. The ongoing relationship between them was evidence of that transformation and the value each placed on the testimony of the other. For Keisha, Adam was both a villain and a savior. She paradoxically received life-giving answers because he killed her father. Although the meeting was clearly beneficial for Adam, the sole focus was on Keisha and what she needed from him to close her wounds. This singularity of purpose was demonstrated by the fact that Keisha, ironically, knew nothing about Adam by the end of the meeting except that he was an alcoholic and had a son.

A number of contradictions and dissonance-generating circumstances stimulated the energy flow within Keisha and between Keisha and Adam. These included her awareness of having a father only because he had been killed; the exposure of lies that generated dissonance which propelled her to seek the truth about her genealogy; the recognition that her father's life mattered because it did not matter to anyone at the trial; her anger at Adam for killing her father while recognizing the similarity in their behavior as alcoholics; her anger at Adam for his lack of remorse while understanding his position as a defendant; her desire to share with him in the meeting alongside the possibility of more emotional abandonment; the need for safety alongside Keisha's inability to assess Adam's receptivity; using the man who killed her father as a catalyst to bring her father to life by sharing with Adam; and Adam's acceptance of Keisha's pain and willingness to respond as a surrogate father in response to a history he did not cause. By allowing these dissonance-fueled energies to flow, Keisha was able through the dyadic interaction to unearth the blocked energy from her childhood circumstances, bring her father to life, mourn his death, bury the sorrow and regret of never having him, and emotionally forgive and bond with a man who received her pain and as a result brought release and healing to her.

PEARLE'S STORY AND ANALYSIS

A few days before Christmas Pearle's mom was kidnapped, forced to drive to a wooded area, and strangled to death. It took 12 days to find Jean's body. From the beginning, Pearle felt it was important to relay to Hal that he took a life, sharing video and pictures at the sentencing and making eye contact. Pearle described her healing as long and throughout the journey she participated in every experience that came her way. She saw VOD as just the next stage in her journey, and during preparation Hal confirmed he had felt a connection to Pearle since the trial. There were many coincidences, which reassured Pearle she had made the right decision. The VOD resulted in an authentic connection and ended with a hug between two people deeply connected and fulfilled by their meeting.

My mom was forced into a car by a man named Hal with a knife, while she was Christmas shopping. He made her drive into a distant wooded area, get out of the car and then he strangled her. We knew she was missing because someone was using her credit cards. People went looking for her all over town. The police gave up their holiday for us and let us sit with them as they took calls about her whereabouts. A hiker found her body 12 days after she was killed. We had her cremated. No one saw the body because it had been sitting in the woods for so long.

When they found her body, I just kept screaming and thinking, "What do I do now?" I'd walk myself through my day just trying to figure, "How do I go on?" Fortunately, me and my two siblings managed to keep our closeness for the whole year and a half of going through the criminal justice system without a falling out. I stayed in a state of functional shock for months. That meant that I could function in the world but I was living with the shock that someone could do this to a 75-year-old woman. I had a lot of feelings for my mom. She was afraid of driving. I remember spending hours in the bedroom with my brother trying to comfort me.

Hal had absconded from parole in California. The police caught him on tape at a gambling casino using my mom's credit cards. He pled guilty and was sentenced to true life. For my victim impact statement, I prepared and showed a 14-minute video of my mom's life with photos from everywhere. I also made lots of eye contact with Hal during the sentencing hearing.

Of the three siblings, I was the one who healed most. I did a great deal of counseling. My mother and I were estranged. In fact, I'd been estranged from my whole family for nine years except for weddings and funerals. So here she was missing, gone, murdered and I hadn't reconnected with her. I had a lot of regret about that because I love my mom but I'd lost sight of that love over the years. I started looking at mother–daughter love and how complicated it is. I would happen upon movies like *Remains of the Day, Shadowlands,* and *Into the Woods* that made me think about love in another way. For example, I kept realizing that my mom absolutely did the best she could, given all the circumstances. She made me who I am. She was a homemaker all her life, which is a lot of work. I just kept making the connections between the things I do in daily life and what she taught me.

Besides counseling, I did peer counseling and astrological work. I also participated in a community-based ritualistic healing ceremony. I had discovered that the ceremony was to be held on property that was owned by a gay and lesbian community. It just happened to be next to where my mom's body was found so I called the community and said, "My mother was killed close by to your property. I'm a lesbian and I practice Wicca and I want to come." The ceremony lasted 24 hours. At the end, we walked the path that Mom was forced to walk. We did a ritual where her body was found and left items on the side of a logging road. So my healing was quite intense and thorough. I approached it based on what came into my life and what I saw about more ways to heal.

This process happened with my decision to do a VOD. Most of my feelings after my mother's murder were about her and what she went through. My feelings about Hal came up later. I couldn't forget him and thought of him at least monthly over many years. I wondered what had happened to him and actually worried about him but I didn't think about meeting with him. I learned about the VOD program while serving on an state advisory committee for VOCA (Victims of Crime Act). I began researching it and out of the blue I decided to call the program director. Although we talked for an hour, I realized later that she was basically interviewing me. She asked, "Why do you want to meet with this guy?" I said, "I don't know. It seems like the next thing to do." So my call and conversation with her just happened with no planning.

The VOD program director also assessed Hal to see if he was acceptable for the program. She told me that she had said to him when she met him at the prison, "I'm here because of the VOD program and one of the children of Jean wants to meet with you." He knew which one of us it was because he had had the same connection with me at the sentencing that I had had with him. That was mind blowing. I went to see a former therapist as part of preparing myself for the meeting. In that therapy, I took a journey into very deep parts of myself which I wouldn't have done except for my anticipation about the upcoming meeting at the other end of the journey. I chose not to tell any of my family members what I was doing. I felt I needed to do the VOD for myself and couldn't take them along. They'd want to know all the details so I kept it a secret until two years after the meeting.

The preparation took seven-and-a-half months. Two facilitators were assigned to work with Hal and me. We talked on the phone every three weeks and met together three times. It took me a while to feel comfortable and trust them. I can be very intense. In contrast, they were quiet and soft spoken. We finally bonded when we had dinner together the evening before the actual meeting. The facilitators had also visited with Hal at least three times. He got confused at one point and came to one of the preparation visits thinking it was the actual meeting between us. He was very upset during that visit and everything seemed to break loose for him. He was talkative and really candid and ended up sharing a lot of himself. The details that the facilitators shared about that visit gave me a clear picture of what he was going through.

I decided to write Hal a letter. I told him I appreciated him for where he was coming from. I didn't know his motivation so I asked him why he was doing the VOD. He wrote back and I read his response together with Josephina who was my partner, the VOD program director, and our facilitators. I could see from what he wrote that he was open and had put himself out in answering my question. So there was some relationship being developed before we had even met physically. There were also a number of strange coincidences. Hal had the same first name as my son. His middle name was the male version of my partner's name. Moreover, Josephina and her former partner were prison guards at the prison where Hal is housed. So they knew him from afar. Josephina went to the meeting as my support person.

On the day of the meeting, I was calm because I had a very complete agenda, which I had shared with everyone. I went into the room first. I wanted to cleanse it so I did a ritual of walking counter-clockwise three times and said prayers to remove any negative energy. Then everyone came in. I put Josephina in a corner because I knew that would be a safe place for her and told the others where I wanted them to sit at the table. I insisted there be no guards present that we could see. When Hal came into the room, I stood up. He was so much smaller than he had been at the sentencing hearing. He had shaved his head and looked all clean and shiny. We exchanged silly grins. We sat directly across from each other. Once we got started, everyone else disappeared. Inside of me was a deep calmness and a profound readiness to do the dialogue. He knew what I wanted to say and what I wanted to ask him. I knew that he was in that same place. Everything fell away except him and me.

One of the facilitators introduced the purpose of the dialogue and gave the ground rules. I made a very brief opening statement that included what I wanted to cover in the meeting. Then I said, "Well, Mr. Habert, is there anything you'd like to say to me before I jump in?" There was a long pause and he started crying. Tears were streaming down his face and he got all red and said, "I am so sorry—so, so very sorry." Tears were streaming down my face and I realized he was expressing all this regret. Indeed, his deep remorse was so totally evident that it set the tone for the entire meeting.

I told him all about my mom from her birth to her death. Josephina told me later that he just listened. He listened and listened. Then, I wanted him to tell me about his background from his birth to the present moment in time. He was confused. He didn't understand why I cared and why I wanted to hear about him. I reassured him about how important it was to me to learn what his life had been like. I just let him talk. If he needed encouragement, I'd say, "No, no. Go on. I really want to hear this." So the morning was all one-way communication for each of us. Then we broke for lunch. My partner and I had a bizarre picnic lunch in the hotel room and processed the morning. She commented that I hadn't gone very deep with him, which was true. After lunch, I asked him to describe the crime in detail, from his parole in California until the sentencing. He said, "Are you really sure you want to hear this?" I said, "Yes, I really need to hear this." I said this in part because my counselor had said, "Pearle, if it were me, I'd really want to hear every single detail." I agreed. Throughout his story, Hal checked in with me about whether or not I wanted him to continue. I would just ask him a few questions and he'd go ahead with the specifics. I got to hear about my mom's last words and how he strangled her. He told me she revived two times. He also told me, "It's not easy to strangle somebody to death. It's not what they show on TV."

When he was finished, I told him what had happened to our entire family starting with my brother's call that Mom was missing all the way through to the sentencing. Somewhere along the way, we started to go back and forth in learning about each other. It was very spontaneous and such a dialogue. That's where the authentic connection happened that resulted in true intimacy. The most amazing thing was how much we had in common. I'm a recovering alcoholic and he's in recovery. As we started to talk back and forth, he asked, "Well, didn't you ever get mad? Weren't you mad at me at some point?" I answered, "Well there was a point 14 months after my mom's death when I came home and discovered my dog had chewed up this book. I went into the garage and I got the horse's lunge whip. It stands six feet tall and there's a whip part that's another six feet so you can whip the end of it behind the horse. I was going to kill the dog but the minute I started whipping the whip, the dog disappeared. Right in front of me was this old, old cherry tree. I started whipping the tree and I completely lost it. I was enraged. I was yelling and screaming at the top of my lungs for around five minutes. In the process, all the rage dropped away." When I finished telling Hal the story, he said, "Well, I love dogs too and I'm never going to be able to touch another dog." He started crying again and I, too, just cried and cried because dogs are my love. I couldn't imagine being without one. So we went back and forth revealing ourselves to one another with lots and lots of tears. When all this was finished, I realized I was done. There was nothing more I needed to say or hear from him.

In terms of my agenda, there were three things I kept to myself because I didn't know if they would happen or not. First, I told Hal that I had talked to my therapist about forgiveness and in our discussion realized that I had already forgiven him. I had let go and released him as a human being. I'd clearly seen him as enough of a person that I could forgive him. However, the minute I said the word "forgiveness" to him, he got beet red and tears started streaming down his face. I said, "There's a part of you that murdered my mother I cannot forgive." He said immediately, "Well, of course not. I was a horrible person. I did a horrible thing." Then I told him what I had said to my therapist, which was that "I couldn't really forgive the crime but 79 percent of me can forgive you." I told Hal that I shared that line with everybody and he kind of chuckled. I tell folks that the forgiveness came to me over a long period of time and had nothing to do with the facilitated dialogue.

Second, I asked Hal to do something, even in prison, to make a purpose out of his life and perhaps help other inmates. Third, I told him that I'd continue to think about him and send him good energy and that I'd like to shake his hand. He got a funny look on his face and stood up but without moving an inch. The big chaplain got down from his perch where he was sitting on the sink counter and stood up as well. I walked slowly around and put my hand out to take his hand but without thinking I took his hand in both my hands. Then, spontaneously, I just embraced him. The embrace lasted around ten seconds, not very long. Then I let Hal go and stepped back. I needed to step back so as not to compromise security. After that, we just spontaneously started debriefing what had happened during our meeting. It was stunning to debrief about dogs in prison and all that. As soon as I used the word "forgiveness," however, and he started crying, I began questioning whether or not I made it up because it is something all inmates want to hear. But I didn't do the forgiveness for any effect. I was only going to say it if the dialogue went well and there was sincerity. I hadn't told anybody but Josephina.

Usually I would just leave because we were done. But we sat around debriefing for half an hour. It was like having finished an intense running race but then you had to keep walking to cool down. In describing our meeting, Josephina said, "It felt like rappelling where you've got somebody on the ropes and somebody going down a cliff face. You're trusting the person at the top with your life. But for the two of you it was like you were rappelling but then switching places. One would hold the line and the other would go down. Then that person would hold the line as the first person went further down the cliff. And you did this together until you both reached the bottom safely." It just summed it up.

This experience turned my life around completely. Because Hal acknowledged and took full responsibility for the evil thing he did, my whole life changed when I walked out of that prison. My whole life changed to the core of my being and I was in a state of grace. I felt like a totally new person. The burden of everything in the universe had lifted from me. I stayed in this state for 36 hours. When I went to see my counselor, I said, "I gave him his life back." The next week, I said, "I didn't realize this, but he gave me my true life back." There's no way that would have happened without direct eye-to-eye contact.

Some time after the meeting, I asked permission from the VOD Advisory Committee to speak about the meeting publicly. The committee talked about it among themselves and then talked with Hal. Although we had signed a strict confidentiality agreement, Hal was alright waiving it on two conditions: first, he did not want his name used and second, he asked me not to share something he told me. He told the committee, "She will know what that is" and I did know. The committee also allowed me to write him a year or two later. He answered me back and I wrote him again. I wrote him a second letter a couple of years ago but he never replied. That's all that will ever happen.

Analysis: Crime story and its aftermath

The murder of Pearle's mother, Jean, violated social mores at every level. Jean was elderly. Hal had broken parole. He was on the prowl for someone to kill. The murder happened in a small town where the residents otherwise looked out for each other. The murder happened when Jean was buying gifts for others at Christmas, a special and sacred time of peace. Having killed Jean, Hal used her credit cards to gamble, an act that was repugnant to Pearle— "I'm just so morally opposed to gambling." Hal forced Jean, who was afraid of driving, to drive out of town into the woods where he killed her. Hal left Jean's body to rot on the ground for 12 days before she was found.

Pearle felt lost and functioned robotically for a long time just trying to comprehend how someone, with no forethought, could murder an aged woman. Jean's death, however, laid bare the unfinished business between Pearle and her mother. Pearle not only had to grieve her mother but also had to face the fact that she had not done the work to reconnect with her prior to her murder. Her regret was intensified by recognizing her unabated love for her mother such that she started to do the work, herself, to internally reconcile herself with her mother. Her opening herself to that work was part of her letting the universe direct her healing as a new homicide survivor. Indeed, whatever she met on her healing path became, for Pearle, a sign of what she should do. Pearle believed, therefore, in synchronicity and that opportunities appeared, in effect, for a reason. Her job was to recognize and take advantage of each prospect as it presented itself.

For example, she discovered a healing ceremony on property next to where her mother was killed and owned by a group that mirrored her own sexual identity. She literally took the death walk her mother took and performed rituals where her mother's body was found—"I approached my healing based on what came into my life and what I saw about more ways to heal." Each thing she did opened her to more possibilities. For instance, Pearle had thought regularly about Hal but didn't consider meeting with him until she discovered the opportunity to do so while serving on a committee for crime victims.

Preparation

The value she gave to her intuition and letting the path guide her was evident in her response to the VOD program director's question about why she wanted to meet with Hal. "It just happened. It seemed the next thing to do." In commenting on her process, Pearle said, "I approached my healing [such] that it was things just coming into my life of more ways to heal." This philosophy fit well with the preparation process and the goal of becoming more open to the upcoming meeting with Hal. She struggled, however, with trusting the facilitators because she and they were temperamentally different but she felt they bonded just prior to the meeting.

Pearle worked to make herself be more and more open to the process. For example, she elected to do much of her preparation with her therapist to help her to be fully mindful during the meeting. "I intuited I needed to do this myself." She therefore harnessed her energy for the dialogue, in part by being highly selective and self-protective about the details of her therapy and her decision to meet with Hal. Indeed, she did not tell her family what she was doing until two years after the dialogue. Several incidents occurred that increased Pearle's openness and responsiveness to Hal. Hal was transparent in his response to Pearle's letter and her question about his motivation to meet with her. Hal's upset and reaction to mistakenly thinking that a preparation meeting was the actual VOD broke him open. As such, it gave Pearle an authentic portrait of who he was and helped humanize him in her eyes. There were several coincidences about names and relationships that confirmed Pearle's belief that meeting with Hal was the correct next step in her journey, for example, her partner's former employment as a prison guard. The conduit between Pearle and Hal was already being laid, prior to the meeting, through letters and knowledge of each other through the facilitators. Indeed, the information exchange and trust building that preceded the VOD played an important role in allowing the meeting to start strong and end quite personally.

Dialogue

Pearle entered the space for the meeting centered and inner connected. She established the space as sacred through the ritual she previously performed and as safe by assigning seats and insisting that the guards remain out of sight. Her anxiety about the unknown was reduced because she knew what would be said and asked in the meeting, as did Hal. Indeed, she felt calm, in part because she had stayed true to the dictates of her own process throughout. The silly grins exchanged between Pearle and Hal expressed their mutual awareness that they were the two main actors and what was to occur in the meeting was solely between them. "There was a deep calmness and a profound readiness" to do this. Pearle also experienced that she and Hal were entering a different zone of existence—"I realized it was a falling away of absolutely everyone else except him and I." Indeed, their being together physically was like an energy sigh of relief, "At last."

Within this conduit, Pearle requested a statement from Hal. He responded with sorrow, tears streaming down his cheeks and a deep apology. The emotionality of his statement likely brought Hal, psychologically, fully into the room but was importantly an indicator of the pain he already bore and accepted even without specific knowledge from Pearle about her pain. He listened intently to Pearle's description of Jean, the woman he had killed. Pearle requested and encouraged Hal to reciprocate by sharing his background. This turn-taking helped establish the mutuality of their endeavor. Hal's attentive listening and Pearle's encouragement further solidified their investment in one another.

In the first part of their dialogue, Pearle and Hal were establishing the base for Hal's sharing the specifics of how he killed Jean and how she responded. In the second part, they completed the full story of the murder for each other that included Hal's story and the discovery of Jean's disappearance and the impact of her murder on Pearle and her siblings. A subtle tipping point was reached during this unfolding, when the energy shifted from one-way reporting to a free-flowing interchange between Pearle and Hal marked by mutual comfort, honesty, trust, and curiosity. Within their mutually constructed climate of safety and acceptance, they allowed the exchange process to guide them and found commonalities through what they revealed to each other, such as doing art, being in recovery, and a love of dogs. The growing momentum of this back and forth energy was fueled by the reciprocal influence of the topics as well as the emotional resonance they felt between them. "The true back and forth dialogue is what resulted in the true intimacy." Josephina described this shift in energy during their dyadic volley as holding the rope for each other so each person could climb further down the cliff. Her analogy underscored that neither could have climbed down or done it safely without the other.

Another tipping point occurred after Pearle expressed forgiveness both verbally and spontaneously through her embrace of Hal and he started crying. She knew she had forgiven Hal for herself but was otherwise testing him throughout the meeting to determine if he had earned the right to know about it. Indeed, she wanted the giving and receiving of her forgiveness to be meaningful and genuine. Although her expression that "79 percent of me can forgive you" reflected her singular decision prior to the VOD, it took the experience of Hal in the meeting to be able to release or forgive fully.

Even though she did not verbalize it, Pearle had to trust the genuineness of his remorse and the authentic quality of his character through their dyadic interaction before she could release herself and him fully and be moved past the crime and likely past the limit of 79 percent to a place of emotional forgiveness. It was her movement in the dialogue with him that allowed this fuller sense of forgiveness. As such, the change grew out of the dialogue and required the conversation. The back and forth flow between them took the dialogue to a new level of intimacy which consequently provided a meaningful grounding for their interchange about forgiveness and Pearle's embrace. This building process helped transform the pain and, in effect, allowed each to give the other back a freer and fuller life.

Although the momentum was building throughout the meeting, the positive energies created by their dyadic volley caused a bonding dynamic, which was further actualized in the half hour debriefing after the dialogue. Indeed, there was no formal ending of the meeting other than Pearle's embrace while she and Hal were both standing, which, in effect, marked the finish of their business together. Rather than leaving, however, Pearle and Hal spontaneously began to debrief and the others in attendance joined the conversation. It was as if no one wanted to leave because they were still caught up in the combustion of positive energy that arose with the raw emotion and human connection precisely because the negative energy fields had been dealt with and had dissipated.

Pearle felt a strong sense of completion but also excitement because the impact of the VOD went so much further than she expected. There was no unburdening because she didn't go into the meeting feeling encumbered. However, she felt "to the core of my being, my whole life changed" because Hal acknowledged "the evil thing he did and took complete responsibility," that is, transferred the pain to himself. Beyond just the murder, she felt as well that "everything in the universe had lifted from me." Pearl's reinstatement of Hal was expressed in a myriad of ways including the easy back and forth flow of conversation between them, her face-to-face sharing of forgiveness because he was worthy, her embrace, his active participation in the debriefing, and her desire for additional contact through letters after the dialogue.

Pearle's healing, including her participation in the VOD program, was directed by the universe. Indeed, she let the universe dictate her process including astrological work, her work with her therapist, the Wiccan healing ceremony, sharing the story about the horse's lunge whip, her decision not to share with her family, her embrace of Hal, and her writing Hal after the meeting. Because her mode was to live in the middle of the process, she trusted it implicitly and worked continually, therefore, to remain open to wherever it led her. Also, Josephina played an important role throughout as observer. Her feedback to Pearle underscored the importance, for example, of Hal's rapt engagement as listener while Pearle spoke about her mother or the need for Pearle to go into deeper territory, such as the details of the murder itself that would be more productive. Although the dialogue belonged to Pearle, her life-partner accompanied her through this significant venture, which made her an active part of Pearle's healing journey.

Pearle experienced little, if any dissonance in her reactions to her mother's death, the motivation to do a VOD, or during the meeting with Hal. Perhaps the only dissonance was the fact that she thought that she had the forgiveness issue under control and that she had given Hal her forgiveness by reporting to him about her therapy. However, her experience of him during the meeting unexpectedly moved her to a fuller acceptance and forgiveness of him as a person. The dissonance did not bother her, however, because of her basic commitment not to fight the dissonance but rather to resolve it by going along with whatever element was pushing her in a new direction. Similarly, she felt some dissonance about keeping her meeting a secret from her family with whom she otherwise shared her life. She managed the dissonance by contending that she did not want to sully the dialogue and, therefore, had decided to keep it to herself. She eventually told them about the VOD, however, which again resolved the dissonance.

KALICIA'S STORY AND ANALYSIS

Kalicia's adult son, Darnell, was the victim of a DUI [driving under the influence] hit and run. Kalicia struggled not only with the loss of her son, but the indifference of the driver and the subsequent media attention which placed some of the blame back on Darnell. Kalicia's situation was unique, because the judge allowed her to stipulate VOD in the offender's plea agreement. Less than a year later she and her husband met with Ahmad. Although the dialogue was authentic and productive, the centrality of Kalicia's focus on Ahmad and his lack of follow-through after the meeting left her frustrated and disappointed. Although the negative energy increased, Kalicia preserved her hope and humanizing of Ahmad by placing responsibility for his backsliding on external influences.

A hit-and-run driver named Ahmad killed my 28-year-old son, Darnell, when he was bicycling with a friend. Darnell was hit from behind and thrown in front of the other bicyclist. The driver was picked up about an hour later. He had ditched his car but told the police he'd been carjacked.

Because he was drunk, he was charged with manslaughter 2, vehicular assault of a bicyclist, DUI, felony hit and run, and reckless driving.

I found out about the crash when a police chaplain knocked at my door at 5:00 in the morning and repeatedly called out, "Is this the family of Darnell Stanford?" I was completely clueless. When I finally opened the door, the chaplain told me that Darnell had been in a hit-and-run crash and had died. The second cyclist was at the hospital with injuries. He sat with me while I called the medical examiner's office to find out what had happened and made arrangements for his body. I also called my children who live out of town and they all came right away. The chaplain and I watched the news together because it was the third bicycling fatality in two weeks and the second hit and run. My daughter and my husband plus my best friend, my sister, and her friend went with me to the scene of the crash. It was very, very sad. When we got home there were news vans and I decided to talk with them. Up to that point, my son was nameless. The news referred to him as an unidentified, deceased bicyclist. I changed all that by going over to the newsman, introducing myself, and telling him what I knew had happened. I also talked about how horrible it was for both our family and the family of the driver. The driver was 18. I never had any anger towards him, only at what happened. I never blamed or hated him. I never wanted him dead or run over, like I hear some people say. I was just terribly sad for both of our families.

I had to face things I'd never thought about before. For example, no one told me it was necessary to go to the morgue so I never considered seeing him. Because he'd been on a bike without a helmet, thrown 175 feet and died of blunt force head trauma, I just assumed we wouldn't be able to see him or that we would want to. But the funeral director assured me that he was perfect. The death evidently was caused by a severe whiplash that knocked his skull off his spine, just separated it. He had a minor abrasion across the top of his head but there were no other visible injuries except on his hands. He also had some lung issues and his sternum was cracked in half. He didn't have any broken legs or arms, just a junk of meat taken out of his thigh when it got caught in the headlight.

A number of people felt that Darnell's death was his own fault because he was out at night without a helmet. Those comments, plus the "what if" questions, made me extremely angry. For example, "Wouldn't it have made a difference *if* he wore a helmet?" Moreover, the police erroneously told the local newspaper that the deceased bicyclist, Darnell, was not wearing a helmet but the bicyclist who survived was. That message left the impression that Darnell would have been okay if he'd had a helmet on. The truth was that my son was hit full force, straight on at 50 miles an hour whereas only the mirror on the side of the car hit the other bicyclist. When I checked with the medical examiner, he verified that a helmet would have made no difference because Darnell was hit so hard.

I started researching crashes because I couldn't believe how often they happened and I was mad at people for blaming my son. I also focused on the court system, which really needs help. We were advised to accept a plea bargain for criminally negligent homicide because it would be hard to get a conviction. After all, no one had witnessed the crash and Ahmad, the driver, wasn't driving his own vehicle. For the plea bargain, my prosecutor asked me to specify the conditions for drug treatment and how much time Ahmad needed to serve. He had already done drug treatment for harder drugs like Ecstasy and this was his second hit and run. I wanted conditions in the plea, therefore, that would teach him life skills so that he would be a more responsible and safe person when he was released. I asked for as much rehabilitation as possible. Moreover, I'd discovered the VOD program by surfing the Internet and introduced my prosecutor to the idea. She agreed so we put Ahmad's participation in the program as one of the conditions of the plea. We had an awesome judge. At one hearing, both families sat at a table facing each other with the judge between us. As part of the personal conversation with us he said to Ahmad, "I see you completed a year of treatment. How do you feel you did with that?" Ahmad answered, "Oh, I did good." The judge said, "Well, apparently not, because you're here for a DUI that killed someone."

Ahmad went to prison and I took a couple of months to just wind down. Three months later, I contacted the VOD program director to begin the preparation process. We were assigned two facilitators and it all happened quickly from there. I was recently married, so my new husband and I attended bimonthly meetings for seven months. The facilitators would meet with us and then meet with Ahmad. At one point they brought a letter he had written to us, which was very nice. I was thrilled with their support and their insights about Ahmad. Of course, they couldn't tell us about the content of their talks with him but they were able to give us their impressions. They suggested I make a list of questions to ask Ahmad. When they saw my three-page list, they said, "Ahmad is a little bit on the immature side and rather introverted so this kind of a list would likely overwhelm him. Why don't we go through it, narrow it down and pick out the most important items?" The facilitators helped me be more realistic in my expectations.

The meeting was scheduled right before Darnell would have turned 30 years old. My husband and I felt very prepared. Frankly, I was anxious to be done with it. I had learned through the police reports and the media that

Ahmad didn't have much positive support so I was wary that he might pull out. Indeed, I felt that without that support, he wouldn't move in the positive direction I was hoping for. I liked meeting with the facilitators so I was somewhat unhappy that the preparation was over. I surmised that finishing preparation might be a let down for Ahmad as well.

I was pretty nervous about the meeting. I had a lot of concerns. My husband was my support person but Ahmad refused to have anyone present on his behalf. I wondered if, in hindsight, I had made a total fool of myself by giving advantages to Ahmad in the plea bargain. Honestly, I was never really angry with Ahmad. Rather, I was upset and actually devastated about the circumstances. Family members and Darnell's friends were very vocal. They'd say, "He should be put to death." "He should be run over." I knew many of them could not understand my attitude. I too worried that I might be wrong. I thought, "What if they are right and this person doesn't deserve to be forgiven? What if they think that I'm stupid for caring and that Ahmad is just saying what is necessary to get himself the lowest sentence?" Because of these misgivings, I needed Ahmad to demonstrate to me that I had not misplaced that hope.

We did a visit to the prison before the meeting and were shown the room for the VOD. At the meeting, Almad seemed to be quite open and receptive. He was quiet and listened thoughtfully as I told him about Darnell and showed him pictures from his life. I described how the crash and his death had impacted our family. Throughout the meeting, Ahmad seemed very, very interested and was extremely attentive. The meeting was focused more on us and our loss than on who he was. However, he talked about his family and his little boy who, at the time, was just a few months old. He also opened up a bit and said, "I'm sorry. I don't know how this must feel for you but I've got my own child now." After lunch, Ahmad shared some pictures and other things that he had brought to share with us. He apologized for what he had done and stated that when he got out of prison, he wanted to speak to youth to stop them from repeating his mistakes. He really wanted others to learn from his poor decisions.

I loved what Ahmad wanted. I really felt committed to him, to his wish to turn his life around and to preventing this conviction from ruining his life forever. I had already expressed these thoughts to him at the sentencing hearing. They grew out of my conviction that people who want to help themselves attract other people who would love to help them. I felt that if he had the right attitude, even a homicide conviction on his record would not stop him from being successful. At the meeting, I got the sense that he was going to have the attitude that I wanted him to have. We all felt so good about it that we agreed to continue talking for another couple of hours after lunch. We ended the meeting by hugging and deciding that we both wanted to meet again. Ahmad asked if he could keep the pictures of Darnell that I had brought to the meeting. Although I had a nagging sense that he didn't fully understand what he had done, Ahmad was remorseful. He had done some reflecting, was truly sorry, and really wished the crash and my son's death hadn't happened. We both were a bit tearful. My husband and I left the meeting feeling very, very positive. I was actually ecstatic. I even had the nerve to ask Ahmad if he would speak with me on victim impact panels when he was released. He said that he was a little shy and nervous but we were both hopeful.

I never felt there was anything to forgive. Ahmad didn't deliberately pick my son or hurt him intentionally. He was just a stupid kid making the same kind of stupid mistake that 10,000 people a year make. After all, he was only 18 years old. Ahmad, however, brought up forgiveness. When I commented that he had the opportunity to make positive things happen in his life, he said, "I hope you can forgive me." I figured that he brought up forgiveness because he realized that if our situations were reversed, that it would be a huge thing for him to forgive me. Alternatively, he may have introduced the idea because he assumed that saying it was the appropriate thing to do in our society.

I had several fantasies about Ahmad. I assumed that if he were in the public eye, he would get attention from people who would want to help him. Then, he'd see that the crash didn't have to define his life forever. Moreover, he'd probably have opportunities that he otherwise couldn't get. There is a Native American legend that if a man killed a chief's son, then that man was obligated to become the chief's surrogate son. I was prepared, if Ahmad had the right attitude, to be a mother-type support for him. I would go to bat for him as long as I felt that he warranted that type of backing. Actually, I was willing to take him in and love him just like a son if he reciprocated.

Several years later, I set up a second meeting but without any facilitators. I had gotten concerned that things weren't going the way I had hoped they would. At this meeting, Ahmad complained about things he didn't want to do and asked for my help in getting back his driver's license. His explanation was that "I want to be able to drive my little boy around." I didn't know what he was thinking when he made that request. I have no pull with the Department of Licensing. I can't go to them and say, "Hey, I know he killed my son but can you give him his license anyway?" Indeed, my response at the time was, "My little boy never gets to drive again. I think you can ride a bike." That's when I started to feel negative. Although he was remorseful, I felt that he didn't really "get it." Ahmad was starting to feel sorry for himself, wanted to get out of prison and forget about what had happened.

He'd gotten married between the two meetings. His wife was significantly older than he was and had a lot of influence over him. She was not willing to change her life or lifestyle to accommodate the things he had previously said he wanted to change such as the people he hung out with. When I met him the second time, he wasn't willing to make the kinds of changes he had expressed the first time. He wasn't interested in doing any kind of public speaking. I felt let down. The facilitators, however, had mentioned his immaturity level several times during the VOD. His desire to just move on with his life and put the crash behind him was congruent with the facilitators' assessment.

I had more anger toward him as I got further away in time from the crash and his release date got closer. The injustice of my son's death dawned on me as I realized that my son was dead and gone forever while Ahmad at age 22 was just getting out of prison and would have his whole life in front of him. I recognized that he hadn't served much time. He got a five-year sentence but was out in four years, ten days. If I had been assured about how Ahmad would handle his future, I wouldn't have wanted him to have any time at all in prison. But I felt my son deserved some measure of justice and I didn't feel confident about Ahmad. He left my son on the side of the road like he'd hit a possum or a squirrel. He didn't even stop to see if Darnell was okay. How can one human being leave someone else like that? I talked about the incomprehensibility of what Ahmad did in our VOD. He said he was so drunk he didn't even know he'd hit someone. Indeed, the prosecutor kept referring to his state of mind at the crash as completely "blotto."

I've had no direct interaction with Ahmad's family. I have gone to their Facebook pages and seen a Mickey Mouse tattoo with his eyes cut out. Underneath the tattoo it says, "Snitches die." There was mention in the police report of possible gang activity and I didn't get a good sense from his family. Although I've had no contact with Ahmad since he was released, I was shocked to get a request from his wife on Facebook the other day. I feel negative toward her because she was influencing Ahmad not to take seriously the commitments he made to himself and me during the VOD. I knew as well that while Ahmad was lying to the police and saying he was carjacked, Ahmad's wife (then girlfriend) and mother were standing just a hundred feet from where my son was dead on the pavement and lying to the police as well. I realize of course that she was lying for Ahmad to get him off. I just felt from the beginning that she didn't want him to take any responsibility for anything that had happened. I'm angrier with her and his mother than I am at Ahmad for not telling the truth. Had the situation been reversed, I cannot picture myself trying to get Darnell off for what he did. I'd be saying, "Oh, my God, Darnell, what happened? Let's get you the help that you need to make what happened as good for everyone as possible." I can't even imagine Darnell trying to get off because he was a very responsible person.

I have no idea about Ahmad's life or what visions he has in his head about what happened. I am a little disappointed but I don't necessarily feel angry. I just wish he had the wherewithal within him to follow through because I think it would be good all the way around. I'm thinking about responding to Ahmad's wife. I want to ask her, "What is your purpose in reaching out to me? What are you hoping to gain from this?" I might be willing to meet with them in public at a restaurant. I'm still hopeful that the crash and the VOD would turn into something good for the families. But if it doesn't, that's okay too. I do show Ahmad's picture when I do victim impact panels, not to disparage him but so folks can see that what happened was awful for both families. I never say anything about him on TV because I don't want to make his life harder.

In terms of the VOD, I felt like we were both somewhat vulnerable to each other because we mutually felt a sense of trust. We were both there for a positive outcome. My children also hoped he'd have a good outcome. They agreed with my telling him, "I hope this doesn't ruin your life. I'd like you to have a happy life." I felt that if he had a happier life, he'd be a safer person and be able to raise his child better. He'd also do better in life if he didn't hold onto some kind of grudge because we did this to him.

Analysis: Crime and its aftermath

Kalicia lost her son in a hit-and-run crash while he was bicycling. The driver was "blotto" and so wasted on drugs that he claimed not to have known that he had hit someone. This was not his first crash. Indeed, he had been incarcerated and received drug treatment for a prior hit-and-run offense. Kalicia initially minimized Ahmad's history and his efforts to dodge responsibility for the crime. Specifically, both Ahmad and his girlfriend claimed that Ahmad, who had ditched his car, had been carjacked as an excuse for his whereabouts. Ahmad's mother did nothing to counter her son's story. Instead of having outrage at Ahmad, Kalicia's anger was focused on the injustices she experienced from the criminal justice system and from the media's depiction of her son as responsible for his own death. She initially spent time, therefore, researching the frequency of crashes with bicycles rather than concentrating on the loss of her son or on Ahmad. The research filled a lot of her time—"I talked about it a lot, so I'm sure people were quite bored with me or stressed that I wasn't recovering." Indeed, the stored, negative energy she carried came more from these injustices than the actual crash.

Being an activist, Kalicia quickly identified the flaws in the criminal justice system and responded to the invitation from the prosecutor to contribute ideas for the plea agreement. Although she had reason to be upset with the circumstances that hampered obtaining a conviction, she again concentrated on the larger issue, which was to provide Ahmad with life skills that might prevent harm to others and instill a stronger sense of responsibility. In that regard, Kalicia was extremely aware of Ahmad's young age and the odds he would face in overcoming the trajectory of a criminal record associated with drugs and two hit-and-run fatalities. "I really did want this young man to…turn his life around… I expressed that to him in the sentencing phase, that I hoped that he could just be wholeheartedly out there afterward." Kalicia never had negative feelings toward Ahmad—"I don't want to say it was an accident because it wasn't, but it's not like he went and picked out my son or did something to him deliberately."

Kalicia, therefore, used the plea agreement as a treatment plan for Ahmad with the goal that the crash and her son's death not ruin another youth's life. The prosecutor let her specify the amount of time to be served, drug and alcohol treatment, etc.—"Of course, I threw all of that stuff in there." Indeed, Kalicia discovered the VOD option herself and proposed it be included as well. She clearly felt some responsibility toward Ahmad because he was so young. Her appreciation for his situation was likely informed by her experience of raising several sons and the challenges they faced as young adults. Moreover, the judge at the trial partially set the stage for the VOD by bringing the key stakeholders together at a table, engaging in conversation with Ahmad, and challenging the authenticity of his motivation. Specifically, after Ahmad's statement that he had done well in treatment for his first hit-and-run offense, the judge said, "Apparently not, because you're here for a DUI that killed someone."

Preparation

Ahmad had only served two months of his five-year sentence before Kalicia initiated the preparation process. She resented her preoccupation with Ahmad and felt that completing the VOD might help refocus her energies on Darnell. Having recently married, she and her new husband attended preparation sessions for seven months. Throughout this time, Kalicia worried about Ahmad. Even though Ahmad agreed to the meeting, she was aware that she had engineered doing the VOD as part of the plea agreement and was anxious that he might back out. He had little backing, if any, from his family or from anyone in the prison and elected not to have a support person at the meeting.

Kalicia, therefore, went through the preparation with a lot of apprehension and dissonance. She found herself thinking more about Ahmad than Darnell or her other children. She now had a self-imposed obligation to care about yet another person's life. She also put a lot of her energy into anticipating what Ahmad would do with his life in the future. During both the preparation and the meeting, therefore, Ahmad became a kind of project. Specifically, Kalicia's decision to do the VOD early in Ahmad's incarceration was based on her fear about Ahmad's participation. She continually worried, during and after the first meeting, that some outside threat would interrupt or stop the process for him. That worry was reinforced, somewhat, by the facilitators who cautioned her to shorten her three-page list of questions because it might overwhelm Ahmad. More, Kalicia recognized that he lacked positive support generally and therefore had additional anxiety when the preparation was finished because the support they both had received from the facilitators during preparation was removed.

The relationship between Kalicia and Ahmad was fairly well established because of the plea agreement and the preparation process. Ahmad had written a letter to Kalicia during preparation, which further personalized their connection. Their openness to each other and the VOD process appeared promising. Kalicia was deeply invested in Ahmad and his future and Ahmad had been cooperative and receptive in getting ready for the dialogue. There were some critical caveats, however, that likely influenced the quality of the openness between them. Specifically, the startup of the process occurred shortly after the conclusion of the criminal justice process. Little time was given, therefore, for either Kalicia or Ahmad to process the crime, their feelings, or what impact it had made on their lives long term. Indeed, Kalicia's motivation was tied up with her agenda for Ahmad rather than her own personal healing. Moreover, Ahmad was still an adolescent and under the influence of older people in his life. Because the VOD was part of a plea agreement, the legal mandate, although agreed to, likely influenced the timing and perhaps pre-empted the sense of need as well as the voluntariness of each person's participation. These dynamics likely shaped the nature of the engagement between Kalicia and Ahmad both during preparation and in the meeting.

Dialogue

Kalicia had two meetings with Ahmad with vastly different outcomes. She felt that the actual VOD went well. Both she and Ahmad were vulnerable to each other. Kalicia talked to him about how the crash had impacted the family. Kalicia felt that Ahmad expressed genuine remorse. Kalicia brought pictures of Darnell so Ahmad could know him better and Ahmad asked if he could have them for himself. Ahmad also shared pictures of his new baby son and talked about wanting to help other youth learn from his mistakes. Everything that occurred in the first meeting seemed authentic and congruent with what Kalicia had wanted. She left feeling "very, very positive," "a very extreme sense of hopefulness," even "ecstatic." Kalicia felt so buoyant that she proposed that they speak together at victim impact panels in the future and fantasized about being a mother and loving Ahmad "just like a son."

For Kalicia, the concept of forgiveness was almost irrelevant. She harbored no anger at that point and had chalked up the crash to a mistake made by a developing adolescent. Indeed, when Ahmad had stated during the VOD that he hoped Kalicia could forgive him, she dismissed his statement as relevant to anything she thought or felt. She could only understand it as something he might feel if their roles were reversed.

Kalicia, however, had some lingering doubts because of the dissonance between her optimism and some of the incongruences she experienced throughout the process. For example, the facilitators had warned her about Ahmad's immaturity. Because of his young age and lack of positive support, she worried that Ahmad might not follow through on his commitments to her and instead be negatively influenced by others. Even in the dialogue, she felt that he really did not understand the gravity of what he had done. Kalicia's uncertainty began to rise. Her optimism after the VOD was based on the belief that Ahmad would follow through on his commitment and would develop the right attitude for success so that he could flourish when he left prison. Kalicia and Ahmad had agreed in the VOD that they wanted to meet again so Kalicia initiated a second unfacilitated conversation two years later. She had no specific agenda other than to check in and assess Ahmad's progress.

Kalicia left the second meeting feeling frustrated, offended, and disappointed. Ahmad had no interest in doing any kind of public speaking himself or with Kalicia. Moreover, his attitude had changed such that he felt sorry for himself, was ready to move on from the crash, and wanted her help to get back his driver's license. He was no longer willing to make the changes he'd committed to in the VOD. The negative energy engendered by this encounter shattered Kalicia's positive feelings. For the first time, she began to feel anger and resentment that Ahmad had been given such a short sentence and would soon be released—"My thought was, 'That's not fair,' over and over. 'That's not fair.'" She began to realize that Ahmad had not cared enough to stop after he hit Darnell and that Darnell deserved something more after Ahmad left him "on the side of the road like he'd hit a possum or a squirrel." In spite of the results from the second meeting, Kalicia worked to maintain her optimism. She did not doubt the authenticity of the VOD or her hope for Ahmad. Rather, she placed the responsibility on his wife, his family, and other negative influences—"I am a little disappointed that he doesn't want to do this but I don't feel necessarily really angry. I just wish he had it in him to do it, because it would be good all the way around."

The second meeting magnified the dissonance between Kalicia's past positive response and the reality of Ahmad's limitations. In hindsight, the initial success of the VOD was ephemeral. Kalicia doubted her perceptions, wondering if others, who were more sceptical about Ahmad's motivation, might be right. Darnell's friends, for example, wanted Ahmad put to death or run over. In response, Kalicia wondered, "What if I'm wrong and this person doesn't deserve to be forgiven?" She questioned if Ahmad might be gaming her and thinking, "God, she's just stupid to even believe that I care." Indeed, Kalicia felt a little like a chump after Ahmad reneged on his promises. He was not willing to devote his life to the wrong he had done or to give the crash the priority that Kalicia gave to it by becoming a strong advocate for victim rights. Kalicia's worry about misplaced hope reflected her reliance on Ahmad to change. She needed him to fulfill her expectations in order to resolve the dissonance between her optimism and doubt. Without his shift in attitude, Kalicia's sense of resolution remained incomplete.

Although real to her, Kalicia's idealism and positive response to the first meeting masked the gaps that likely influenced her incompleteness. For example, the motivation for the VOD did not evolve from Kalicia's felt need or pain. Rather, it derived from her concern for Ahmad and what she could do to steer him in the right direction. Consequently, there was not a full unburdening of the pain and negative energy associated with the crash. Indeed, Kalicia began to have stronger negative reactions after the second meeting when Ahmad wanted his driver's license back and as time moved closer to Ahmad's release date. The positive energy associated with the first meeting gave the impression that dyadic shifts in energy had occurred when, in fact, there was a limited expression of need by Kalicia and little direct transfer of the pain to Ahmad. Although the conduit had been established between them for the back and forth flow of energy, the transformation of the pain was somewhat inconsequential. Kalicia felt hopeful that Ahmad was motivated to move in the right direction and that was enough. When he backed down, Kalicia did not have enough relief from her own pain to sustain what she had gained from the VOD. Indeed, she did not report any quality of life changes, no sense of being unburdened or of feeling complete.

Kalicia moved onto other activities to distance from and manage her disappointment with Ahmad. She already was strongly committed to being an advocate because of the meaning it gave to her life. Now, however, she re-subscribed to her mission of righting wrongs and making something better come out of her loss by greater involvement as a speaker on victim impact panels and leader for crime prevention activism in her city—"I usually do five to six victim impact panels a month and have formed a group to express our urgency to the lawmakers and city officials that they need to be more proactive about this stuff."

Kalicia seemingly moved on from Ahmad. However, when Ahmad's wife friended her on Facebook, it triggered the negative energy and lack of resolution Kalicia still carried. Rather than ignoring the request, Kalicia considered meeting with Ahmad and his wife at a public place like a restaurant to find out why his wife reached out to Kalicia—"I'm still hopeful that maybe this would turn into something good, for the families. But if it doesn't, that's okay too." Indeed, Kalicia continued to have many private conversations in her mind with Ahmad. She noted that she shows his picture when she speaks and wonders if someone in the audience might recognize him. "I have had numerous people come up to me and say, 'Hey, I knew Darnell' so there have to be people who knew Ahmad." Because of the wife's outreach, Kalicia's hope and agenda were reignited as well as her doubt. She did not want more disappointment but felt pulled to make contact because she felt incomplete. Likewise, if she did not respond to Ahmad's wife, she might miss an opportunity. If she engaged, though, she might feel manipulated.

The distortions that flanked the VOD process were evident as well in the explicit and implicit dialogue about forgiveness. There were nonverbal implications, for example, of an energy shift between Kalicia and Ahmad. They hugged and exchanged pictures. Ahmad's remorse was authentic. Moreover, Kalicia reinstated Ahmad in many ways. Her intent was to move him past the crash so that he could be an active and valued member of society. She asked him to join her as a speaker on victim impact panels. In truth, whatever forgiveness occurred was conditional and based on Kalicia's agenda for Ahmad. The examination of forgiveness, therefore, varied based on what happened in both meetings and the difficulties with sustaining the results from the VOD.

In the aftermath of the second meeting, Kalicia was left with even greater dissonance that remained unresolved. Although she now had specific knowledge of Ahmad's limitations, she refused to accept that Ahmad had been inauthentic and, instead, maintained that others were responsible for his backsliding and poor judgment. This positioning preserved her hope but kept her trapped in the unpredictability of Ahmad's decisions. His shifts in attitude and her focus on external influences on Ahmad and on him rather than on herself increased the negative energy and distorted the VOD process. In actuality, the scheduling of the VOD was out of sync with the time necessary for integration of the crime and the events associated with the criminal justice system. Indeed, Kalicia likely needed more time to process her son's death before meeting with Ahmad so that her personal needs specific to her pain took priority. Ahmad likely needed to mature so that he could address the consequences of his actions more thoroughly and with greater self-accountability.

Moreover, the context and motivation for the VOD was a part of the plea agreement, which legally mandated that Ahmad had an obligation to meet with Kalicia. The mandate, in effect, distorted the voluntariness of the VOD and the spirit of giving and gifting between two individuals who freely decide to meet. Kalicia's control in constructing the conditions in the plea agreement likely set the stage for her to assume she had more control of Ahmad than she actually did. Instead of finishing their contact at the end of the VOD, she felt compelled to monitor his commitment to her. Moreover, there was little stored or negative energy based on Kalicia's personal reactions to the loss of her son or toward Ahmad to propel movement toward each other. Indeed her movement was based on following through on one of the conditions of the plea agreement and her fear that Ahmad might back out. For Kalicia, therefore, the VOD was a part of the criminal justice process, which she felt she needed to complete before she could move forward.

TAMARA'S STORY AND ANALYSIS

Tamara was the victim of gang violence and survived three potentially life-threatening gunshot wounds. From the very beginning James, the shooter, expressed remorse for his actions but not in ways that allowed for dialogue with Tamara. Because of the nature of the crime, James was sentenced to 37 years in federal prison, a system that has no formal VOD process. It took over ten years, two wardens and some covert operations until James and Tamara finally arranged by themselves to meet. Their dialogue completed a process of accountability that had remained unfinished for years. Besides learning details about James that solidified her understanding of him and the shooting, Tamara committed herself to an inseparable and enduring relationship with James as "son."

One night I pulled into the driveway of my home, not realizing that I had been followed by a group of four boys until I saw their car stop in front of a house several doors away. I didn't open my garage door or go into my house because I knew my four-year-old son and his nanny were there alone. Even though it was drizzly and dark, I tried to watch what the boys were doing. Suddenly I felt somebody standing next to me. I looked and there was James, a young man with a gun. I threw my car into reverse and floored it. He unloaded his .38 into my car hitting me three times. I didn't want to stop and go into my own house because I thought I was going to die and I didn't want to die in front of my four-year-old. So I pulled up to the neighbor's house and got out. Then I tried dialing 911 on my car phone but I couldn't get through because I lived in a military neighborhood. Everybody there recognized gunfire so they were all calling 911. I didn't realize three of the boys were in the cul-de-sac turning around. They were still firing. But the neighbors rushed out, grabbed me, and ran me into their house. I found out later that James hid in the bushes across the street until all the commotion died down and then he ran away. He had walked over to my car at one point, looked in, and saw blood all over my face so he presumed I was dead. He didn't meet up with the other boys until later that night at their girlfriends' apartments. At the trial, the other boys testified that James was in tears because he thought he had killed me and didn't mean to.

I was transported by EMS to the hospital and kept overnight. Eight detectives came and tried to show me pictures. It had been so dark and fast and happened in a split second. I have no clue as to why I threw my car into reverse. You always think you will freeze in a situation like that but I didn't. I also don't know how I survived the gunshots other than that God was in the car with me. One bullet grazed across the top of my shoulder. One bullet went into my left shoulder and hit the scapula bone and broke it and went back out the same hole it came in on. That was a miracle. Finally, one bullet went in the base of my neck on the left and landed in the base on the right side. They took the bullet out six weeks later. The surgeon said that if it had landed one centimeter one way, I'd have been dead. If the bullet had landed a half a centimeter the other way, I'd have been paralyzed from the neck down. There are no other scars. Today, I am perfectly fine.

The boys were all members of a gang. There were two 14-year-olds, a 17- and an 18-year-old. They caught two of the boys trying to steal another car with the same gun they used on me. They started pointing fingers and ratting each other out. Eventually the police arrested all four of the boys. The two 14-year-olds were juveniles and so they were released early. The 17-year-old was adjudicated to be an adult. The 18-year old was already an adult. We went to trial 13 months later. The case was tried in a federal court because carjacking is a federal offense. Specifically, my vehicle was traced back to being partly manufactured in Canada and then brought into the United States through Detroit where it was a simple hold crossing state lines into Nevada where I bought it.

The boys faced charges of federal carjacking, conspiracy to commit carjacking, weapons, and enhanced gang activity. I gave testimony at the beginning of the five-day trial but was otherwise kept at the top of the federal building for my safety because what happened was a gang-related crime. I was allowed, however, to attend the final arguments. The two older boys were convicted. James, the shooter, was given 55 years in a federal penitentiary with no parole. The driver was given 30 years with no parole. They were both given an opportunity to speak. James stood up in front of the court and apologized. He looked me straight in the eye, which according to my friends and family was the first time he had looked up from the courtroom floor. He looked first at me and apologized, then at my family, his family, and the judge, and apologized in turn to everybody. The judge lowered his sentence from 55 to 37 years. In contrast to James, the driver just said, "Well if I did have anything to do with it, I'm sorry." He's actually in maximum security up north somewhere. He'll probably never see the light of day because he keeps committing more crimes in prison. Both of his parents were already incarcerated. James' parents were at the trial and sentencing. His father was Black and his mother was Filipino. They came up to me after the sentencing. His mother was crying and asked if I would forgive James. They wanted to stay in touch with me. I said, "I don't know about that at this point."

Five years later, James went back to court on appeal to lower his sentence ten years. I had an opportunity to speak and I did. Then James spoke and told the judge, "I didn't ask for this hearing. I don't want this. I don't deserve any time off. I deserve to serve every day I received for what I did to her and her family."

I was in therapy for eight years. I knew there was something different about James. He was very remorseful from the beginning. I tried to do a VOD but it was not possible because the program had not been adopted in the federal system. The State of Nevada, therefore, tried to help me. They went to bat with the Federal Bureau of Prisons and got permission for me to do a VOD. I went through preparation and all the paperwork, which was about one-and-a-half feet high. The folks from Nevada made a presentation to the warden of the prison but he said "no." That decision put a screeching halt to everything I was trying to do. The warden argued that James had rights too but they never even asked him if he wanted to speak to me.

After that, I began to participate in an in-prison restorative justice program called Bridges to Life that brought together offenders and crime victims. I found that program gave me the surrogacy of a VOD because it involved offender participants. There, I could work with and learn to talk to offenders as well as care about them. It helped me realize that they were real people who were no different than I am. They just made some bad choices. So, my preparation was many years in the making. I knew I was doing it on my own. I thought a lot about it. I wrote a lot of things down. I had a list of questions for James to answer. A lot of those questions were "Why, why, why, why, why, why me?" So my preparation lasted from 1995 to 2011.

I tried to meet with James for a second time ten years after his appeal. Again the State of Nevada stepped in to help me. They were even willing to facilitate the VOD. I got another "no" from the warden. I reported what had happened to the offenders and crime victims at Bridges to Life. I said, "I'm not giving up. I'm going to get into that prison one way or the other." At this point in time I was divorced and my boys were all grown and in college or married. I had just sold my house and my ex-husband was helping out by picking up the mail. Out of the blue, I got a phone call from him that I had received a letter from James Arbuckle. He read it to me and by the time he finished, both he and I were in tears. The letter was absolutely incredible and beautiful. I was not sure what to do. I sat on it for a week or two and talked to some advisors about it. I talked to a woman from the Federal District Attorney's office about possible ways to contact James. She said, "Well, I guess as long as nobody knows [what you are planning to do], no harm, no foul, right?"

So, James and I emailed and wrote back and forth for about three months. Then he said that he wanted to call me. I still remember that call and how weird it was to actually talk to him. He didn't tell me a whole lot because he wanted to tell me everything face to face. I said to him, "They're probably not going to let me into prison." He said, "Well, it can't hurt to try." So he sent me papers to complete on a Monday so I could get on his visitor list. I sent them back right away. James had told me that it would take at least three weeks before I was approved but everything went through in three days. It's unheard of to get approved that quickly. I think the administration at the Department of Corrections did not know I was the victim. I had remarried and my name was changed so they put the paperwork through. I was so grateful that I was finally going to get to see him.

On Saturday morning, I drove down to Three Hills Federal Penitentiary and had my first visit with James. There was no formal preparation or facilitation. It would just be the two of us using our time together to do what otherwise happens in a VOD. When I got to the prison, people seemed to know who I was. They knew I shouldn't be there but they weren't going to stop me. They wanted to see what would happen so they watched James and me while we met in the visiting room for the whole time. When James walked in, he gave his ID and turned around and looked at me. He walked over and we hugged. Then we just sat and talked for the next six hours. We laughed, cried, and talked. It was the most amazing six hours I've ever had. I learned that he was never offered the opportunity to meet with me. Two different wardens never even approached him with the possibility. I learned that James was now doing a chaplaincy stint at the facility. He had been at Three Hills for ten years. He'd never told his story until we started talking. He told me everything—his whole life, how he ended up in such a dark place, how he ended up in the gang, the events that happened the night he shot me, and how he really lost it when he thought he had killed me. He actually threw away the gun that evening and then went back and got it. Otherwise, he'd probably never have been caught. But he felt that he would likely be dead today if he had not been caught.

At our first meeting, I made him tell me everything from the beginning. "I want to know it all," and he did. At the time of the shooting, James was in a very dark place. He knew that his mother, when she was in the Philippines, got pregnant from a man in the United States military who was already married. He left her alone with James when he returned to the States. She married another man in the military when James was four years old and moved to the United States. James became a citizen and had several siblings. He was a straight A student and excelled in sports. His stepfather, however, would not allow his mother to show him much affection and was not very kind. No one in the family showed up to celebrate his accomplishments or make a big deal about his good grades.

By the time he became a teenager, he got himself wrapped up in gangs where he was loved and cared for. James' goal was to rise to the top of the gang. He told me awful things that he did that he's not proud of but wanted me to know everything. I had learned from the trial that the four boys were on drugs and smoking cigarettes laced with embalming fluid. However, James told me point blank that he did not do drugs that night. He was completely stone cold sober. He was just angry. Apparently a rival gang had tried to kill him the night before. The four boys wanted to steal my minivan so they could go retaliate and the rival gang would never see them coming. Who would think that a gang member would be in a minivan? That's why they had targeted my car.

Although I got all the answers I asked for, I didn't want to hear that James shot me without being on drugs. I had always used that excuse, "Oh, well they were on PCP." If someone is on PCP, they are acting outside of what they would normally do. I would share that piece when I told my story and everyone would respond, "Oh, yeah. That's why he did it." When I found out he was cold sober, that was hard to hear. However, I prefer the truth straight up and to my face. Knowledge is power, period. It was gut wrenching, however, knowing the truth and hard, as well, for him to say. There were a lot of tears during that visit on both sides. Every light at every end of the tunnel, every piece of closure that anybody ever talks about, I felt all that day. Although what he shared was scary, I saw more that he was capable of the truth and remorse. I walked out of that prison, probably as whole as I will ever be.

After he told me about his life, I told him about mine. That's when we began to really start bonding like mother and son. We started sharing and laughing and talking. It was almost silly and giggly. It was like the child who has just told his mom all the little bad things he did and now it's time to go for ice cream because he told the truth. He heard my side of it too and what had happened to me in my life. That included the destruction of my marriage, the drugs, and the addiction one of my sons was thrown into. He needed to hear all that ugliness and it hurt him because he had a responsibility in it. As much as I cared about him, I also needed him to understand the weight of what he did and what I told him was harsh. I had a lot of years getting through the shooting. At one point, I was suicidal and almost jumped off of a penthouse patio. I went through a drinking binge of about nine months, where I don't think I was sober. I neglected my children while I was trying to put the pieces back together. There were a lot of repercussions from what he did and I didn't excuse any of them.

By the end of the first visit, he and I were inseparable. It was the most powerful day of my life. I got the answers I needed, which was why. Why did this happen? I got the truth, the real, honest-to-God truth. I learned about his whole life, the darkness, the blackness, and how he ended up. James called me after I left there. He told me that when I walked out of the visitation room the guards were all in tears. So everybody watched us talk and was absolutely blown away. I visited him for about a year before somebody ratted us out. Even the warden knew what was happening but when another inmate brought it to people's attention, the prison had to stop it. But we still talk every week. He calls me every Friday and we still email. He calls me "Mom." I call him "son." We shared everything. In fact, there is probably nothing that we don't share at this point. We tell each other everything. It's very strange, very weird. My family was a little concerned, especially my boys. But after they read his letter, saw the peace this has brought me, and heard how amazing my visits are with him, they can't wait to meet him.

I don't know how to explain that people have choices like he did and still choose to do the bad things when they know better. After hearing all the stories of offenders with Bridges to Life, however, you see the similarities and begin to understand why some of the inmates like being in gangs and doing things like what happened to me that particular night. Then you see James who had lived with abuse and pure neglect and realize that all a child ever wants growing up is to be loved, accepted, and acknowledged. He never got, "Good job."

I do forgive what happened and I've learned to put it all in perspective and in place. My getting shot broke me to my core and the feelings I have about it will never go away. They just become a part of who I am. I wanted to meet with James so I could find some peace and a place to put what had happened. Although I wish there were things that hadn't happened, when I look at my life today and my children today, I wouldn't change a thing. I have been a Christian the majority of my life. I cried out to God that night in the car. I always felt that He picked me for a reason and that there was something He wanted me to do. I still believe that to this day. I never really thought about forgiveness or what it means but I grabbed a magazine one day in my therapist's office. It flopped open to a very short article by a professor whose mother had been brutally murdered. I was beaming when my therapist came to get me for our session. He looked at me and asked, "What?" I said, "It's been here all this time. I got it. I got it. I've forgiven him but I didn't even know I had." The article said that forgiveness is when you no longer wish ill will on somebody for what they've done to you. I knew I was way past that time. I remember being so angry at the beginning. I remember asking the detective if I could have ten minutes in a room with James. I never really knew what forgiveness was until then. I had so much weight lifted off me that day with James. The honesty with which he told me everything just solidified everything for me. I heard the real, honest-to-God heart truth that was so pure that it solidified it all.

The hardest thing for James was forgiving himself. He's still working on it. He holds himself accountable for what happened. When you see that quality in somebody, you know there is a real, good-hearted person in there. Somebody just needs to love them so it can come out. I told him I forgave him but he struggles with understanding why I forgave him. He has to let go of it because he did it and there's nothing he can do to take it back. He just has to do better moving forward. He's been in prison so long that I don't think he has had enough life skills with non-criminal people.

For me, forgiveness is letting go of the anger, hurt, and pain. You shouldn't forget that it happened, however, because everything that happens makes us the person we are today. I believe we should allow those things to become part of us and let us be who we're supposed to be. I believe that not forgetting prevents us from getting back into the same situation or position. Even though I did nothing wrong that night, I am hyper-vigilant to my surroundings. I don't want to be like those people who live in the bubble and go, without thinking, to get a gallon of milk at 10:00 at night. I wouldn't go out to get that milk because it's not worth it to me. You would think I was perfectly normal but I don't live like other people. I have fears and security issues. I don't park in parking garages. If somebody's walking towards my car, I will immediately get out of the way of them. Everything in my house has to be locked. I bought a gun and learned how to shoot it right after the shooting. But the gun scares me to death.

After my first meeting with James, I invited his mother to dinner. We sat and talked. I told her I had forgiven James, which gave her some peace. That's all she had ever wanted. She never tried to defend him or give excuses. She just listened. We talked a lot about James and where he is in his life right now. I haven't talked to her since. I somewhat blame her for what happened to James and that's why I don't want to have an ongoing relationship with her. I guess it's a little strange that I forgive him but hold her accountable. I have no desire to meet his stepfather because I know what he did. Yet James I hold so dear. I don't understand it. I really can't explain it.

Our meetings were exactly what I thought they would be. I just never imagined loving the man who tried to kill me. What I had hoped for was just peace. I didn't know that along with that peace, I was actually going to get an amazing person in my life for the rest of my life. I think that's the best part. I look forward to the day he gets out. I do plan for him to be completely and totally in my life, part of my family and probably will come and live in my house. I think he and I telling our story of peace and forgiveness can change lives. He's amazingly bright and intelligent. It's so sad that this happened but both of us feel the same way. We wouldn't change a thing. We're trying to write a book together. It's hard to get his stuff out of the prison to me. I have to keep track of all emails that he sends so I can use them. That first night that I met him, I just didn't see anything in his eyes. They were empty. I see everything in his eyes now. I don't know how to explain what an amazingly open and beautiful heart he has.

Analysis: The crime and its aftermath

Tamara was the direct victim of a gang-related aggravated assault that nearly took her life. The unexpected shooting occurred outside her home and in a quiet neighborhood where most of the families were connected with the military. One of the bullets almost killed her. Although severely injured, she had the foresight to put her car in reverse, floor it, call 911, and not escape into her home where her four-year-old son was waiting. She wanted to protect him from witnessing her death. She miraculously pulled through even though the bullet was within centimeters of killing or paralyzing her from the neck down.

From the moment of the shooting, James was unique in his response. After seeing the blood covering Tamara's face and body, he assumed she was dead. He cried because he did not mean to kill her. He and the other boys only planned to take her car. At his trial, he offered no defense and publicly apologized to her directly. He disagreed with his attorney's efforts, at the appeal hearing, to reduce his sentence, stating publicly that he deserved the time he'd been given for what he did to Tamara and her family.

Tamara waited 15 years and pursued a number of avenues before she was able to meet with James. During that time, she went through numerous medical procedures and sought years of therapy to address the physical and psychological trauma she endured. She went on a drinking binge for nine months and struggled with being suicidal—"I had a lot of years getting through it." In her efforts to put all the pieces together, she found that she neglected her children, all of whom had serious problems because of what happened to their mother. Her marriage could not survive the immensity of the trauma and violence associated with the shooting. Tamara became hyper-vigilant about her surroundings. To this day, she will not park in parking garages and has a concealed handgun license to carry a gun—"I learned how to shoot right afterward… But the gun scares me to death."

The primary issue for Tamara, however, was not the physical injury to her body or the emotional scarring but, rather, her compelling need to talk with James. Although she had given victim statements at his trial and the appeal hearing, it was his outreach and recognition of what he had done to Tamara's life that touched her. Indeed, James held himself unabashedly and publicly accountable to her at the legal proceedings where attorneys were zealously fighting to ensure he did not spend most of his life behind bars. Although there had been no meeting yet between them or verbal expression by Tamara of the pain differential, James had visually seen what he had done when he peered in the window of her car and saw her bloody face after he had shot her. That visual and the fear that he had killed her were not distorted by drugs and made a lasting impression on his mind. James' voluntary and honest acknowledgment of what he had done was, in effect, the beginning of the pain transfer. Moreover, he made his comments directly to Tamara. She felt the surge of positive energy that he conveyed at both the trial and the appeal hearing such that the energy flow between them began to construct the conduit for future ongoing communication.

The core dissonance for Tamara, however, was created by her desperate need for a dyadic engagement with James for her healing and the restricting impediments she faced from the criminal justice system, which, rather than helping her, blocked her ability to heal. Indeed, James was already trying to have dialogue with her when he saw her at the legal proceedings but neither could get to the other. James was trying to communicate his remorse and deservedness of punishment to Tamara in a setting in which he had to fight the system to do it. Tamara heard his comments as meant for her and likely felt them in a way that cemented their ongoing connection. Their desired dialogue, however, remained stalled and frozen because neither James nor Tamara had an avenue open for completing it. Although James made meaningful statements in court to Tamara, he had no way to assess her response, which left him empty. Likewise, Tamara had no way to communicate her reaction to him, which also left her empty. This circumstance created a gulf between them. Indeed, the yearning for completion but with no outlet was the primary source of frustration and stored energy. It increased as Tamara encountered ongoing resistance in her efforts to arrange for a VOD with James.

The statements made by James produced an unusual dissonance. Usually it is the victim who holds the offender accountable. James, however, held himself accountable, even going against the position of his own attorney who wanted to lower his sentence. He knew that he owed something directly to Tamara and reached out to her first and in a variety of ways. This shift on his part resulted in Tamara never seeing him as a monster. She had to work around the system to meet with him but she did not possess the anger that most victims otherwise feel toward the offender.

Preparation

Tamara did extensive formal and informal preparation over many years before she was able to meet with James. Initially, the Department of Corrections in Nevada agreed to help because the federal facility was located in Nevada and the Federal Bureau of Prisons agreed to allow the VOD. Consequently, Tamara went through the formal preparation process, which involved reflecting on and completing numerous self-assessments that probed her reactions to the crime and to James as the offender.

When the warden at the federal facility refused to allow the VOD, Tamara began volunteering for Bridges to Life as a substitute opportunity for meeting with James. Tamara's involvement with offenders gave her extensive exposure to their backgrounds and struggles and began to erase the line that otherwise divides crime victims and offenders—"I could work with, talk to, and learn to care about these offenders and realize that they are real people." In many ways, Tamara's experience with Bridges to Life was her first major energy shift. She understood how the stories of offenders aligned with the theme of making bad choices because bad environments such as gangs surrounded them. Although this experience served to open Tamara up emotionally and psychologically to the realities of an offender's world, she was aware, throughout, that the offenders in the Bridges to Life program were stand-ins for James. In that process she was limited because she could only transfer her knowledge to James mentally. However, she remained internally in dialogue with him all the way through.

James' statements to Tamara conveyed both remorse and empathy and his deservedness to face whatever punishment was necessary to atone for what he had done. Tamara's respect and admiration for James established her openness and receptivity to him early on. The knowledge gained from the offenders in the prison program helped humanize James and gave her clues about why he was involved in a gang and such dangerous activities. Tamara's openness to James, as well as her determination, were generated, however, by her anger with the criminal justice system. Indeed, the more rejection she experienced, the stronger was her desire to connect with James. The opposition from two wardens ultimately joined her and James against a common enemy even before they met.

Indeed, because James had behaved in such an unusual way, which Tamara actually normalized through her positive contact with the Bridges to Life offenders, she was able to have a positive experience in her preparation for meeting James. In contrast, the behavior of the wardens diminished the significance of James' allegiance to holding himself accountable because they responded as if he was a stereotypical criminal they were warehousing. Consequently, their response was dissonant with the person James had already shown that he was. That dissonance propelled Tamara forward in her determination to get into the prison to see James no matter what.

Dialogue

It is difficult to guage the start of the dialogue between James and Tamara. James' statements in court, his letter to Tamara, their written correspondence, and telephone call occurred before they ever met in person. Moreover, because of the wardens' refusal to allow the VOD, there was no preparation that included James or the facilitators shuttling back and forth between the participants that otherwise occurs. Indeed, before they ever met at the prison, they had schemed together to get Tamara into the prison. Their mutual determination was already propelled by the energy flow between them. Consequently, the conduit for energy transfer was well established. Although they had been bridging toward each other for a long time, the strength of their dyadic will finally brought them face to face. In many ways, the outcome of the visit could have been predicted. They just had to fill in the pieces. Their hug at the beginning of the visit was further evidence of the shift in the relationship that had been present from James' initial apology and subsequent stand against serving less time.

Tamara's primary need was to get answers to her longstanding questions—"I made him do just like I do [with the offenders] in Bridges to Life program. You tell me from the beginning. I want to know it all." Consequently, James took the lead and described in detail what happened the night of the shooting, how he got into gangs, his family background, and the countless wrongdoings and harms he had caused as part of his history. Tamara got the answers to her questions. Indeed, it was only through their face-to-face contact that she could see his eyes and how he had changed. James too needed Tamara to directly see his remorse. For example, he did not want to talk to her over the phone about the shooting. He would share his story only in person.

Tamara most appreciated his honesty and accountability both to himself and to her. Tamara's reciprocal sharing of her hard and painful truth helped humanize each to the other and complete the dialogue that had started years ago at James' trial—"I walked out as whole as I will ever be." Their mutual truth-telling served to clean out the negative energy. It worked like an acid to cut through the stored-up ugliness of the past as well as a healing balm but it was harsh, raw, and real. The honest-to-God, gut-wrenching truth dissipated the negative energy as shown by the fact that both Tamara and James were able to laugh, cry, and talk, and begin a bonding process. Tamara described it as "kind of like mother and son." Indeed, at one point, "It [was] kind of almost silly and giggly."

James' resourcefulness in writing the letter and advocating for their visit along with the work he'd done on himself changed the ownership of the meeting from it being "hers" to it being "theirs." They became co-conspirators with a shared narrative. Their single-mindedness actually brought their relationship to fruition and continued it past the initial meeting at the prison.

Although Tamara had prepared for years, she was shocked to discover that James was stone cold sober when he shot her. This admission erased any illusion or excuse that Tamara might have had to explain what had happened. She struggled with the dissonance that he had chosen to shoot her alongside her belief that he was a good-hearted person. She partially resolved the dissonance by recognizing that his choice was about getting the car, not about her. She also resolved it by understanding that his drive to hold himself accountable and to confess his life to her was connected to trying to give back to her what he took when he shot her. Their mutual unburdening, in effect, helped unburden Tamara.

Tamara had struggled with forgiving James during her therapy. James' mother had asked her to forgive him right after the trial. However, Tamara was not sure what forgiveness was or how to get there. Her reading of the article by the psychologist helped her first to identify that the critical issue was letting go of the anger or vengefulness and second to discover that she had already accomplished that. Although she logically derived that she had forgiven James, she felt the full impact of her forgiveness after James conveyed his whole story with such honesty. "Everything just solidified. I had so much stuff, so much weight lifted off me that day." Indeed, the nature of James' sharing showed Tamara how deserving James was of her forgiveness. Her response to his invitation and her giving of herself and her pain to him reflected her sense of James as worthy, which may be partly responsible for the lifting of the weight from her shoulders. For Tamara, the larger issue, however, was the difficulty James had with self-forgiveness. She recognized that James' honesty and insistence on self-accountability held him hostage in ways that made it difficult for James to left go of the pervasive negative toxic elements, which is what Tamara learned was necessary for forgiveness.

Over the years, Tamara worked on the idea of acceptance and the belief that in letting go of the negativity, it made room to accept what had happened so that it could be absorbed—"When we forgive then what we're forgiving just becomes a part of who we are." She applied that same philosophy to the horrific event that happened to her—"I don't think you ever get closure. An event that drastic never goes away. It becomes part of who you are." As such, the meeting with James allowed the dialogue about the crime and its impact on both their lives to come to completion so it could be absorbed and shared. This meeting and their coming together, in effect, transformed the pain Tamara otherwise carried. A major shift for Tamara, therefore, was accepting that her losses and the impact from the crime, including her relationship with James, had become a part of who she is. The transformation was not loud and intense. Rather, it was manifested quietly as a sense of peace.

Because of the circumstances, the guards and staff of the facility witnessed the meeting in the prison's visiting room. They sanctioned it with their amazement and tears and made it safe by keeping the secret about Tamara's status as victim until it was exposed and they were forced to stop their visits. Tamara's reinstatement of James took many forms. She continued to meet with him five more times. She continued to correspond with him and have weekly calls after she could no longer see him. She planned that he would be an active part of her world when he was released and laid the groundwork with her sons to accept him as a family member. Finally, Tamara and James decided to write a book together about their shared experience of the shooting and its aftermath.

MONIQUE'S STORY AND ANALYSIS

Monique's 19-year-old brother, Eduardo, was killed while working security at a local convenience store. Edwardo lived for 21 days in the hospital before succumbing to his injuries. The family scrambled for details of the crime and the shooter but it took more than a year before law enforcement disclosed they had caught the perpetrator, Manny, and he had already been sentenced. Monique's motivation for meeting with Manny was based on his impending release from prison. She saw him as a monster who deserved prison and never to see the light of day. Through the dialogue, Monique began to humanize Manny and restructure her understanding of the crime. Manny paradoxically gave Monique her freedom by guiding her to live in ways that moved her forward but with her brother's memory beside her. Years later, she gave that freedom to another offender who, unbeknownst to her, had witnessed her brother's shooting and subsequently became a hostage of guilt and self-recrimination.

When I was 24 years old, my 19-year-old brother, Eduardo, was killed while working as a security guard for a convenience store. There was a confrontation in a huge parking lot between three guards, including him, and a crowd of 50–75 people who were not supposed to be there. The guards were White and the crowd was mostly Black. People in the parking lot felt that the guards were racist because they had arrested three young kids who had stolen beer from the store. The crowd started pushing and shoving. In the confrontation, one of the guards, who was in a pick-up truck, grabbed his shotgun and fired into the air thinking everyone would scatter. But a man in the crowd pulled a gun out of his car and, in response, fired into the crowd. My brother was stuck in the back where the bullet hit his shoulder blade and then came out the front. It could have been so much worse but my brother was the only one hit. Finally, the guard in the pick-up truck fired back and peppered the shooter's car and the shooter.

The police, who were three blocks from the store, were called over 50 times to come to that parking lot but no officer showed up until after the shooting. Eventually, the crowd dispersed and my brother and the shooter ended up at the same hospital but we did not know that fact. I learned what happened from my mother and we all went down to the hospital.

Everyone who was in the parking lot at the store had ended up in the hospital parking lot. It was just chaos. People were yelling and screaming at us and calling us names. We had no clue what was going on. By the time we figured it out, the police had cleared the hospital parking lot and everyone settled down. There was so much confusion that, initially, nobody knew who shot whom first. The hospital released the shooter within a few hours. My brother lived for 21 days but there was so much damage that his body could not survive it.

The police told us nothing about the shooter, whose name was Manny. We kept pushing to get details. We wanted them for my brother during those 21 days because he could not remember anything about that night. We were denied at every turn. I think I was discounted because I was just a sister. The truth was that I had raised Eduardo as if I were his mother. I would go to the District Attorney's office just begging, "Please, just tell me something. Have you arrested somebody?" After a year, the lead detective contacted us and told us that the police had arrested a man shortly after the shooting and he'd been in jail ever since. He decided to take a plea bargain and got a 15-year sentence. We had had no communication with the criminal justice system. That started my mission to meet Manny.

At first, I was angry with the shooter. My brother and I were so close and Manny took him. A nagging question played repeatedly in my mind. "How does somebody get to the point where they think shooting another is okay? What goes on in their life so that this is the answer?" Eventually I moved from the anger to just wanting answers and ultimately, "the" answer. When I would tell others about my desire, they would think I wanted to do something bad to him but that was not my intention.

My brother's murder really did a number on the whole family. Everybody who was in a relationship ended up divorced because they and their partners were not on the same page. My mother and I both divorced. I ended up being a single mom raising two kids. I felt like I went on autopilot. It was the only way I could continue to raise my kids and not let grief totally consume me but it just kept coming out in different ways. I was really depressed a lot, just going through the motions, and not really living a life. I tried to shelter my kids but they were affected as well. The truth was that they could see how shut off I was and not the happy mom they had known. I was so wrapped up in my loss that I didn't realize what was happening to them.

Indeed, I was pretty fixated on the shooting. I knew Eduardo was a great guy. I adored him. He was nothing but friendly and loving. I felt like I was chasing my own tail, however, because I couldn't get answers about Manny, nor could I see for myself who he was. All my thoughts were very negative and I was almost obsessive about what had happened. My fear held me hostage because that was all I could think about. For example, I'd sit and feel the loss and how horrible this world felt without my brother. I'd wonder how anyone could take his life. Then I'd get angry about it because Manny only got 15 years. I began thinking, "Maybe if I talk to him and he sees what life he took, he won't want to do this again." Indeed, I felt that if you take someone's life, you should know whose life you took. Who are they? What were they about?

So I started sharing with everybody and anybody who would listen that I would like to meet Manny. Indeed, I even talked to his parole board when it was time for his review. I said, "You know, I really wish I could meet him. I need to know more about him and I want him to know about my brother." That's when I learned about the VOD program. That was also the point when I learned, for the first time, some facts about Manny. The parole board told me that he was going to school and hadn't been in trouble. A staff person connected to the parole board sent me the paperwork to complete. I signed up for the program even though I was convinced that Manny was "probably not going to do it." I was thrown for a loop when he agreed to it. Sometimes when you say you want something and it happens, you're not quite sure that's really what you want because it's scary. I'd never been in a jail or prison. I'd never been in trouble. So, going into a prison to meet my monster was terrifying.

I had two reasons for wanting to meet with Manny. The police reports were so sketchy that I felt driven to know what had actually happened the night my brother was killed. When you have that many people in a parking lot and take everyone's statements, it's amazing how different the accounts are and how difficult it is to figure out whose recollection is correct. I needed answers that I could understand, know, and be at peace with. My other motivation was my fear. Manny got a very short sentence of 15 years for a deadly weapons charge and I didn't think that was right. Moreover, he only had to serve half of the sentence. I was deathly afraid, therefore, that he'd get out and commit another crime. I was scared for society. Because I'd been fighting his parole for years, I even told the parole board, "No, no. Please don't let him out until after the VOD." Indeed that fear kept me wrapped up for many, many years.

I went through preparation for six months. I loved my facilitator. She felt like a friend. She counseled with both Manny and me and cared a lot about us. She wanted to be sure Manny and I were on the same page. Every time I got scared and thought, "I don't know if I can do this," she'd bring me back saying, "But this is really what you wanted. You asked for this. So think about it before you don't do this." She would sit with me, let me go through my fears, and talk it out. I'd respond saying, "You're right. I do want to do this. It's my one chance to do this in a safe environment. I could have hunted him down when he got out but this was a safe way to do it."

I went on a tour of the prison the day before we met. It was terrifying to go into a maximum security facility. There were guards and all the wire and dogs. I was deathly afraid. My facilitator helped me. She kept me calm and breathing. "I'll be here the whole time with you and we can do this." In the prison visit I got to see how Manny worked and lived. On the day of the meeting all my apprehension melted away as soon as we got to the meeting and I was faced with him. I thought to myself, "That's the guy that I've been having nightmares about for ten years?" I had made him up to be a big monster in my head but when he walked in, he was just a guy. So why was I so afraid?

The facilitator introduced us to each other and I shook his hand. That was an awkward moment. How do you greet someone who has harmed your family in that way? We then sat down across from each other. The facilitator talked for a minute about the sessions she had had with each of us. We had both written letters about what we wanted to get out of the meeting and even though that information was known, the facilitator read the letters out loud so we could hear in each other's presence the expectations of one another. That procedure helped calm our fears. Actually, Manny was more afraid than I was. He's told me many times that he didn't know what I wanted to say to him.

I asked Manny to start by telling me where he came from and how he was raised. I also wanted to tell him about our childhood, how we were raised and who my brother was. So we kind of went back and forth with childhood stories and what led up to the night of my brother's murder. We kind of held back, dragging our feet about the night of the murder because both of us were a little nervous to talk about it. We needed time to warm up to the idea of going there.

I brought a photo album to the meeting that I had arranged in chronological order. Toward the end of the album I had my brother's autopsy report and a picture of the headstone I had made for him. I also had pictures of when we were with him in the hospital. He was awake and talking at one point. Because he was a macho man there were many pictures where he was saying, "I'm going to make an album so I can pick up girls because I've got this gunshot thing." The photo album was important because Manny could see the actual damage he had done. When he saw the pictures, he cried. I felt for him. I realized that in all the chaos that night, it could have been anybody who was shot. I can't imagine being responsible for someone's life and being brave enough to own up to it. So my heart kind of switched at that moment. I told him, "You are so brave for agreeing to meet with me, not knowing what I was going to say to you or do to you when we got in here." He answered, "I'm not going to lie. I was scared. I didn't know."

Because I could share the actual event with him, he could answer more questions for me. I didn't know, for example, if he was actually trying to kill my brother or not. He told me that he had just fired into the crowd because he heard someone else shooting. He also told me he was very heartbroken when he found out that he had hit my brother with the gun because he liked him. He had known him slightly because he had been in the store where my brother worked many times, but they weren't friendly. That made things a little easier for me to absorb. I could see the emotions warring in him when I pulled out the autopsy report, my brother's pictures, and the headstone. It made it more real for him. He told me that since he had been locked up, he had tried not to think about it a lot. He explained that when you're in prison, you are just trying to survive and you cannot be weak and let all those emotions take over. So I saw that he hadn't had time to properly absorb what had happened. Later he expressed to me that the meeting was a great help because he could actually digest what had happened and work through it.

As we started just opening up about our families, the mood in the room shifted. I felt like I was just meeting somebody for the first time and having a really nice conversation with the person. There was definitely a shift from us both being scared and then recognizing that we were really both human. We weren't there to hurt each other. Once the apprehension melted away, we began talking like we were just swapping stories. I learned so much about him and his past and could see where the road took him. I do not condone what he did, but I could see how he reacted out of fear. I think I might have done the same thing.

We spent seven or eight hours together that day. We laughed and cried. It was a beautiful experience. At one point, we broke for lunch and went right back to it. It was just a life-changing experience for me. He was very accountable for what he did. He was curious about my brother and wanted to know more about him. That made the meeting easier for me because there wasn't any hostility and I could share fully about Eduardo. Moreover, I was able to get the answers from him that I needed to fill in the blanks about the night my brother was killed. For example, I always had wondered about Manny's life. In the meeting, he told me about himself so I could understand his background and how he ended up thinking that firing into the crowd was the answer. That helped a lot. People always wondered why I cared. I'd respond, "I do care. There's something that happened to him in his life that made him think that it was okay to behave the way he did." I needed to understand what that was. I think I wanted to know so that I could feel more sympathy and empathy for him. After the meeting, I didn't have to feel bad about having caring feelings for him because now I had an accurate picture of what it was I was feeling.

During the meeting, Manny asked if I could ever forgive him. I had to take a break to compose myself because it was a topic I hadn't considered much. By the time I rejoined the meeting, I had decided that forgiveness was on the table and it was something I wanted to do. Before we left that day, I hugged him and told him I forgave him. That felt like such a tremendous relief. I can't say I believed it 100 percent the first time I said it. I wanted it to be true and I knew that I would have to work at it to make it more permanent. For example, there are days that come back as a reminder that I'm missing my brother, that he's not in my life, and that Manny took the person from me that was so precious. Now I remind myself that the forgiveness was never for Manny or to tell him it was okay what he did. That was my twisted thinking. I even thought that if I didn't forgive him, I would have a power over him. I gradually realized that was false and, in fact, I would be imprisoning myself. Indeed, something during the meeting changed in me. I realized forgiveness wasn't about him, that I could keep myself hostage with all that negative energy and I didn't want it. I saw that forgiveness was about setting myself free. I also saw that I had to separate him from his actions. I had to realize that we all do things that are not right, all the time. Does that make us a bad person? It just means that we did something dumb or stupid and out of character even for us. So we have to forgive people for stumbling and making mistakes. Forgiving him was empowering for me. When you're actually able to do it with the person, it just makes forgiveness a hundred times stronger because both people find peace that way.

Before the meeting, I was robotic and shut down emotionally because I had all these bad feelings and I didn't know what to do with them. It was just easier to function by shutting them down. That meant everything was on lockdown because I couldn't feel one emotion without feeling guilty about not feeling another emotion. Lockdown included joy, happiness, and love. However, when I walked out of the meeting, I thought, "Wow." I felt alive again. It was absolutely wonderful. I told my facilitator, "That was the most beautiful experience I've ever had in my life." I've had kids but the meeting just topped that. It healed me in so many ways. I was able to actually feel safe again, let my guard down, and feel what I was feeling without all this guilt.

The negative energy was no longer in me. I think it slowly faded away during those hours we were together. Before I had no way of knowing if all the negative thoughts I'd had were true. A typical person doesn't go to jails or prisons all the time. You only hear the media stories, the sensationalized cases and you think that everyone in prison is just like those cases. Suddenly you see that's not true because you can clear up all those unanswered questions and speculations. Perhaps we could have written letters back and forth without meeting but it would not have been as profound as when we sat down across the table from each other and looked at each other when he talked. We could see the emotions on each other's face and go through those emotions together. I needed to see Manny. I needed him to know who my brother was. It was safe for us both. If we'd met on the street, it would have been in total panic because neither of us would have known each other's intentions. This way, we both knew going in what to expect.

I think of the time that I did the VOD as a positive time in my life. There was such a shift inside of me when it happened. It met every expectation I had and then some. The core shift happened during the VOD. I'd had no interaction with anybody who had ever been to jail or prison. The meeting taught me that even though you're incarcerated for a crime, you're still a human being. You're still a person. You're not a monster. You're not garbage. At the time of the VOD, everybody, in my opinion, who was in prison was a horrible monster, deserved to be there, and should never see the light of day. Now I don't feel that way at all. Manny, like other offenders, made bad choices and hurt people but they can change that reality. The meeting put things in a better perspective for me. When I left the meeting, one of my first phone calls was to the parole board that was reviewing him. I said, "Okay, no more. Please let him out."

The meeting was difficult because some of my family members were not pleased that I did it. They were still stuck with their anger and tormented by my brother's loss. They still are. Although I'm free from all that negativity, my family doesn't see Manny the way I do. Because I forgave the man who murdered my brother, my family feels I've betrayed Eduardo. My mother barely speaks about my brother at all. It's like he never existed. I couldn't talk to her while I was preparing and doing the VOD because she didn't want to know about it. Now through the years, she has been somewhat curious. Manny and I wrote several letters to each other after our meeting. He even wrote a letter to her. I gave it to her but I don't know if she's read it because we don't talk about it. Indeed, I've watched my family stumble through life still feeling that anger. It's hard for me because if they would open their heart a little bit and look at this, they wouldn't have to feel all those negative feelings. I think they could find some peace in what happened.

After the meeting, my facilitator suggested I participate in Bridges to Life, an in-prison restorative justice program for crime victims and offenders. I've been active in the program for ten years. I get to almost relive my experience with Manny over and over again because Bridges to Life is done with offenders who can't have VODs with their victims. So now I'm using what was a negative thing to produce a positive thing. My brother didn't just die. He still lives on and I think his story helps people. My family's reaction has been worse, unfortunately, since I decided to go back to the prison after my meeting. I told them "It's what I need to do. It's what I'm called to do." I have since remarried and my husband is very supportive of what I've done.

One night when I was at a Bridges to Life meeting, I spoke to a group of 70–80 men. I was telling the story of my brother. When I got done I asked the inmates if they had any questions. This gentleman stood up. He was openly weeping and very upset. I worried about what I had said. "Why is he crying like that?" I know my story is sad but he was really touched by it. Then he started telling me specifics about that night, specifics I don't usually share. At first I felt afraid. "Who is this man? How does he know all this?" He knew my brother's name, the gas station, the name of the street. He knew it all. The whole room just stepped back. It's like the men were all thinking, "What's happening? How does he know this?" It turned out that this inmate was standing in front of my brother when he fell. He was 15 and just watching and experiencing what was happening. His life spiraled out of control after he witnessed my brother's murder. He started drinking and doing drugs more. He just didn't care any longer about his life. He was never implicated in the crime but he was definitely there and involved. After I listened to him, I walked over and hugged him and told him, "I forgive you too." He was still trapped living in the murder when both Manny and me had already gotten past it. Yet here was this other person that we didn't know or think about who was suffering.

Manny and I stayed in contact for almost a year after the meeting. We'd write back and forth two or three times a month. He had promised to do whatever I asked him to do including finishing his education, which was really sweet of him. I've talked to him a few times on Facebook. He's out now and had a child about a year ago. He was going to college. I always tried to be encouraging of him and believed he could do school and change his life if he wanted to. I was proud of him for doing it.

Everything has just changed for me. It's been night and day. The guilt has gone away. I managed to put myself through school and raise my kids. Manny had told me at the meeting that he had to live for himself and my brother and he wished that I would do the same thing. Life became happy again. I fell in love with doing prison ministry because it gave me the chance to do something positive with all this ugly. If I hadn't done the meeting with Manny, this would not have happened. Instead, the meeting gave me the first step up to really look at people in prison in a different way. I'm thankful I did the VOD. I'm just sad more people don't know about it.

Analysis: Crime and its aftermath

Monique lost her younger brother, whom she had raised as a child, in a racially charged random exchange of gunfire that unintentionally resulted in his particular death. Indeed, the shooter, Manny, did not know the identity of the victim until sometime after the shooting. Monique and her family members attended Eduardo for three weeks in the hospital, but he could not survive the extensive damage done to his body. This touch-and-go situation was particularly grueling because it kept the family teetering between hope and despair for days.

The chaos associated with shooting and near-riot crowd made it difficult to get accurate information. The police withheld details so that Monique knew nothing for a whole year—"We were denied at every turn." When she did get some specifics, she learned that the shooter was at the same hospital at the same time as her brother and that he had been arrested and jailed since the shooting. This poor treatment by the criminal justice system was compounded by the fact that Monique felt disenfranchised because she was only a sister to the victim—"I don't know how many times I heard from people, 'Well, you're just a sister.'" Consequently, Monique had a difficult time finding support groups that would make room for her. She did not fit into Parents of Murdered Children and was told directly that even though "I raised my brother but that didn't matter because I was only his sister."

Eduardo's murder had a huge impact on the family. According to Monique, everybody who was married got divorced, including Monique. She managed to function and raise her children by suppressing her grief but that took away the mother they had known. Indeed, her shut-down closed off all of her other emotions as well, which left her numb—"I couldn't feel one emotion without feeling guilty about feeling another emotion, so it was just easier not to feel anything at all."

Monique was depressed for many years. She would obsess about losing Eduardo, question how someone could have taken his life, and then get angry because Manny only got a 15-year sentence. Eventually, that the shooting was incomprehensible became dominant but she could find no answers. The eyewitness accounts were contradictory and police reports were sketchy so it was difficult to reconstruct what had actually happened. Monique's questions, however, went deeper than any information she could obtain. She truly needed to understand how Manny got to the point where it was permissible to shoot another human being—"Something happened to him in his life that made him think it was okay to behave that way." She concluded, within herself, that having the answers would allow her to understand, which would bring her some peace. Only Manny had those answers.

Monique also worried about Manny's release. She feared that his short stay in prison would do little to stop him from killing someone else. In her search for something that might prevent another egregious crime, she began thinking that talking to Manny about her brother and the life he took might be a strong enough incentive to stop him in the future. She had tried to protect society by fighting his parole. However, the desire to meet with him remained constant over many years. She learned about VOD only after voicing her wish to the staff person who was interviewing her for Eduardo's next parole review. Monique signed up for the program never expecting that Eduardo would agree to their meeting.

Monique had voiced her wish to talk with Manny repeatedly over the years. Her wish was driven by the stored energy that accumulated from the grip of anger, obsessiveness, and shut-off emotions that otherwise careened around internally with no outlet. It wrapped around and consumed her for many years. She also had dissonant feelings that needed resolution. On the one hand, Manny was a monster that had malevolently shot her brother. Monsters are dangerous and less than human. They should be avoided. Yet, Monique yearned for greater understanding about how he could have done it in hopes that answers to her questions might put to rest what was otherwise incomprehensible.

Preparation

Although Monique wanted to talk to Manny, she was also scared because she truly pictured that he was a monster. Her family, who disapproved of her decision to meet with him, fed her apprehension—"I have family members who are not pleased with me…They see that I have betrayed my brother." The facilitator, who prepared her for the meeting, however, was extremely supportive and caring—"She would sit with me and let me go through my fears." During the six months of preparation, the facilitator regularly reminded Monique of her desire to meet, which strengthened Monique's yearning and resolve and dissipated some of her family's influence.

Monique, however, also had an internal battle about being open to Manny and whatever might occur when they met. She was plagued by deeply held societal stereotypes about offenders. Besides seeing Manny as "the worst monster on the face of this planet," she felt that he "deserved to be in prison and never see the light of day." She recognized that the understanding she so desired ran straight into these deep-seated judgments, causing a war of emotions between vengefulness and empathy. She had to walk through the fire of all that negativity, which continued until she met Eduardo. Although she was in internal conflict, Monique went ahead because of her trust in the facilitator and the positive clues she received from Manny, such as his willingness to meet with her. Each time she took a step back, the facilitator would push her gently forward.

Dialogue

For Monique, the real picture about Manny and his life started with the tour of his world at the prison. Going into a maximum-security prison escalated her apprehension because she was being introduced, for the first time, to a netherworld of guards, wire, dogs, and monsters. At the same time, she saw for herself how Manny lived and worked. When Manny walked in for the meeting, Monique immediately experienced the distance between the fabricated monster movie in her mind and the immediate reality that "he was just a guy."

During the first part of the meeting, Manny and Monique carefully constructed the conduit between them before they talked about Eduardo's murder. They drew each other in by reciprocally sharing their childhoods. As each communicated something about themselves, the other responded with a similar piece of information. Their resonance to each other was deep and likely accelerated the continuing reciprocity of their sharing. For example, Monique learned that Manny was afraid like she was. Indeed, "he was more afraid than I was." The reading of their expectation letters by the facilitator made the process trustworthy because it joined them in terms of hearing what each wanted from the meeting.

Monique, however, discovered that although she initially was scared of Manny because of the unknowns in meeting a "monster," Manny didn't know her either and was terrified of what she might say to him. In explaining how they spent the first part of their time together, Monique again recognized their commonality and said, "Both of us were a little nervous about getting there. It did give us more time to warm up to the idea" of talking about Eduardo. By first building the connection between them, it set the stage for later sharing the most important information. Moving together toward discussing the killing of Eduardo was gradual. The slow pace was not the result of a psychological blockage or mistrust of each other but rather because of the deeper emotions they both carried and the honoring of their respective pain and shame by inching their way into the territory—"We had to go through the emotions together."

Monique communicated the pain differential by showing Manny pictures of her brother in the hospital so he could see the actual damage he'd done. Her showing the autopsy report and Eduardo's headstone brought the reality of his killing Monique's brother closer to the surface. Monique watched and listened as Manny absorbed what he had done. She saw his struggle to control his feelings as she pulled out the autopsy report. Monique felt his remorse as Manny received her pain onto himself, cried, and expressed his willingness to do anything she asked him to do. At that moment, Monique opened up to seeing Manny differently. She recognized that he never intentionally shot her brother. In fact, Manny liked him. The shooting of Eduardo, therefore, was a random event. The fact that Manny had unknowingly shot someone he liked created a heavy burden and internal dissonance for him as well. Monique saw his struggle but also began to realize that although he had taken Eduardo's life, he was brave enough to meet with her and face what he had done. It was like raising a curtain and behind it, she saw a human being— "He's just a person. He's just a human like me." As Monique woke up to who Manny was, she experienced a major transformation in how she saw and related to him—"There was a shift inside of me when it happened that met every expectation I had and then some."

Moreover, Manny answered many questions for Monique so she could make better sense out of what happened. She learned that he shot into the crowd without targeting her brother, that he was bereft when he found out he'd shot Eduardo. This meeting was his first chance to actually digest what had happened. For Monique, the switch in her heart was the turning point. She felt no more fear or guilt. The negative energy was gone. Most important, she could feel again. She described the transformation and shift in energy as taking something ugly and allowing it to become beautiful. It literally gave her back her ability to feel joy.

Monique also experienced a major shift in how she thought about forgiveness, which was not a conscious issue for her prior to the meeting. Manny's initiation of the topic, however, forced her to consider it. She "decided" to forgive him but regarded it as one-way and as an act or gift that one person gives to another. She had already experienced deep forgiveness toward Manny on an implicit level. She felt tremendously compassionate given what had happened between them in the meeting and there was no remaining negative energy for her to address. The shift for Monique, however, was her realization that her gift of forgiveness was actually a gift to herself. Instead of forgiveness setting Manny free, she set herself free from the bondage of all the negative energy. Besides feeling unburdened and complete, Monique's reinstatement of Manny was profound. She literally humanized him fully in her mind, feeling that the shift happened because of their dyadic process and what they went through together.

Indeed, part of her feeling freed was due to Manny's guidance, which was to live both for herself and her brother as he himself does. Instead of warring emotions, which created ongoing dissonance between moving forward and remaining loyal to her brother, this "both/and" model became a way to stop the burden of having to make an impossible choice. Her acceptance of his advice absolved some of the guilt that otherwise attended any positive emotion that she felt—"Life became happy again." Monique recognized the importance of their mutuality. She forgave him and he helped her recognize that it was okay to let go and be free of the ways she held herself hostage. Paradoxically, therefore, the person who was a monster in her eyes provided her with her freedom through both taking responsibility and telling her how to live in a "both/and" way. In describing her forgiveness experience she commented that doing it together, or as part of a dyadic rather than singular process, made it more significant because "both parties find peace that way." As part of her forward direction and evidence of Manny's reinstatement, they exchanged letters. Rather than a rehash of the past, their ongoing communication focused on their present lives and plans for the future, including Manny's education.

Even though the VOD was liberating, Monique continued to live with the fact that her meeting with Manny was unacceptable to her family. Indeed, they were unable and unwilling to consider that he was anything but a monster. Monique, therefore, was faced with conflicting needs. If she tried to move forward with her life she would incur her family's disapproval. It she stayed where she was, she would remain stuck and negative. Monique resolved some of that dissonance and also found a unique way to move forward while remaining close to her brother with Bridges to Life. Besides reinforcing her new outlook, the program let her do something positive through her continued contact with, and humanizing of, offenders who would not have had the opportunity she gave Manny. Bridges to Life, therefore, became a ministry for her that also sustained the impact from the VOD. The irony of meeting one of the men who was involved with and present when Eduardo was killed was an exemplar of the ripple effect from her meeting with Manny. She was able to see how Eduardo's murder had changed and stalled the man's life and how badly he needed the burden lifted so he could go forward as she had. She forgave him too, both explicitly and implicitly, by her statement, "I forgive you too" and her hug of acceptance and reinstatement that was witnessed by all the Bridges to Life participants that night.

3

MAPPING DYADIC FORGIVENESS

An Analysis of Positive Energy Shifts in Restorative Justice Dialogue

1 ▓

CRIME AND ITS IMPACT

The inflicting of bodily harm, including death, is associated with an act that is violent, unexpected, and intentional. Figure 3.1 shows the impact of crime on the victim participants. The negatively charged energy associated with seriously violent crime has a pervasive and toxic impact because it shatters the fundamental principles that bind us together as human beings. Namely, we cannot survive alone and rely, therefore, on a shared code as a species that ensures our safety and ability to live together. Seriously violent crime maims the shared reverence for life that otherwise places limits on those behaviors, such as anger, that might otherwise cause dire, deadly, and destructive results. The principles that bind us together are embodied in legal and religious doctrine. Their preeminent stature is a commentary on the immense power they hold over all of us and how we live together. When they are violated, we commonly feel horror and outrage.

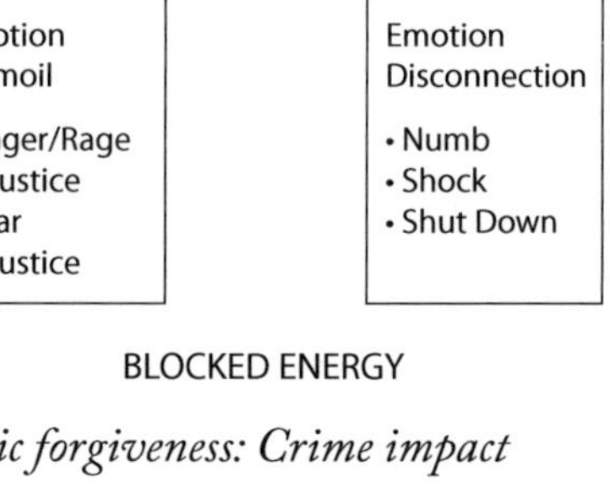

NEGATIVELY CHARGED ENERGY

```
                    CRIME
                    Impact          - - - - - - - ->


      ┌───────────────────┐      ┌───────────────────┐
      │ Emotion           │      │ Emotion           │
      │ Turmoil           │      │ Disconnection     │
      │                   │      │                   │
      │ • Anger/Rage      │      │ • Numb            │
      │ • Injustice       │      │ • Shock           │
      │ • Fear            │      │ • Shut Down       │
      │ • Injustice       │      │                   │
      └───────────────────┘      └───────────────────┘
```

BLOCKED ENERGY

Figure 3.1: Process of dyadic forgiveness: Crime impact

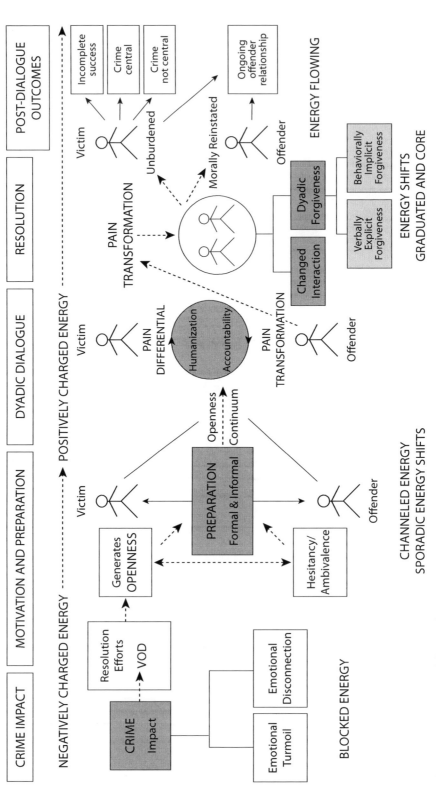

Figure 3.2: *Process of dyadic forgiveness*

Participants described the impact from the crime as debilitating. Clynita, for example, said, "I dropped about 30 pounds… just kind of withered away to not much. I couldn't sleep and was starting to kind of deteriorate…my office manager thought I was having a stroke…my left side was numb. I was thin. I was pale. I couldn't talk right." For most participants, the negatively charged emotional energy attached to the crime had a compounded effect because there was no viable outlet for their reactions. Micaela described being continually overwhelmed with grief and panicked about her own and her child's survival. Norman talked about the dominance of his anger that, aside from a periodic release, was continually building and destroying him and those he loved. Lila noted that she felt like the walking dead and was loaded with guilt and regret for what she should have done to save her daughter. She repeatedly and compulsively visited the apartment where her daughter was killed to make sure she wasn't there. These blockages associated with negatively charged emotions disrupted the natural energy flow, sealing in pain and fear, and reinforcing victims' negative thinking and anger. Lila described the build-up inside as "…a balloon that you blow up and it gets bigger and bigger, like you're about ready to pop." Negatively charged energy tended to manifest itself either as emotional turbulence or emotional disconnection.

EMOTIONAL TURBULENCE

Emotional turbulence included anger/rage at the offender, a sense of injustice often associated with the criminal justice system, and extreme fear.

Anger/Rage

Unrelenting anger and rage were common reactions to the crime. Maria said that her hatred and anger were so large that she wrote off the world at large. For Paula, her fury over the lies and betrayal from the offender were fed by the thwarting of her needs from the members of the criminal justice system. Her anger would zoom out with no warning, pushing away the people who might otherwise support her. She felt an endless feedback loop where her fear activated her anger, which activated a sense of impotence, which re-activated still more fear. Several of the victims had family members who were also homicide survivors of other murders. Randell, for example, had watched his grandfather turn from a mellow man into a mean, violent alcoholic after his son was killed. Portia had watched her aunt and uncle die from hate and anger after their son was killed by his wife—"They got sick and the doctor couldn't find anything wrong with them… The effects of hatred and anger just destroys everything inside your body."

Injustice

Besides anger at the offender, many of the participants experienced a profound sense of injustice that included feelings of betrayal, disappointment, fury, and powerlessness. Briana, for example, recognized that her son's death was caused by his hitting his head on a rock but her primary reaction was about the unfair advantage Big Jon gave himself by hitting her son after her son thought he had successfully quelled their impending fight. Kalicia's fury was not with the young offender responsible for hitting her son while he was biking but rather with the media's unfair insinuation that "Darnell would have been okay if he had a helmet on." For Keisha, the discovery of her father's murder exposed countless injustices done to her through her childhood by her stepfather whose lies robbed her of a possible relationship with her biological father. For many of the victims, the sense of injustice focused on their experiences with the criminal justice system. Monique felt discounted because she was referred to derisively as "only the loved one's sister." Tamara endured years of arbitrary refusals by prison officials to allow a facilitated dialogue between her and James. Lizette described living in limbo because there was no finality with the civil court system about adopting her deceased daughter's child and no finality with the criminal court system about the boys who had murdered her daughter.

Fear

Anger was frequently mixed with fear. Fear was often manifested in sleep disturbances. Paula, for example, was scared to sleep for fear she'd see her father's wounds. Her anxiety would escalate further when she imagined Jessie trying to kill her after he was released. She was plagued by flashbacks from the trial after learning that her father had been stabbed 85 times and hit over the head with a hammer. Clynita reported that her sleep was disturbed by "flashes of what I knew had happened. I knew he had chased her. I knew certain pieces and…these visions would pop through my head." Portia knew that Jackson was a serial rapist and had been released by mistake three months before her daughter was killed. Her fear manifested in her being hyper-vigilant and keeping a close and almost obsessive watch over Jackson so he wouldn't slip through the cracks again.

Participants tried to manage the emotional turbulence even as it grew. Briana overate to quell the pain of losing her only son. Cassandra held onto her anger for ten years as it grew and spread over more and more of her life. She tried to control it by insisting no one mention her significant other. Maya compartmentalized her grief, leaving work at noon each day so she could let it out by crying at home before she returned to her job.

Norman did kickboxing as an outlet until he injured his back and the anger over his mother's murder returned. Terri Ann plotted her suicide to get relief from having to wake up in the morning without her son. None of these mechanisms provide a release from the emotional hold of negatively charged energy.

EMOTIONAL DISCONNECTION

In contrast to the turbulence of overwhelming and escalating emotions, some of the participants described emotional states of numbness and disconnection. They, in effect, distanced from their emotions in order to continue functioning.

Shock

Many, if not most of the victims described feeling shocked initially by the crime. Lizette commented, "I felt absolutely empty inside for a long time… I remember just a feeling of hollowness…and the dry mouth." Pearle talked about the fact that she remained "in this state of functional shock that went on for months."

Numb

Participants also described that they felt very little or felt life in muted ways. For example, Clynita stated that she never felt any anger but "found myself absolutely numb like at the dentist. It was like I'd left my body and was looking down at me…" Indeed, with her weight loss and physical reactions, she felt her energy evaporating. For others, their numbness reflected the fact that their lives had stopped and were frozen in time. Lila commented that she felt that she was in a deep fog. Micaela noted that "I didn't cry or get hysterical. I was just suspended in an alternate reality." Monique reflected on the past ten years after her brother was murdered. "I was robotic and shut down emotionally because I had all those bad feelings and I didn't know what to do with them… That meant everything was on lockdown… Lockdown included joy, happiness, and love."

Shut-down

For some, their emotional disconnection from life was so steady and gradual that they barely noticed their hardening and removal from life. Portia said, "I got lost in myself. I walked around brain dead for 12 years."

Monique commented that she "…went on auto pilot. It was the only way I could continue to raise my kids and not let grief totally consume me." Lila described how she stuffed her feelings so she could hold up everyone else. "I had to put on this face, this mask and pretend I was handling it and everyone kept telling me that I was so strong." Indeed, several of the participants described how they kept their emotions at bay by compartmentalizing their lives. Lizette, for example, determined to give little of her energy to the boys who killed her daughter because "…I had my granddaughter to raise now." Maya limited the time she would give to grieving and consciously decided to keep the residue from the murder of her daughter tucked away. In referencing where she put her pain she said, "I've gotten to the point where…it's sort of like that closet you have that's just full of all sorts of crap you just don't want to deal with. And when that door cracks open, boy, I slam it shut, unless I'm really ready to deal with it."

BLOCKED ENERGY

The strength of the negatively charged energy from the crime was evident in both the size of the emotional turbulence and degree of emotional disconnection reported by participants. Indeed, they described their reactions in extreme terms, almost as if there was no language powerful enough to convey the netherworld they entered. Portia described the permanence of its impact. "Murder…just invades every fiber of your being… It's just always there. It just changes everything about you, changes the way you think, it changes the way you do things, it changes the way you treat people. It changes the way you even think about people… You're more cautious and suspicious and, you know, it's just something that is there from now on."

Portia's description coupled with participants' accounts of emotional turbulence and emotional disconnection strongly suggests that the negatively charged energy from the crime is particularly potent because it has no outlet. Consequently, the energy gets readily blocked and has an erosive effect on victims' lives over time. Several participants noted the lasting imprint made by the negatively charged energy from the crime. Monique observed that everyone in her family, including herself, had gotten divorced after her brother was killed. Norman vividly portrayed how he carried immense anger for 26 years. Indeed, the anger of the man who murdered his mother was now implanted in him. Moreover, he realized that he was passing it to the next generation by how he was treating his son. Randell reasoned that his cancer diagnosis and heart condition were products of his hate. "Hate becomes a drug. You become addicted to it. You learn to hate something so bad that's constantly in the mind 24 hours a day, every time you're awake. [It's there] even subconsciously in your sleep."

Energy that is blocked does not move from place to place or freely. Because the very nature of energy is movement, the suppression of emotions created, in part, by their displacement or lack of appropriate outlet, or unresolved negative emotions produces stagnation that can ultimately lead to disease, disconnection that impacts perception, and disruption in feedback systems that can inhibit mental processing. Most of the participants in this study referenced pronounced energy blockages in how they reacted to the crime. These blockages, like clogged arteries, generally narrowed how they lived over time.

2 ■

MOTIVATION AND PREPARATION

Efforts to Resolve Negatively Charged Energy

Many participants realized, after some time, that they would struggle with the noxious aftermath of the crime unless they did something to specifically combat the negatively charged undertow. Without any available outlets for its release, the negatively charged energy would likely defeat their efforts to move forward. Participants used a variety of mechanisms both by themselves and in combination with other mechanisms to move beyond their anger or to making something constructive or meaningful out of the horror of their past. In some cases, their efforts were precursors to meeting with the offender or helped shape the dialogue itself. Figure 3.3 shows efforts made to resolve the negatively charged energy and dimensions of formal and informal VOD preparation.

EFFORTS AT SELF-CHANGE
Therapy
Pearle, for example, made the decision to use therapy to work out her estrangement from her mother. In describing off and on counseling, the Wiccan ceremony and ritual she performed where she walked the same path her mother was forced to walk right before she was murdered, peer counseling, and astrological work, she remarked, "My healing was quite intense and thorough." As part of her journey, Pearle determined not to resist, but to allow whatever came into her life to direct her healing. That decision included doing intense therapy prior to meeting with the offender—"I took a journey into very deep parts of myself...a deeper journey than all my

healing…a journey that would never have happened without this meeting [with the offender] at the other end…"

Activism

Some of the participants became activists. They deliberately redirected the negatively charged energy from the crime toward projects and causes that reduced its negativity. Beyond an acute stress reaction, Duncan never stated that he experienced negatively charged energy from the murder of his daughter. He had outlets for his feelings because of connections with leaders in his community and became an active part of providing positive direction to his community in how they responded to the tragedy. Moreover, he helped envision the VOD concept for himself and other survivors. Lizette was majorly committed to the principle of non-violence. She left a support group because she felt that the members were keeping her in a state of anger. She was vested, however, in promoting restorative justice even to the point of recording her dialogue so it could be used to advance VOD generally.

Personal philosophy

Similarly, Cassandra developed a strong personal philosophy about how to live positively after her partner was killed. After a ten-year absence from her home town, she returned to find "…all the people doing the same thing they were doing ten years ago. I thought, 'You people have so much hatred and so much anger… I don't find joy in it.'" Cassandra's decision grew, in part, out of an epiphany she had when she discovered that the mother of the man who killed her partner worked in the school cafeteria and served lunch to her daughter—"Her family and friends would say, 'Cassandra, his mom is serving your daughter lunch.' They'd get really angry and try to rile me up about it. I'd say, 'So what? She's a woman who's out here and everybody knows her son killed a man. She's had to live with that burden and that stigma and for us to continue that… Let go. Let it go.' Her son's life has been on pause mode for a long time and it just didn't make sense to me anymore to continue holding on to such anger."

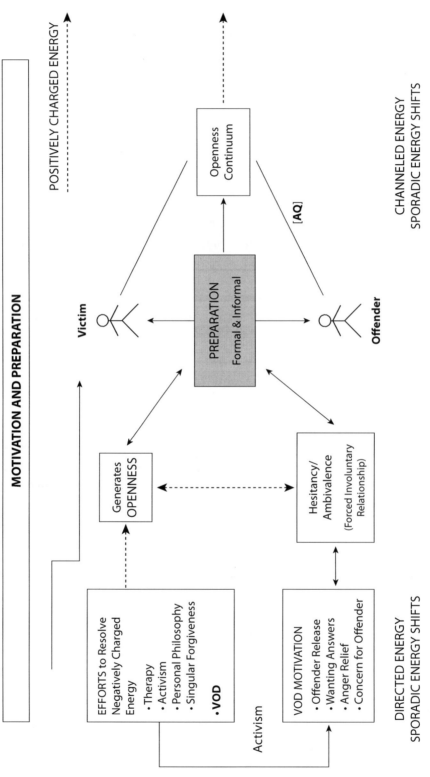

Figure 3.3: Process of dyadic forgiveness: Motivation and preparation

Singular forgiveness

Cassandra's determination to cultivate compassion and not contribute to the suffering of the offender or his mother was mirrored by 33 percent of the sample. Indeed, a number of the participants worked at decisional or pre-forgiveness to keep their anger at bay. At the trial, for example, Maria had told Donny that she forgave him—"But as the years went on, I knew that I hadn't because he was on my mind too much." Lizette decided not to let anger over the loss of her daughter build up inside or determine her future—"One definition of forgiveness is letting go of any negative emotional power that something holds over you. I had done that long, long, long ago." Portia related that she had zero motivation to forgive. However, in her conversation with God, she was directed to forgive Jackson's being or soul but that did not include forgiving what he did in killing her daughter. Theresa noted that "[T]he whole idea of forgiveness was on the scene pretty quickly for me… I knew this was going to have to be part of the journey but it was going to have to be an honest one." Although she struggled with it, she convinced herself that she needed to give it in order to receive it from God and that it would further her path with her children as well as with herself.

ENERGY SHIFTS

Participants' efforts at self-change included therapy, activism, positive personal philosophies, and decisional or pre-forgiveness. These actions pushed for their greater openness to life and the unfamiliar, and the consideration of feelings and thoughts that contradicted the direction of negatively charged energy associated with the crime. As such, they began to redirect the energy. In addition, there were specifically identified energy shifts for some of the participants as part of their self-change efforts. For example, James' remorse and public apology to Tamara in the courtroom generated a deep connection long before they actually met for the VOD. That shift continued as a result of Tamara's involvement with Bridges to Life, a restorative justice in-prison program with offenders—"There, I could work with and learn to talk to offenders as well as care about them." Theresa's shift occurred as part of her unexpected anger outburst with her husband when she finally recognized the impact her sister's murder had had on her life and others—"That awareness was a really, really big relief because I knew all my feelings were just sitting in this big pressure cooker waiting to blow up and I had to deal with things before that happened." Maria's initial shift happened when she read the poem "Two Mothers"—"After I read it again, I heard from within myself the declaration, 'I want mothers whose children were murdered and mothers whose children have taken life to come together and heal.' At first I thought, 'No. That can't happen. I don't want it to happen. It's not going to happen.' I threw the idea away. But over the years, that declaration was all I kept hearing." These examples of pre-dialogue energy shifts were sporadic among participants but powerful in changing the direction of the negatively charged energy.

VOD MOTIVATION

Although some participants made self-change efforts to remove energy blocks that led to their decisions to pursue a meeting with the offender, many participants sought out doing a VOD without any self-change precursors. In some instances, they recognized that they were blocked and felt a compelling need for something only the offender could give them. In other instances, they felt an obligation to share or give something to benefit the offender that was vital to their personal agenda.

The catalyst for movement

Regardless, all participants had some crisis or awareness that served to motivate them to meet with the offender and move the negatively charged energy from being blocked to have some outlet. This motivator of crisis or awareness served as the catalyst that started the drive for the VOD. Indeed, at some level, all participants had a sense that meeting with the offender would make some difference to themselves alone or to themselves because of a difference it might make to the offender. Micaela's partner, Joel, had been in recovery. When it came time for Ronald to be released, she said, "I knew enough about AA and recovery to know that he needed to make amends to me. A missed opportunity to do so could become the catalyst to continue his life of drinking and drugs." Lila knew she wanted to meet with Jake soon after learning her daughter was killed. She felt the need for information about exactly what happened but also wanted to know if he had any remorse. Indeed, she felt he "owed" her. When she learned about the VOD program, she pounced on it and demanded a meeting with the facilitator—"I went up to her and I asked her, I told her, 'I've always wanted to meet with Jake and how do you do that?'" Randell was determined to get the truth out of Baird about how his son died. He felt haunted by his grandfather as he watched himself "…turn into that same person, a vile angry man. But I wasn't drinking." He also realized that his cancer and heart condition were taking away his life and were directly fed by his anger and hatred of Baird. Duncan felt driven by his vision of what he could do, as a professional and a victim, to develop and promote VOD as a restorative justice practice. As a direct recipient of the practice, he wanted a relationship with Gregory that was mutual and eventually helped to reintegrate Gregory successfully back into the community.

The role of dissonance

These deep desires for mending and completion were activated, in part, by the presence of opposing forces that generated an uncomfortable dissonance for participants. This dissonance was not recognized or named but was threaded throughout participants' accounts of what helped to generate movement. Briana, for example, experienced dissonance during the trial when the judge remarked on the difference between her son and Big Jon—"You couldn't have two young men who were brought up so dissimilarly." Briana struggled with the injustice of her son's death and the social inequities in Big Jon's background that played some role in her son's death. She remarked, "I felt very sorry for Big Jon because he lacked the loving and kind environment Felix had as well as a meaningful relationship with his mother. I knew then that I wanted to talk to Big Jon and learn more of his story so I could understand where his rage came from and how he could hit Felix so hard that it would cause his death." Maya had little motivation to meet Gregory. Her husband, however, had already contacted a facilitator about doing a VOD. Maya reported that "[I]f Duncan went alone…he'd never give me all the specifics."

Consequently, Maya felt she had to go, despite her disinterest, to get the important information given her husband's proclivities—"I remember thinking, 'I'm going to want to know *everything*, all the fine points, facial expressions, body language.'" Clynita felt tremendous ambivalence about meeting with Tyrone but she felt desperate—"I'd have visions in my head trying to figure out what had happened. I felt like I was truly starting to deteriorate." Clynita struggled because she was dependent on the person who murdered her daughter, a person she never wanted to see again and yet someone she needed.

Specific motivators

Each participant had specific reasons and needs for meeting with the offender. In some instances, those reasons and needs were combined.

Offender's release

A number of victims were concerned that the offender would soon be released from prison. Cassandra and Bret were from the same small community—"I pondered over the fact that when he got out, he would come back here and we might run into each other. What would happen if I saw him? Would I grab a can of peas and hit him over the head?" Paula "…knew about the VOD program but had huge reservations… It began to dawn on me, however, that Jessie would be getting out of prison soon and I'd never get a chance again to meet with him." At first, Micaela was interested in a meeting because she was curious about how Ronald was doing—"That changed [because] Ronald could get out at any time and I might run into him." Terri Anne too was worried that Chester might get out soon—"I got a notice 11 years into Chester's sentence that he was up for parole review. That letter took me to my knees. I was balling and squealing and frankly hysterical… It became a reality, at that point, that he might get released." Theresa acknowledged that she had a number of reasons for meeting Gerald. However, "I knew he would be released soon and hoped this meeting would take him further down the road to some kind of peace." Kalicia knew that Ahmad would serve a short sentence as part of his plea agreement. She pushed to include the VOD so that Ahmad "…could be a more responsible and safe person when he was released." Similarly, Monique felt that Manny had a short sentence "…of 15 years for a deadly weapons charge and I didn't think that was right. Moreover, he only had to serve half of the sentence. I was deathly afraid, therefore, that he'd get out and commit another crime. I was scared for society." Monique hoped that by meeting with Manny, she could prevent another family from having to feel the horrendous pain she lived with.

Wanting answers

Participants also wanted to meet to get answers to their burning questions. In many cases, participants were trying to make meaning out of their loved one's murders and could not make sense out of what happened without the full context. The available information from the investigation or the trial was not available, or was contradictory. Without it, victims lived with an incomplete story, which left them feeling incomplete as people. They eventually realized that the only witness to their loved one's final moments or last words was the offender. The only way they could get the information was to meet with the offender. Moreover, the information and conveying it was not easy to access because it was attached to powerful emotions and reactions for both the victim and offender.

Some participants were particularly interested in understanding more about the offender and his behavior. As regards the offender, Terri Anne was plagued by the question Why? After all, Peter was giving Chester, who was a stranger, a ride to see his sick mother—"Why, why, why, why, why? That was my cry. Why did you do that? Peter was trying to help you. How can you be that mean?" She read voraciously, trying to understand the offender's thinking and resolve the discrepancy that someone could kill a person who was helping them—"I read books about criminals…to try to understand how someone could do something so terrible when someone was nice to them and gave them a ride." Similarly, Cassandra could not figure out why Bret had killed David. Although Bret owed David money, David would have readily given him chores to do to help pay off his debt. Bret's behavior therefore made no sense.

Other participants wanted specific details about the crime itself. For Monique, the eyewitness accounts of her brother's death were contradictory. The police reports were sketchy so it was difficult to reconstruct what had happened. Her questions, however, were deeper than any information she could obtain. Clynita struggled physically, in part, because she literally had no information to hold onto—"I had no idea what had happened. I continued to feel like I was coming apart. I had the front of the book and the back of the book but knew nothing about what was inside the book. Why? How did it get to this point? Did anyone see what happened? I knew no details. I spent hours combing through the police files, autopsy pictures and asked a ton of questions but it was never enough. It just made no sense to me." Lizette, Theresa, and Paula wanted to know about particular aspects of the crime. Lizette and Theresa were most interested in learning what their loved ones went through in the last minutes of their lives. Theresa said, "Gerald had her last moments and I wanted to know what she had gone through." Paula had lived for years with the media's portrayal of the crime, that her father was killed because he had sexually attacked Jessie. Paula had to know if that was true.

Anger relief

Some of the participants wanted a meeting with the offender in order to convey their anger directly to the person responsible for the loss of their loved one. Sometimes the anger was specific to a particular event. Duncan, for example, only expressed once in a single sentence his truth, which was that Gregory had raped his daughter. In contrast, Norman had spent his childhood and adulthood "…angry, angry at the world, at God, and everything else." Norman worried that he might lose his current marriage unless he did something about his anger—"I had to confront the demon that had controlled my life. I…planned to rid myself of every bit of hate and anger that had built up for decades by spewing it onto Raul. I wanted to pour it on him like hot tar... After all, he was the rightful source of my rage." Keisha too wanted to give Adam the anger she carried from the various chapters of her life, including not knowing her father and the specific anger she had about Adam's robbing her of the opportunity she would never have now because he was killed. Randell was furious with Baird for his lies and leaving his son Cameron "...on the side of the road like he was a piece of trash..." He wanted to do a VOD to get the truth—"I saw him as evil incarnate and felt he was evil to have walked away leaving my son on the interstate dead."

Concern for offender

In some cases, participants wanted to meet to get a more complete understanding of the offender. Their desire usually was connected to learning something about the person responsible for the crime that began to humanize them. For example, Briana noted, in contrast to herself, that Big Jon had no support at any of his hearings or at the trial—"At first I was curious about the lack of support but then I began to wonder about his family. I wanted to know, 'What does a mother look like whose son would hit somebody they don't know so hard?'" Briana learned that Big Jon had been in foster care since he was 11 because his mother was a drug addict—"I knew then that I wanted to talk to Big Jon and learn more of his story so I could understand where his rage came from and how he could hit Felix so hard that it would cause his death."

Concern for the offender, however, was not enough of a motivator. Rather, it was the debate about who the offender actually was, that is, human or monster, and the inability to know for sure, or to reconcile two opposing images that pushed participants toward wanting to meet the offender. Maria, for example, was ambivalent about meeting Donny. She noted, for example, that the first thing the facilitators said was, "Maria, he's such a nice guy... I wanted to hear that he was an ogre." Maria attended a program for victims and offenders prior to meeting Donny. She said, "By the time it was over, I was thinking differently about offenders and murderers because I had heard their whole story." She also learned about a murderer who had been released to go and share the children's books he'd been writing while incarcerated. Although Maria knew that she was impacted by these experiences, she remained reluctant about Donny until they met.

Maya and Duncan both felt pity and compassion toward Gregory. Duncan described part of his motivation to meet with Gregory—"Who were these guys What was their motivation? What prompted this? What put this in motion?" He learned about him from friends who were teachers in the alternative school where Gregory had gone.

Micaela and Keisha both were familiar with alcoholism and recovery and felt some understanding, therefore, of the issues in their offenders' lives. Micaela, for example, knew about Ronald's alcoholism and the fact that he'd had 20 prior alcohol-related offenses before his drunk driving accident that killed Joel. She first thought about meeting Ronald after thinking a lot about him at Christmas time—"I began to wonder, 'How is he doing with this? Is he feeling as horrible as I am? I need to go see him.'" Keisha was angry with Adam for killing her father and knew his blood alcohol level was high. However, "I also had empathy and understanding because of my own circumstances. I, too, had been an alcoholic… I identified with him because I too had drunk and drove but hadn't gotten caught." Keisha also understood Adam's obstinacy over taking full responsibility—"As a private investigator, we tell our clients to keep their mouths shut in court, fight like hell, and appeal anything you can to avoid 35 years in prison."

Participants' humanistic responses and desires to know the offender were generally mixed with other agendas such as the need for information or to assess if the offender was truly remorseful. In some instances, their concern for the offender was in response to the criminal justice system and its punitive response to crime. Duncan, Maya, and Lizette were committed to restorative justice, which philosophically is opposed to the dehumanizing practices of the current system. The motivation of these three participants to do a VOD with their offenders was guided, in part, by their deep faith in restorative justice practices. Kalicia also was guided to meet with Ahmad, in part, because of her response to the criminal justice system and awareness that Ahmad, when he was released, would face more hardship because he would have to overcome the trajectory of a criminal record.

The pursuit of a meeting with the offender was a possible outlet for the negatively charged emotional energy that participants carried, to varying degrees, without resolution. It became an option, alongside some of their self-change efforts, to move past stuck or blocked energy. Not all participants felt stuck. Duncan, for example, saw a clear path for himself from the beginning that included VOD. Similarly, Lizette carved her way through by deciding to take a non-violent path. Her decision to pursue a VOD with Gamal was motivated by wanting to experience the healing that other victims reported they felt after meeting with their offenders. In hindsight, however, Lizette acknowledged that although she was happy, "I had that hole there that was never going to be filled in"—"I…felt that I had had enough of my own personal healing but when I realized more could happen, it made me go from not needing to feeling that talking with either of the young men who killed Karmen would be the ultimate completion of my healing process." Consequently, both Duncan and Lizette went after doing a VOD because they believed it would move them forward in their respective journeys.

Participants' decisions to meet with their offenders did begin to harness and direct the energy that was otherwise blocked. Once they elected to proceed, they felt focused and committed to going down an unfamiliar path but one that held potential for greater healing and an outlet for an engagement with the offender that would leave participants with more than they previously had. The "more" might be getting crucial information about the crime, information about themselves, their loved one, or feelings that they wanted to share with the offender, the chance to see for themselves if the offender had regret for what they had done, or the opportunity to do what they could to prevent more harm to others in the future. Just realizing that they wanted to meet and then taking steps to actualize what they wanted was important because it shifted the energy away from being blocked to being directed. In that regard, the drive to meet the offender and the motivator for the meeting started the openness process. Indeed, participants had some sense that meeting would make a difference. For many of the participants, however, the decision to meet was monumental and might not have happened without their feeling that the offender's time in prison was running out or that their personal situations were so precarious that they had little choice.

PREPARATION

In making the decision to pursue meeting the offender, participants, consciously or otherwise, opened themselves to territory that was unfamiliar and dissonant with culturally dominant and traditionally based adversarial norms. Their drive to go a different direction was motivated by their beliefs that engaging with the offender could bring relief or a sense of completion that would help them move forward in their healing. However, there was no guarantee. They did not know how the offender would respond to their requests to meet or how the offender would behave if he agreed to meet. For many participants, this sense of the unknown felt risky and precarious. Moreover, for the VOD to be effective, participants had to be open to hearing details they did not know, experiencing the offender anew and apart from the courtroom, sharing what had happened to their lives in ways that made them more vulnerable, and talking about their loved ones with the offenders who had killed them. This pull toward meeting and the need for openness was met, in some instances, by counter feelings of hesitancy and ambivalence. Indeed, participants felt it from themselves as well as from some offenders who also felt dubious about encountering each other face to face. These opposing forces were moderated, to various degrees, by what happened during the preparation process, which included prescribed protocols and activities unique to participants' individual needs. For many, including the offender, the debate between moving forward and backing out or questioning the advisability of meeting continued right up to the time the parties met in prison.

Openness

Openness generally refers to being receptive to new ideas, people, or experiences. Moreover, being receptive refers to being willing to receive something or to hear or learn something new. Although participants' decisions to meet with the offender reflected this openness and receptivity to what was unfamiliar or unknown, their openness was not necessarily to the offender as a person. As participants went through preparing themselves for the VOD, however, some of them had experiences that challenged some preconceived ideas about the offender, which opened them up to greater receptivity.

Participants varied greatly in the degree of openness they had before they met face to face. Clynita, for example, wanted only information about what exactly had happened to her daughter—"In preparing for the dialogue, I was clear that my agenda was to find out what had actually happened between Tyrone and JoEllen to cause her death. I had to talk to Tyrone to get answers. I warned folks that I would stay the whole time if Tyrone was honest with me. But if he wasn't, I'd leave and never come back."

Theresa found that she was starting to feel alive once she was able to allow in and then release the pain from her sister's death. Having closed herself off in her efforts to live a "normal" life, she yearned to feel again. Her openness to meeting with Gerald was, in fact, part of her decision to open herself to her grief. Similarly, Portia percieved that God had instructed her to forgive Jackson, not what he did. She struggled to be open to and work with herself about what otherwise seemed an impossible task. Otherwise, she had little time for Jackson—"…I went into the meeting believing that I would be there…to tell him I'd forgiven him." Randell was consumed by hatred. He helped other victims prepare for their VOD meetings and saw the positive impact. His witnessing helped him be open to the possibility that a VOD could help but he was otherwise not open to Baird. Instead, he used the reports from others to convince himself that it was possible to have a positive experience without more pain and suffering. Theresa, Portia, and Randell recognized that the offender was important to their journeys, but their openness was not specifically directed to the offender personally.

Pearle's openness was generally to the process of her growth and whatever was necessary to do to further that growth. Like following a trail of breadcrumbs, she let the universe guide her, going down various paths, for example, astrology, peer counseling, ritual, and therapy that for her were interconnected. Each of the paths opened her still further to the next one, including the meeting with Hal. In contrast to some of the other participants, Pearle's openness did include being receptive to Hal as part of her commitment to her own ongoing healing.

For some participants, their openness was focused on what they could do for the offender. They were, therefore, open to learning about and knowing the offender but they did not expect to be personally impacted. For example, Micaela approached Ronald, open to how she might help him but with little awareness that the meeting could help her. Likewise, Kalicia was open to helping Ahmad and whatever she could do to steer him in the right direction but she didn't expect much for herself beyond the sense that she'd make a difference in Ahmad's life.

There were also participants whose determination produced greater and greater openness. Duncan was literally inventing the VOD process prior to meeting with Gregory and was deeply invested in opening himself up to an ongoing relationship with him. His openness increased as he participated in the meetings and observed the success of the process. Tamara knew early on that she had to meet with James. However, the more rejection she received from the criminal justice system, the more joined she felt with James in their mutual determination to meet and in being open to what they could give to each other.

The openness generated solely by participants' decisions to meet was pivotal to their redirecting the negatively charged energy from the crime to go in a different, more positive direction. The target of their openness varied as did their goals and their receptiveness to being personally impacted, even changed, by the meeting.

Hesitancy and ambivalence

Indeed, there was tension between the pull to meet and not to meet. Participants realized that meeting required some level of receptivity to the offender, a willingness to engage, and the subsequent impact of the offender response on their lives. Some participants were more ambivalent and guarded than others about entering this territory.

Before learning about the VOD process, Cassandra wrote a letter to Bret asking if he would meet with her in the visitor's room at the prison because it was a safe, controlled environment. She kept it but never sent it because, arguably, the activation of a connection with Bret generated more fear and concern for her safety—"I kind of forgot about it until I realized that he was getting close to his release date." Maya wanted details about her daughter's murder but was not particularly interested in meeting with Gregory—"I can honestly say that all through the preparation, I still wasn't committed to the idea of meeting with Gregory. I was just going along to learn about his present life." Paula had known about the local VOD program but was concerned that "Jessie was still a liar, that I might feel even worse after meeting with him or that he would hurt someone else and I couldn't stop him." Paula spent two years fighting with her hesitation and "…pulling on myself to be as receptive as possible." She went through a long process "…of getting close and then putting back." Kalicia too was hesitant about having pushed for a meeting with Ahmad—"I was nervous about the meeting. I had a lot of concerns… I wondered if, in hindsight, I had made a total fool of myself by giving advantages to Ahmad in the plea agreement." Monique vacillated all the way through between her decision and the actual meeting. "Sometimes when you say you want something and it happens, you're not quite sure that's really what you want because it's scary… Going into a prison to meet my monster was terrifying."

It wasn't just the participants who wavered in their decisions and remaining open to the process. Some of the participants remarked that offenders were also hesitant. Jake initially refused to meet with Lila. "I don't need her to come in and shame me and blame me anymore than has been done. I can't put my family through this. Tell her that I'm sorry. I would trade places with her if I could." During preparation, Terri Anne wrote long letters to Chester but his response was cold. She waited as he kept changing his mind. "Chester backed out six times until the facilitator was persuasive enough that Chester consented to meet." Indeed, he wrote a letter the night before the meeting to Terri Anne that said, "Don't expect me to cry. I'm a grown man. I know what I did when I killed that kid."

Chester's struggle with being receptive in the upcoming meeting demonstrates the same tension that participants felt between being open or not. These opposing pulls reflect the depth and volatility of feelings associated with the crime and immensity of facing what happened with the person who was responsible for the pain or the person whose life was shattered because of it. Indeed, the pull toward greater openness associated with the decision to meet is, arguably, an openness to experiencing the pain together, which may be a prerequisite to shifting the energy that otherwise has been carried by the victim alone.

IMPACT OF PREPARATION ON OPENNESS AND HESITANCY

Participants did a variety of activities or had experiences that moderated the tension between their openness and hesitancy. For some, their formal preparation for the dialogue consisted of regular meetings with the facilitator and might include some exchange of letters or other supervised communication with the offender. Indeed, part of their readiness and the readiness of the offender, from the facilitator's perspective, was focused specifically on increasing their openness to one another by providing information about each to the other to convey a more accurate picture of the person in the here and now. Others had experiences, prior to meeting, that were not part of the prescribed protocol that were, however, pivotal to increasing their openness or reducing their concerns.

The facilitator's actions and relationship with many of the participants helped diminish their apprehension and actually begin the dialogue with the offender indirectly before they ever met. Lila reported, "The facilitator would visit with Jake and give me an idea of some of the things he'd said and then share with him some of my questions that he should think about. We kind of got to know each other through her. That helped a lot." Jake was so hesitant that he made himself sick with the prospect of meeting Lila. His relationship with an older inmate that he trusted "…told him that he had an opportunity that 'many of us will never be able to do.' This man gave him the courage to meet with me."

Preparation for Maya and Duncan was lengthy. Because of Gregory's appeal process and the experimental nature at that time of the VOD program, the facilitator took longer than usual to prepare them. They repeatedly rehearsed everything that would happen in the meeting so there would be no surprises. The facilitator also shuttled back and forth between Maya and Duncan and Gregory, bringing information about Gregory so they would be prepared for his way of speaking, which was principally in monologues. The lengthiness of the preparation gave Maya time to consider everything and helped humanize Gregory, which both relaxed her and opened her up to the possibility that the meeting could be useful, not damaging or a waste of time.

Norman's meeting with the facilitator over eight months seemingly did little to lessen the intensity of his fury. Norman had told the facilitator that his goal was to let Raul know how badly he had impacted his life and how much he hated him—"I just wanted to spew out every bit of hate and anger and everything that I had built up for decades, just wanting to pour it all on him, like hot tar." When he learned that Raul was willing to "…accept my venting in the way it was going to be presented," Norman felt he could go forward with what he needed to do.

Cassandra's concerns about Bret had to do with safety. She had worried about running into him after he was released and didn't know what she might do. She was fortunate that the facilitator and support person for Bret were both people she had known previously. The facilitator had been her girl scout troop leader and she'd slept at her home many times. The support person for Bret was the same priest who officiated at David's funeral and was her priest growing up. The trust she felt toward both these individuals increased her sense of safety considerably and, arguably, her receptiveness to Bret.

Monique was terrified to meet Manny. Based on her upbringing, she truly saw him as a monster. She struggled between her feeling some beginning empathy for Manny and her sense of vindictiveness. The facilitator patiently worked to nudge her closer to the dialogue that she had requested—"She would sit with me and let me go through my fears… We would talk it out…Every time I got scared and thought, 'I don't know if I can do this,' she would bring me back and say, 'But this is really what you wanted… You asked for this so think about it before you don't do this.'"

In addition to what facilitators did, participants were influenced toward greater openness by the offender's responses or what they knew or learned about the offender during their preparing for the VOD. Jackson and Portia exchanged some letters prior to the dialogue. Although Portia, at the time, claimed that she wasn't interested in apologies, his apologizing seemed to interrupt her one-track agenda, which was to give Jackson the forgiveness that she perceived that God had commanded her to do.

Paula had serious concerns about the viability of a meeting with Jessie because she saw him as disingenuous and a liar. The facilitator videotaped an interview with Jessie that dispelled many of Paula's concerns. The impact "…was really, really big because it showed his appearance and how it had changed… He was just talking about everyday things. It prepared me for what he was gonna look like, what he was gonna talk like. The facilitator asked him, 'Is this something you really want to do?' And he said, 'Yes, this is something I really want to do.' It indicated that he wanted to make it right somehow or do something for the better out of this. That made a big impact on me."

Pearle had a number of serendipitous and coincidental experiences that she interpreted as spiritual confirmations of the rightness of her decision to meet with Hal. For example, "…the offender's first name is the same name as my son. His middle name is the male version of my partner's name, and my partner was a prison guard at the prison where Hal is." She also wrote a letter to Hal asking him why he was willing to meet with her. "I realized he was just being very open and answering my questions, and putting himself out." Pearle also reported that Hal had mistaken a preparation meeting with the facilitators as the actual dialogue. The facilitators reported back that "…he was very upset and everything broke loose for him…they shared everything with me about him and I got this picture of him and what he was going through… I thanked him and appreciated him for where he's coming from."

Tamara and Maria both went through prison programs where they interacted with offenders and learned more about their lives both before and during their incarcerations. Not knowing whether or not she'd ever get a VOD with James, Tamara "…got involved in Bridges [to Life] and doing Bridges gave me that surrogacy with having those offenders that I could work with and talk to, and learn to care about, and realize that they were real people…that was my first encounter with trying to understand that offenders are no different than I am." Terri Anne read countless books about criminals and the criminal mind to help her better understand Chester. Keisha literally investigated everything possible about the father she'd never met and everything about Adam's trial. The more she learned, the more open she was to meeting with Adam. "I need to face him. I need to see him. I need to tell him that my father's life mattered to me, and it mattered to me probably the most out of anybody." Although Keisha decided to wait to judge Adam's sincerity until they met, she was ready, if he was authentic, to share about her father, the impact of not having him in her life, and what her life had been like as a result.

Although formal preparation is considered a critical component of VOD, many of the participants did not emphasize it in describing their pre-dialogue experiences. Indeed, some of the participants had little preparation time. Randell, for example, only had two meetings with a friend who was a facilitator. Because Jackson's execution was to occur within two weeks, Portia had almost no time for preparation. Tamara never went through the formal protocol because she was not allowed access to James for a VOD. Micaela met several times in person with the facilitator and did the rest by phone. They did, however, emphasize the critical events, whether a part of their formal preparation, their relationships with facilitators, the pre-dialogue interaction with offenders, or events in their lives that were relevant to the upcoming meeting that impacted their openness to the VOD process.

OPENNESS CONTINUUM

The openness of individual victims and offenders to the upcoming meeting is dependent on numerous factors including their histories of pain and healing, inner and social resources for coping, the nature and impact of the crime, the growth from the preparation process, intentions for sharing, and hopes and yearnings for what is possible. Preparation, whether prescribed or informal, is a time, after the actual decision to meet, that mingles together the negatively charged energy from the crime and its impact and positively charged energy connected to participants' efforts to move blocked energy and redirect its negative charge. It is a time of pushing and pulling, a time when the anger and sense of injustice is dissonant with the hope for relief and even resolution with the offender. Keisha, for example, felt the dissonance between needing to put everything she had learned about her father—his death, the trial, and her missed opportunities—in a safe place, and yet she could not assess Adam's availability to receive what she wanted and needed to offer. Maria felt conflicted toward Donny because the facilitator's comments about his being a nice guy inhibited her from concluding that he was an ogre.

Participants, consequently, fell at different points on a hypothetical continuum of openness that was anchored at one end by authentic openness to the meeting and the offender and anchored at the other end by guardedness. Although offenders' reports about their experience were not part of this study, it is evident from the participants' narratives that offenders too fell at different points on this hypothetical continuum of openness. The preparation phase of a VOD meeting begins to bring the victim and offender together. Whether this only occurs in the mind of the participant, occurs through the facilitator who serves as a bridge, or involves an exchange of information about the parties or sending of materials between them, where victim and offender fall on their own continuum of openness has different meaning when the two continuums are put together. Indeed it is useful, in the context of assessing their readiness to meet, to construct a two by two table that reflects the relative openness and guardedness of each to the other (Figure 3.4). Given that the purpose of coming together is to redress the harm suffered by the victim, the openness of victims and offenders to give and receive from each other is a critical dynamic to the success of the VOD. If one or both parties are closed or guarded, they will impact each other differently than if they are both open.

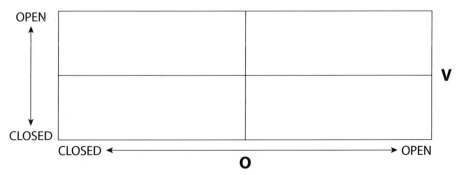

Figure 3.4: Continuum of openness

Participants in this study recognized that the work they needed to do with the offender required some shift in what they needed to share or hear from the offender. Many of them were ambivalent about meeting. After all, their relationship with the offender was forced upon them because of the crime. None of them would have entered the relationship voluntarily. And yet, they were electing to meet and share, in many cases, their deepest pain with the person responsible for it. Although they had plenty of reason to be guarded, they also recognized that what they needed from the offender required them to be forthcoming and open to what they needed for their healing.

3 ◼

DYADIC DIALOGUE

The meeting between victim and offender is the culmination of a lengthy process that includes the crime and its impact, the victim's decision to move forward with a VOD in order to shift the negatively charged energy associated with the crime, some beginning movement toward the offender, which may be countered by their ambivalence about the meeting, and formal and/or information preparation for the dialogue. The actual dialogue also marks the start of the dyadic process itself. Some of the components that influence the quality of the victim–offender interaction may begin before the parties meet but they are not brought to fruition until the dialogue. Figure 3.5 is an illustration of the dyadic dialogue process.

DYADIC ENCOUNTER

Many of the participants emphasized the importance of what happened to them when they first saw the offender. In some cases, these initial glimpses set the emotional stage for the dialogue. Cassandra commented that she had watched Bret age over 17 years by following his prison photos. However, when he came into the room for the meeting, "my whole body got hot and I could feel my chest expand. Then I felt an overwhelming sadness because I saw a man who took a life and in the process damaged his own." Participants noted changes in the offender's appearance from when they last saw them in court. Pearle, for example noted that Hal had shaved his beard and looked all clean and shiny. Micaela similarly observed that Ronald "was not as skuzzy as he was in court." In reference to Big Jon, Briana said, "I had expected a young man who looked wild and crazy but instead he walked in like a regular kid. My heart just broke because he looked like any other kid that Felix would have brought home to stay at our house. In fact, he looked smaller than the six-foot four, 190-pound buff man I had met in court."

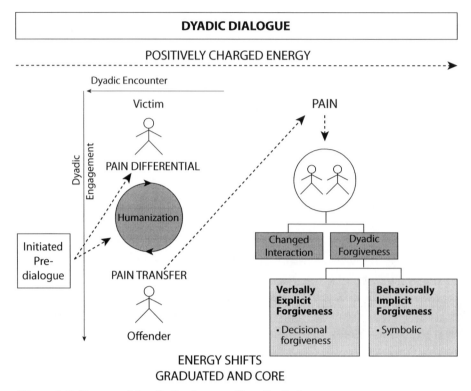

Figure 3.5: Process of dyadic forgiveness: Dyadic dialogue

Participants resoundingly watched for or were strongly impacted by the offender's initial responses to them. After commenting on her apprehension and tension in going into the meeting room, Portia said, "It was nothing like what I thought it would be. I sat down and then he sat down…and started crying…he was remorseful… He had changed in a lot of ways and I could see the changes." Portia's experience was replicated over and over again by other participants. Randell commented that Baird "…was afraid and scared of me, someone who was broken, ashamed, and hurting." Duncan shared that Gregory was remorseful and crying from the beginning for what he did.

These initial encounters sent strong messages to the participants, often expressed through the offender's eyes. Keisha said that Adam "had the softest, most loving eyes," suggesting that Adam was receptive, welcoming, and kind. Randell relayed that he "…could see the remorse in Baird's eyes" suggesting that Baird was suffering and regretted deeply what he had done. Indeed, many participants were struck by the offender's inability to even look at them. Clynita noted that "…the whole time he couldn't look me in the eye. He sat with his head down and his hands in his lap. I remember thinking, 'Why hasn't he said he was sorry…Why isn't he crying…'"

Clynita interpreted his behavior negatively—"He looked so hardened. There was no emotion." Lila described that Jake kept his head down throughout the meeting. She felt that a person's eyes are the mirror to their soul. At one point she insisted he look at her. Jake responded, "I don't feel I have the right to." Once Jake explained what he felt, Lila said, "He was feeling the remorse and guilt. It made him more human to me. He talked about the shame he brought on his family and his not wanting to look at me."

Participants frequently portrayed the dyadic encounter as one of the shift points. Sometimes the shift had to do with humanizing the offender. Other times participants suddenly felt things in response that were not expected. Norman, for example, said, "I felt like crying. As soon as he sat down, God filled my heart with love, compassion and forgiveness... As he started talking, I interrupted him and said, "I don't need all the details. We all know what you did and why you're here. We know why I'm here... I just want to stop the hate. We have to stop the cycle." Clynita shared that "Tyrone walked in and I was shocked because he wasn't shackled. He sat across from me with his head down. I began to cry. Everything that had happened just came back on me. I couldn't stop crying and I couldn't breathe. It took five minutes before I could compose myself."

DYADIC ENGAGEMENT

The phases of the dyadic dialogue were not discrete. For some participants, the initial dyadic encounter or visual absorption of each other stood out and apart from the rest of what happened during the meeting. For others, the spoken or verbal dyadic encounter literally started the dyadic engagement or interaction. Dyadic engagement included the communication of the pain differential by the victim and the pain transfer to the offender as well as the pain transformation. Dyadic engagement, therefore, refers to the sharing between victim and offender about the crime and its impact on their lives. This sharing includes information about the participant and what happened to their lives that the offender does not know, but it also includes information about the crime itself and its impact on the offender's life that the victim does not know. Although the stories victim and offender give to each other fill in missing pieces, including the offender's response to what he did, they also elicit emotional reactions because both parties are experiencing each other along with the shared information and are learning things they never knew before.

This sharing in the context of a face-to-face encounter and dyadic engagement was responsible for the significant energy shifts participants reported in the study. For some participants, the shifts were life changing whereas for others, the shifts were quieter but generally positive. Moreover, the level of their engagement with each other varied from low to high, based on the relative openness of victims and offenders and how they saw and impacted one another, the nature and history of the crime, the time between the crime and the dialogue, and the participants' agendas. Finally, the storytelling of each to the other played a pivotal role in substantiating or shifting the meaning each person carried about the crime and each other.

Pain differential

The pain differential refers to the victim's pain as a result of the crime and the fact that there is a disparity between the parties in the amount of pain each carries. Indeed, the offender has little or no visceral awareness of the pain either in terms of the damage he has caused or the immensity of the ripple effect on the victim's life. The victim cannot resolve the pain that embodies the negatively charged energy because it actually belongs to the offender who caused it. Efforts made by the victim to move the negatively charged energy have been somewhat futile because, although they carry it, the pain is not their responsibility to heal. The offender, however, cannot know the full dimensions of that pain without learning about it from the victim.

In this study, some of that learning happened in the dialogue but it also happened, for some participants, prior to the actual meeting. Facilitators, for example, shuttled between victim and offender and shared information with discretion based on what they felt would help victim and offender in their readiness to meet. They also had parties write letters to each other.

Participants communicated their pain in a variety of ways. Most of them literally told the offender how they had learned of their loved one's death and what impact it had on their lives and the lives of other family members. Theresa, for example, told Gerald her story of finding her sister's body—"I told my story but I told it differently to him than I had anyone else because now I had the eyes and ears of the person responsible. Telling him how his actions impacted me was empowering. His listening, eye contact, and head nodding at the right times felt genuine." Keisha told Adam about the father she had never met, the abuse she had endured in her life because of his absence, and how Adam's killing him had affected her—"I made clear that Adam was responsible for [her father] not being in my life and taking away the opportunity to have found him and confronted him or possibly to have had a restored relationship with him." Tamara told James about how his shooting her had destroyed her marriage and thrown her son into a life of drugs and addiction—"He needed to hear all that ugliness and it hurt him because he had a responsibility in it… I needed him to understand the weight of what he did and what I told him was harsh."

Some of the participants brought items to make what had happened more real. Monique brought a photo album to the meeting—"I had my brother's autopsy report and a picture of the headstone I had made for him. I also had pictures of him when we were with him in the hospital…" Monique wanted Manny to see the damage he had done—"When he saw the pictures he cried." Briana brought pictures and cards she received from her son for her birthday and on Mother's Day. I wanted Big Jon to know the person he took from me…after he finished looking at the cards, he put his head down on the table and cried."

Pain transfer

Pain transfer refers to moving and sharing the pain and suffering that the victim incurred and have it carried by the offender to whom it belongs. It is a transfer of the negatively charged energy from the victim to the offender. It also refers to the offender's response as the offender experiences what the victim has endured, and through reliving the victim's anguish takes on the burden of the pain and the responsibility for what they have done. Symbolically, the pain becomes theirs. This movement allows the pain to be shared.

Briana used the cards her son had sent her to help Big Jon understand the depth of love she and her son had for each other. He had taken away that love by fighting with Felix—"After I showed him all of my Mother's Day cards, he was visibly crying. His head was down on the table and I knew he was sorry… I cried too but I talked to him." Briana used Big Jon's openness to having received her pain to carry his learning into his future. She said, "When you marry and have a baby, I want you to remember me sitting here talking to you…and I want you to be a good dad. Hold your babies. Be there for them. Not until you hold that baby in your arms will you know what you took from me."

Besides the murder of her father, Paula's pain centered on Jessie's dishonesty, including his claim that was sensationalized and broadcast by the media that his killing her father was justifiable because her father sexually assaulted him. Paula had a list of 40 questions and asked Jessie every one of them—"Jessie answered all of them. He admitted my father never attacked him… He openly apologized for what he did… He didn't have to be sorry. He didn't have to own any of it. He owned all of it… He told me he was never going to do something like this again… I actually believed him."

In Randell's case, Baird started the VOD by apologizing. He told the story of his life, not as an excuse, but to suggest how he had learned that drinking was his right and how he had learned to abuse others and how not to be responsible—"I could see the remorse in his eyes. I was getting some of the answers I needed about Cameron." After forgiving Baird in the parole hearing, there was a second VOD. Randell shared with Baird that he needed his help very badly—"He spoke and I felt like we were hearing the truth for the first time. The pain began to melt away. It's like you take an aspirin for a headache and it starts to go away…some of that was being lifted, the weight we had carried from all the stories we'd heard about our son [from Baird] that were not true."

As Norman shared the anger he had lived with his whole life, Raul "… was willing to take whatever I was going to dish out, including beating up on him, because that's what God said he needed. Raul gave to me with his actions, mannerisms, and the way he handled himself in the meeting. It wasn't his words, therefore, but his demeanor of acceptance that was so powerful. Our souls talked. It was as if God brought us together to make both of us stronger."

Accountability

A major part of the pain transfer is offenders taking responsibility for what they did. In this study, offenders held themselves accountable by telling the full story about what they did, showing regret for their behavior, being truthful, and responding to participants' expectations for their future behavior. Indeed, the offender's remorse and the taking of responsibility had little weight until it was shared with the person it was intended for, namely the victim. As such, the victim's witnessing and receiving of the offender's responsibility helped complete the offender's giving or contribution. Indeed, what they received from the offender and how they responded to the offender dyadically tied into the offender's capacity to give remorse and accountability back to the victim.

When they met, Lila first showed Jake an album of pictures of her daughter—"He was squirming in his seat but I felt that was right. He should. I wanted to see if what had happened meant anything to him." As Jake told the story of what had happened, he said, "She looked really, really bad." Lila said, "I could hear it in his voice, on his face that he didn't forget. He said that he thought about Loretta every day." He was clear that what happened wasn't Loretta's fault or Lila's fault—"He took full ownership… he was taking it. He listened… I felt like I was literally handing over all these burdens to Jake and he was willingly taking all that from me so I didn't have to live with it."

Gerald told Theresa all the details of how he raped and murdered her sister. Theresa shared the impact of her sister's death on her. Gerald apologized saying, "I know this means really nothing in some ways but I want and need to say it. I am really, really sorry." Although their interaction was a little stiff, Gerald sent a letter a few years later in which he wrote more specifically 26 different things that he was sorry for. He said, "These are things I couldn't express in the meeting but I need to express them now." Theresa said, "He apologized for every one of them." He also shared that he had given up his right to a trial about being committed to a long-term facility. In so doing, he held himself accountable for his proclivities and the fact that it was not safe for him to be in the free world.

After being cold and dismissive during the formal preparation process, Chester literally cried all the way through the dialogue. Terri Anne expressed that "…he had opened up to me and would have done anything in his power to bring Peter back. He said to me, 'I wish I could give you something. I don't have anything. I don't have nothing.'" Terri Anne used his yearning to heal her to give him ways he could change and be accountable to her. "I said, 'What you can do for me is turn your life around. I know how you've acted in prison. You've attacked the guards and choked them. You've been a terrible person. You don't have to do that… You can go to college in here. You can make something of yourself. That's what you could do for me.'" Chester responded to Terri Anne's request. He wrote her every day and did not get in trouble in the prison as long as they were able to maintain their connection.

Offender accountability was central to participants feeling that their words and expressions were trustworthy. Accountability was healing for both victims and offenders. For victims, it was another expression of true ownership. For offenders, it demonstrated that they were willing to face themselves as well as the person they harmed. Indeed, for participants, offender accountability was an active demonstration and application of the remorse they had shown. Jake did it by being definitive about the fact that only he was to blame for Loretta's death. Gerald did it in the letter he wrote enumerating the specific things for which he was sorry and giving up his right to a trial. Chester did it by changing his behavior based on Terri Anne's request that he better himself in prison.

Humanizing the offender

Although many participants had begun to see the humanity in the offender before their face-to-face meeting, they also found themselves responding differently after the offender either showed genuine remorse or accepted the pain that the victim had otherwise carried alone. In other words, many, if not most, of the participants showed shifts in their attitude in response to the offender's remorse, story about their background in accounting for what they did, and willingness to take real responsibility by holding themselves accountable for their horrific acts. Participants' humanization countered their prior opinions of the offender as "monster," which removed the offender from the position of "other" and placed themselves in a position of caring for the offender.

Before they met, Randell saw Baird as the "devil incarnate and felt he was evil to have walked away leaving my son on the Interstate dead." He insisted that Baird come to the meeting in handcuffs and shackles. As Baird told him about his upbringing, the family legacy of drinking and abandonment, the abuse everyone suffered, and the lack of any male figure, Randell said, "His story began to break me down. I was overwhelmed at what I was hearing and seeing… I had to get out of that room. So we took a break and I asked the guard to please remove the handcuffs and shackles… I wasn't expecting to feel empathy for Baird but I did. I grabbed hold of my wife's arm and said, 'I have to try to help this guy now. I have to do something.'"

After they told each other childhood stories and "…what led up to the night of my brother's murder," Monique shared the photo album she had made of her brother's last days in the hospital so Manny could see the damage he had done. She did not know if shooting her brother was intentional or not. Manny cried and shared that he had just fired into the crowd and that "…he was very heartbroken when he found out that he had hit my brother with the gun because he liked him." Monique could see the emotions warring in him when she pulled out the autopsy report—"It made it more real for him. He told me that since he had been locked up, he had tried not to think about it a lot. He explained that when you're in prison, you are just trying to survive and you cannot be weak and let all those emotions take over." Monique explained that understanding Manny's background and how he ended up thinking that firing into the crowd was the answer helped a lot— "After the meeting, I didn't have to feel bad about having caring feelings for him because now I had an accurate picture of what it was I was feeling."

Lizette described that "…Gamal was so remorseful and started crying from the very beginning. He never cried when he talked about his own upbringing and his abuse at the hands of others but he sure cried when he talked about what he had done. It was just more than he could bear… The new piece that came out of the dialogue…was Gamal's sharing the information about Karmen's last words… The last thing she said was, 'I forgive you and God will too.' The last moments of her life were the hardest for me to think about. It was a place I never went. Learning what happened at the end was amazing and incredibly helpful… [Later] we talked about our own family and ourselves and the impact the murder had had on all of us. It was painful for him to have to hear about all the damage and ripple effects of what he had done…it was hard for me to see his response because it felt a little like the football penalty where they all pile on top of the player."

These examples show that when offenders shared critical information about who they were, clarified their intentions at the time they killed participants' loved ones, or demonstrated that they were feeling remorse including the pain that the victim had otherwise carried alone, participants responded humanely and with a recognition of their shared humanity. Indeed a number of participants responded to the needs of offenders and literally began to parent them. Maria lovingly lectured Donny about his need to shed tears even though he was a man—"Your tear ducts are my tear ducts. There's some things that you can just get rid of in your life. They may be small or they may be big. You just need to shed some tears and let some things out." Duncan explained that Gregory's parents had died and he was the only visitor Gregory has. He hopes to speak in his favor before the parole board—"I have a lot of respect for Gregory particularly because of the way he speaks about his work, his respect for the staff, his roommate, and the mentor he has become… I trust him because he's done no more harm. I'm gaining deeper respect and trust as he talks about his other offenses including stolen property and taking responsibility for what happened." Terri Anne talked about parenting Chester after she handed him a tissue from across the table—"He just shook his head. He couldn't speak because of the tears. It was unbelievable that I had any bit of kindness in me but we went on for hours… I talked to him like a mother. "Terri Anne became relentless in her encouragement to break through Chester's low opinion of himself. Besides showing him that someone from his own housing project could be a successful author, she said, "You can make something of yourself, better yourself… I don't care if your mother used to smoke dope with you, you can make something out of yourself."

Humanizing the offender was not always positive. Theresa saw who Gerald was. She credited him with his willingness to meet with her. However, she also saw his limitations. Similarly, Clynita met with Tyrone's father before the dialogue. She learned about his past, his inclinations as a child and declared to her that "Tyrone never had a chance." Clynita was grateful for Tyrone's honesty about killing her daughter and was able to remove the negatively charged energy because she saw, in the dialogue, exactly who he was and accepted who he was. He had no emotion as he talked and yet was telling her the truth about what he did. Just as a dog cannot help being a dog, Tyrone also could not help being who he was. As such, she was able to understand and humanize him but in a more negative direction.

Energy pulls between accountability and humanization

Participants' stories show numerous shifts in the energy as the pain they carried alone (e.g. pain differential) was now shared with the offender who accepted responsibility for it (e.g. pain transfer). The stories also demonstrated that getting the missing pieces, such as information about the offender's past, their feelings and reactions to what they did, and vital details about the crime itself corrected and completed participants' accounts and satisfied their longing to know about what happened. The movement in positively charged energy, however, was dependent on the two core dynamics of offender accountability and victim humanization of the offender. In this study, these dynamics were intertwined. The self-reported, positive shifts of participants were frequently embedded in their humanizing responses to offenders, which only occurred after offenders showed some measure of accounting for their actions. Participants' expressions of humanity and caring, however, also served to elicit stronger, fuller, and more personalized statements of accountability. This reciprocity, along with the sharing of stories and information, generated a channel that connected the victim and offender but also provided a passageway for the energy flow and pull of each party on the other.

Participants described the channel. Cassandra said, "Once we got the dialogue going, it flowed. Everyone who surrounded us at the table faded away. It was like having tunnel vision." Micaela depicted it as "…a strange bond between us that grew out of the fact that Joel's death had impacted both our lives… I felt like what happened between us was spiritual. I could feel the energy in the room…that was bigger than the two of us." Pearle commented that "[o]nce we got started, everyone else disappeared. Inside of me was a deep calmness and a profound readiness to do the dialogue. He knew what I wanted to say and what I wanted to ask him. I knew that he was in the same place. Everything fell away except him and me."

PAIN TRANSFORMATION

For most participants, the flow and interaction in the dyadic dialogue moved the charge associated with the energy from the crime from negative to positive. Indeed, as offenders acted to reduce victims' pain, victims felt differently. Paula felt safer because there were no more lies to have to figure out. Jessie had been honest about what had happened to her father and truly wanted to help her. Clynita felt resolved because Tyrone told her everything he'd done in killing her daughter. She also experienced his rage, the same rage that killed her daughter when she announced, as her daughter had done prior to her death, that she never wanted to see him again—"It confirmed that's what happens to him when the control is taken from him." Cassandra felt more settled because Bret assured her that his killing David had nothing to do with David—"He had not been a jerk or a bad guy. In fact, in Bret's eyes, anyone could have been the target that day."

For the most part, these changes generated greater openness between victims and offenders. They often felt joined as if they had been on a shared journey together. Victims felt visible, acknowledged, and empowered because they were truly seen by the offender, the person responsible for their pain. Based on participants' accounts, offenders seemed more whole because they had been accountable through their stories of the crime and their remorse to the person they had harmed.

Instead of a quiet culmination, the dissipation of negatively charged energy and expansion of positively charged energy served to produce a change in the interaction between victim and offender and some of the largest energy shifts for participants. Indeed many of these shifts culminated in both explicit and implicit expressions of forgiveness.

Changed interaction

Victims and offenders shared differently after the pain transfer and shift from negative to positive in the victim's energy. For many participants, the transformation they experienced allowed for a higher quality of engagement. It became more natural and spontaneous. Their interaction with their offenders was looser, relaxed, informal, and intimate. Indeed, once the pain was transformed, there was space for a more conversational process or for answering the question, "Now what?" There was also space for a changed relationship if that was wanted and appropriate. In many ways, victims and offenders felt more joined. For example, Maria and Donny talked about Donny's school experience and the similarities between Donny and Marcus—"Marcus was reading at a 12th grade level in 6th grade and so was Donny. Marcus had to dress differently because he went to a private school and Donny's mother sent him to school in suits." Portia and Jackson shared notes about Jackson's drug history and the changes he was trying to make while he was in prison. They also discussed some of the things he did during his sentence, like his efforts to get new trials or to donate his organs post his execution, efforts that Portia had opposed.

Lizette and Gamal talked about their backgrounds and common likes and dislikes. Gamal told Lizette that the family of another inmate had "adopted" him as a member of their family. Lizette talked about her own family.

Tamara and James shared information about their lives. "That's when we began to really start bonding like mother and son. We started sharing and laughing and talking. It was almost silly and giggly. It was like the child who has just told his mom all the little bad things he did and now it's time to go for ice cream because he told the truth."

Pearle and Hal discovered how much they had in common—"I do watercolors and he does sketches in art. I'm a recovering alcoholic and he's in recovery… At one point as we were starting to talk back and forth, he says to me, 'Well, don't you ever get mad? Weren't you just mad at me?'" Pearle shared with Hal that she was ready to whip a dog with a horse's lunge whip because the dog had chewed up a book—"I was going to go out and kill the dog. But dogs aren't going to stick around." Pearle continued her story and told Hal that she ended up whipping an old, old cherry tree and yelling and screaming at the top of her lungs. After that, all the rage dropped away. Hal responded that he too loves dogs but because of prison, "I'm never going to be able to touch another dog." This kind of exchange went "back and forth… this revealing ourselves to one another, and lots and lots of tears."

DYADIC FORGIVENESS

Forgiveness, as a concern, was central for several participants prior to the dialogue. In some cases, offenders made requests for forgiveness during the dialogue and particularly toward the end of the meeting. In other instances, participants did not see the relevance of forgiveness to their journeys. Indeed, in terms of verbally explicit forgiveness, participants ranged from no forgiveness to decisional forgiveness to conditional forgiveness to emotional forgiveness. In terms of behaviorally implicit forgiveness, there were numerous close and emotional interactions between victim and offender that manifested the positively charged energy and the magnitude and meaning of the shift to participants.

Verbally explicit forgiveness

In this study, features of verbally explicit forgiveness were manifested in participants' shifts from decisional forgiveness, which occurred prior to the meeting, to emotional forgiveness, which occurred toward the end of the dialogue. Aspects of verbally explicit forgiveness were also seen in the requests for forgiveness made by offenders and in participants' experiences with partial or conditional forgiveness. In some cases, verbally explicit forgiveness had no bearing on the meeting or anything that happened directly between victim and offender except as it might help an individual's healing outside of the dialogue.

Decisional forgiveness

Some participants came to the dyadic dialogue with agendas about forgiveness. In court, Maria told Donny that "I'd forgiven him, but that was just lip action…as the years went on…he was on my mind too much." Maria went through a process with God where she repented for all the negative things she had said or felt toward Donny. She felt directed "…to change my thinking and I had to pray for him. And then every time I heard his name, it's like you need to speak it out loud that I choose to forgive him." However, Maria wasn't sure if her decisional forgiveness was real. "I don't think I really recognized a heart change."

Portia also had had an encounter with God about forgiveness. After asking God how she could ever forgive Jackson, she remembered God's answer—"You don't have to forgive what he did. You have to forgive him." Portia claimed that it took her five years before she could do this and she fought it all the way. She initially thought that the purpose of the meeting was to tell him she had forgiven him. She planned to say, "I can never forgive you for what you did, but as a person, I have to forgive you."

Tamara talked a lot with her therapist about forgiving James long before she met him—"I knew I was going to do it but I didn't know how I was going to get there." Tamara found a magazine article on forgiveness and felt, based on what she read, that she no longer harbored anger and therefore had already forgiven James—"I never really knew what forgiveness was until then."

Maria, Portia, and Tamara, however, had significant emotional experiences with their offenders during the dyadic dialogue that shifted their decisional forgiveness, done without the offender, into emotional forgiveness. Maria described how at the end of the meeting Donny asked her for a hug. When she walked around the table to give it, she became "…hysterical… I was falling… and he had to hold me up, not allowing me to fall to the floor… I think there was a bond made at that time… He whispered to me, 'I believe you're gonna be the person to help me to cry' and I said, 'Yeah, I'm gonna be that person.' When he left the room I bent over and I was sad. I just hugged the man who murdered my son." Maria had a powerful energy shift immediately after Donny left the room. As her support person lifted her up, "I began to feel whatever was moving in my feet…kind of stirring, and it was moving up, and moving up, and moving up. I felt that leave me… And instantly, all that anger, the hatred, the bitterness, animosity, all that stuff was gone… I knew it was over with and I have been free ever since."

Portia described how she expected to tell Jackson she forgave him and for the meeting to last 30 seconds. She really did not want to hear anything he had to say. It lasted, however, five-and-a-half hours—"He sat down in front of me and he just started crying. And…and eyes. I could actually see life in his eyes…it was something that hadn't been there before. And he was remorseful. I could tell. When I told him I forgave him, he said, 'Well, I don't deserve it.' I said, 'No, you don't but you have it.' And then we just started talking and it felt so natural…it just felt like this is where I'm supposed to be at this point in time." Portia then felt a powerful energy shift like Maria. "My whole demeanor just changed. I felt a peace come over me…like somebody had put a blanket over my shoulders. And I started breathing…and my brain came back… I was able to think clearly for the first time in 12 years… I say it was a transformation. I say that literally because I came back to life…right there on death row." Portia had struggled, prior to the meeting, with God's mandate to forgive Jackson as a person. She did not know what that meant. Over the five-and-a-half-hour dialogue, Portia claimed, however, that "…with the grace of God I was able to really see him as a person rather than as the monster that I had seen 12 years earlier." Her acceptance of his personhood allowed her to complete God's bidding—"I finally did get to the point that I could forgive Jackson. My completion of forgiveness happened on death row. The completion when I saw his eyes and I saw his remorse…and when I saw he was a human being and not a monster."

Tamara felt she had done most of her forgiveness before she ever met James in prison. She learned, however, that when he shot her he was not on drugs as she had always assumed but was cold sober. That fact shattered the story she had told herself and made what he did to her an intentional act. "[W]hen I found out he was cold sober, it's kind of like, whoa! Okay! But even though that was hard to hear, I prefer the truth straight up and to my face… It was gut-wrenchingly hard to hear and hard for him to say. There were a lot of tears during that part on both sides… It was powerful. She acknowledged, however, "…that really, truly the honesty with which he told me everything just solidified for me…it wasn't that I was hearing the pleasantries or whatever. It was that I heard the real honest-to-God, from the heart truth…that was so pure that it just solidified it all."

Offender requests

A number of offenders asked participants for forgiveness toward the end of the dialogue. Some, but not all of the requests were made after powerful energy shifts had occurred. Kalicia did two meetings with Ahmad. She never felt that she had something to forgive him for—"He didn't mean to do it…it's not like he went out and he deliberately picked my son… He was 18 years old." Near the close of the dialogue she told Ahmad that she hoped he would make some positive things happen in his life—"He responded, 'I hope you can forgive me.'" Kalicia was confused—"I had never expressed that I was unforgiving…it led me to believe that maybe he thought that if the situation were reversed, it would be a huge thing for him to forgive. Or maybe he just knew that in society…that's what you say to people." Although Kalicia left the meeting feeling very, very positive and hopeful, she had a negative energy shift in the second meeting because Ahmad backed down on his commitments to her. He wasn't interested in any public speaking as he had wanted to do in the VOD. He just wanted to get out of prison and forget about what had happened.

During the dialogue, Monique felt that "the negative energy was no longer in me. I think it slowly faded away during those hours together." Manny "…brought it up first and he asked me if I would ever be able to forgive him…When he asked me that, I had to take a break because I really had to compose myself and think about whether I could do that… I didn't realize that forgiveness was about setting myself free…when we went back in [to the meeting room] I had decided that forgiveness was definitely on the table and that it was something I wanted to do. Before we left that day, I hugged him and told him that I forgave him… I can't say that I, 100 percent, believed myself when I first said it. I wanted it to be true and I knew that I would have to work at it being true." Monique clarified that she felt in a bind. If she forgave him, she was telling him it was alright to have done what he did. But if she did not forgive him, she felt she was holding power over him—"That's really false because you're imprisoning yourself with all that ugly… I'm so thankful that I had that opportunity… I would like to think that I would have eventually got there on my own but probably not… Something in the meeting changed in me, and I just realized that it wasn't about him. It was about me, keeping myself hostage with all that negative energy… It dawned on me during the meeting that we all do things that are not right, all the time. But does that make us a bad person? It just means we did something dumb or stupid or out of character for even us. So we have to forgive people for stumbling and making mistakes."

Jake did not initiate the focus on forgiveness but Lila asked him, toward the end of the meeting, if he had a faith life and if he had asked Loretta, the girl he killed, to forgive him. "Jake said, 'Oh, I couldn't do that. I couldn't do that.' I just looked at him and said, 'Yes you can.' That surprised me. It's like 'Did I just say that?' But I did. I didn't plan to do that. Forgiveness was a foreign word to me. It felt that it wasn't up to me to forgive. That was up to the Lord." Lila noted that her voice changed during the dialogue. "I know my voice got softer when I talked to him…it was almost like I was talking to another child… He was human and I thought, 'Here he is at this age, but he was a child at 19 [when he killed Loretta].'"

At the end of the dialogue with Jessie, Paula said, "He asked for my forgiveness… I was surprised by that. I said I wasn't ready to give him forgiveness yet, that I may eventually and it may take time but it's not where I was at or feeling." Paula was angry. The facilitator had warned her during preparation that she did not need to give forgiveness until "…it's something you really, really, want to do. You're going to get emotional and don't get caught up in that and do something you don't want or say something you don't want to. If that's something you want to say to somebody be careful with that." Jessie had been given the same warning—"So it upset me that he went and did that because…we agreed that we weren't going to do that. But then I thought, this is big for him. This is his one chance like this is my chance to get questions answered, and this is bothering him." Paula remembered that he had gotten caught up in her sister's threats that she said at sentencing. She had told him to rot in hell and the whole courtroom cheered—"That clearly was bothering him…so it was kind of a revelation that he was pretty certain he was going to burn in hell. So when he asked for forgiveness he specifically mentioned that incident… For me, a kind of grace happened, a compassion happened, some type of forgiveness happened where I was allowed to see things from his eyes in a way that I've never allowed myself to before…the same thing happened for him and it was big. It was huge. Is that forgiveness?"

The requests from offenders for explicitly verbal forgiveness clearly threw the participants, including Lila who initiated the topic, into territory they had not planned to enter. Although each person responded differently, the impetus to raise the question seemed to evolve out of the energy shifts that had occurred in the dialogue and were part of the pain transformation for the parties. Consequently, participants, even if they were initially offended, were thoughtful and sensitive to offenders in their responses. In this regard, they continued to nurture the positively charged energy between themselves and the offenders.

Conditional forgiveness

Some participants offered verbal forgiveness to offenders but were hesitant to give it fully. Although the dialogues went well and participants felt positively toward the person who had harmed them, they either were not confident about the offender's resolve to change or were not ready to let go of their hold over the offender or their negative feelings.

Theresa struggled with forgiving Gerald but found a way to do it so that it did not have to be complete. Theresa viewed the meeting with Gerald as a forgiveness journey but she struggled with it—"It felt wrong, basically… It felt like such a big thing to forgive…it took a life. It devastated my parents and my family." It was a spiritual journey—"I wanted to do it because it just seemed like it was going to open up my whole world again to other people… I was going to be able to care about other people better… The dialogue was the culmination of a forgiveness journey." At the same time, Theresa did not want to emotionally connect with Gerald "…so he felt any kind of a bond with me. I was really scared of that actually." The dialogue was principally victim centered and there was little back and forth conversation between them. Towards the end of the meeting, there were some things that I just did spontaneously… I didn't know if the forgiveness words were going to actually come out of my mouth…" When asked about any last thoughts or feelings, Gerald made eye contact and earnestly said he was. Theresa remembered reading about a victim who, after the offender apologized, did not say, "I forgive you" and had regretted it ever since—"I wanted to say it and I wanted it to be genuine but I didn't really know… And then I just looked at him and I said, 'I forgive you and I will need to continue to be on that journey probably the rest of my life.' For me, it felt like a clean break from any lingering hatred that would remain in me." Her caveat about forgiveness being an ongoing journey instead of a closed event allowed her to give forgiveness, as she had wanted to do, as authentic and done with integrity.

Toward the end of the meeting, Micaela began to feel that she needed to give something to Ronald. They had shared a lot during the meeting—"He started to seem like very pitiable person. His life history—a lot of loss and he seemed like a very lost person…my heart just went out to him." When the word "forgiveness" came to her, she reacted—"Oh, my God. I don't know about that. I didn't know what to do with it. I said to Ronald, 'I want you to know that if you go on and you get the help that you need, and you stay clean and sober, then I want you to know that I have forgiven you. If you don't do those things, then I don't.' That was as good as I could do at the time." Micaela worried that by giving forgiveness Ronald might think that everything was all right now. She also struggled with the gratitude she felt toward him because it might be a betrayal of Joel. Ronald left the room when they were done but Micaela realized she'd likely never see him again. She called him over to her to shake his hand and thank him—"I can still see the vision in my head of our hands, of shaking his hand [while thinking that] I'm touching this man who killed Joel." Eighteen years later, Micaela learned that Ronald was back in prison for a DWI. During that time, she had followed a father whose daughter was killed in the Oklahoma bombing by Timothy McVeigh. The father had commented that McVeigh owed him nothing. When she heard his words she knew that she needed to take away the condition that she had placed on her forgiveness with Ronald—"I wanted to have that real release of him…that conditional thing I said to Ronald kept me attached to him." Micaela sent him a letter saying, "I wish you well. I hope you have a good life. But you have nothing to do with me anymore. So live the life that you choose, and I wish you well." With that letter, Micaela acknowledged the significance of the dialogue but cut the emotional attachment to him.

Randell did two VODs with Baird. At the end of the first meeting, he felt that his hatred and anger began to fall away—"I was still kind of angry but I was getting some of the answers I needed." When the meeting ended, Baird reached out to shake his hand. Randell accepted his apology. Ronald felt positively about the meeting—"Everything that I had hoped for in the VOD was met and far exceeded, because he began to tell the truth. All I wanted was the truth, to know what happened, how my son died, and why he acted the way he did. And he was very honest." However, his cancer and heart problems persisted. He also was plagued with questions about forgiveness from attendees at the victim impact panels he did—"Forgiveness is something that's really hard to do… Forgiveness is a complete, total let-go. It's not, 'I forgive and I still hate.' Forgiveness means you've released it, all of that." Randell ultimately told the parole board he wanted to tell Baird he had forgiven him fully. At the hearing, he told Baird, "I forgive you. But that's not meaning that there might be some days I might not like you. There might be some days I'm not willing to talk to you. But I want you to know that forgiveness means it's over. I can't take it back because it wouldn't really be forgiveness, would it? Forgiveness has to come from the heart, has to mean you're done, you've reached the end point." Baird broke down in tears and said, "I will do anything Randell wants me to do."

Theresa, Micaela, and Randell struggled with being explicit about their verbal forgiveness. It did not feel quite right to any of them because of their associations with the meaning of the term and their expectations about where they needed to be emotionally. Each of them took steps to behave in ways that were congruent with their beliefs and feelings. In so doing, they met expectations or removed conditions on themselves and on the offenders that otherwise impeded doing what was needed in a complete way. Theresa turned an event into a process. Micaela removed the condition so she could release the sense of bondage. Randell came to terms with the fact that the event that had poisoned his life was indeed over. He expressed its finality by conveying that forgiveness established the end point of the crime.

Irrelevance of forgiveness

Although all participants associated the concept of explicit forgiveness with meeting the offender, some of them felt it was not relevant to the meeting or their journey. Lila, for example, felt that forgiveness belonged to God and suggested that Jake ask Loretta for forgiveness. Maya relayed that she and her husband had no conversation about forgiveness prior to the dialogue. Maya, however did not want to spend her life "a sad, mean, bitter old person who just can't get over it, get beyond. I made a conscious decision that they were not going to take my life too. I think that's part of that forgiveness. I'm not going to carry that around." Maya saw forgiveness as a private decision, "a gift you give yourself." Duncan also saw dyadic forgiveness as irrelevant. He did not carry a sense of vengeance or anger. He felt that forgiveness belonged with God rather than between individuals. He had studied it philosophically and psychologically for years. At the time of the study, he felt that the core issue for him was not forgiveness but compassion—"I'm moving beyond forgiveness to the area of compassion. We've been able to establish some mutual compassion for the suffering both of us have as a result of [the crime]." Duncan also shared the opinion, theoretically, that people try to move away their pain by forgiving, but, in fact, the pain is always there. What matters more is reducing the suffering, which can be done through mutual compassion. Duncan's ongoing relationship with Gregory reflects his efforts to feel and act on that compassion.

Summary

Explicitly verbal forgiveness took many forms. Some participants revisited the decisional forgiveness they started outside of the dyadic dialogue. In many cases, the revisiting happened after there had been significant energy shifts as a result of the dyadic engagement. In the context of the actualized relationship between victim and offender in which participants received new information, the offender's remorse, or acknowledged the offender's humanity, participants moved from decisional to fuller and more emotional expressions of forgiveness. In some cases, participants received requests from offenders for forgiveness. Because the desire was expressed at the end of the dyadic engagement with the offender and often occurred after there had been significant energy shifts, the context around the requests influenced how participants responded. Indeed, the reactions from the participants were grounded in their changed perceptions and feelings toward the offenders as a result of what had happened between them as a result of the meeting. Some participants wrestled with partial or conditional forgiveness. They wanted to give to the offender and yet felt restricted from a full expression of letting go. As participants recognized that the conditions were hurting or could hurt them, they framed or redid their expressions of forgiveness in ways that left them free. Finally, some participants eschewed any substantial involvement with the concept of dyadic forgiveness because forgiveness was either only relevant to a person's relationship with God, a personal, private, and individual matter, or a false way to reduce permanent pain. Outside of decisional forgiveness, participants' experiences with explicitly expressed forgiveness occurred in the aftermath of the offender's accountability and the victim's humanizing of the offender, and in the context of the transformation of the pain.

Behaviorally implicit forgiveness

Not all participants expressed forgiveness in verbally explicit terms. Arguably, many of them expressed their feelings through facial expressions, their eyes, and body posture. Occasionally, they reported their own behaviors in the interviews done for this study. They described crying with the offender, speaking in comforting and caring tones of voice, feeling emotionally pulled toward the offender as they learned more about them, their lives, and their reactions to the crime. A number of them felt grateful for what the offender gave them and the immense relief they felt as pieces went into place. Unfortunately, much of the actual data about their nonverbal behavior is missing because there was no way to capture it other than through their retrospective reports.

In some instances, participants did describe, in detail, what happened physically and symbolically between themselves and the offender that manifested itself as behaviorally implicit forgiveness. Similarly to verbally explicit forgiveness, these instances occurred primarily after or as part of the transformation of the victim's pain and toward the end of the dialogue. They spontaneously occurred and were connected to intense emotional reactions from the victim to the offender.

Most expressions of behaviorally implicit forgiveness were physical. Victims and offenders shook hands or gave hugs as part of acknowledging that the dyadic dialogue had been meaningful, even pivotal, to their healing. But physical touch was important as well because it symbolically expressed the positively charged energy that now existed between them. Moreover, physical touch was a powerful gesture, an internal giving, made by victims to offenders, that they saw the individual as worthy and acceptable, as humanly touchable. Notwithstanding the horror of the crime, it also conveyed that matters between them were settled, or that things were "alright." In some cases, the message expressed a sense of compassion in both directions that overrode the limitations of a strictly verbal response and sped up the positive energy flow between victims and offenders.

Physical touch

Cassandra, for example, talked about the shift in energy during her dialogue and her openness to Bret. "It lightened me... I sort of wished we would have exchanged phone numbers. I wouldn't mind seeing him again...just to catch up, seeing what he's been doing...if I wanted to say, I could give him a hug. We took a break [during the dialogue]. I went outside to have a cigarette and he joined us and I hugged him outside."

Kalicia described that after Ahmad talked about being sorry for what he had done and his desire to speak to youth so they would not make the same mistakes he had, they were both tearful. "[W]e ended the meeting by hugging and if it was possible we wanted to meet again... I thought the meeting with him was extremely positive."

After Monique responded to Manny's request for forgiveness, she gave him a hug. "I had decided forgiveness was definitely on the table and that it was something that I wanted to do... Before we left that day, I hugged him and told him I forgave him... That was such a tremendous relief." As an extension of and ripple effect from the dialogue, Monique told the story about the offender in the Bridges to Life program who coincidentally was a part of the crime and saw her brother fall. He was openly weeping as she told the story of her brother and meeting Manny—"I walked over and hugged him, and I told him, 'I forgive you too...' He was still trapped living in that murder when both myself and the gentleman who did this had already gotten past it."

Symbolic gestures

Some of the participants and offenders had unexpected and significant responses after their physical expressions of thankfulness and caring. Maria and Donny shook hands at the end of the dialogue. Then Donny asked if he could hug her and she said yes—"I don't know why I said yes, like he said, he don't even know why he asked me. He walked around the table and I was hysterical." As Donny held her so she wouldn't fall, they made a pact that Maria would help Donny cry. Maria then had an epiphany in which she felt all the negatively charged energy leave her body. She tested the permanency of her forgiveness each time they met for additional meetings. In retrospect she commented, "I had already done all the work that allowed God to do the work in my heart...but I knew that this was the time that the forgiveness took place... I just felt totally different... I just knew that all that junk was gone. It was over with."

Terri Anne described how, at the end of the meeting, she gave Chester a book as part of encouraging him to do more with his life. She had surmised that he had no reason to believe in himself. "[H]e was sitting across the table with his head down, just shaking his head [in disbelief]. God said [to me], 'Terri Anne, put your hand across that table.'" Terri Anne replied that she couldn't do it because she'd be holding the hand that held the pistol that killed her child—"I said, 'God, I can't do this by myself.' I had my eyes closed and I stretched my hand out across the table. Chester took my hand in both of his. He pulled my hand under his face and he washed our hands with his tears. At that moment, I let out a guttural scream of anger, hate, and rage that I had contained for 13-and-a-half years… It was the most spiritual thing that has ever happened to me in my life…at that moment, the rage and hate and anger was just lifted. It was gone."

For Terri Anne, touching Chester started a chain reaction. Chester felt tremendous love and gratitude for how she had mothered him throughout the dialogue. Her reaching out to him with her hand was meant to comfort him as he sat at the table unable to fathom that someone could truly care that much about him. His tears over both their hands were healing. Just as she had touched his soul and helped heal, through her mothering, the wounds he had carried from his childhood, he held her pain and anguish from the loss of her only child whom she loved fiercely. As that happened, Terri Anne was able to release all the pain she still carried. In some ways, everything in Terri Anne's dialogue with Chester was about forgiveness. She reinstated him over and over again through her love and encouragement. Chester absorbed it with tears of remorse for killing Peter and tears that broke down his hardness from years of just surviving. With his tears, he pulled on Terri Anne's pain so she was able to finally release the rest of the negative energy she held within her.

Pearle talked about her comment to Hal about forgiveness—"[T]he minute I said the word to him, once again tears started streaming down his face and he got beet red and tears started streaming down my face. I said to him, 'There's a part of you that murdered my mother I cannot forgive.' Hal said immediately, 'Well, of course not. I was a horrible person. I did a horrible thing.' I told him that I told my therapist that I could forgive 79 percent of it so Hal kind of chuckled about that. I asked him to make something of his life in prison and than I said, 'I'd like to shake your hand.' He got a funny look and stood up. I walked slowly [around the table] and put my hand out to take his hand, and then my other hand goes to take it [his hand] in both hands. And then, spontaneously, I just embraced him. I think that embrace lasted five seconds, ten seconds…then I let him go and I stepped back…and then we started spontaneously debriefing about what had happened [in the dialogue]… I didn't do the forgiveness for any effect… He gave me my life back and I gave him his life back." Pearle was clear that she had forgiven Hal long before the dialogue but she was not going to share it unless the dialogue went well and there was sincerity. "I had let go. I released him as a human being. I had forgiven him as a person." Pearle's behaviorally implicit forgiveness surprised even her. She was clear that she could not grant complete forgiveness yet she embraced Hal in such a full way that she elevated him in the room as a full human being. He subsequently entered the debriefing with Pearle and the others as an essential player, which he had been throughout the dialogue.

Pearle's partner described the quality of their giving and receiving so both of them could heal—"What it felt like to me was rappelling, where you've got somebody on the ropes and somebody going down the cliff face and you're trusting the person at the top with your life. But for you two, it was like, you were rappelling but then switching places. So one would hold the lines and the other would go down. And then that person would hold the line as the first person went down further on the cliff." In her statement, Pearle's partner was referring to her observation that Pearle and Hal became one during the dialogue and that both were working to help heal the other. Although initiated by Pearle, their mutual embrace showed their deep gratitude, appreciation, and partnering so that something better could come out of the tragedy.

Keisha also started her conversation about forgiveness with Adam by claiming that she could not forgive him for killing three people but she could forgive him for never being able to have the answers she would have liked from her biological father because of his death due to Adam's drinking and driving—"I can truly, truly live with not having those answers." Adam cried and cried. He had bowed his head, conveying to Keisha that he was not worthy of that forgiveness. Keisha worked to reassure him—"God's forgiven me for so many things that I have done in my past and the harms I've caused other people and I can forgive you… I was trying to tell him that he could let it go, the slate's clean. This has been burdening me too long. This has been burdening him too long."

Adam had started the dialogue by reading her his letter of apology and Keisha asked for it—"As I reached for the letter in his hands that was all folded up, I laid my hands on top of his hands…and he started to pray… For the first time in my life, the man, he prayed for me. He prayed for my healing. He prayed for my heart. He prayed for my protection. He prayed for my safety. He prayed for my comfort. He never once prayed for himself. He prayed for me. That's how we ended the meeting." For Keisha, their encounter was magical—"I've never been in a situation where I have had to earnestly really forgive someone for something that had such a powerful impact in my life… It was just something that happened. To have him pray like that was so genuine and so honest. It was so healing… [My] journey all came to an end right there and then."

Maria, Terri Anne, Pearle, and Keisha had experiences of forgiveness that were deeply emotional and profoundly healing. Although there were expressions of verbally explicit forgiveness, the power lay in what happened for each of them behaviorally. The embrace between Maria and Donny led to a covenant that the mother of the man Donny killed would help him cry. Maria arguably felt his need for her and the hunger in his soul for relief and knew through her doubling over in pain that she was releasing the rest of the negatively charged energy in order to move forward with Donny. Terri Anne had poured her caring into Chester throughout the dialogue, eliciting more and more of his pain and remorse. When they met and Chester bathed their hands in his tears, she allowed Chester's deep remorse to touch and pull out her remaining anger. Pearle had embraced Hal as a show of her forgiveness but what emerged was the mutuality of their caring and what they had done for each other. They helped each other descend into the depths of where each needed to be to heal themselves and each other. Keisha worked to carve the opening within Adam so that he could receive her forgiveness. In return, he, like a strong, protective and comforting father, prayed over her for everything she would need to move forward and safely in the world.

These expressions of behaviorally implicit forgiveness carried symbolic meanings that impacted participants viscerally on both emotional and physical levels. It became almost impossible to decipher where their dyadic actions started and went because they were so intertwined. Although the forgiveness focus is usually on the forgiver, in these cases, the focus truly moved from the victim to the dyad. Indeed, the behaviorally implicit forgiveness was exceedingly powerful because it so encompassed both parties such that the engagement and healing, the giving and receiving were truly mutual.

ENERGY SHIFTS

Many participants had experienced some shifts from negatively to positively charged energy prior to meeting the offender. These shifts came as a result of the following circumstances: participants' reflections about the offender, information about the offender, experiences with offenders, and their compassionate character. The shifts occurred also because of events during the preparation process such as information shared by facilitators about offenders, offenders' letters, or offender's willingness to meet with participants. Although these shifts happened independently of dyadic interaction, some participants were already moving in a different direction and brought that shifting energy into the dyadic dialogue. In these instances, there were graduated energy shifts in which what happened in the meeting built on what had gone before. There were also graduated shifts during the dialogue. Regardless of the number of energy shifts in a particular case or their graduated nature, participants usually identified one core positively charged shift that was pivotal to their healing or sense of release and unburdening.

Graduated shifts

Participants easily related to the idea of energy shifts. This terminology seemed to match well with their experience. Consequently, they self-identified, with little prompting, when and where the shifts occurred, in what order, and their significance.

Maria, for example, felt that the initial shift happened when she discovered and read the poem "Two Mothers"—"I opened up to a book and it fell on a page that had a poem entitled "Two Mothers." She fought against its message, which was to bring together mothers of victims and offenders, but it kept returning. The next shift happened when she attended a prison program where offenders told their stories—"By the time it was over I was thinking differently about offenders and murderers." A friend who showed her a video about a murderer who was writing children's books followed this shift and introduced another—"I know that changed something in me, watching that, cause I wondered what it was like in prison. So I got to see him in prison and some of the changes and things he went through and I was like, 'Wow.'" When Maria went into the prison to meet with Donny, she saw that the prison staff brought no cup for him to have water like the others in the meeting had. She said to the guard, "Well, what does that look like, us sitting here drinking water when he can't... I didn't realize it at the time [but] something had changed." While waiting for Donny to come into the meeting room, Maria noticed that the prison guard had brought her lotion for her dry hands in a bottle that said, "Beyond Belief"—"I'm just like, 'God, what is going on here.'" Maria commented that she was ready for a change. Something had to change—"It had started. The forgiveness had started and I may not have been aware of it."

Paula also was able to trace a series of shifts. For years she debated whether or not to meet with Jessie. Her decision to go forward was the start of her shifts. She replicated that ambivalence throughout her preparation, and it took two years before she decided to go forward. The movement was because of information she got from the facilitator about Jessie and her realization that meeting with her was a free choice for Jessie—"At the core of it, the most important thing was he doesn't have to do this process. He chose to do this. He might be willing to give me the answers I want so I have to be open to this process to receive anything from it." Paula experienced another shift when the facilitator showed her a tape of Jessie—"It was really, really big because it showed his appearance and how he had changed… It prepared me for what he looked like and what he was gonna talk like… One of the questions [the facilitator] asked him was, 'Is this something you really want to do?' He said, 'Yes, this is something I really want to do.' It indicated that he wanted to make it right somehow or do something for the better out of this." The final shifts for Paula were getting reassurance from Jessie that he would not attack her when he was released and that her father never sexually attacked Jessie—"The thing that made the biggest difference was the change in my mindset about my personal safety and the change in my mindset about the homicidal attack. Those two things were instrumental in me being able to feel safe again… The whole way home I cried. It wasn't crying full sorrow cry. It was like tears of release or joy, of finally having some peace for many, many of those questions that I'd had for 25 years."

Briana mapped out the series of shifts she experienced. It started with noting that Big Jon had no one at any hearing to support him. She asked the victim advocate, "Where the hell is his family? I want you to find out where his family is." At the sentencing, "my side is totally filled up with family and friends of Felix and I thought, 'Wow, it's gonna be nobody over there again. The poor kid. What is going on?" Briana found herself feeling sorry for Big Jon as she learned his extensive history in foster care. Briana felt another shift when Big Jon walked into the room. Instead of looking wild and crazy like his picture "…he walked in like a regular kid, and my heart just broke." Another shift happened for Briana as she talked to him about what he missed in his life and what he needed in the future—"Hold your babies. Be there for them. It's what you didn't get. It's why Felix is not here." Briana commented, "I didn't even know I was going to say this, but when all was done I said, 'Not until the day that you hold that baby in your arms, not until then will you know what you took from me. This isn't about what you took from Felix. It's what you took from me.'" After the dialogue, Briana commented, "It was extremely positive in my life. I thought it was going to help Big Jon not do it again, but it actually did help me. It calmed me. I got everything said to him that I would want to say and he accepted it all. He took responsibility and he said he was sorry and would try to live a better life because he took my son. He also said to me that he didn't understand why he didn't learn this stuff before. Why did he have to kill Felix for him to learn it? He was sorry that it took me losing my son for him to learn it. That was unfair to me."

Maria, Paula, and Briana all demonstrate the gradual and graduated movement from pivotal event to event that shaped the dialogue and how events in the dialogue resulted in solidifying their shift from negatively charged to positively charged energy. They all had clear agendas going into the dyadic dialogue about what they needed and wanted to come out of meeting. They were surprised by some of their reactions to offenders during the dialogue because they felt more open or responded more humanely than they expected. Their shifting during the dialogue was based on what they experienced with the offender, which in some instances surprised them. Paula did not expect Jessie to be so honest and forthcoming. Briana did not expect to use the analogy that came to her in the dialogue about Big Jon holding his baby in the future to powerfully impact him. Maria did not expect to be concerned about the prison's treatment of Donny or to care about him. In the aftermath of the dialogue, these small occurrences were indicators, to participants, of the genuine emotional shifts they were making internally.

Core shift

Participants were able to identify an event during the dyadic dialogue or a pivotal time, if the shift occurred before the dialogue, that marked their change or feeling that what they needed to do, or what had happened, was instrumental in their moving positively forward. As noted, the core shift often was preceded by a graduated series of shifts. In contrast, however, the prior shifts were not complete. Rather, the core shift, as presented by the participants, was permanent. It was maintained even in those cases where offenders backslid after the dialogue as participants found creative ways to hold onto their gains.

Tamara's core shift was in finally being able to meet James and complete an accountability process dyadically that had started many years earlier with James' public apology in court. James had waited years to finally account for himself and what happened the night he shot Tamara. He knew he had to do it directly with Tamara since she was the person he harmed. James' confession that he was not under the influence of drugs and had intentionally shot Tamara and her ability to face that truth was a pivotal dynamic in putting all the pieces together.

Norman's core shift was in shifting the burden of the intergenerational anger he carried to Raul. He felt the anger go directly into Raul's soul. For Norman, there were few shifts that he consciously knew about prior to the meeting. Instead, he claimed, "In a blink of an eye it changed. As soon as he walked into the room and sat down, God filled my head. God filled my heart with love and compassion and forgiveness. All I could do is forgive him. And he cried." After declaring to Raul that he had to drop his anger, he then proceeded to thank Raul for killing his mother because of the life he would have led otherwise. "[H]ad you not killed my mom, I would either be dead or in prison because I was growing up in the biker lifestyle. And God removed me from that situation by taking my mom." Norman commented that Raul was in awe of what happened as he was, that his spirit and soul were starving, begging for forgiveness. He felt what he got from Raul was priceless—"The meeting changed everything. It absolutely changed me."

Lila's primary shift happened during the meeting with Jake. She felt an initial change when he walked into the room—"I had this image of a monster in my head. I didn't give him a face. But when he came in, that mask that I put on him came off. It came off immediately and I had to see him as a human being. I was not prepared for that." After telling Jake what she had been through, he commented, "I was so messed up." He then confessed that he had had his hands around other girls' throats and knew he was going to kill somebody. It made no difference who it was. Lila was deeply impacted by his taking ownership—"It's like he is taking all this that I was hanging onto, and he's taking it. Then he said, 'It wasn't her fault.' And he said, 'It wasn't your fault.' He said again, 'And it wasn't your fault.'" Lila felt the balloon that had been ready to pop inside her deflate—"As he and I were talking the balloon got a little smaller and smaller and it was releasing somehow… I felt like I was literally handing over all of these burdens and things to Jake and he was willingly taking it. I felt like he was willing to take all that from me and live with it… He knew he couldn't give me my daughter back, but he gave me something, some kind of peace." Lila felt that Jake had gone to another zone in talking to her. "He went through something too… He felt that remorse, the guilt, all those things. It made him more human to me. I needed to know that it mattered to him. He wasn't the cold killer that I imagined."

Lizette had had a long history with restorative justice and involvement in VODs with other victims. She saw the meeting with Gamal as a finishing touch on her healing process—"I just felt really comfortable with the process by then." The one piece she never wanted to think about, however, were her daughter's last words—"Those last moments of her life are always the hardest to think about…it was just a place I never went. I wouldn't allow myself to go there…I wasn't actually asking him to go there when he did… But once he started down the road… I found it hard to stop him. Gamal shared that when Karmen realized she was about to be killed, she said, 'I forgive you and God will too.' I never knew that. That was amazing and incredibly helpful." Gamal's sharing about Karmen's last words was pivotal for Lizette. She was also impacted by the fact that he was exceedingly remorseful. He never cried when he talked about his own upbringing or abuse—"…but he sure cried when he talked about what he had done. It just seemed more than he could bear."

Randell's goal in doing the dialogue was to rid himself of the intense anger that was literally taking his life. His cancer and heart condition were directly related to his obsession with hating Baird. His core shift occurred when, after the first dialogue, he shared his forgiveness with Baird, which was followed by Baird's full transparency in the second dialogue. He shared that he wanted Baird, as part of his parole, to join him on victim impact panels. He told him he forgave him fully—"I can't take it back, no… It wouldn't really be forgiveness, would it?" In the second dialogue, Baird shared all the details about the accident that he caused. Randell said, "I thanked him for letting me know the truth, because the truth was something I really had to have. I needed the truth…when you're hearing the truth for the first time that you've been looking for, for so long…some of that pain began to melt away… It felt like some of that was being lifted, that weight that we were carrying from all the stories that we heard that were untrue about my son… [Baird] carried that weight too… People who lie and tell stories…it has to be eating on them as well…he did confirm it, that it was a nightmare that he lives as well."

The core shifts for Tamara, Norman, Lila, Lizette, and Randell are exemplars of what went on for most of the participants. In the interviews, participants selected the critical events that allowed them to move into a different space, a space of positively charged energy. The movement happened both because their needs were met but also because of how offenders gave to them. Indeed, most offenders offered them their sorrow, their remorse, and their humanity. Participants were amazed both to receive what they needed from the person responsible for their pain and to experience the internal and visceral shifts after so much time had passed. Most, but not all, participants described their reactions in very positive ways. Maya and Duncan had unique experiences. Duncan and Maya never felt the energy block reported by the other participants. Duncan's motivation was to establish an ongoing relationship with Gregory. Maya wanted to be part of Duncan's process but soon decided that she had no more need to attend their ongoing meetings. Her healing happened outside the context of meeting with Gregory. In many ways, neither Duncan nor Maya felt the anger, sense of injustice, fear, or lasting disconnection that other participants expressed. The context for their dialogues with Gregory, therefore, was not shaped by the same conditions and they did not report core shifts in energy.

4

RESOLUTION AND POST-DIALOGUE OUTCOMES

RESOLUTION

Participants reported many positive outcomes from the dyadic dialogue, both for themselves and what they witnessed in offenders. Within the framework of restorative justice, dyadic forgiveness refers both to the victim's letting go of negatively charged energy but also to the reinstatement of the offender. Participants' verbally explicit and behaviorally implicit expressions of forgiveness were, in effect, accounts of morally reinstating the offender. Many participants felt that they had received what they wanted from the dialogue and described their internal changes in glowing and uplifting terms. Something had come to rest and there was a sense of completion. Their energy was now flowing because the blockage had been removed and the negative charge had shifted in a positive direction. As such, many of them felt affirmed and energized in whatever direction their lives took. Figure 3.6 shows the positive outcomes for victims and offenders.

Unburdened victims

Although participants' experiences varied widely, they were quite uniform in how they described their feelings and the energy shifts they experienced. Their reactions exposed the weight they had carried from the crime and how little relief that had felt prior to the dyadic dialogue. Their dyadic engagement with the offender clearly was a demarcation that separated blocked from flowing energy and negatively charged from positively charged energy.

Monique, for example, remarked that prior to meeting Manny, she was robotic and shut down emotionally. After the meeting, she was

"…able to actually feel safe again to just let my guard down and feel what I was feeling… For so long, it's like when you shut down your emotions… everything was shut down. That was the only way that I could function was to shut everything down. That meant joy, happiness, love, it was on lockdown because I couldn't feel one emotion without feeling guilty about not feeling another emotion. So it was just easier not to feel anything at all. Going through mediation allowed me, once we got to the end of it, to really go back and feel all of those feelings." Monique commented "…it was okay for me to have these feelings without having all this guilt wrapped up around it."

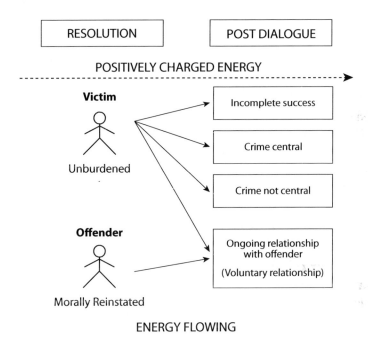

Figure 3.6: Process of dyadic forgiveness: Resolution and post-dialogue outcomes

Tamara declared, "I walked out of that prison probably as whole as I will ever be. [It was] the most powerful day of my life. Got all the answers I needed which was why I got the real honest to God truth. Peace. So much weight lifted off." Pearle echoed Tamara's comments about feeling unburdened. She said, "He acknowledged and took full responsibility for the evil thing he did. I felt like a totally new person. The burden of everything in the universe was lifted from me. He gave me my life back." Similarly, Keisha claimed, "It was freeing, this burden. I had no idea how heavy that burden was when I walked in there [to the dialogue]. But when I walked out, it wasn't there anymore."

Portia was graphic in her self-portrayal. She said, "I felt like someone had lifted 1000 pounds off." Her intense focus on Jackson for over 12 years had been infused with negatively charged energy, which bound her to him and reinforced her sense of powerlessness. As that energy was transformed into something positive, she experienced the release. Terri Anne also described the conversion of negative into positively charged energy—"We came to a place of peace. Through God, [our] converted hatred was turned into doing something worthwhile."

Theresa met with Gerald as part of facing what actually had happened to her sister. Her vow to live "normally" had stopped her from facing all the pain and messiness that came with her sister's murder. After the dialogue, Theresa's unburdening was manifested by her determination to live differently—"Now I feel like I want to live engaged and I don't necessarily want just normal life." Theresa acknowledged that after the dialogue she had more grieving to do because what she learned opened up more processing for her to do. However, she said, "The biggest impact is the no-turning-back impact that I still see plays out in my life." In describing Gerald, she said, "I'll never be able to go back to just seeing him as a ruthless animal. He's always human to me now. I'm not saying 'human' in the best terms of being human. I mean that I see him as a human being who has his own journey. I see it a bit more realistically. And that's never gone away. That has just always stayed."

Although there was a strong consistency in participants' accounts of the emotional outcomes, there was some variation. Duncan, for example, did not feel unburdened, likely because he never felt that he was emotionally blocked as a result of his daughter's murder. His resolution was to keep Gregory in his life forever. Indeed, his sense of completion is that he completes himself through contributing from his experience with Gregory back to the professional community in terms of knowledge about the VOD process in restorative justice.

Clynita deliberately worked not to engage with Tyrone during the dialogue. She only wanted information and was clear that she would end the dialogue if it felt unproductive. After announcing to Tyrone that she did not ever want to see him again and experiencing his resulting rage, she left immediately. However, she still felt the kind of relief described by the other participants—"I didn't come up there to forgive him...but I think he thought that was gonna happen. I was coming up there for closure and peace of mind and to fill in the blanks and that was exactly what I got. I left that prison feeling a huge lift. I hadn't felt that good in two years... I could breathe again...it was relief. It was brightness in my life again. It was moving forward."

Kalicia's initial response to the VOD was positive. In describing her husband and herself, she said, "We both left feeling very, very positive about the meeting. We both were very hopeful and feeling that he truly was sorry for what had happened... I was ecstatic. I even had the nerve to ask [Ahmad] if...he would be willing to do some speaking like at victim impact panels with me... It wasn't until that second meeting that I started feeling negative." Kalicia discovered that Ahmad wanted her to help him get back his driver's license and had no interest in pursuing public speaking. She felt let down. Instead of questioning the VOD or feeling disillusioned, she maintained her optimism—"I don't feel necessarily really angry... I just wish he had it within him to do it, because I think it could be good all the way around." Indeed, when she was contacted by Ahmad's wife, she considered responding to her or even meeting her at a restaurant, hopeful that "...maybe this would turn into something good, for the families."

These accounts demonstrate participants' energy shifts and the staying power that accompanied them. Participants clearly felt internally resolved about the events, questions, and feelings that had plagued them about the crime and its impact. Their feelings of being unburdened had a solidity that did not budge even when offenders behaved in ways that might have diminished the impact of the dyadic dialogue.

Offenders' moral reinstatement

Current research suggests that crime is a violation of values presumed to be shared (Wenzel and Okimoto, 2010). In this context, restoration refers to restoring those values through re-establishing the social consensus with the offender. In this study, participants and offenders engaged in a process that furthered accountability, remorse, and even reparation. As a result, the forgiveness from participants was commensurate with being reinstated in the community a moral citizen (Van Biema, 1999) based on participants' perceptions that offenders did, in fact, share relevant values with them. Indeed, as offenders showed through their remorse and contrition that they were not monsters but rather, deserving and credible as human beings, the reaffirmation through the dyadic dialogue of what they shared together likely reassured participants of their common commitment and adherence to a morally derived social compact, which allowed participants to reinstate offenders as humanly worthy.

The road to reinstatement is best exemplified by participants' humanization of offenders after they held themselves accountable for the harm done. However, participants' behavior at the end of the dialogue, or reflections about offenders after the meeting was finished, is a stronger commentary on the position they accorded the wrongdoer. Cassandra commented that she wished she'd had more contact with Bret and wished they had exchanged phone numbers so she could see how he was doing post release. Her desire to have connection with Bret outside of the safety of prison suggests that she saw him as a safe citizen.

Jake had a lot of shame about his behavior. He could not even look at Lila during the dialogue. When she asked him to look at her, he said, "I don't feel I have the right to." Lila surprised herself by suggesting he ask Loretta for forgiveness. When he declared, "Oh, I couldn't do that. I couldn't do that," Lila answered, "Yes, you can. Yes, you can." In this interchange, Lila conveyed to Jake that she saw him as worthy and as deserving of forgiveness, a giving that she felt belonged to God. Jake later acted on her belief in his goodness by calling his grandparents—"He got on the phone and called his grandparents he was very close to, to let them know that he did something good, something they can be proud of him for, for owning it... I think he held his head a little higher." Lila's reinstatement of Jake was powerful because her sense of his worthiness cut through his low self-esteem.

Some participants reinstated offenders by creating relationships outside the dialogue itself. Randell, for example, indicated that he wanted Baird to talk with him on victim impact panels, which he did over ten times. Although the relationship was maintained on prison grounds, Duncan continued the relationship with Gregory over 20 years, intends to speak to the parole board in his favor when it is time for Gregory's release, and plans to help him re-acclimatize and integrate into the community. In Norman's meeting with Raul, he elevated him to the position of spiritual brother and guide. Noting the difference between them, Norman said, "He would have been okay. He would have still continued to grow with Jesus and he would have gotten out... He would have continued to pray and he would move on with his life...With me, it changed me. There's no denying it... Raul was already walking on the right path...and God brought us together." Indeed, after the dialogue, Norman started to go to church and has maintained a relationship with Raul since he was released—"I asked that the lifetime no-contact order be lifted between Raul and me...so that he and I could remain in contact. Randell, Duncan, and Norman all reinstated the offenders by maintaining relationships post the dialogue. Moreover, participants included them in the personal areas of participants' lives that were most meaningful. Their actions sent ongoing messages that they saw these offenders as worthwhile and valued who these offenders were in their lives.

The moral reinstatement of offenders was significant to them. Indeed, as participants conveyed how they saw them after the dialogue, offenders reacted in ways that often exposed just how unworthy they felt. This gap only appeared when participants gave them back their stature as honest, decent "citizens." Theresa gave Gerald a medallion from a halfway house where her sister worked, a copy of the New Testament because it had brought her peace, and attempted to shake Gerald's hand. These actions were part of feeling good about their meeting and reinstating him, to the extent possible, as a worthwhile human being. In response to shaking his hand, however, "…he just right away said no." Gerald later told the facilitator that he did not want Theresa to touch his hand because he "just felt really dirty."

Tamara reinstated James through forming a tight bond with him over time and making future plans to have him in her life when he was released. Although she explicitly forgave him, "…he struggles with understanding why I forgave him…he really holds himself accountable for what happened…he just doesn't think he deserves it."

Terri Anne reinstated Chester by encouraging him to turn his life around. She talked to him about what he deserved as a child and still needed. After the dialogue, she sent him books and wrote him letters to help him move forward. Chester "…looked at me just incredulous…it never crossed his mind that anybody would ever take an interest in him and care. He wrote me a letter that said, "…I felt more love in that room the day I met you than I've felt my whole life." Gerald, James, and Chester clearly felt seen in new ways, different from how they saw themselves, and felt participants' efforts to reinstate them as moral citizens. The distance between participants' views and their own perceptions of themselves was noteworthy. Participants' changed opinions of them are a further manifestation of participants' forgiveness, as defined within restorative justice, and the positive energy shift that happened for participants.

POST-DIALOGUE OUTCOMES

In the aftermath of the dyadic dialogue, participants went in four different directions relative to the offender and the centrality of the crime in their ongoing lives. Participants were generally thriving according to their self-reports. They had few, if any, regrets about having done the dialogue, regardless of the post-dialogue outcome.

Outcome 1: Crime remains central

Some participants who completed the dialogue continued to keep a central focus on crime and offenders even though they felt finished in their work with the individual wrongdoer. Maya continued to know about Gregory because of Duncan's work and ongoing relationship with him. She herself determined, however, "I've just had enough" in terms of continuing to meet with him and her husband—"I just didn't see any more need." She felt good about closing the door because "…for so many months, maybe years, it was just falling out all over the place." Maya's current focus is on gun violence victims and families of offenders—"I'm working with groups that are working to end gun violence. One of our common things is to ring a bell in the garden down by the town lake for violence victims and gun violence victims."

In Portia's case, Jackson was executed, which, in her opinion, was the appropriate response to the murder of her daughter. Portia attended the execution at Jackson's request—"We witnessed the execution and he told everybody he was sorry. He told me he loved me and thanked me for the last two weeks of his life…" After the execution Portia met with his foster mother and learned that his mother had sexually abused him since he was eight years old. Portia said, "That was a different story for me then… The execution was already over and I thanked God for that but my heart just broke for [his foster mom]. She saw something in him that evidently no one else had ever seen." Portia has been a tireless advocate for restorative justice ever since the dialogue. After the execution, she got involved in numerous restorative justice projects and used the story of her daughter and meeting with Chester to educate criminal justice professionals throughout her home state.

Outcome 2: Crime not central

After the dyadic dialogue was finished, many participants seemed to move forward with few, if any, ties to the offender. Moreover, in the interviews, they made little reference to crime generally. Although their loved ones remained a vital part of their lives, how they lived and their daily activities appeared to have no connection to the crime.

Paula commented that she felt very exhausted after the dyadic dialogue. She has no more nightmares but "I still don't watch any scary movies because I will still have nightmares." Paula feels a lot of peace, "…the peace that comes with having answers to questions that you never ever had for 20 years…the peace that comes with not being afraid and living in fear. The peace that comes from…having the truth about what happened that night. The peace that comes from being more self-assured and knowing kinda where you stand with your loved one and that you did right by them." Paula said that after the dialogue, there was a shift in her relationship with her husband, "…because he went through the process with me. He understood much better…because it's something else to see somebody face to face…

We did that together… He felt at peace too because we allowed him [my husband] to say whatever he wanted to." Paula's husband told Jessie never to hurt his family or come near them—"They kinda had a man thing where that is not an issue. That gave my husband great relief too."

Briana said, "I don't have any regrets…like I wish I would have said that to him, or I should've said that to him… She reminisced about her son, Felix—"[Everybody says] 'Well, you were a good mom.' I say I was and I wasn't done yet, because I really wanted to do it a whole lot longer… But I learned to appreciate that I did have him for 22 years because there's people who don't have anything like we had with their kids and they've had their kids their entire life."

Cassandra talked about the centrality of her philosophy both in guiding her to meet with Bret and how she has used it with her daughter post the dialogue—"We live on the north side now. We hear gun shots all the time but the neighborhood kids love to come over here from age 5 to age 17. They flock here to my porch… I embrace it because I feel like it's an opportunity to maybe tell these kids some things. I have a few rules… When you're on my porch you can't fight with each other, you can't yell at each other, you can't be mean to each other. You wanna play with something take turns… They don't know how to act, how to behave. Should I run around selling drugs for bitches and hot clothes or should I be a nice person because how often do they view those messages to be kind, to be nice. You don't hear that often." Cassandra also shared how she incorporates her philosophy into raising her young daughter—"I told [my daughter] that I loved her more than anything but I was gonna hurt her. [When I hurt her], unless she told me, I might not ever know that I hurt her. She has to let me know…so I can apologize and change the behavior. Otherwise I might continue on…" Cassandra explained that "…if I change the behavior it means I value you as a person and our relationship now. If I continue with the behavior it means I don't care if it hurts you."

Outcome 3: Ongoing relationship with offender

Almost half the participants had some level of ongoing relationship with the offender. Although the original relationship was established by the crime and was forced upon them and involuntary, the relationship post the dyadic dialogue was voluntary. It emerged from their interaction with the offender during the dialogue but took on its own momentum and history afterwards.

Monique got very involved with a prison program called Bridges to Life after the dialogue where she told inmates the story of her brother and doing the dialogue. Being a part of the program allowed her to use "…what was a negative thing to now be a positive thing. So that my brother didn't just die… He still lives on and his story helps people." In addition, Monique maintained contact with Manny. They wrote back and forth while he was still incarcerated about two to three times a month—"We weren't rehashing what happened. We were talking about what the plans were for the future." Monique also talked to him on Facebook. Monique was clear in the dialogue that she wanted him to continue his education—"I felt that was important and he had promised to do that. He wanted to do whatever I asked him to do, which was really sweet of him." She shared that Manny got released, is now in college, and has a child—"I always tried to be encouraging of him, that he could do it. He could change his life if he wanted. I was proud of him for doing that."

Norman described his amazement with the results of the dyadic dialogue, how God-directed it was and God helped establish an ongoing connection between him and Raul—"All I could do was forgive him. I couldn't do anything else. He cried. Everyone in the room was in awe of what had just happened because that's not what was expected… I was amazed at what happened and I feel it every day. That's why Raul and I keep in contact. He said that I affected him in such a way that it reinforced his faith in God… and in humanity… Now he looks up to me as a mentor to Christ to him because I did something he doesn't think he could do. I want to keep in contact with him. A lot of people think that it's so I can keep an eye on him… That's not why I want to keep in contact with him. I want to keep him updated on how my son is doing in his sports and athletics… He says that whenever I call him, he seems to be really struggling with something. All of a sudden I call him, and he finds that he could get through it."

Terri Anne continued her relationship with Chester after the dyadic dialogue. He had had 153 disciplinary cases written up by prison officials when she met him. She had challenged him during the meeting to go beyond the limitations imposed by poverty and the violence of his background. She promised to write him and try to help him get an education while in prison. After the dialogue, they continued to communicate. Chester called Terri Anne his godmother and said that he loved her. Terri Anne sent him books, wrote him letters, and put money in his trust fund—"As long as I communicated with him, he was not in trouble. He did not get another disciplinary case at all. None, zero, zilch… He wrote me a letter every day…and I would write him one letter a month." Unfortunately the person in charge of prison services for victims made Terri Anne quit writing to him. She believes that banning contact with Chester sent him spiraling downward—"Someone had seen value in him…he wanted to live up to that…he didn't want to disappoint me." Terri Anne felt that Chester lost hope again—"Nobody cared. Nobody came. Nobody bothered with him." Chester attacked a prison guard and has been in trouble ever since. Chester had initially told her, "When I get out of prison, I'm going to come and take care of you." Terri Anne answered, "No, that's not what this is all about, Chester. This is about you taking care of yourself."

Outcome 4: Incomplete success

Two participants had post-dialogue experiences that disturbed the sense of success they had had immediately after the meeting. In both cases, the participants remained confident that the dyadic dialogue between themselves and the offender was genuine and the benefits they felt were sustained. In humanizing the offender, they both were able to maintain perspective, compassion, and understanding about what likely happened for the offender. They accepted the realities of their lives and character and were able to protect and not doubt their gains.

By including the VOD in his plea agreement, Kalicia hoped that Ahmad, who was 18 years old, could turn his life around—"When people want to help themselves, people love to help them… I thought, and I still believe, that if he has a right attitude, it's not going to stop him from being able to be successful." Kalicia felt that at the end of her first meeting with him, "I got the sense that he was going to have that attitude that I wanted him to have." In the second meeting, Ahmad reneged on what he had said he would do. Kalicia began to have reactions to the crime that, until then, had not occurred. She felt angry that Ahmad had left her son "…on the side of the road like he'd hit a possum or a squirrel… He didn't even stop to see if Darnell was okay." She began to feel the injustices, such as the fact that they did not test Ahmad for drugs and alcohol and that he got a short sentence. Kalicia put most of the blame on the bad influences in Ahmad's life—"His reaction is probably more the normal reaction. He probably just wants to move on with his life and put this behind him… I don't feel necessarily really angry… I just wish he had it within him to do it because I think it could be good all the way around."

Micaela felt a strong spiritual connection with Ronald during their dyadic dialogue—"It was an incredible event in my life, meeting with him… I was just in so much pain and having that experience was a relief. It was a release…of wanting a man to be dead or obsessing about him, thinking about him and wondering about him… I felt freer." Fourteen years after the dialogue, she learned that Ronald was back in prison. She sent a friend to meet with him to find out what had happened. The friend advised her not to see him again. He told her that Ronald had distorted the dialogue and believed things about Micaela that were not true—"I was a crack addict and Joel should not have been driving." Micaela described her response to Ronald's changes—"I told myself I don't want what happened then to take away what I experienced of him 14 years before. I didn't want to lessen that… I just said that's who we were then, and that's what happened then." Micaela explained what she thinks happened to Ronald—"If he continued to drink and do drugs, which he apparently did…he just started losing more and more of himself… I imagine for him to live with killing someone, what do you do? You make it less your fault. So he created rationalizations and stories in his head so he didn't have to feel responsible. I get that. I understand that."

There is no ranking of the four possible post-dialogue outcomes from this study. All participants were pleased with their dyadic dialogues. All participants sustained the positive effects, regardless of subsequent events, including offenders' disappointing behavior in their lives. Consequently, participants' efforts to resolve the negatively charged energy through a VOD were successful. Participants no longer felt the anger, vindictiveness, obsessiveness with the offender, or fear associated with blocked energy. Moreover, they were no longer impeded in their ability to move forward. As such, their involvement in the preparation and dyadic dialogue removed the unforgiveness that many, if not most, felt initially. If shifts from negatively to positively charged energy are indicative of forgiveness or changes in attitudes toward offenders, it is possible to suggest, based on these post-dialogue outcomes, that explicitly verbal or implicitly behavioral forgiveness was present for those participants who were in this study.

5

DYADIC FORGIVENESS

INTRODUCTION

The purpose of this project was to study dyadic forgiveness through a quantitative study of change in VOD participants and a qualitative study of energy shifts in the accounts of victim participants who engaged in a VOD with their offenders. Most studies of forgiveness have focused on forgiveness as an individual phenomenon that occurs outside the context of the victim–offender relationship. The change process is done solo and involves cultivating an empathic perspective that results in changes in the victim's perception of the offender. The vast majority of the studies are experimental rather than applied or address the impact of interventions to promote forgiveness on victim change. In those studies, forgiveness may be decisional or emotional (Worthington *et al.*, 2007). Decisional forgiveness is focused on the victim's intent to respond differently to an offender. Emotional forgiveness is considered as the replacement of negative emotions (i.e. anger, vengefulness) with positive other-oriented emotions such as empathy. There is sparse literature on dyadic forgiveness. Studies have concentrated on offended relationship partners in ongoing, committed relationships and the restoration of interpersonal closeness (McCullough *et al.*, 1998). Most of these studies again are experimental rather than qualitative, have focused solely on the person offended, the quality of the pre-existing relationship, shared history, and the variables principally of rumination, empathy, and apology.

This project proposes that dyadic forgiveness is a product of the interaction between victim and offender. It occurs in the context of the dyadic relationship. The word "dyadic" refers to two elements: the structure of the relationship and a bilateral process where both parties give something to the other and receive something from the other. Hence, they need each other's presence and participation to achieve the forgiveness experience. The relationship, though created by crime, therefore, is needed paradoxically for resolution of the negatively charged energy associated with the crime.

MUTUAL AID: GIVING AND RECEIVING

The bilateral process in dyadic forgiveness stimulates change, in part, because of the dependence and impact each person has on the other. Victims need information about the crime from offenders in order to complete the story. No one else knows better what happened than the offender. Offenders need to tell the truth about what happened. In effect, offenders need "to confess" to the person specifically harmed for the confession to be complete. This accounting includes the offenders' feelings about what they have done. Indeed, offenders need opportunities to demonstrate human qualities such as pain and remorse. The victim's presence is a necessary component to the "confession." This mutual aid or need for each other is symbiotic. Each party leans on the other. Each party gives. Each party receives.

In relating the truth, the full story, to the victim, the offender gives. In hearing the victim's account of the impact of the crime and feeling remorse for what he did, the offender gives again. Specifically, the offender takes on the pain for the crime and its devastating impact, a reality that only the victim could know and a reality that has, up to this point, been carried alone by the victim.

In a victim's desire and willingness to meet with the offender, there is some acknowledgment of the offender's existence. The victim gives, as well, in their humanization of the offender, which, in effect, is an acceptance of the offender as other than a monster. The victim's listening and response to the offender's truthfulness is also a giving. It allows the offender to unburden themselves of the shame and guilt they may carry from committing the crime and knowing the wrong that they did. Often their self-hatred and loathing appears as well but is harder to release.

Alongside their shared giving is their mutual receiving. The person harmed receives the offender's remorse. Not only do victims feel that what happened to them and their lives matters to the person responsible for the harm, but the offenders' remorse is also expressive of their humanity toward the person harmed. Indeed, victimization is deeply dehumanizing. Remorse transforms victims as objects to victims as human.

The offender receives the victim's humanity as well. It may show as a shift in the victim's attitude toward the offender, in an expression of empathy for the pain embedded in the offender's background, in the provision of parental guiding and advice, and in a hug or taking of the offender's hand.

Dyadic forgiveness, therefore, requires victim and offender to be emotionally available to each other. Otherwise the giving and receiving will not occur and the healing will be reduced. Because both people are necessary to this process, the forgiveness that occurs, consequently, is co-created. Moreover, both victim and offender are involved in a bilateral process where they mutually impact each other. The interchange may set off a change reaction of influence with feedback loops that energizes and possibly accelerates movement.

SHIFTS IN ENERGY

Dyadic forgiveness is implicit and a part of the interaction. It is not dependent on a verbally explicit claim of "having forgiven" or the occurrence of particular behaviors. It can happen subliminally, that is, a person is influenced by another but the influence is not recognized or understood consciously. It can consciously occur but not be claimed or asserted by the victim. Consequently, dyadic forgiveness cannot be examined directly but through shifts in emotional energy as revealed, in this project, through victims' accounts. Indeed, energy shifts in the movement from negatively to positively charged emotional energy is the language of dyadic forgiveness. This project, therefore, focused on the flow and course of emotional energy. It used victims' reports of their own and offenders' emotional energy shifts during the dyadic dialogue as the medium for examining forgiveness in a dyadic context. These shifts in dyadic forgiveness were voluntary and helped change the direction and quality of the energy.

Dyadic forgiveness is a process rather than an event, as shown by the series of graduated energy shifts reported by victims. Indeed, they described shifts in motivation, attitudes toward the offenders, responses to the dyadic encounter and engagement, and post-dialogue outcomes. Many of these shifts were additive. They built on each other and built over time. For example, many victims did not humanize offenders until they experienced offenders' remorse or the taking ownership of what they did in their story of the crime. The core shift, therefore, frequently emerged out of victims gently moving themselves forward first through more minor shifts.

The findings from the qualitative study support the quantitative findings and vice versa. Specifically, the only outcome for VOD offenders that showed a significant change over time was gratitude. This variable contained two statements that offenders rated based on their level of agreement: (1) "I accept myself as a human being like the victim." (2) "I have so much in life to be thankful for." This finding arguably demonstrates an energy shift for offenders. It likely reflects the offender's emotional response to feeling accepted by the victim and facilitator, having engaged in a process of accountability, remorse, and reparation, and being symbolically reinstated by the victim as a moral citizen.

Similarly, the quantitative study showed energy shifts for the victim as demonstrated by an increase over four time periods in empathy, forgiveness, physical functioning, physical role, general health, vitality, emotional role, and mental health. Positive changes in these variables are a likely reflection of the victim's positive shift in negatively charged emotional energy related to the crime and its impact and the release of bitterness and vengeance during and after the dialogue.

Finally, the quantitative findings provide some support for dyadic forgiveness specific to the positive influence that each party has on the other, which helps shift the negatively charged emotional energy. In that regard, it is notable that the mediator's rating of the offender's readiness for the dialogue was a predictor of the victim's rating of success. This finding suggests that the overall success of the dialogue occurred in the context of the dyadic process and that the process was additive, that is, each part built on the other. The readiness of the offender for the meeting likely meant that he was open to sharing information, receptive to hearing the impact of what he did, and willing to express some level of remorse, regret, and sorrow.

MOVEMENT IN NEGATIVELY TO POSITIVELY CHARGED ENERGY

The movement in shifting from negatively to positively charged emotional energy as a result of the VOD is somewhat linear. It begins with the crime, its impact, and the residue of negatively charged emotional energy. Victims are traumatized by the crime and then held in a suspended state by the criminal justice system. There is no viable or constructive outlet for their intense emotions. Consequently, the negatively charged energy is *blocked*. For most victims, this phase reinforces their powerlessness and sense of being stuck.

At some point, VOD victim participants make attempts to resolve the horrific pain and discomfort they live with. This negatively charged energy is commonly referenced as a state of "unforgiveness" (Worthington and Wade, 1999). The decision to pursue the VOD option may be activated by the offender's pending release, the desperate need for information, and answers to unresolvable why-related questions, the toxicity of anger, or concern for and curiosity about the offender. At this point, the energy, although still blocked, is *directed* toward a goal. Indeed, there is the possibility that meeting with the offender will relieve some of the victim's ongoing torment.

During this time there are also sporadic energy shifts because of new insights or personal decisions made by victims about how they will face the future.

Victims' preparation for the VOD may be formal and/or informal. Regardless of the methods used to ensure readiness, the negatively charged energy is now *channeled* in the direction of the upcoming dialogue. Depending on the facilitator and procedures followed in different states that have VOD programs, victim and offender may exchange letters, pictures, and video-taped interviews with the facilitator about the future meeting. Facilitators may also carry information about each person back and forth to the other as they prepare for the dialogue. In some instances, victims' responses to the offender may begin to be somewhat less negative. In the cultivation of greater openness, they begin to consider aspects of the offender or that person's response that they previously would have disregarded or written off. As such, there may be some mixture of negatively and positively charged energy that starts to emerge. This phase may also include some sporadic energy shifts based on new information or personal decisions made by victims about going forward.

The dyadic dialogue brings together victim and offender. This actualization of all the pre-work and the interplay between participants allows for the possibility of negatively charged energy to be *released*. Indeed, the sharing of the pain through expressions of remorse, anger, and deep sorrow as well as the stories of the crime and its impact provides the outlet that was never available during the first phase of the crime's aftermath. Although there may be numerous small energy shifts throughout the dialogue, a pivotal or *core energy shift* occurs as the pain caused by the crime is transformed for the victim. This usually occurs after the offender has taken some measure of affective accountability for the crime.

The core energy shift is also called "pivotal" because it allows the blocked energy to flow again. The victim's sense of being unburdened refers to the release of negatively charged energy. The offender too likely feels unburdened because his actions helped relieve some of the pain he caused the victim and he, too, has had the opportunity, through his truth-telling, to release the negatively charged energy he too carries as a result of the crime he committed. The critical dynamic, however, for the offender is his shift in status from monster to human being in the eyes of the victim. The victim's reinstatement of the offender as a moral citizen in the same realm as the victim is "pivotal" because it releases the offender also to move forward. Hence, for both parties the sense of resolution and post-dialogue re-engagement in the world reflects that the *energy is flowing* again.

Behaviorally, the shift is reflected in the quality of the interaction between victim and offender. Specifically, there is a dyadic exchange of information related to the pain differential and pain transfer. Both victim and offender may be open to giving and receiving but there is limited back and forth movement between them. After the pain transformation, however, the interaction changes. Victim and offender feel safer, more available, and even closer to each other. There is space, now, for a more conversational process. The quality of the flow is more open, spontaneous, and triggering of each other's responses. Pearle's story about her rage, wanting to beat the dog she loved and flogging the tree instead triggered Hal's love for dogs. "…[D]ogs are my love. I couldn't imagine being without one. So we went back and forth revealing ourselves to each other with lots and lots of tears."

ROLE OF DISSONANCE IN ENERGY MOVEMENT

Dissonance refers to discomfort associated with holding two or more contradictory beliefs that conflict with a person's existing beliefs, ideas, or values (Festinger, 1957). Dissonance creates a field of energy due to the tension of opposing forces. The energy provokes movement to reduce the opposition created by contradictory elements. In dyadic forgiveness specific to VOD, there was pre-dialogue dissonance that propelled victims' efforts to resolve negatively charged energy by electing to pursue a VOD. The decision to move forward resolved some of the dissonance associated with feeling blocked but also generated new pre-dialogue dissonance because of the requirement for greater openness to the offender. Indeed, this dissonance did not resolve for many of the victim participants until they actually saw and could assess, for themselves, the offender's authenticity.

Once in the meeting, victim participants were faced with additional dissonance-generating experiences caused by the dialogue. For example, they received new information from the offender that conflicted with their prior understanding of the crime-specific details. They also experienced the offender differently than they had during the trial. What they expected and what actually happened frequently threw them. For example, Keisha never expected that Adam would be kind and generous toward her. Likewise, Monique never expected that Manny felt bad because he had known her brother and liked him. Victims also experienced dissonance between their commitment to the past and the pull of the future. Micaela felt that she wanted to express gratitude to Ronald for the meeting but felt that doing so would betray Joel, her deceased partner. Maya wanted to close the door on the unresolvedness of her daughter's murder but could not do that if she continued to join Duncan in meeting frequently with Gregory. Victims had to make decisions about these opposing pulls in order to resolve the immensity of their discomfort. For the most part, their choices reflected decisions to move forward. These decisions about what to believe, what to honor within themselves, and who to trust played a powerful role in their energy shifts during the dialogue. Indeed, it is hypothesized that as participants shift in response to the dissonance-generating discomfort, what victims felt or believed previously dissipates because it is absorbed by the new attitude or understanding.

ACCOUNTABILITY IN DYADIC FORGIVENESS

The essential component in dyadic forgiveness is the offender's accountability to the victim. The offender's willingness to accept responsibility and account for his or her actions is, without question, the core factor that generates movement. As it relates to dissonance, the offender's apology, sorrow, and regret contradict the victim's belief that the offender is evil or a monster, which pushes the victim to see the offender anew. The exchange of accountability statements and humanization or empathy-building statements is at the heart of what disarms the power of the past and allows both victim and offender to move toward a different future.

According to the model advanced by this project, the victim, prior to meeting with the offender, unilaterally carries the pain caused by the offender (e.g. pain differential). That differential is sustained by unshared stories or experience and intensified by the victim's ongoing discomfort, which creates a highly charged energy imbalance. During the VOD, wrongdoers authentically accept responsibility for what they did and, consequently, transfer the pain from the victim to themselves (e.g. pain transfer). Many of the participants in the study reported that even before the dialogue began, the offender was steeped in remorse. Indeed, the offender's pain from the onset of the meeting set the tone for the VOD and was responsible for the initial energy shift in the victim. For the most part, participants' shifts in attitude toward the offender occurred after there was some expression of accountability, some shouldering of the pain that began to rebalance the inequity or pain differential between them. These victim shifts humanized the offender and allowed a stronger connection between the parties.

Although victim participants shared their pain in telling the offender about the impact of the crime on their lives and the lives of their families, the remorse of the offender frequently occurred independently of the victim's story. It was as if the offender already knew the horror they had caused and was anxious to show and express how sorry they were to the victim. In many of the cases, the offender demonstrated the extent of their accountability by sharing the entirety of the crime they committed with the victim. The offender's accountability, therefore, might reflect their feelings about the damage they did, a recounting of exactly what happened, their decisions and their actions in committing of the crime, and their response to learning what the victim endured as a result.

Participants' responses were heavily dependent on the authenticity of the offender's story and feelings. Indeed, it was the genuineness of the offender that touched the humanity of the victim and helped open them up to a different experience of the offender. Accountability that was believable also made the experience of being with the offender safer. The offender did not just give them information about the crime. Rather, the story was expressed honestly and with regret and sorrow. Moreover, the sharing was done in the context of a relationship that was, in fact, formed by the crime and both the victim and offender's connection to the person who was murdered. The offender's accountability in the context of such intense history and engagement also made it more viable and trustworthy. Consequently, how the information was given was as important as the information itself. Truth-telling was raw, naked, honest, and conveyed with integrity.

DYADIC FORGIVENESS AND MEANING-MAKING

The pain transfer, as reflected in the offender's accountability, shifts the pain differential for the victim. Indeed, as the offender acts on the victim through taking on the pain, it elicits a different and humanizing response from the victim. This movement by the offender actually begins to transform the victim's pain. The victim's humanizing of and response to the offender is one manifestation of the beginning transformation. Humanizing refers to how people use their own basic humanity, their essential strength, decency, and compassion as a human being to identify, bond, and join out of sameness with others. This movement by the victim is recognition of the offender's humanity and, in effect, is a refusal to demonize him any longer. The pain transformation also elicits the forgiveness response, verbally or behaviorally, from the victim.

All of these shifts in attitude and position between victim and offender reconfigure the meaning of the crime. Indeed, the narrative about the crime has a different ending because of the VOD. It moves the grammatical "period" about the horrific event to a new place. The future is no longer defined by the negatively charged emotional energy but, rather, is defined or influenced by the transformation of negative to positive energy. This shift creates a changed openness to what is possible.

As victims learn the true story of what happened to their loved one or receive knowledge about the background or motivation of offenders, they have the missing puzzle pieces and are finally able to put the puzzle together.

They now can "make sense" out of what happened. The new information allows victims to have some measure of internal resolution. Moreover, the dialogue itself is a meaning-making venture between the two parties about the crime, its aftermath in both their lives, and who they become to each other as a result of the meeting. Based on the victim participants' accounts, offenders too went through a transformation as a result of the interaction with the victim. Victims often worked to positively guide offenders, offering advice and showing concern for their wellbeing. Consequently, the meaning made during their encounter is a product of this shared process between them.

Based on the findings in the qualitative study, the new meaning is powerful in that it sustained itself even when participants had post-dialogue experiences with the offender that were disappointing. Kalicia, for example, discovered that Ahmad would likely not keep the commitments he made to her during their meeting. Micaela discovered that Ronald had reoffended and had badly distorted the reality about their VOD meeting. In both cases, the victims maintained the positiveness they received from the VOD and did not question the offender's authenticity as human or the viability of what happened in the meeting.

DYADIC FORGIVENESS AND
LEVELS OF ENGAGEMENT

Victims and offenders varied in the quality of the dyadic engagement during the VOD. Based on the openness continuum, some victims were more guarded than others. Some offenders were more emotionally expressive than others. In some of the VOD meetings, victims worked to pull out offenders. In other cases, victims were less active. Across the board, victims and offenders make choices about how much of themselves to give to the other.

These dynamics affect the quality of the dyadic engagement and, perhaps, the degree of satisfaction felt by each of the parties. Roughly half of the victims in the qualitative study had some ongoing contact with the offender after the dialogue was completed. This post-dialogue outcome is notable because engagement with the offender, in some instances, becomes voluntary. Although heavily informed by the crime, the ongoing nature of the relationship is forward looking and both parties are electing to play some ongoing role in each other's lives.

Indeed, a number of victim participants formed parenting type relationships with the offender. Adam, for example, became a type of father figure to Keisha. Donny became like a son to Maria. Lizette watched over Gamal's wellbeing. Tamara expected that James would join her family when he was released. In these cases, the dyadic forgiveness took on a quality of unconditional acceptance. Victim participants did not minimize or forget what the offender did to their loved ones or their own lives. Rather, with the shift in meaning about both the crime and the offender, victim participants carved out a new place in their lives for the offender and for the meaningfulness of their relationship.

DYADIC FORGIVENESS AND THE SENSE OF INJUSTICE

Wenzel and Okimoto (2010) assert that the sense of injustice experienced by victims of crime refers to the fact that societal values presumed to be shared have been profoundly violated. Those values are personified by the concern for the welfare of others, a communally understood moral standard that tempers self-centeredness and instills safety. Wenzel and Okimoto maintain that any response to crime, such as a VOD, must restore those values through re-establishing the social consensus with the offender about the values violated. In dyadic forgiveness, the social consensus is restored by the offender's behavior and the victim's experience of the offender during the dialogue. Again, the offender's verbal and affective expression of accountability to the victim for what the offender did and took from the victim helps show the victim that the offender genuinely regrets his behavior. In many cases, the victim may even be able to forgive the offender explicitly or implicitly but the offender cannot forgive himself for the violation.

Wenzel and Okimoto (2010) hypothesize that forgiveness is motivated by more than a decision or an emotional response but is also an attempt to restore a sense of justice based on trust in a consensus with the offender about shared values. Victim participants saw that offenders were remorseful, shared information fully in an effort to help the victim, gave credible explanations for their behavior, wanted to give and repair what they could, cared about them, heard them fully, responded to their needs, and took accountability for the pain they caused. Although this study did not address directly the issue of justice, victim participants' responses to offenders who fully held themselves responsible for the crime suggest that victims felt that they were closer to being on the same page with offenders morally. Their anger receded and even disappeared. They felt safe again. Indeed, they responded to offenders as human beings rather than monsters but, more importantly, victim participants reinstated offenders as moral citizens in a variety of different ways. Offenders moved from being "other" in victim participants' eyes to human beings who had worth, who, like themselves, had made bad mistakes and for whom they wanted a better future.

THE PROJECT'S LIMITATIONS

The purpose of this project was to explicate dyadic forgiveness in victim offender dialogue (VOD), also called victim offender mediated dialogue (VOMD), by studying behaviorally implicit forgiveness and the process of victim and offender shifts in energy from the time of the crime through the restorative dialogue. Because dyadic forgiveness is a bilateral process that creates change in both victim and offender as a result of their impact on each other (Umbreit and Armour, 2010), the findings from the qualitative study are limited. They reflect only the voice of victim participants. Consequently, information about energy shifts in offenders is incomplete and available only through participants' reports about offenders. Likewise, the facilitator's voice as observer and witness to the dyadic engagement between victim and offender, their shifts, and the pain transformation is missing. Over 85 percent of the victim participants were White/Caucasian. Moreover, the accounts of what happened in the dialogue process are retrospective. In some cases, the dialogues happened years ago. Indeed, 30 percent of dialogues occurred before 2000. Consequently, the accuracy and completeness of the accounts are open to question. Finally, there was no member checking of the researchers' interpretations of victim participants' stories or the researchers' analysis of the cases.

There are some similar limitations in the quantitative study. For example, 75 percent of the victim participants were White. The scope of the study was regional, which, along with the issue of random sampling, raises questions about representativeness of the sample and the generalizability of the results. Moreover there was no control group.

IMPLICATIONS OF THE PROJECT

Dyadic forgiveness as a bilateral process is an important addition to the field of forgiveness research. Heretofore, studies have concentrated on close relationships and the victim's unitary decision to forgive. Interaction between the person responsible for the harm and the person harmed has not been the focus of inquiries. Although it might be ideal, in addition to interviews, to observe victim–offender interaction directly, this project contributed beginning theory about the process of dyadic forgiveness, particularly in restorative justice practices. A major part of the contribution was the focus on emotional energy shifts as manifestations of movement from negatively to positively charged energy. Making energy shifts instead of verbally explicit claims (e.g. "I forgave him"), the language for dyadic forgiveness recognizes its reality yet respects the out-of-the-way status of forgiveness in restorative justice. It also allows its implicit nature to be identified and examined.

Besides its contribution to forgiveness research, dyadic forgiveness has application to many other areas. For example, mental health providers commonly work with clients who struggle with accumulated injuries, or with couples or family relationships where harm and wrongdoing remain unresolved and stuck. Restorative justice interventions have appeal beyond the criminal justice context and could be used to help generate energy shifts as documented in the qualitative study. Besides possible micro-level use, dyadic forgiveness has much to offer international conflict, which is frequently plagued by monsterizing the "other," strong feelings of vengefulness, massive mistrust, and a lack of openness to seeing and hearing something different from what is believed. The same dynamics color relationships between community members and law enforcement in the United States. Interventions such as VOD that foster, as shown in this project, the conditions for dyadic forgiveness might provide possible avenues for moving or even transforming energy that is stuck or blocked.

Future research should focus on testing the theoretical model of dyadic forgiveness in a variety of different contexts. It should also include the voices of offenders and facilitators. Indeed, the shifts in energy for offenders may be quite different than for victims. Including the facilitator's perspective would provide eye-witness accounts about what occurs between parties, which would help validate or propose changes to the process documented by the qualitative study.

CONCLUSION

This project proposed and tested a model of dyadic forgiveness by studying VOD, a restorative justice program for victims and offenders of severely violent crime. Guided by forgiveness theory, as proposed by Worthington and Wade (1999), the project examined victim participants' movement in the aftermath of crime from "unforgiveness" as manifested by negatively charged energy to feeling unburdened as manifested by positively charged energy. The movement involved a series of phases that included blocked energy as a result of the crime's impact, directed energy after a decision to pursue a VOD, channeled energy during preparation, and changed energy after engagement in a dyadic dialogue with the offender.

Strong energy shifts were evident for both victim and offender in the quantitative study results and clearly and specifically identified by victims in the quantitative study. A beginning model of dyadic forgiveness was proposed after a review of archival materials and applied in analyzing victim participant stories in the qualitative study. Findings from a cross-case analysis of the victim participant stories and analyses were used to rework and dimensionalize the origianl model. Although many of the concepts identified for the beginning model were substantiated by the victim participant accounts, their narratives helped refine the model and added depth and understanding. The narratives also gave meaning to the construct of dyadic forgiveness so that its dimensions could become more visible.

Dyadic forgiveness is a much needed construct in a world rocked by trauma, victimization, gross inequities, and violence. Most of the available interventions for healing are focused on the individual and intrapsychic change, which does little to repair the violations to relationships and the glue that holds us together in ways that redeem our belonging to and need for each other. Attention to dyadic forgiveness and the bilateral process it requires is an antidote to the historically individualized focus on forgiveness. It also offers victims and offenders, persons hurt by wrongdoing and those responsible for the wrongdoing, a courageous challenge, a promising opportunity, and a way beyond the pain and torment that distorts our love for each other, diminishes our hope, destroys our vital connections with one another, and erodes the trust in relationships that are necessary for our mutual survival. The journey back truly can only be done together.

REFERENCES

Festinger, L. (1957) *A Theory of Cognitive Dissonance*. California: Stanford University Press.

McCullough, M.E., Rachal, K.C., Sandage, S.J., Worthington, E.L., Jr., Brown, S.W., and Hight, T.L. (1998) 'Interpersonal forgiving in close relationships II: Theoretical elaboration and measurement.' *Journal of Personality and Social Psychology 75*, 1586–1603.

Umbreit, M.S. and Armour, M.P. (2010) *Restorative Justice Dialogue: An Essential Guide for Research and Practice*. New York: Springer.

Van Biema, D. (1999) 'Should all be forgiven?' *Time 153*, 55–58.

Wenzel, M. and Okimoto, T.G. (2010) 'How acts of forgiveness restore a sense of justice: Addressing status/power and value concerns raised by transgressions.' *European Journal of Social Psychology 40*, 401–417.

Worthington, E.L., Jr. and Wade, N.G. (1999) 'The psychology of unforgiveness and forgiveness and implications for clinical practice.' *Journal of Social and Clinical Psychology 18*, 385–418.

Worthington, E.L., Jr., Van Oyen Witvliet, C., Pietrini, P., and Miller, A.J. (2007) 'A review of evidence for emotional versus decisional forgiveness, dispositional forgivingness, and reduced unforgiveness.' *Journal of Behavioral Medicine 30*, 291–302.

APPENDIX

1 ■

STUDY METHODOLOGY

INTRODUCTION

The purpose of this study of 20 VOD victim participants is to examine manifestations of dyadic forgiveness through a focus on the shifts from negatively charged to positively charged energy in the personal, retrospective accounts of crime victims who engaged in a restorative justice dialogue with offenders responsible for crime and ensuing harm. Although forgiveness is not necessary or an expectation in restorative justice dialogues, restorative justice processes tend to create conditions that may be conducive to forgiveness. To date, the theoretical and experimental examination of forgiveness has been restricted to explicit manifestations of forgiveness usually arrived at singularly or without input from the person responsible for the harm. Restorative justice, however, provides a unique opportunity to investigate new dimensions of forgiveness. For example, because forgiveness in the restorative justice field is not considered an explicit or prescribed goal, unless desired by the victim, it requires that forgiveness be examined indirectly, both through shifts in negatively charged energy related to the crime and through implicit expressions of those shifts between victim and offender. Moreover, because restorative justice is a dyadic process, it allows the emphasis on forgiveness to move from the individual or singular decision to forgive to a focus on dyadic processes or how victim and offender influence positively charged energy shifts in each other.

METHODOLOGY

This qualitative research study uses a narrative approach to collect and analyze crime victim accounts of their participation in a restorative justice practice and its impact on them and their lives. Narrative research is based on the supposition that humans are storytelling organisms who, individually and socially, lead storied lives (Connelly and Clandinen 1990). As such, narrative is both phenomenon and method. The study also uses template analysis to chart changes in the flow from negatively charged to positively charged energy for crime victims based on their accounts of participating in and benefiting from a dialogue with their offenders. Description of the process used needs to remain to show the rigor involved specific to template analysis (Crabtree and Miller, 1999). In this instance, the theory, specific to implicit and dyadic forgiveness, derives from the analysis of archival data. Figure 1.1 shows the process model, formulated before this study was conducted of shifts from negatively charged to positively charged energy.

The purpose of this research, therefore, is to map the interaction between victim and offender and subjective responses to that interaction from the perspective of victim restorative justice participants who, as a result of the dialogue process, experience major positive emotional shifts (e.g. implicit forgiveness) toward offenders. The primary research questions are as follows:

1. What is the emotional, cognitive, and behavioral dyadic change process between victim and offender that fosters the experience of implicit forgiveness?

2. What factors influence positive intrapersonal movement during pre-dialogue preparation and during the dialogue itself?

3. What are intrapersonal and relational indicators of implicit forgiveness and how is it communicated behaviorally?

Context for the study

The crime victim participants for this study have been participants in victim offender dialogue (VOD), a victim-initiated intervention for seriously violent crimes, for example, homicide, aggravated assault and rape. Engagement in a dialogue with the offender generally requires extensive preparation of at least six months for both victim and offender followed by an intensive facilitated dialogue about the crime and its impact on both participants. The VOD is not stipulated by the court but is entered into voluntarily by both parties. It occurs post conviction during incarceration.

In many cases, the offender may be incarcerated for years or a lifetime. The purpose of a VOD is to create a safe space so that both parties can ask questions, share information, and express feelings such as anger, sadness, and remorse as part of an effort to move forward with their healing. Close to 30 states use their Department of Corrections as home base for the VOD intervention. Because of the uniformity in intensity of seriously violent crimes and the consistency in the structure and delivery of the intervention across states, the VOD intervention creates a naturalistic laboratory setting for examining dyadic forgiveness from victim participant accounts. The study was approved by The University of Texas at Austin Institutional Review Board.

Recruitment and sample

Participants were recruited from restorative justice facilitators in Central Texas, Minnesota, Wisconsin, Oregon, and Colorado. Eligible participants included victims of seriously violent crimes who speak English and who had participated in a restorative justice facilitated dialogue (VOD) with their offender and experienced major emotional, cognitive, and/or behavioral shifts as a result of the dialogue and letting go of negative/life-depleting energy. Descriptive statistics are presented in Table A1 (see below). The sample comprised 20 crime victims, including 19 individuals who had a loved one murdered and one person who was the direct victim. Two of the participants were married but were treated as separate cases for this study. Women were disproportionately represented (n=17, 85%), and primarily White. The majority of participants (55%, n=11) had a college degree or higher and 80 percent had some college or higher education (n=16). Most participants were currently married (n=11, 55%), while others were single, divorced, or widowed (n=7, 35%). At the time of the crime, 75 percent of the victims were younger than 29 years old (n=15) and they were evenly split for gender. For the participants, 25 percent were between 40 and 49 years old (n=5) and 45 percent were 60 or older (n=9). Parents and children of the victims were the largest categories of participants (n=9, 45% and n=6, 30%). Half of the crimes occurred in the 1990s. The majority of the victims did not know their offender prior to the crime (n=15, 75%) and similarly 70 percent of participants did not know the offender (n=14). The dialogues occurred across a large span of years, relatively evenly distributed across decades: 30 percent in the 1990s (n=6), 30 percent in the 2000s (n=6) and 40 percent in the 2010s (n=8).

Table A.1: Sample demographics

	Number	Percent		Number	Percent
Current age			**Age at time of crime**		
20–29 yrs	0	0	0–9 yrs	1	5
30–39 yrs	3	15	10–19 yrs	1	5
40–49 yrs	5	25	20–29 yrs	5	25
50–59 yrs	2	10	30–39 yrs	2	10
60–69 yrs	5	25	40–49 yrs	9	45
70+ yrs	4	20	50–59 yrs	1	5
Not available	1	5	Not available	1	5
Gender			**Age of loved one**		
Male	3	15	10–19 yrs	7	35
Female	17	85	20–29 yrs	8	40
			30–39 yrs	0	0
Race			40–49 yrs	0	0
White/Caucasian	17	85	50–59 yrs	2	10
Black/Afr. American	1	5	60–69 yrs	0	0
Hispanic/Latino/a	0	0	70+ yrs	1	5
Asian/Pacific Islander	1	5	Not available	1	10
Not available	1	5			
Relationship status			**Gender of loved one**		
Single	3	15	Male	10	50
Partnered, never married	0	0	Female	10	50
Married, not separated	9	45	**Year of the crime**		
Separated/Divorced	3	15	1980s	6	30
Repartnered	2	10	1990s	10	50
Widowed	1	5	2000s	2	10
No Answer	2	10	2010s	2	10
Education level			**Participant knew offender**		
Less than high school	0	0	Yes	5	25
Completed GED	1	5	No	15	75
High school graduate	2	10			
Some college	5	25	**Loved one knew offender**		
College degree or more	11	55	Yes	6	30
No answer	1	5	No	14	70
Relationship to loved one			**Year of the dialogue**		
Parent/Stepparent	9	45	1990s	6	30
Spouse/Partner	2	10	2000s	6	30
Child/Stepchild	6	30	2010s	8	40
Sibling	2	10			
Self	1	5			

Data collection

Data were collected through semi-structured in-person interviews conducted face to face or through Skype by Umbreit and Lewis. Interviews lasted approximately one-and-a-half hours. They were audio recorded and transcribed for analysis. An interview guide was developed and consisted of nine questions with probes. Questions focused on the details of the crime and its impact, the victim's decision to meet with the offender, preparation for the dialogue, the actual dialogue, and participants' accounts of the impact of the dialogue on their perceptions and wellbeing. Participants also completed a 13-item demographic questionnaire. Copies of the interview guide and demographic questionnaire are in Appendix 3 and Appendix 4 respectively.

Data analysis

Data were analyzed using both narrative and template analysis. As noted earlier, Armour, Lewis, and Umbreit developed a preliminary model for this study from a review of archival materials that included victim and offender participant transcripts, case notes, videos of dialogues, and transcribed interviews with an experienced facilitator who developed a large VOD state program. This theoretical model was a beginning formulation of the flow and shifts in negatively charged energy from the crime through the dialogue process. It was used as the template for *a priori* coding of concepts in each case.

After each interview, Lewis reviewed the transcription and did an initial analysis of energy shifts and events associated with the shifts over time using the preliminary model and *a priori* codes as the basis for his review. Lewis sent the transcription and his analysis to Armour. Armour completed three readings of each case. The first time, she read through all interviews once and developed a five-item self-reflection questionnaire that could be used as a summary of the case and for culling out critical events and decision points affecting the flow of energy, for example, What parts of the theory were substantiated? What new information specific to the theory was presented for reflection/theory modification? The reflection sheet is in Appendix 2. The second time, Armour read through all interviews again, mapping the narrative with attention to the transition points in participants' stories, and completed the self-reflection questionnaire at the end of reading each of the individual accounts.

The third time, Armour applied the template to each case by first summarizing the narrative from the perspective of the participant and then coding the case based on the *a priori* codes from the preliminary model and additional codes that had emerged from analysis (see Figure 1.1). Cross-analysis of the case summaries and analyses was done using NVivo (Qualitative Research Software, International). Cases were coded based on the *a priori* concepts from the preliminary model and additional codes that had emerged from the analysis. A list of the *a priori* concepts can be found in the glossary in Section 1. Additional codes are included in Figure 3.1 and described in Section 3. Data supporting each concept or additional code were retrieved and used to support, modify, and describe the key dimensions of the final theoretical model of energy shifts in implicit and dyadic forgiveness.

Section 3 reports the findings from the cross-case analysis of the victim participant stories and analyses. It has five parts: (1) Crime and its impact, (2) Motivation and preparation, (3) Dyadic dialogue, (4) Resolution and post-dialogue outcomes, and (5) Dyadic dialogue. The analysis of each case in Section 3 applied the model of dyadic forgiveness originally developed from archival materials (See Section 1). Figure 3.1 is a revision of the model of dyadic forgiveness based on the analysis of the victim participant cases in Section 2 and findings from the cross-case analysis in Section 3.

REFERENCES

Connelly, F.M. and Clandinin, D.J. (1990) 'Stories of experience and narrative inquiry.' *Educational Researcher 19, 5*, 2–14.

Crabtree, B.F. and Miller, W.L. (1999) *Doing qualitative research.* Sage Publications: Thousand Oaks, CA.

2 ◼

PARADOX OF FORGIVENESS
Reflection sheet

Name:
1. What critical events impacted the dialogue process?
2. What parts of the theory were substantiated?

3. What information negated the theory or was missing?

4. What new information specific to the theory was presented for reflection/theory modification?

5. What are new thoughts or ideas to explore?

3 ▪

PARADOX OF FORGIVENESS
Interview guide

1. I don't know much about your story of the crime. Could you please tell me what happened starting at the beginning?

2. What were your initial thoughts and feelings toward the offender?

3. Tell me about what your life was like after the crime.

    Probe: What aspects of the crime seemed to resolve themselves over time?
    Probe: What areas of your life or issues remained unfinished? How did the unfinished business affect your life?

4. Tell me the story of how you decided to meet with the offender.

    Probe: How did you first learn about the dialogue process? What were your initial reactions? How did they change, if at all, over time?
    Probe: What were your hopes?
    Probe: What were your reservations and why?
    Probe: Tell me about your inner dialogue in deciding to move forward.

5. Tell me the story of going through the preparation process.

    Probe: What changed, if anything, in your thoughts or feelings toward the offender?
    Probe: What changed, if anything, in how you thought about the crime, including new questions and clarity about things to say to the offender?
    Probe: What changed, if anything, in your openness to or concerns about moving forward?
    Probe: What did you consider as possible outcomes of the meeting? What did you want most to happen in the meeting?

6. Tell me the story about meeting the offender, doing the dialogue, and the process that occurred between you in detail.

    Probe: What was the most important/impactful thing that happened between you in the meeting?

    Probe: What episodes happened during the dialogue, if any, that are memorable and why?

    Probe: Describe times, if any, where you and the offender were on the same wavelength.

    Probe: What conversations happened between you that were not planned or surprised you?

    Probe: What was new—information, perceptions, reactions? What effect did these new realizations have on you, if any? How did they influence you during the dialogue?

7. What took place between you and the offender at the end of the dialogue?

    Probe: How did you feel toward the offender at the end of the dialogue? How were those feelings conveyed?

    Probe: What was your perception of how the offender felt toward you? How were those feelings conveyed?

    Probe: Describe any agreements made between you and the offender. What did you want in the agreement and why was that important to you?

    Probe: How was gratitude, if it occurred, expressed? Who felt it?

    Probe: Was there physical touch or the desire to do so between you? If so, describe and give your reaction to what happened or the wish for something more.

8. The word forgiveness can mean different things to different people. Was there ever any talk of forgiveness in the preparation or the meeting? Please describe.

    Probe: If yes, describe your reaction/the offender's reaction when the forgiveness topic came up.

    Probe: If no, do you think a type of forgiveness happened in the meeting? Please describe.

    Probe: If negative about forgiveness, what other concepts are more meaningful and applicable for you?

9. What has been the importance of the dialogue in your life?

    Probe: What differences did you notice in yourself, if any, after the dialogue?

    Probe: Were there more insights for you or shifts in how you felt generally or shifts in your reaction to the offender after the dialogue? If so, what were they and how did they impact you?

4 ■

PARADOX OF FORGIVENESS

Demographic and background survey

Code   _____

Date   _____

1. **What is your current age?** _____

2. **What is your gender?**
   a. Male   ☐
   b. Female   ☐

3. **What is your race/ethnicity?**
   a. Black/African American   ☐
   b. Hispanic/Latino/a; Chicano   ☐
   c. White Caucasian   ☐
   d. Native American/Alaskan Native   ☐
   e. Other (please specify) _____ ☐

4. **What is your relationship status?**
   a. Single   ☐
   b. Partnered, never married   ☐
   c. Married, not separated   ☐
   d. Separated, or divorced, not repartnered ☐
   e. Separated, or divorced, repartnered   ☐
   f. Widowed   ☐

5. **What is the highest level of school that you completed?**
   a. Less than high school   ☐
   b. Completed GED   ☐

    c. High school graduate   ☐

    d. Some college, no degree   ☐

    e. College degree or higher   ☐

6. **Based on the crime, how old were you at the time of the crime?** _____

7. **Based on the crime, how old was your loved one (if a crime victim) at the time of the crime?** _____

8. **What was your relationship to your loved one (if a crime victim)?**
    a. Parent/Stepparent   ☐
    b. Spouse/Partner   ☐
    c. Child/Stepchild   ☐
    d. Sibling   ☐
    e. Grandparent   ☐
    f. Grandchild   ☐
    g. Close friend   ☐
    h. Other (please specify) _____ ☐

9. **What was the gender of your loved one (if a crime victim)?**
    a. Male   ☐
    b. Female ☐

10. **When did the crime occur?** _____/_____/_____ (00/00/0000)

11. **Was the offender known by you?**
    a. Known   ☐
    b. Not known ☐

12. **Was the offender known by your loved one (if a crime victim)?**
    a. Known   ☐
    b. Not known ☐

13. **Time since sentencing:** _____ Years _____ Months

SUBJECT INDEX

accountability
  in dyadic dialogue 268–9, 272
  in dyadic forgiveness 309–10
  and humanizing of offender 272
activism
  and negatively charged energy 245
ambivalence
  and preparation 256–60
anger 239
  as motivation for victim offender mediation 250–2
Armour, Marilyn
  and dyadic forgiveness project 26

balance
  description of 27
Briana's story
  crime and aftermath 54–5, 57–9
  dialogue 55–7, 60–2
  preparation 55, 59–60

Cassandra's story
  crime and aftermath 62–3, 65–6
  dialogue 64–5, 67–9
  preparation 63–4, 66–7
Clynita's story
  crime and aftermath 78–9, 82
  dialogue 80–2, 83–5
  preparation 79–80, 83
completion
  description of 27, 29
concern for offender 252–4
conditional forgiveness
  in dyadic dialogue 278–80
conduit
  and dyadic forgiveness project 29
crime and aftermath
  Briana's story 54–5, 57–9
  Cassandra's story 62–3, 65–6

Clynita's story 78–9, 82
Duncan's story 112–13, 116–17
Kalicia's story 197–9, 203–4
Keisha's story 178–9, 182–4
Lila's story 85–7, 90–1
Lizette's story 159–61, 163–4
Maria's story 46, 49–50
Maya's story 103–5, 108–9
Michaela's story 120–2, 127–8
Monique's story 222–4, 230–1
Norman's story 131–2, 135
Paula's story 60–70, 73–4
Pearle's story 187–8, 193–4
Portia's story 149–50, 154–5
Randell's story 95–6, 99–100
Tamara's story 210–11, 216–18
Terri Anne's story 139, 144–5
Theresa's story 168–70, 173–4
crime impacts
  dyadic forgiveness process 237–43
  in energy flow dynamics 37

decisional forgiveness 18–19
  in dyadic dialogue 275–6
dialogue
  Briana's story 55–7, 60–2
  Cassandra's story 64–5, 67–9
  Clynita's story 80–2, 83–5
  Duncan's story 114–16, 118–19
  in energy flow dynamics 38–40
  Kalicia's story 200–3, 205–9
  Keisha's story 180–2, 185–7
  Lila's story 88–90, 93–4
  Lizette's story 162–3, 165–7
  Maria's story 47–9, 52–3
  Maya's story 105–8, 110–11
  Michaela's story 123–6, 128–31
  Monique's story 225–30, 232–4
  Norman's story 132–5, 136–8
  Paula's story 72–3, 76–7

AUTHOR INDEX